HISTORICAL GUIDE TO CHILDREN'S THEATRE IN AMERICA

HISTORICAL GUIDE TO CHILDREN'S THEATRE IN AMERICA

Nellie McCaslin

Foreword by Jed H. Davis

GREENWOOD PRESS

New York • Westport, Connecticut • London

Library of Congress Cataloging-in-Publication Data

McCaslin, Nellie.
    Historical guide to children's theatre in America.

    Bibliography: p.
    Includes index.
    1. Children's plays—Presentation, etc.—United
States. 2. Children's plays—Presentation, etc.—
United States—Bibliography. I. Title.
PN3159.U6M3 1987   792'.0226'0973   85-12684
ISBN 0-313-24466-9 (lib. bdg. : alk. paper)

Library of Congress Catalog Card Number: 85-12684
ISBN: 0-313-24466-9

First published in 1987

Greenwood Press, Inc.
88 Post Road West
Westport, Connecticut 06881

Printed in the United States of America

The paper used in this book complies with the
Permanent Paper Standard issued by the National
Information Standards Organization (Z39.48-1984).

10 9 8 7 6 5 4 3 2 1

Contents

Illustrations

Foreword

It is true of any field of endeavor; to know where you're going, you need to know where you've been. I am quite sure no one knows more about where we've been than Nellie McCaslin. Her unusually comprehensive view of the field of drama and theatre with and for children has been built over many years and through many diversified projects. Her 1957 doctoral dissertation gave us the first complete account of children's theatre history in this country, and it was followed in 1971 by publication of the nation's first book on that subject. Sparked by these works, other researchers followed suit; subsequent years saw the publication of a number of directories aimed at updating the McCaslin information. In the present volume, McCaslin has built upon all these earlier sources and given us a valuable retrospective look at over eighty years of progress in the field.

With a firm belief in the truth of Mark Twain's observation that "children's theatre is one of the very, very great inventions of the twentieth century,"[1] we welcome the addition of this reference work to our shelves. Those of us who have pursued advanced study in children's drama know how elusive historical information can be, how fraught with inconsistencies are the accounts of any single event, and how unreliable is the hyperbole that permeates the ephemeral sources we are so often forced to use. So it is with some relief that we can now point to this volume, painstakingly assembled from all those ephemera (luckily before they all disappeared) and, of course, from what hard sources existed, as a definitive body of information on which to found the trends and premises of the future.

What is recorded here is much more than a simple chronicle of the times through which children's drama has passed. McCaslin has brought her historical account up through the mid-eighties, noting the principal companies, organizations, and people who have contributed significantly to progress and recounting their aims and ambitions, their pretensions, foibles, and idiosyncracies as well as acknowledged accomplishments. It was important to bring us into the eighties with this account, not just to update the record but to link recent, more mature developments with the sketchy, struggling, but optimistic past. While those hardy pioneers of the teens, twenties, and thirties had little reason for optimism, they hung on—and passed on to us a legacy of stalwart effort, dedication, and enthusiasm that could quite possibly be unparalleled in any other art community.

McCaslin's organization of this vast body of material seems particularly wise. Part One is an overview of the developing art form presented in convenient time increments. This section chronicles the main events in children's theatre development from the first efforts in the early 1900s on into the sixties; then she expands upon that base and notes important events in more recent years that could well become the trends and directions of the future. While the influences of those early groups and people are, from our perspective in time, relatively obvious, the ultimate importance of the more recent ones will be proved by time alone. Even so, McCaslin's selections are based on a broad understanding of the field and are quite likely to prove valid.

Part Two is an alphabetical listing of companies and organizations that have exerted influence on the progress of the profession. Some groups will feel slighted by her choices. Others may be surprised to find themselves included; but they are there because they represent a genre or special feature that requires mention or because they exerted influence on others over a period of time. Instead of a simple, factual listing, McCaslin has included, where possible, a narrative account of origin, development, purposes and goals, physical plant, and touring operations. That many of these entries are brief underlines the hard facts of life and death in this profession. What makes this section unique is the inclusion of historic, not necessarily extant, companies. I doubt that one would be inclined to read this section cover to cover at one sitting. It is a reference work, a badly needed one, one of the very few in our field that gives a comprehensive view of what was and is done, by whom, and to what stated purpose.

Among the useful appendixes is a chronology of events, by year, highlighting the development of theatre for young people in the United States. Another appendix, a Personality Roster, provides entries on people who have made significant contributions to the field, either through directing, managing, entrepreneurship, publications, or organizational work. A Geographical Directory is a handy locator for the companies and organizations previously described. Users will be able to find extant and past children's theatres listed in this section by state, and then can check the full description in the alphabetical entries in Part Two. Several useful bibliographies complete the volume.

In the preface, McCaslin notes a change of attitude toward theatre for children in the United States from what existed thirty years ago, when she first began collecting data on this cultural phenomenon. I assume that this change is one of increased respect for serious artistry demonstrated by producers today. Perhaps there is also a higher respect for the scholarship of the field. It could also be admiration for our survival instincts, for our will to persist in spite of scorn and derision, and for our determination to improve as artists and educators. Signs of this improvement are everywhere, if we just look for them. And surely the addition of this important reference to our bibliographies will take our cause one more step up the ladder.

Jed H. Davis

NOTE

1. Winifred Ward, *Theatre for Children* (New Orleans: Anchorage Press, 1958), p. 76.

Preface

There can be no more challenging and, at the same time, frustrating task than the compilation of a reference work in which the inclusions appear, only to disappear suddenly and without warning. Such a phenomenon is children's theatre. Like the blinking lights on a plane after dark, a children's theatre company will open, shine brightly for a season or two, then vanish when interest or financial support is withdrawn, often leaving no trace of its existence. Fortunately, however, some of these theatres for young audiences endured long enough to inspire other communities to establish theatres of their own, thus strengthening an American tradition begun soon after the turn of the century.

In my preface to *Children's Theatre in the United States: A History*, published in 1971, I stated that children's theatre in this country was "a dream for many, a reality for some, and a challenge to all" who produced or sponsored it.[1] Looking back over the fifteen years that have passed since the publication of that book, I should describe it in exactly the same words today, though there have been significant changes, some of them greater than in any other period of comparable length since the founding of the first children's theatre in America in 1903. These changes are apparent in origin of companies, playscripts, styles of production, and performance skills. As to the attitude of the public toward theatre for children, there have been changes here also, though I cannot yet say with assurance that the American people consider the performing arts to be central to the lives of their children. Lip service has been paid, according to the 1977 Rockefeller Report, *Coming to Our Senses*, but this expressed belief in the value of the arts has not yet been transformed into many widespread, ongoing programs.[2] Recession and inflation have eroded many fine enterprises that, had the favorable circumstances under which they were founded continued, might have survived. On the one hand, we see history repeating itself; on the other, some accomplishments have proved too strong to be easily toppled. It is quite a different picture that we see today from that of thirty years ago when I first began my research. The genesis of this book was a doctoral study at New York University, completed in 1957, which, fifteen years later, was revised and rewritten as the text on theatre history previously noted. Once again I have returned to the subject of the development of children's theatre in the United States, this time as a reference work focused on the individual histories of companies and organizations; and once again I have researched these histories but with emphasis on the last fifteen years.

As in the earlier research, I have been fascinated with the accounts of dramatic activities, frustrated by the many missing links in the chronology, and awed by the dedication of the pioneers and first practitioners. The data throughout the children's theatre movement in the United States are plentiful, but they are fragmentary and scattered. Although theatre for children is no longer regarded with suspicion and is, in fact, today welcomed in most communities, it is still not given the respect accorded its adult counterpart. With few exceptions, it remains a second-class citizen and lacks sufficient financial support and overall professional competence. Despite these limitations, however, I do detect a change in attitude; and while the purpose of writing this book is to assemble a concise reference work on the subject, the underlying research reveals a number of significant trends and changes over the past eighty years.

Perhaps the greatest difference between theatre for young people and theatre for adults is the audience. Whereas the adult audience is interested in the playwright or star, the child audience is concerned with a good story, honestly told by believable characters. Elaborate settings and costumes are added attractions but not essential elements. Indeed, a familiar title has more drawing power than the announcement of a new script, a fact that accounts in part for the popularity of traditional tales.

This book gives a brief historical overview of children's theatre history in Part One. Alphabetized profiles of both early and current producing companies and associations comprise Part Two. In view of the wide variation that exists among professional and nonprofessional producing groups—quality of material, structure of organization, performance skills, extent of touring programs, number of performances given during a season, and thrust and style of production—some criteria had to be employed to determine which companies would be included. Obviously, not every group that produces plays for children qualified, however good the work may be. It is hoped that this reference book will provide useful information about companies that have served or are currently serving the public in a significant way. So far as the historic companies are concerned, the inclusions are more easily determined. Those that survived over a period of time are a part of the record; those that failed or shifted their focus are among the little known or forgotten. Contemporary companies, on the contrary, are more difficult to assess. While one cannot predict the future of even the most successful enterprise, the fact that a company has been operating on a regular basis for a period of five years or more and is well known to sponsors establishes its credibility. Certainly such a company has made its mark and is qualified for inclusion in a historical context under any circumstances, should future activities be suspended.

At first I had thought of categorizing performing groups and associations separately; however, the frequent relationship of one to the other made such an organization impractical and confusing. The decision to combine both theatres and associations in a single list seemed the better solution, and that is the way they have been handled. As to the historic companies, those about which the most information is available, have lasted the longest, or have served as models for subsequent ventures have been included. In determining which contemporary companies to include, a different set of criteria was employed. No qualitative judgments were made. Rather, all Equity companies listed at the time the data were assembled were included, and all educational, community, and commercial groups that have been in existence for at least five years and offered fifty or more performances in a season were selected. This does not imply that they are superior; it is simply a way of distinguishing between companies that engage in extensive touring programs or have their own facilities and perform on a regular basis, and the vast numbers of clubs and community groups that produce an annual play or perform occasionally for young audiences. In many instances the occasional play may be excellent, but, as children's theatre is not the major thrust of the organization, the practice may be discontinued at any time. Such groups are of value, but they are different from established ongoing programs.

An exception was made in the case of child drama programs certified for Winifred Ward Scholars. A number of these programs present fewer than fifty performances a year but are recognized for their excellence. They have therefore been included.

Some profiles are longer than others, depending on the information that was available. Length in itself is not an indication of either quality or importance, though in most cases the longer a company has been in operation, the more data there are about it. Where groups and companies have changed their names or locations, cross-references are given to help the reader find the information he or she seeks. No addresses are given for companies that are known to have closed or for which no current address was located. When the location but not the name of a company is known, the researcher may find it listed in the Geographical Directory. If it does not appear there, either because of length of operation or qualifying number of performances a year, further information may be obtained from state arts councils or from the American

Association of Theatre for Youth (AATY) (q.v.). The reorganization and incorporation of the Children's Theatre Association of America as an independent entity during the final stages of work on this manuscript caused serious problems for the researcher; every effort has been made, however, to update information and fill in areas left incomplete by the sudden demise of the American Theatre Association.

Missing data have been my major concern, a concern also voiced by the committees of the Children's Theatre Association of America in reports of their national surveys conducted in 1968 and 1978. Whereas the first survey listed 701 companies in operation at that time, the second listed only 476. There are several possible explanations for this drop in numbers, but one suggestion was the growing professionalism of children's theatre. Equity contracts, increased production costs, sponsors' reduced budgets, and the competition of television are all factors that have affected children's entertainment, improving it in quality but at the same time causing the demise of weaker groups. Whereas the CTAA directories listed companies in existence at the times the surveys were made, the present reference work describes companies both past and present that have contributed significantly to the movement.

Primary sources have been used whenever possible. Newspapers, periodicals, and scrapbook collections were the most fruitful sources of information regarding the early years. Interviews with producers and sponsors have likewise been illuminating and have led to the use of unpublished material from files in some cases. Considerably more information was available after the 1940s than in all the preceding decades, for there was vastly more activity in all parts of the country after World War II, and much of the activity is well documented. The *Children's Theatre Review*, a publication of the Children's Theatre Association of America, and the various regional newsletters of the association offer the most accurate and comprehensive information on work done until the spring of 1986. Despite the most careful screening, however, some groups have undoubtedly been omitted; this is because addresses have changed and mail was not forwarded or because repeated efforts to obtain information were unsuccessful.

Other sources include state, county, and city arts councils, the American Council for the Arts, Actors' Equity Association, and the Theatre Communications Group, who have also cooperated in making available their current lists of professional performing groups and information from their files.

Cross-references are provided. *See* references help the reader locate groups that may have undergone name changes. Q.v. following the name of a theatre or group indicates that it is profiled in Part Two. Appendixes to this volume include a Chronology of Events significant in the history of the children's theatre movement in America, a Personalities Roster, and a Geographical Directory. The Personalities Roster lists the names of persons active in children's theatre during the same period of time, identifying their various contributions. Although the book is a historical reference work and not a directory, I thought it helpful to include a geographical listing to show where theatres were and are located in the fifty states. Street addresses are not given for theatres no longer in existence. Readers desirous of obtaining information regarding current groups will find addresses in the profiles under the names of the producing organizations. In addition, I have compiled a list of extant companies that did not return my questionnaires or respond to my requests for information. In some instances, the information given was inadequate to write a profile; in others, my unopened letters and questionnaires were not returned, giving reason to believe that the companies are still in operation.

At this time I should like to express my appreciation to the many persons who have cooperated in the collection of material. Particular indebtedness for historical data is acknowledged to Constance D'Arcy Mackay, Winifred Ward, Dorothy McFadden, William Kolodney, and Sara Spencer, all of whom were alive at the time I began my research in the mid-fifties. Frances Schram of Briggs Management, the Association of Junior Leagues of America, the American National Theatre and Academy, Margaret Lynne, executive director of the American Theatre Association at the time of this writing, regional governors of the Children's Theatre Association of America and directors of state arts councils have all been generous in their contributions of published and unpublished material. Jed Davis and Gayle Cornelison, who chaired the committees responsible for the CTAA directories cited, Lin Wright, who edited the 1984 survey on *Professional Theatre for Young Audiences*, and Sister Kathryn Martin, who was responsible for the 1979 *Theatre Resources Handbook/Directory* for the National Endowment for the Arts, have helped enormously as I checked my findings with theirs. Finally, I want to thank the editors of the University of Oklahoma Press for granting me permission to draw to an unlimited extent upon the content of my *Children's Theatre in the United States: A History*, published in 1971.

It is my hope that this book will be of value and interest to persons concerned with this youngest branch of the American theatre, a branch that has experienced hardship and neglect as well as a fierce and caring concern in its ongoing struggle for existence.

NOTES

1. Nellie McCaslin, *Children's Theatre in the United States: A History* (Norman: University of Oklahoma Press, 1971), p. ix.

2. *Coming to Our Senses: The Significance of the Arts in American Education*. A panel report, David Rockefeller, Jr., Chairman (New York: McGraw-Hill, 1977).

PART ONE

Historical Overview of Children's Theatre

INTRODUCTION

Children's theatre is a branch of the American theatre, similar in its elements but vastly different from adult theatre in the objectives of its producers and sponsors and in the expectations and response of its audience. Whereas adult playgoers make a conscious decision in their choice of entertainment, the child is taken individually or in a group to see a performance deemed appropriate to his or her age and interests. The child, anticipating the magical hour or so that lies ahead, goes without preconception or reservation. In general, American children's theatre has remained outside and independent of the adult theatre, though it has reflected many of the same styles and trends.

Like its parent, which is often described as "that fabulous invalid," children's theatre has shown itself to be the hardiest of the performing arts. Through the years companies have been founded, sometimes to succeed, more often to fail, but always imbued with the determination to continue or resume activities at some later date or in some other place. Periodically, classes in drama have been added to school curricula, then, without warning, withdrawn when budgets were cut. In fact, it is only within the past thirty years that anything approaching stability can be observed. State arts councils, union contracts for performers, better educated producers, university theatre departments that offer child drama programs, and more discriminating sponsors account for the changes. In order to view them properly, however, it is necessary to look at the origins of a movement that from its inception has withstood adversity, if not seeming to thrive on it.

As we consider children's theatre in America as an art form, many questions come to mind: Where did it originate? When was the first play for young people produced? Who was responsible for it? How has children's theatre changed?

The support has come largely through the efforts of amateurs, although there have been some commercial ventures, and a few professional producers have shown interest in its potential. It was the social workers and educators, however, who instigated the first organized programs, but the interweaving of the activities of all of the groups cited constitutes a fascinating chapter in theatre history. By tracing the contributions of the major children's theatre companies, associations, and leaders, past and present, who have been involved in the movement, it is possible to understand its status and characteristics.

From the outset, and in almost every instance, funding has been inadequate; yet, where there has been a strong commitment on the part of the community, groups have managed to survive. Some of them have lasted for periods of ten to thirty years where interest and leadership have been constant. There is no doubt, however, that continuing financial problems have affected the quality and character of children's theatre in America, resulting in conservatism and mediocrity in far too many instances. Until the sixties very little experimentation took place, for the simple reason that well-known titles attract the child audience, and few producers or sponsors were willing to risk new plays on contemporary themes presented in unconventional formats. The fact that the first recorded groups were located in community centers and educational institutions rather than on the commercial stage further explains the direction that the movement took.

These first theatres for children were established with three clearly stated objectives, which may be described as follows: to provide whole-some entertainment for children in urban neighborhoods devoid of rec-reational and cultural resources; to provide another way for the children of immigrants to learn the language and customs of their adopted coun-try; to provide a gathering place for immigrant families. Social workers at the turn of the century had observed that storytelling and dramatic play were favorite activities of the children who came to the centers; and, while there were adult drama clubs, there were no counterparts for the children. To meet what they perceived as a need, social workers organized classes in the performing arts. Some of the classes were taught by staff members, but more often they were led by volunteers with a background in amateur theatricals and an interest in social service.

A group that has been active from the beginning was the Association of Junior Leagues of America (AJLA) (q.v.). A women's organization dedicated to social service, the league became the first national organi-zation to plan and carry out a large-scale drama and theatre program. Since then other organizations have played a significant part in the growth of the movement, but Junior League chapters throughout the United States have maintained a strong interest, teaching classes in acting and puppetry, telling stories, and presenting plays for young people in communities where there was no live theatre. While the league has changed and modified its emphases during the past eighty years, it has continued to support theatre for children in various ways in hundreds of communities throughout the nation.

Although today theatre for children may be found in suburban and rural communities, it is still a popular activity in inner city neighborhoods where its values are recognized as important to the quality of life, and as an antidote to the mass media. By the thirties, schools, colleges, and universities were beginning to assume responsibility for children's the-atre; today it is to these institutions that we look for guidance.

The American Educational Theatre Association, later renamed (The American Theatre Association [q.v.] or ATA) was founded in 1936. It gave professional recognition to this growing field of interest and thus put a stamp of approval on the subject as worthy of serious study. Less than a decade later the Children's Theatre Conference (CTC) was formed as a division of ATA. Its regional organization brought leaders and teachers together in central locations in all parts of the United States; their sharing of work and ideas was a turning point in the development of educational theatre. Since the sixties, government funding has made possible some large-scale projects through which students, teachers, and children have all benefitted. These projects include workshops in creative drama, movement, and puppetry as well as children's plays. Programs vary widely according to local needs, but under the guidance of educators, children's theatre entered a new era. The professional companies gathered strength through grants provided by arts councils and private foundations and by working more closely with schools that booked their productions and follow-up workshops. For the first time in history some children's theatre companies flourished.

The values of theatre for children have been stated and defended by its advocates from the beginning, and these claims have changed little, except in phrasing and ranking order. Appropriate entertainment for children and youth, an opportunity for learning, the development of an appreciation of the performing arts, and social awareness are the four most frequently stated reasons for presenting plays.

Today's high costs of production and the competition of television, however, pose new threats to producers and sponsors. On the other hand, the living theatre in one form or another has survived for 2,000 years; children's theatre, despite the differences between it and the parent art, shows the same resilience and capacity to satisfy deep human needs.

THE EARLY YEARS

The Precursors

Theatrical productions for children appeared in this country as early as 1810, according to periodicals of the period. During the next few decades performances of such plays as Joseph Jefferson's *Rip Van Winkle*, *Little Lord Fauntleroy*, and Mark Twain's version of *Tom Sawyer* were reported. *Mother Goose*, a mid-nineteenth-century operetta, was given numerous community productions and was apparently acted by children themselves. Another enterprise, cited in a scrapbook collection at The New York Public Library, was the Grand Duke's Theatre.[1] It was organized by a group of teenaged boys, but the entertainment was given for adults. The name was said to have come from the Grand Duke Alexis of Russia, who happened to be in the audience one night in the year 1872. His pleasure in the boys' showmanship prompted him to patronize a performance, after which the group called themselves the Grand Duke's Players. Like many other groups, it enjoyed a brief period of popularity, but there was no later record of activity. Under any circumstances this could not be construed as children's theatre, for the plays were given for adults, and the performers were of high school age.

Various settlement houses in New York, Chicago, and Boston also reported dramatic activities during the second half of the nineteenth century, but these did not develop into programs of regularly scheduled plays. The concept of entertainment planned and executed for the purpose of giving children wholesome pleasure and exposure to an art form belonged to the twentieth century.

On the elementary school level, few included the performing arts in their curricula; where they were found depended on the interest of the individual classroom teacher. The Dewey School of the University of Chicago (1896–1903) cited dramatic play in the study of literature and social studies as "a radical departure from the notion that school is just a place in which to learn lessons and acquire certain forms of skills."[2] The Ethical Culture Schools of New York, also oriented toward an experimental philosophy, held festivals and pageants in which children took part. With few exceptions, however, the public schools did not include dramatic activities of any kind.

Little more was being done on the college level, although there are occasional references to dramatic clubs and the production of classics in periodicals and professional journals of the time. Courses in drama were seldom included in the curriculum; instead, students were offered a limited choice of electives such as elocution and public speaking. Only occasionally were modern plays presented, and plays for the child audience were not even considered. Among the first universities to recognize theatre as a discipline worthy of academic study were the University of Pennsylvania, Yale, Harvard, Radcliffe, Columbia, Barnard, Vassar, Bryn Mawr, Smith, and the Women's College of Baltimore, all located in the East. Few courses in either dramatic literature or history of the theatre were offered, and only classic works were reported as having been presented to student audiences. Some of the large state universities in the Middle West and in California also gave productions of Shakespearean plays, but apparently they were rehearsed without faculty guidance or supervision. Unlike England, America lacked a tradition of support for the theatre arts; hence, it was not until there was a change in the attitude of the public that the performing arts were accorded the respect given the visual arts and music. While this did take place in time, it was in the community centers of our large cities that the first pioneering efforts were made.

According to all accounts appearing in periodicals and scrapbook collections of the period, the first important theatre for children in America was The Children's Educational Theatre (q.v.), founded in 1903. It was established at the Educational Alliance, a community center located on the Lower East Side of New York. The founder was Alice Minnie Herts, a social worker who was hired by the Educational Alliance to direct its recreation program. Noting the interests of the people who participated in the various activities included in the program, she soon realized that one of the most popular with both children and adults was drama. She also saw that it had little supervision and no artistic direction. As the existing drama club was composed of adults, Herts decided that a counterpart for children was needed and would be a good addition to the after-school program. She wanted to offer productions that, besides having value for the players, would provide a better quality of entertainment for children than she saw being performed at the Alliance and by the professional companies who brought their shows to local stages.

Herts' goals were in keeping with the objectives of the Alliance: to help young people learn the language and customs of their new country; to meet the social needs of the community by providing a place for families to gather; and "to help people create an idea from within rather than impose one on them from without."[3] These have been the major goals of children's theatre and creative drama leaders throughout the history of the movement, though they are ranked in importance according to the priorities of the producing groups.

Pioneering Programs

The Children's Educational Theatre opened officially with a highly successful production of *The Tempest* in October 1903. It was followed by *Ingomar*, *As You Like It*, and *The Forest Ring*, all of which received enthusiastic receptions. Children and adults were cast in the plays, a practice that aroused some controversy but which was consistent with Herts' point of view. The next season opened with *The Little Princess* by Frances Hodgson Burnett. All of the scripts selected for public performance were by Shakespeare or were children's classics. One of the most popular plays presented by The Children's Educational Theatre was Samuel Clemens' *The Prince and the Pauper*. Clemens' enthusiasm for the project and his approval of the production of his work led to his accepting an appointment on the board of directors. As news of the group spread, there was pressure to introduce a touring program in the metropolitan area in addition to the scheduled performances at the Educational Alliance. Increased costs as a result of this expansion could not be met, and so, six years after its founding, the first significant theatre for children in this country was forced to close. The excitement that it had generated continued, however, resulting in a restructuring, called the Education Players. The new group adhered to the original principles but operated under different management. The performers were adults, with children involved only as spectators.

The reputation of The Children's Educational Theatre spread rapidly, particularly among social workers and recreation leaders, who saw the values of the performing arts in the pursuit of their own goals. One settlement with a record of achievement in this area was Hull House (q.v.) in Chicago. Under the direction of Jane Addams, programs in the visual arts, music, and theatre had already been introduced. The first art exhibition had been held in 1891; a music school was founded in 1893; and productions of *Snow White*, *Puss in Boots*, and *Mat Tyler* were mentioned during the early years of the twentieth century. Before the thirties six dramatic clubs had operated at Hull House. Unlike the Educational Alliance, these clubs were begun for the youngest children who came to the center, but the popularity of the activity spread to all age levels. Hull House was fortunate in having a well-equipped auditorium for family entertainment; plays presented in it included *The Tempest*, *A Midsummer Night's Dream*, *Alice in Wonderland*, and some of Molière's comedies.

During the same period The Henry Street Settlement (q.v.) in New York was pioneering programs in dance and drama. Carried on informally in the beginning, they became the forerunners of the later well-known Henry Street Festivals. The director of the settlement, Lillian Wald, believed strongly in the value of the performing arts for disadvantaged youth and, like Jane Addams and Alice Minnie Herts, subscribed to the same objectives. Two New York philanthropists, Irene and Alice Lewisohn, gave money for a beautiful 500-seat theatre on Grand Street, designed to serve the people of the Lower East Side. This was the Neighborhood Playhouse, a name that has been associated with education in the performing arts and Off-Broadway theatre to the present time. It was officially opened in 1915, not as a children's theatre per se but as a home for theatrical activities of all kinds and for audiences of all ages.

The year 1903 also saw the founding of Nettie Greenleaf's Children's Theatre (q.v.) in Boston. It differed from those of the social settlements in intent and objectives. Children from the Dorothy Dix Home for Stage Children performed in plays that were popular with matinee audiences. It has been suggested that the theatre might have continued had it not been for the stringent new fire laws resulting from the tragic Iroquois Theatre fire in Chicago that same year. Nettie Greenleaf's building was considered unsafe and so was closed, not to reopen.

Franklin Sargent, director of the American Academy of Dramatic Art in New York, was also interested in establishing a theatre for young audiences. He was supported by playwright Edward E. Rose in his contention that there was a potential audience, if plays of superior quality were available at reasonable prices. Sargent initiated activities in 1899, using child actors in dramatizations of such well-known stories as *Jack the Giant Killer*, *Alice in Wonderland*, and *Humpty-Dumpty*. The audiences he hoped to reach did not materialize, however, and as an alternative, he began a second season with plays like *Oliver Twist*, designed for the entire family. After the third season the project was dropped, but its importance lay in Sargent's concern for young people and his attempt to reach them.

Although Broadway has never concerned itself with the establishment of a theatre for children, it has occasionally produced plays to which children have come. *Peter Pan* is an example of a play that has been seen with different casts six times in the past eighty years. The first production starred Maude Adams in 1905. Since then Marilyn Miller, Jean Arthur, Mary Martin, and Sandy Duncan have all played the title role to enthusiastic audiences, and Eva Le Gallienne's Civic Repertory Theatre gave a production of the play in the twenties. *The Blue Bird* in 1910 and *The Wiz*, a musical version of *The Wizard of Oz* in the seventies, captivated children able to pay the high price of admission. Stock companies in many cities around the country offered occasional entertainment billed as appropriate for the whole family. *Rebecca of Sunnybrook Farm*, *Mrs. Wiggs of the Cabbage Patch*, *Little Women*, *Uncle Tom's Cabin*, *Daddy Long Legs*, and *The Little Minister* were among the most popular titles. These productions could not be construed as children's theatre, but they do reveal producers' awareness of a young audience and the kinds of plays that would appeal to it.

Although more growth was to take place in subsequent years, the period between 1910 and 1930 was to see phenomenal growth in the nonprofessional theatre. Civic or community theatres, many of which included plays for children, were given encouragement and support from a new source, The Drama League of America (q.v.). Founded in 1910 in Evanston, Illinois, the Drama League considered a junior department of sufficient importance to bring in a specialist, Cora Mel Patten, to direct it. It was not long until children's programs sprang up in many large cities with both plays and pageants as popular activities. Founders of the league came from both the professional and non-professional sectors. Percy Mackaye, a playwright and enthusiastic advocate of the pageant, was a strong supporter of community and regional theatre. He was equally critical of Broadway for exploiting theatre and of the schools for their exclusion of it. Mackaye was convinced that it was only in the communities that America would be able to achieve an art form worthy of the name.

In addition to establishing centers throughout the United States, the Drama League published a magazine, *Drama,* which carried information and critical articles. Three well-known professors on its staff were Walter Pritchard Eaton, George Pierce Baker, and Barrett Clark; their regular contributions indicated the interest of educators in this burgeoning new movement. The Educational Drama League, established in 1913, was an extension of the Drama League and was created to introduce dramatic activities, or upgrade those that already existed, in schools and settlement houses. It published collections of plays for children and in 1915 published a play index entitled *Plays for Children,* edited by Kate Oglebay. This was the first reference work of its kind in America.

Chapters of the Drama League grew in size. Four years after its founding, the Boston chapter alone had 2,300 members. George Pierce Baker of Harvard was its president, a fact that may have accounted for the appeal of the organization to educators. Years later Winifred Ward, a Northwestern University professor of drama and one of the founders of The Children's Theatre Association of America (q.v.), stated, "In the awakening of general interest and dissemination of knowledge concerning children's plays, the Drama League of America deserves highest credit."[4] She went on to say that the history of children's theatre in America began with this organization.

Playgrounds and recreation centers were also recipients of the league's stimulation and support. While there were fewer organized or ongoing programs in these centers, the references to plays and pageants that appeared in the pages of *The Playground* and *Recreation* (magazines) are further proof of the league's influence. In spite of the enormous growth of the organization and the support it extended to all amateur efforts, the Drama League ceased operation in 1931. There has been speculation as to why such a positive force should be withdrawn, but Mrs. A. Starr Best, one of the founders and its first president, expressed her belief that the league had fulfilled its mission. It had raised the consciousness of the public as to what community theatre might be, and it had helped countless groups become self-sufficient. Its job done, the league suspended operations, leaving its members to continue the work in their own schools and communities.

No description of these early years would be complete without acknowledging the contributions of the Association of Junior Leagues of America, a national women's organization dedicated to volunteer social and charitable service. Junior League members as early as 1912 were engaged in storytelling and informal dramatic activities with and for children in slum neighborhoods. In 1921, however, the Junior League initiated a children's theatre program that was later recognized as one of the most important contributions ever made to the movement. A theatre consultant was hired and given an office at the national headquarters in New York, though most of her work involved travel to the various branches throughout the country. Both theatre and puppetry fell under the consultant's jurisdiction, but because this book is concerned only with the former, puppetry will be excluded from the discussion.

To mark the founding of the program, an elaborate production of *Alice in Wonderland* was given in Chicago. This took place in a large auditorium downtown and was highly publicized. The performers were women, all amateurs, but the staff and backstage crew were professional. The success of this venture generated future productions of such plays as *The Little Princess, The Land of Don't Want To, The Wizard of Oz*, and *Racketty-Packetty House*. Other cities followed the example of the Chicago league until, by 1928, fifty-two leagues were reported to be producing children's plays. Lavish settings and costumes were an important component of the productions.

It is here that the work of the Junior League revealed its new direction. Plays were performed by adults rather than by children; and in order to meet production costs, tickets were so high-priced that only children from well-off families could afford to buy them. Recognizing this situation, blocks of tickets were reserved for the disadvantaged, thus maintaining a practice of social service. Meanwhile, community theatres in smaller cities and suburbs were serving the interests of the middle class, while the settlement houses were implementing their programs with informal dramatic activities. A statement supporting the Junior League's move into formal production was made thirty years later in the following words: "Theatre meets a fundamental need of human beings. It allows them to enter worlds larger than their own, to encounter people different from themselves, and to share experiences that may never exist in everyday living."[5]

A unique theatre, begun at this time and later to become world famous, was the Karamu House Children's Theatre (q.v.) in Cleveland. The founders, Rowena and Russell Jelliffe, came from the University of Chicago in 1915 to direct the activities of the Karamu House, a small Negro settlement. Unlike the majority of institutions of its kind, Karamu House was a center for the visual and performing arts. Three years after the Jelliffes' arrival, they took the first steps toward founding a children's theatre. They began with informal classes in story-acting and puppetry, moving gradually to public performances of scripted plays performed by young actors. One of the interesting aspects of the development of the Karamu theatre was that the children's plays preceded the adult plays, contrary to the usual pattern.

The first plays were dramatizations of stories the children brought with them from the South to their new home in the Midwest. "How Come Br'er Rabbit Do No Work?," "Saturday Evening" (an animal story), and "Shoes for the Feet"were three of the earliest stories to be dramatized. The migration of southern Negroes to the large northern cities brought new needs and pressing social problems. At Karamu House the arts served many of these needs and, in so doing, promoted interracial cooperation and creativity. The reputation of the work spread beyond the city limits, bringing not only neighborhood people but university students and interested residents of Cleveland suburbs to the little theatre in the heart of the Negro ghetto. In the thirties a new building was erected to provide more audience space, rehearsal studios, and backstage operation. Within a few years of its founding, the Karamu was on its way to becoming the most distinguished Negro art theatre in the world, and this included the children's component. Anne Flagg, later to join the drama faculty of the Evanston, Illinois, school system, developed a program of creative drama for the younger children. Although the staff was increased and there were changes throughout the years, the Jelliffes remained in charge until well into the fifties, a factor which accounted for the stability and clear direction of the program. Indeed, their interest continued beyond their retirement, and while severe racial problems were to beset the city in the sixties, the Karamu managed to survive. Rowena Jelliffe, still a resident of Cleveland, recalls the hard times and the highlights of this extraordinary institution.

Once public consciousness had been raised and a few successful ventures were launched, it seemed as if the idea of presenting plays for children spread overnight. Known producing groups are described in Part Two of this volume, though there were undoubtedly many more that functioned briefly with little or no publicity. Among those mentioned before 1920 were the Community Theatre of Duluth (q.v.), The House of Play (q.v.) in Washington, D.C., Roxbury House in Boston, Stuart Walker's Portmanteau Theatre (q.v.) in New York, the Children's Civic Theatre of Chicago also known as the Municipal Pier Theatre in Chicago, and the Children's Theatre of San Francisco State Teachers

College (q.v.). As Roxbury House placed its stress on creative drama and storytelling rather than on the formal production of plays, it served a different though equally important function. It was never a producing center but was important for its educational contribution. A short-lived enterprise at the Century Theatre in New York was reported, as were a 1912 professional production of *Snow White* by Winthrop Ames and a 1915 production of *Treasure Island* by Charles Hopkins; however, none of the three developed as the producers had hoped. After the openings there was no further mention of the last two, whereas the Century Theatre project closed at the end of its first year.

Two other institutions must be cited in a review of pioneering programs, although neither one developed an ongoing children's theatre program. The first of these, Greenwich House in New York, has included dramatic activities in its children's program from the early twenties. A remarkable aspect of it is that the program remained under the leadership of one woman for forty years. Helen Murphy, the director, did not approve of public performances for children, believing instead that classes in which process rather than product was stressed contributed more to the growth of the participants. While she did give occasional plays, she selected classics, and the major roles were played by high school students. The other institution was Peabody House in Boston. In 1920 a production of *Aucassin and Nicolette* was given with a cast of children drawn from the settlement and the Buckingham School. Of particular interest here is that Edith King and Dorothy Coit, teachers at the Buckingham School, were in charge. Shortly after the production they left Boston for New York, where they established The King-Coit School of Acting and Design (q.v.).

Children's Theatre in the Little Theatres

Technically, the civic or little theatres of the twenties and thirties differed from those of the inner city in certain important respects. First of all, they were located in small towns and suburbs of large cities and were generally started by affluent civic leaders. In most cases the children's theatre originated as a branch of an adult organization and had similar aims and practices rather than those held by the social workers of the settlement houses. Their primary aim was to entertain and give children of middle- and upper-income groups an experience in live theatre. Early examples of little theatres offering plays for young audiences were the Scalawags of Columbia, South Carolina, The Children's Theatre Guild of New Orleans (q.v.), The Junior Repertory Theatre of Minneapolis, The St. Paul Children's Theatre (q.v.), the Indianapolis Junior Civic Theatre (q.v.), and The Omaha Children's Theatre (q.v.).

The major work of the schools and colleges was to come in the forties

1915 saw the beginning of educational theatre

"Toy Theatre of New York" never materialized (but had elaborate plans for fairtra tals etc

and thereafter, but a few educational institutions offered occasional plays or held dramatic classes for local children in the twenties. A few of these are still in existence, though in a changed form; some have served as models for others that followed.

The Emerson College Children's Theatre (q.v.) in Boston is an example. Founded in 1920, it represented one of the earliest programs under academic auspices and was frequently mentioned in periodicals of the period. Imogene Hogle, the first director, actually began her work in children's theatre when she was an undergraduate. The plays she directed were so successful that after her graduation in 1919 she was invited to return to plan and run a children's theatre program at the college. With few exceptions, her productions consisted of dramatizations of classics, though she used a new script occasionally. On her advisory board were Walter Hampden, Constance D'Arcy Mackay, and Walter Pritchard Eaton. Perhaps the longevity of the Emerson program was due to its solid foundation and concerned professional guidance. Today Emerson College boasts one of the strongest and most modern programs in the United States with an emphasis on theatre in education as well as entertainment.

An enterprise that has intrigued children's theatre leaders to the present day was The King-Coit School of Acting and Design in New York. Established in 1923, it consisted of an after-school program for children aged five to thirteen. An annual production, given in the spring, was the culmination of the entire year's work. Children were the performers, but the scenery and costumes they designed were constructed by professional theatre artists, and plays were given in attractive midtown auditoriums. The procedure followed at the King-Coit School was entirely different from that of any other group of the period, and, indeed, from any that have followed, with the exception of one or two that used it as a model. Some of the plays presented between 1923 and the closing of the school in the fifties were *Aucassin and Nicolette*, *The Tempest*, *Kai Khosru*, *The Story of Theseus*, *The Rose and the Ring*, *The Image of Artemis*, and *The Golden Cage* (from the poems of William Blake).

The Children's Theatre of Evanston (q.v.) is probably the best known of all the early theatres established by an educational institution. It was founded in 1925 and became a model for other communities. Winifred Ward, distinguished pioneer in the field of child drama, was its founder and for many years director and supervisor. A professor in Northwestern University's School of Speech, she established creative drama courses for teachers, a curriculum in creative drama for the public schools of Evanston, and a theatre for the children of this Chicago suburb. It was similar in some respects to the Emerson College Children's Theatre in that it offered Northwestern students an opportunity to act in the plays and work backstage. Unlike at Emerson, however, children in the upper grades of the public schools played the parts of children when the scripts called for them. This resulted in a close relationship between the university and the board of education. Several plays a year were given performances in two of the elementary school auditoriums rather than in the university theatre. This outstanding program lasted until the seventies and was widely praised and imitated for the fine quality of its productions and its service to the community.

Also established in the Chicago area in the same period was the Goodman School Children's Theatre (q.v.) of the Art Institute of Chicago. Muriel Brown, a graduate of Carnegie Institute of Technology in Pittsburgh, was in charge. She combined her background in theatre arts with her interest in working with and for children. Her first season at the Goodman was so successful that it developed into an ongoing program. Roles were played by apprentices (young adult students at the Goodman), and capacity audiences were reported from the beginning.

The University of Tulsa initiated dramatic activities for children as early as 1926. Here college students worked directly with children in Saturday morning classes in play production. The performances were given in the evening rather than during the day, the usual practice elsewhere. Easter and Christmas pageants were also presented and were taken to area churches in addition to the regularly scheduled plays at the university. An article in *The Playground* described the Tulsa enterprise as a pioneer in the furthering of good community drama.[6]

The Jack and Jill Players (q.v.) of Chicago represented one of the first private theatre schools for children. Established in 1925, it served a somewhat different purpose from those already cited. Acting classes for children, a touring program, and regular performances in its own small theatre served thousands of children in the Chicago metropolitan area for many years.

Other theatres for children, established under the auspices of educational institutions, were mentioned in periodicals and newspapers of the times; they included the Minneapolis Children's Players (a high school group); the Richmond, Virginia, High School Players; the Children's Theatre of Illinois Wesleyan; and the Union High School of Bakersfield, California. Vassar, Goucher, Radcliffe, Drake University, Syracuse University, and Texas State College for Women in Denton all gave occasional plays for child audiences. There may have been others, but information is scanty and records are no longer in existence.

One example of a "town-gown" activity was a pageant sponsored by the University of North Carolina. The pageant, *Children of Old Carolina*, was written and directed by Ethel Theodora Rockwell, a member of the faculty. She took as her theme the part that children had played in the history of the state and used youngsters from sixteen schools in the area in the cast. The result was apparently a beautiful production, which

Constance D'Arcy Mackay described as "the first time in America that children have acted a pageant representing their part in the upbuilding of a state."[7]

Professional Theatre for Children

One of the longest lasting and best known of the professional theatres for children in the United States was Clare Tree Major Productions (q.v.). The founder and director, Clare Tree Major, was an English actress who studied at the Royal Academy in London and performed with the Sir Herbert Tree and Benson companies. When she immigrated to New York in 1916 she joined the Washington Square Players, an experimental theatre group in Greenwich Village. The group was composed of young writers, actors, and directors whose ambition and creative energy led to the formation of the Theatre Guild. Clare Tree Major had become interested in entertainment for young people, so instead of continuing with the group, she broke away to establish a professional children's theatre company. Her venture prospered, enabling her to go on with more elaborate productions. In 1922 a new opportunity was presented to her; a high school student, after seeing one of her children's plays, asked her if she could present dramatized versions of some of the literature read in school. Responding to the question, Major consulted the Association of Teachers of English as to the possibility. A positive response resulted in the formation of the Threshold Players, a company specializing in productions suitable for high school audiences. The plays were selected by the New York Association of Teachers of English and Major. This coordination of professional theatre with the public school curriculum was unique at the time, predating a practice that was to become popular in the second half of the century.

Major held a point of view shared by many educators today. She believed in the value of drama classes but thought that they should not constitute the child's total experience. The other part of the experience, in her opinion, was the professional production of plays of literary worth with aesthetically pleasing mounting. Furthermore, she stressed the use of international material as a way of developing interest and appreciation of other peoples and their cultures. Her school plays and her cross-country tours lasted for over twenty-five years, during which time she kept a firm grip on the organization and its artistic direction.

The National Junior Theatre of Washington, D.C. (q.v.), on the other hand, presented Broadway plays of the highest quality that were considered appropriate for children's audiences. These included *A Kiss for Cinderella*, *Quality Street*, *A Midsummer Night's Dream*, and *The Prince and the Pauper*. It was novel in its choice of material; no other group of the period or since has reported a repertory of this type.

Summary

These early years saw the initiation of children's theatre activities in all areas of the country but principally in the large urban communities. Mirroring theatre history, it was the social aspect that first captured the imagination of the public. As time went on, however, this grassroots movement became more formalized, moving from recreation settings into the schools, where it was gradually accepted for its educational value. The professional theatre, never a strong supporter of theatre for children, was represented by Clare Tree Major and a few short-lived commercial enterprises. Yet, despite its haphazard growth, children's theatre had put down firm roots, which were to send up stalks that would become strong and resilient.

1911 - PROSPECT PARK - "PAGENT OF THE PATRIOTS"

1918 - ALICE HAZELTINE PUBLISHED AN INDEX OF CHILDREN'S SCRIPTS IN A ST. LOUIS LIBRARY NEWSPAPER

THE DEPRESSION, WAR, AND POSTWAR YEARS

The economic depression that America suffered during the thirties, closing down many playhouses and commercial theatres, had little effect on theatre for children. Indeed, on the contrary, it was a period of growth. The most obvious explanation was that children's theatre was not dependent on its box office for survival and that the majority of its practitioners were teachers, social workers, and volunteers; only a small minority earned their living as professionals, and they were more affected by the war than by the Depression. It should not come as a surprise, therefore, to find that during the thirties children's theatre continued to thrive.

The transition from the Depression to the war and postwar periods wrought changes in all aspects of American life but, again, children's theatre expanded as it gained new leadership. Because the growth was so steady and the forces so intertwined, these three periods in history may be viewed together. By this time it was obvious that support for children's theatre came from four major sources: national organizations, educational institutions, community organizations, and the professional or commercial theatre. Of these, the commercial theatre offered the least, whereas the schools and colleges were assuming a leadership role.

National Organizations

The three organizations that contributed most to the growth of children's theatre during these years were the Association of Junior Leagues of America, the American National Theatre and Academy (ANTA), and the Children's Theatre Conference.

An active supporter of children's theatre for nearly twenty years, the Junior League continued its interest and programs for the next twenty. Virginia Lee Comer, children's theatre consultant for the league during the thirties, in comparing its early work with its later activities, stated that the touring program was its most successful. The large centralized productions were reconsidered in the light of the children they served. This review resulted in a major policy change. The new direction taken at that time was a touring program, which offered plays on a small and inexpensive scale at little or no cost to the sponsors. "Grand Rapids and Cincinnati Leagues were the first to undertake an in-school trouping program."[8] During the thirties, leagues, PTAs, and community theatres throughout the country frequently cooperated in bringing the performing arts to children.

By the early forties, civic and university theatres were starting to offer more plays for young people in their communities. The league, however, by taking plays on tour, was reaching different populations: audiences not served by either of the others. In 1940 there were forty-seven groups of league players going out on a regular basis to schools, rural areas, settlements, orphanages, and hospitals. When their plays were given in schools during school hours, no fee was charged; when they were given at other times and in other places, there was an occasional fee or admission charge, but it was minimal.

Many leagues sponsored professional entertainment for children, preferring to give their support to companies with high standards rather than perform themselves. This practice has continued to the present day. When, in the sixties, the league touring program was cut back, the sponsorship expanded. Carefully kept records of league programs and audiences during the years 1939–1949 show the extent of the work that was being carried out by league members.[9]

The American National Theatre and Academy was founded in 1935 but did not function until ten years later. Its purpose was to extend the living theatre by bringing the best in the theatre to every state in the nation. Its inactivity at the time of its founding was due in large part to the Depression and the establishment of The Federal Theatre for Children (q.v.). One of the areas with which ANTA was to be concerned was children's theatre. A service organization rather than a research agency, it nevertheless kept records of both adult and children's theatre during those years. In 1948 it listed over 1,500 children's theatre projects in the United States. Though never a strong proponent of this branch of the theatre, ANTA was sympathetic to its goals and cooperative with researchers and producers seeking advice and information.

The Federal Theatre, a project of the Works Progress Administration (WPA), was established in 1935 by an act of Congress. While it was professional in the sense that the performers and technicians were paid salaries and came from the professional sector, it was noncommercial in the sense that it was subsidized and therefore not dependent on box office receipts for survival. The Federal Theatre project was an emergency relief measure that created employment for actors and technicians, while at the same time offering first class entertainment for a public that could not afford theatre tickets. Under the direction of Hallie Flanagan of Vassar College, it was designed to become a decentralized theatre, established in many cities throughout the country. Its leaders envisioned regional producing centers that would recognize the geographic areas, their traditions and interests, customs and occupations. Children's theatre was one aspect of the overall plan, and statistics from the files of the National Service Bureau in Washington showed that theatre for children was presented in the following cities during the three years the Federal Theatre existed: New York, New York; Gary, Indiana; Los Angeles, California; Seattle, Washington; New Haven, Connecticut; Portland, Oregon; Cleveland, Ohio; Denver, Colorado; and Tampa, Florida.

New York offered one of the most extensive programs for young people. *The Emperor's New Clothes* was its first production; following a successful run in New York, it was taken on tour, playing on portable stages in city parks. Within a period of six weeks, over 100,000 persons, mostly children, were reported to have seen it in the metropolitan area alone. The administration was encouraged by this enthusiastic reception and, hoping to establish an ongoing program appropriate to the local audiences, sent out questionnaires to a large number of settlement houses. The results of the survey were the first statistics taken in this country on age level preferences. At the same time, a group of educators from Teachers College of Columbia University made a study of audience response. The policy of the Federal Theatre was that no play should be presented that offered entertainment as its sole objective; substance and a point of view were basic requirements for scripts.

In keeping with this philosophy, the New York Federal Theatre opened its second season with *The Revolt of the Beavers*, a production that caused some controversy because some persons thought it Communist-inspired. Inasmuch as the Federal Theatre was under constant attack of this sort, its directors were not alarmed; however, a statement regarding play selection was made by Hallie Flanagan, further clarifying the principles and practices of the agency: "Washington did not dictate individual plays, leaving such choice to the various directors, with, however, the suggestion of emphasis on new American plays, classical plays, children's plays, and a special program for Negro companies."[10]

Particularly effective children's programs were set up in Cleveland, Ohio; Gary, Indiana; New Orleans; Chicago; Cincinnati; Pasadena; Portland, Oregon; and Seattle; and there were enthusiastic plans under discussion for the future. In spite of its success in many cities, however, there was mounting cricitism of subsidy for the arts and the use of theatre as a relief measure; thus the Federal Theatre was terminated by an act of Congress in 1939, before it had had a chance to fulfill its promise. The suspicion of Communist influence was an ever-present factor in arguments against it; yet it had made a statement and can be viewed in the perspective of time as having made an important contribution to the children's theatre movement in America. One can only imagine how the Federal Theatre might have developed had it been allowed to continue. Within three short years new scripts for the child audience were written and tried out; new techniques were introduced, and many young actors and writers found this branch of theatre an exciting and satisfying experience.

A national professional organization that was to become the strongest influence and most effective force in educational theatre in the future was established in 1936. This was the American Educational Theatre Association (AETA), later renamed the American Theatre Association

(ATA) so as to include the professional, community, and military sectors. While its original concern was drama and theatre instruction in higher education, many members were aware of the growing interest in children's theatre, and to that end established a Children's Theatre Committee in 1944. The following summer Winifred Ward, a professor at Northwestern University, invited eighty members of this committee to her campus to explore the needs of children and to plan a suitable theatre program. Subsequently annual summer meetings were held either on a university campus or in a hotel in different regions of the country. *A Children's Theatre Directory* and a *Children's Theatre Bibliography* were published, and by 1950 a newsletter was circulating. Members of the Children's Theatre Committee (in 1950 renamed the Children's Theatre Conference [CTC]) came from a variety of areas: schools, colleges, Junior Leagues, community theatres, and professional companies. By 1949 between 200 and 300 permanent children's theatre groups were identified as operating in the United States, according to the combined figures of AETA and ANTA. This interest was reflected in the attendance of 248 delegates at the annual convention held in New York that year. Major concerns of the CTC were better scripts, better direction of plays, and a better understanding of the child audience.

The Children's Theatre Conference extended its interest by passing a resolution in regard to UNESCO (United Nations Educational, Scientific and Cultural Organization). It stated that "children's theatres of the United States support the aims and programs of the UNESCO through local activities and through whatever practical assistance may be given to children's theatre programs elsewhere in the world."[11] This concern later resulted in the formation of a new international organization, ASSITEJ (Association Internationale du Theatre pour l'Enfance et la Jeunesse) in the sixties (q.v.). Through that organization the United States attained visibility and assumed a leadership role on the international level.

The Educational Theatre

Winifred Ward's pioneering work in Evanston in the twenties may be viewed as a turning point in drama/theatre education for and with children. By the forties classes in drama and play production had spread on all levels. Whereas before this there had been occasional suggestions that drama might be a valid curricular inclusion, by the thirties it had been taken seriously and could be found on many high school and college campuses. Ward must also be given credit for clarifying and defining the following terms: *creative dramatics* was improvisation and referred to what the child did, and was therefore participant centered; *children's theatre* was what the child viewed as a spectator, and was therefore audience centered. Both were of value, but this distinction helped teachers and administrators to design programs and formulate plans which in time developed into a sequence of courses in child drama. Ward's four books, *Creative Drama*, *Children's Theatre*, *Stories to Dramatize*, and *Playmaking with Children*, were among the first college texts to appear.

Among institutions of higher learning mentioned in the professional journals of the period as offering plays for children in the community were Mills College in California (1931), Syracuse University (1930), Adelphi College (1937), and the University of Iowa (1932). These were followed by dozens of other colleges and universities that included work for and with children as a part of their drama/theatre departments.

The successful program resulting from the close cooperation between Northwestern and the Evanston Board of Education became a model for other universities and colleges. A program that attracted attention and continued to lead for many years in the area of theatre education was begun by Kenneth Graham, a professor at the University of Minnesota. In 1940 university plays were given for school children in Minneapolis in school time. Study guides for teachers were an added feature, a unique resource at the time, although a common practice today. Weekend performances were also given for family audiences, thus proving that theatre could be worthy of a place in the arts for elementary school children, as well as providing entertainment for the community at large.

The University of Denver theatre department sent out one of the first children's theatre touring companies in the Rocky Mountain area. Campton Bell, director of the Children's Theatre Conference in 1949, developed a curriculum in which courses in children's theatre, creative dramatics, and playwriting for young audiences were taught. This was further implemented by a course in creative dramatics for children aged seven to thirteen. In the East at the same time the Children's Experimental Theatre of Baltimore (q.v.) grew out of the creative dramatics classes held at Johns Hopkins University. The founder of the theatre, Isabel Burger, established classes for children in five age groups and, responding to demand, soon afterward added plays and teachers' workshops. By the end of the forties the burgeoning activities of the children's theatre needed new and larger quarters. It was renamed the Vagabond Theatre of Baltimore and took up its new residence in a hundred-year-old carriage house with a suburban branch in Catonsville.

Other educational institutions that announced programs at this time were the Reeder School in Texas, whose program was patterned after that of the King-Coit School (q.v.) in New York; Brigham Young University in Utah (q.v.); the University of Delaware; Baylor University in Texas; and Denison University in Ohio. Some of their programs are among the best known today. Progressive educators of the period viewed theatre as a valuable inclusion in the curriculum, provided that it offered more than light entertainment. Sara Shakow expressed this point of view in an address to the National Progressive Education Association in Chicago in 1940:

A children's theatre today, if it hopes to justify its right to existence, cannot confine its aims to merely furnishing amusement. A children's theatre today, if it expects to exercise its rightful function as a developmental agency and serve effectively as an instrument of education and culture, must offer more than sheer diversion and clean entertainment.[12]

She went on to say that this form of theatre must become a permanent institution, rather than an occasional production under a variety of auspices, and that it should involve itself with other cultural resources in the community.

Children's Theatre in Community and Recreation Centers

The community theatre movement also continued to grow, though at a slower pace than the educational theatre. The two directions it had taken, activity on the part of the little theatre groups and activity on the part of recreation centers, were still apparent. These functions served different purposes and needs and were conducted by persons with different orientations to the arts. Programs that attracted attention for their successful and innovative work were located in Philadelphia, Brooklyn, New York, Boston, Miami, Milwaukee, Palo Alto, and in a number of Texas towns. One of the most unusual, and one that is still a popular resource, was the Children's Theatre of Palo Alto (q.v.). An adult theatre was also housed in a beautiful facility that included, in addition to the children's theatre, a children's library and museum, swimming pool, recreational equipment, and lovely gardens. Its longevity has contributed to its becoming well known, and it has been the site of numerous children's theatre conferences. In addition to articles about it, a book, *Children and the Theatre* by Caroline Fisher and Hazel Robertson, was published by the Stanford University Press in 1950. Aesthetic pleasure and recreation were the goals of this permanent year-round activity.

Newspapers and journals of the period document other programs too numerous to list, but a few deserve mention because of the influence they have had on the movement or for the positions they continue to occupy. Among the latter was the Children's Entertainment Committee of Maplewood, New Jersey, which was the forerunner of a professional enterprise of the late thirties and early forties, "the miracle . . . known as Junior Programs [q.v.]."[13] More will be said of this later. Seattle Junior Programs (q.v.) was founded in 1939 and has continued to offer plays of high quality for area children. It has undergone a number of changes, however, first functioning as a sponsoring organization. Then, when the war reduced the number of available touring companies, it turned to production. Aided by the Seattle Repertory Playhouse, an adult group, the University of Washington, and the initiation of a playwriting contest that gave it national visibility, it managed not only to survive but to become stabilized and thrive.

The Nashville, Tennessee, Children's Theatre (q.v.), established in 1931 by the Junior League, has held steadfastly to its original purpose of presenting a regular schedule of good plays for children. In the sixties it joined Palo Alto in constructing a beautiful theatre building for the production of children's plays. Audiences were bussed to the auditorium, and plays were also taken to outlying communities, a practice that proved so successful that it continues today, on a larger scale. In the seventies an educational program was added, and the official name was changed to the Nashville Academy Theatre (q.v.). Ann Hill, civic leader and a past president of both The Children's Theatre Association of America and The American Theatre Association, was instrumental in its growth and development. Recognition was given her at the time the enlarged and renovated building was opened, and the auditorium was renamed the Ann Stahlman Hill Auditorium.

The Wichita Children's Theatre (q.v.) was formed in 1932. Its growth during the next fifty years was commemorated in the book *The Wichita Children's Theatre: The First Thirty Years*, published in 1977. By the end of the forties children's theatre groups from Maine to California were being reported, with productions, festivals, marionette shows, and storytelling as components of their programs.

Professional Theatre for Children

Several professional companies were offering plays for young people during the thirties and forties. The only one that had been in existence before this time was the Clare Tree Major Productions, established in 1923. The rest, perhaps stimulated by this new movement in the performing arts, or by the possibilities it offered young actors to find employment, were founded during the thirties. As for Major, she expanded operations with the introduction of a touring program, which visited twenty-five cities along the East Coast. By 1940 she was taking her plays across the nation to meet the demands of this new market. Major continued to offer both children's classics and new scripts, with, however, a continuing belief that international material provided the most desirable fare for young audiences. In the forties she added a National Classics Theatre for audiences on high school and college campuses. Her school in Pleasantville, New York, was a training ground for young actors preparing to work in her company. This two-year course, and a summer school for teachers interested in theatre as an art form for students, became regular features.

Although there were other professional companies doing work of high quality, Junior Programs, Inc. (q.v.), was the crowning achievement of the period. It was an outgrowth of the Maplewood, New Jersey, Children's Entertainment Committee, and its phenomenal success must be attributed to the founding spirit, Dorothy McFadden. Junior Programs, Inc. (q.v.), began operations in 1936 as a sponsoring agency with the endorsement of such organizations as the National Congress of Parents and Teachers and the Child Study Association of America. In her statement of purpose McFadden described the project as follows:

1. To make available to every child, rich or poor, productions by the finest adult artists in varied fields of entertainment, which will have real cultural value. Such entertainments should be planned to leave not only happy memories but a high standard for the child's own work in similar fields and a new stimulus and interest in various forms of art and knowledge which before had been outside his field of vision.
2. To educate the parents and the community in general to the need for wholesome entertainment being provided at regular intervals, for every child, at low ticket prices in community supervised auditoriums, and to make them realize that such entertainment can be educationally and morally valuable as well as keeping the child off the city streets and away from harmful occupations, such as gang activities and motion pictures of the more lurid variety.
3. To act as a clearing house for programs for children, and, by means of many conferences, previews and personal assistance of educators, to raise the standards of all offerings for children in the entertainment field.[14]

By the forties ballet and opera had been added to the repertory. In 1943, however, a blow was struck from which Junior Programs was not to recover; the shortage of gasoline and the drafting of actors into the armed forces caused a suspension of performances. These proved to be more than temporary setbacks, for Junior Programs never resumed operation. What was reported to have been one of the finest companies in the history of children's theatre in America lasted only seven years. One member of the ballet company, however, continued, but with a new touring ensemble of his own. This was Edwin Strawbridge, a former concert performer. From 1940 on he devoted himself to children's audiences and became, incidentally, a member of the newly formed Children's Theatre Conference.

Names of other companies that appeared frequently in articles and reviews during these years were Grace Price Productions, Inc. (q.v.) of Pittsburgh; the American Theatre for Children in Los Angeles; the Provincetown Children's Theatre in New York; and Children's World Theatre (q.v.), also located in New York. The last mentioned was described as "one of the brightest hopes of the children's theatre movement in America."[15] Its fundamental purposes were to arouse the imagination through active entertainment; to inspire children with the best in movement, speech, art, and music; and to increase their appreciation of other national cultures and customs. This new venture, which took its shows on the road as well as performing them at the Barbizon Plaza in New York, met with high praise from the beginning. The six members of the founding company were well grounded as both actors and teachers, having qualifications later considered ideal for performers in the field, and, indeed, subsequently required for their counterparts in Great Britain. Children's World Theatre, begun in 1947, ceased operation abruptly in 1955, when its founder/director, Monte Meacham, was killed in an automobile accident. Like Junior Programs, the company never reformed, though the other five members continued to work in the field of drama education for children.

Before leaving this period, one more important event must be noted. This was the founding of the Children's Theatre Press in 1935 by Sara Spencer in Charleston, West Virginia. After her move a few years later to Anchorage, Kentucky, it was renamed the Anchorage Press. Spencer began the small publishing company with only four titles, but thirty years later the list had grown to well over one hundred plays and books on children's theatre. Quality rather than quantity, and tradition rather than experimentation, have been the guiding principles of the Anchorage Press from its inception. In the seventies Orlin Corey, producer of The Everyman Players (q.v.), purchased the press, which is now located in New Orleans.

Summary

In retrospect, it is apparent that educational, community, and professional theatre all advanced during the years 1930–1950, with the leadership gradually shifting from community organizations to schools and colleges. Theatre departments were beginning to offer courses to prepare leaders and teachers of creative drama and children's theatre, mainly for the elementary school level. Publication of plays and textbooks, which had been scanty, was beginning to accelerate; two of the best known texts published at this time were Winifred Ward's *Children's Theatre* in 1939 and *Playmaking with Children* in 1947. Charlotte Chorpenning, Chicago playwright and educator, contributed a supply of good plays, many of which are still in demand. She also designed a set of rules for playwrights in children's theatre. Whereas there had been plays written expressly for young audiences before this, Chorpenning was the first American to study children's reactions, interests, and needs seriously and to offer guidelines for other playwrights to follow. In 1947 Kenneth Graham of the University of Minnesota completed his doctoral dissertation entitled "An Introductory Study of the Evaluation of Plays for Children's Theatre in the United States." While the movement was still far from widespread, interest was growing, and educators were concerning themselves with both the content and teaching techniques that were to influence practices in the years ahead.

The majority of the plays continued to be adaptations of familiar fairy tales and favorite stories, traditionally treated. What was new, however, was a regard for performance skills and education of teachers and directors working in this area. While there was still wide variation in quality, companies were showing a concern for standards. Better scripts, improved performance skills, and a new generation of practitioners, schooled in an educational philosophy and methodology, were visible outcomes of twenty years of growth.

YEARS OF GROWTH, YEARS OF CHANGE: THE 1950s AND 1960s

The years 1950 to 1970 were to witness unprecedented growth and change in theatre for children. There was little change in content and format during the fifties, but some significant events took place that must be noted. The first of these was the Mid-Century White House Conference in 1950, with children's theatre for the first time occupying a place on the agenda. The second was the previously mentioned establishment of the Children's Theatre Conference as a division of AETA (now the ATA) in 1952, with a regional organization that comprised sixteen areas covering the entire United States and Canada. The third event was government funding for the arts on national, state, and municipal levels. Much more will be said of this later, but there is no doubt as to the transfusion it gave to a malnourished, struggling branch of the American theatre and the impact it had on the future.

Educational and community offerings were expanding steadily, and theatrical booking agencies in New York showed both supply and demand for professional entertainment for young people to be at their highest levels so far. Although more imaginative and radical changes were to take place by the seventies, the early part of the period laid the groundwork for what lay ahead.

An International Conference

The First International Conference on Theatre and Youth was held in Paris in 1952. Under the auspices of UNESCO, it was attended by thirty delegates and twenty-three observers from Europe, South Africa, the United States, and the United Kingdom. Rose Robinson Cowen represented the Children's Theatre Conference, later known as CTAA. Public performance by children, appropriate plays for children and young people, and the composition of audiences were among the topics discussed. Future plans were formulated, but it was to be another ten years before the United States became actively involved on the international level. When it did, it was through ASSITEJ (q.v.).

National Organizations

In the fifties the two major national organizations concerned with children's theatre continued to be the Junior League and the Children's Theatre Conference. Conditions throughout the country changed after the war, and the leagues were adapting their activities to meet the needs of children in urban, rural, and suburban communities. Many league members joined the CTC and took an active part in its annual conventions and regional conferences. Because of the relatively limited number of good plays for small touring groups and community theatres, the Junior League established a drama library, which included both scripts and "packages" including sets, costumes, properties, and lighting equipment. In some cities leagues presented plays on local television and radio stations. The Toledo, Ohio, league assisted in a summer workshop for teachers given at the University of Toledo. The league touring programs continued, though sponsorship of professional plays was gaining favor in the interest of obtaining a higher quality of production than local amateur actresses could achieve. A consultant from the national headquarters in New York was also available to local chapters, and drama programs for disadvantaged youth continued to be a priority.

The Children's Theatre Conference, now a full-fledged division of AETA (later ATA), undertook a number of projects that were handled by subcommittees. These included bibliographies, play standards, a directory, publicity kits, and dramatic curriculum studies. Additional committees dealing with a placement service, newsletter, and other topics of concern were added in 1953. The objectives of CTC were stated as follows:

1. To promote the establishment of children's theatre activities in all communities by educational, community, and private groups.
2. To encourage the raising and maintaining of high standards in all types of children's theatre activities throughout America.
3. To provide a meeting ground for children's theatre workers from all levels through sponsorship of an annual national meeting, regional meetings, and conference committees throughout the year.[16]

A foundation for special projects and services, the Children's Theatre Foundation, was established in 1958. Its purpose was to give financial aid to graduate students involved in significant children's theatre research, provide expenses for delegates' travel to international meetings, and supply speakers from outside the association. Regional projects were also established as time went on, but these have varied according to local interests. An example was a New York showcase of professional entertainment for the following season. Excerpts from plays, puppet shows, dance, and one-person performances were presented to sponsors. This popular project became unwieldy, however, as the number of small professional touring companies increased, and it was ultimately passed along to a group of producers, who have continued it under the title of PACT (Producers Association of Children's Theatre). Play festivals, teacher workshops, and conferences on topics such as drama for the special child are among some of the more popular regional projects.

An important event of this period was the formation of ASSITEJ (International Association of Theatres for Children and Young People) in 1964. This world organization, already cited, was founded in England with thirty-three countries in attendance. Sara Spencer was the United States representative for the CTC at the October meeting in Venice, at which Orlin Corey's Everyman Players (q.v.) were invited to perform. ASSITEJ was made a committee of the CTC; it was many years later before it became a separate organization and incorporated as ASSITEJ/USA. Planned at this time, though not to take place until the summer of 1972, was an ASSITEJ mobile congress, the first week to be held in Canada and the second week in Albany, with a two-day excursion to New York City. Improved travel arrangements and lower air fares have enabled more American members to attend ASSITEJ congresses in recent years, and as a result they have seen and been influenced by the imaginative and extravagant productions by some of the European countries. Whereas children's theatre in the United States has been a grassroots movement, operating on a low budget and provincial in its development, it was suddenly stimulated by this exposure to new content, objectives, and forms.

It was in the sixties that government aid for the arts was finally mandated. President John F. Kennedy initiated the action in 1962, appointing August Heckscher as his special consultant on the arts. Further steps were taken two years later by Lyndon B. Johnson, who appointed Roger Stevens to organize and direct the administration's cultural program. The National Council on the Arts was established in 1964 with the following directives: "to recommend ways to maintain and multiply our cultural resources; to encourage private initiative; to advise and consult with local, state, and federal departments on ways to coordinate existing facilities; to conduct studies; and to make recommendations for the future."[17] As it turned out, this was the start of an extensive program of aid to the arts through various agencies established to help educational and community programs, including individual performers and performing groups.

The most far-reaching and important programs, however, were the National Foundation on the Arts and Humanities Act of 1965, which included the National Endowment for the Arts and the National Endowment for the Humanities; and the Elementary and Secondary Education Act (ESEA). Under the jurisdiction of the Department of Health, Education and Welfare, Title I and Title III of ESEA made possible a variety of children's theatre projects. In the same year $31 million (one-half from federal funds and one-half matching funds from private sources) were raised for the building of the Kennedy Center, a National Center for the Performing Arts (q.v.) in Washington, D.C. Children's theatre was recognized with a place in its education department. This action was implemented with a program that offered plays, workshops, and conferences throughout the school year at minimal or no cost to school children and teachers.

In 1969 President Richard M. Nixon asked Congress to extend the legislation that had established the National Endowment for the Arts and Humanities act for an additional three years beyond its expiration date of 1970, and proposed $40 million in addition. This doubled the level of the preceding year and enabled thousands of persons to enjoy music, theatre, dance, and literature. Children's theatre was covered by the program, and while the financial support varies widely from region to region, the program was reported to have helped some areas establish projects they would otherwise not have been able to afford.

The Elementary and Secondary Education Act was created for the improvement of education, but it benefitted children's theatre in a number of ways as well. The projects varied in kind and scope but included exposure to live theatre, participation in creative drama, the experience of working with artists-in-residence, in-service courses for teachers, and after-school activities for children.

One of the largest in-school projects made possible under Title III was located in Huntington, New York. This included a performing arts curriculum enrichment program, which brought artists into the schools. Both performances and artists-in-residence served over 240,000 children and 11,000 teachers from kindergarten through the ninth grade during a four-year period. Begun in 1966, it lasted until 1977.

In Chicago betwen the years 1967 and 1969 there were more than 1,000 live performances of plays, dance concerts, and puppet shows for elementary and high school aged students. These were made possible by the Cultural Enrichment Project and developed by the board of education with the assistance of the Illinois Arts Council, the Illinois Foundation for the Dance, and the Stratford Festival Theatre of Canada.

In New England in 1967, Theatre Resources for Youth (q.v.), or Project TRY, was launched under an operational grant from Title III. This was planned and supervised by the theatre department of the University of New Hampshire and included teacher workshops and classes and touring productions to area schools. According to Judith Kase-Polisini, the director, TRY reached over 50,000 persons in the two years of its operation. Because of the climate and hazardous driving conditions in northern New England during a large part of the school year, it was deemed more practical to take the theatre to the schools than to bus children to the campus. These three examples indicate the different ways in which government funding was used to serve students and teachers in suburban, urban, and rural areas.

CEMREL

As both classroom teachers and specialists were becoming better educated in the theatre arts, the interest continued to grow and new techniques were developed. With government subsidies, additional resources and new agencies became available on a larger scale than in any previous period. One comprehensive program, designed to meet the needs of the nonspecialist, was the Aesthetic Education Program located at the Central Midwestern Regional Educational Laboratory (CEMREL) in St. Louis. It was begun in the late sixties with funding from the United States Office of Education and completed in 1973. This program was soon popular with classroom teachers; indeed, teachers throughout the country sent for the CEMREL aesthetic education materials.

Except for the Federal Theatre of the thirties, which was established as a relief measure, the U.S. government had never taken a substantial role in either promoting or funding the arts. Now it was actively engaged in the support of new ventures through a variety of funding programs. These were to affect both the quantity and the quality of children's theatre offerings thereafter in all sectors: professional, educational, and community.

The state arts councils have probably had the most visibility in the greatest number of communities because of local funding. The first council was established in New York in 1960 and by 1965 had become a permanent agency with an office in Manhattan. Other states followed, until by the end of the sixties all fifty states had arts councils, with thirty-four reporting children's theatre as one area of interest. Support varied widely, as did the services they offered, but within a relatively short period of time councils were helping to implement a vast array of arts programs with money, guidance, and publications. The artist-in-residence program for public schools is a popular feature throughout the country; information about it is available from the state departments of education, and educators and community leaders in increasing numbers have taken advantage of the opportunities that their states offer.

In 1967 the Connecticut Commission on the Arts devised Project Create, a program through which theatre artists were invited into the schools for periods of time ranging from two weeks to a full semester. Theatre was selected because it includes all of the performing and visual arts and hence is the ideal medium for learning in all subject areas. The Paper Bag Players (q.v.) developed a new piece, *Dandelion*, while working in one school and relating its theme of evolution to the school curriculum. The Eugene O'Neill Memorial Theatre Center, the Hartford Conservatory, and Children's Theatre International (q.v.) were among the other groups that followed the Paper Bag Players during the two-year experiment. Selected elementary schools and high schools across the state participated.

The Educational Theatre

Meanwhile, as agencies multiplied and government funding stimulated support from private foundations, the need for better educated administrators, teachers, and social workers with knowledge of the performing arts increased. The colleges and universities, well aware of these developments, introduced courses that would prepare them for the future, and they worked more closely with local schools. Productions for child audiences, teacher workshops, and campus conferences were all manifestations of this new wave of interest and cooperation. A CTC survey in 1950 revealed 69 colleges and universities in twenty-seven states offering courses in drama and theatre; within the next four years, a second survey showed 222.

CTC newsletters of the fifties reported productions for children at the University of Washington in Seattle, Northwestern University, Tufts University, Oneonta State Teachers College, Hunter College in New York, San Francisco State University, Hobart College, the University of California at Los Angeles, Texas Christian University, and Endicott Junior College. The universities of Minnesota, Washington, Kansas, Colorado, and Utah, and Northwestern University continued to dominate, however, in this area of theatre. Within the next ten years new programs that were to become the leading centers for the study of child drama were developed at San Fernando State College (now California State University at Northridge) under the direction of Mary Jane Evans; at New York University with Nancy and Lowell Swortzell; and at the University of North Carolina with Tom Behm. Nat Eek at the University of Oklahoma was one of the most active leaders in the academic community at the time, serving as theatre department chairman, chairman of the ASSITEJ committee, and as president of CTC. Many small colleges were also introducing courses in children's theatre for their students and, at the same time, providing a community service.

A cooperative enterprise, ARTS IMPACT (Interdisciplinary Model Program in the Arts for Children and Teachers) was funded in 1965 under the Education Professions Development Act and administered by the U.S. Office of Education. A million-dollar experiment, ARTS IMPACT was launched by the American Educational Theatre Association, the Music Educators National Conference, the National Arts Education Association, and the Dance Division of the American Association for Health, Physical Education, and Recreation. Alabama, California, Ohio, Oregon, and Pennsylvania were selected as a network to develop and implement teacher training and curriculum improvement programs in the arts to be tested in the schools. In the initial two-year period, CEMREL oversaw the project for AETA.

This national project had specific objectives as follows:

To reconstruct the school's educational program and administrative climate in an effort to achieve better balance between the arts and other instructional areas, and in the learning process, between feelings or emotions and acquiring knowledge;

To develop high quality visual arts, music, dance, and drama education programs in each participating school;

To conduct in-service programs, including summer institutes, workshops, and demonstrations, to train teachers, administrators, and other school personnel in implementing the arts education programs;

To develop ways to infuse the arts into all aspects of the school curriculum as a means of enhancing and improving the quality and quantity of aesthetic education offered in the school and as a principal means for expanding the base for effective learning experiences in the total school program;

To enhance the quality of children's art experiences by drawing upon outstanding artists, performers, and educators from outside the school system.[18]

ARTS IMPACT illustrated a changing attitude toward the arts in this country. While it was agreed that much more needed to be done, this collaboration had an impact on education in the United States and coincided with the establishment of arts councils and support from more private foundations than had been previously available.

Community Theatre for Children

Meanwhile, community theatres for children continued to flourish under a variety of sponsorships. Programs were reported from coast to coast in CTC publications and local newspapers, and some have endured, thanks to the support they received from government agencies and private foundations. Financial aid was crucial in the initial stage of development, while the money for operational costs was being sought. Funding agencies were interested in helping groups they considered serious in their intent and sound in their plans and objectives, but they did not supply money for ordinary running expenses. This policy resulted in more careful planning on the part of applicants, with proposal writing an important factor in obtaining grants.

By the mid-sixties Junior Programs of California was incorporated as a nonprofit organization under whose aegis theatre, puppets, music, and dance were booked into communities throughout the state. Art exhibits and book displays were later added to provide further aesthetic experiences for the audience. Meanwhile, Seattle Junior Programs, Inc., cited earlier, was presenting on a regular basis the best live entertainment to be found to more than 15,000 children in the greater Seattle area. An ambitious program was inaugurated at the Detroit Institute of the Arts in the 1969–1970 season. A four-part series totaling eighteen different programs for children was presented in the museum auditorium. An important objective of Michael Miners, the director, was to help children gain a respect for the theatre by experiencing it in a special place under the best conditions. School auditoriums and all-purpose rooms, community centers, and Off-Broadway spaces rarely offer this element.

One institution that does is The 92nd Street "Y" (q.v.) of New York, which offered a rich assortment of programs for children during the sixties. The Junior Entertainment Committee, under the Education Department, previewed and recommended plays, puppet shows, dance, music, and poetry programs to be scheduled on a subscription basis in the "Y" concert hall during the school year. These programs were given on Sunday afternoons, while, on weekdays, bus loads of boys and girls were brought to the "Y" to see programs selected by their schools. Although children's performances still take place at the "Y," there are fewer of them today than there were in the sixties and early seventies. After-school activities, including classes in the performing arts, abound, however, and summer programs for city children and day camps are popular services.

Arts centers like the Goodman Theatre of Chicago, the Karamu Youth Theatre of Cleveland, the Children's Theatre of Palo Alto, and the Nashville Children's Theatre continued to bring thousands of American young people to comfortable and attractive facilities annually to see plays produced by their own companies. Boston, which had been the scene of some of the earliest activities, was the site of several active drama groups during these years. The Boston Children's Theatre (q.v.), under the direction of Adele Thane, offered classes in creative drama, a production series, and a Stagemobile, which went to local parks and playgrounds during the summer months. The Tribal Players (q.v.), a new group in the Boston area, was experimenting with a different approach called "Environmental Drama," in which children took an active part in developing the piece as well as performing in it. One of its first plays, *Tribe*, by Barbara Linden and the children, was subsequently published by New Plays, Inc., and is still available in script form.

By 1969 the Children's Theatre of Richmond, Virginia (q.v.), one of the oldest producing groups in the country, had become a nonprofit organization. This took place with the help of the Parent-Teacher Association (PTA), the Junior League, Miller and Rhoades department store, and the Richmond, Fredericksburg, and Potomac Railroad. In Greensboro, North Carolina, we find an excellent example of town and gown collaboration. The merging of the efforts of the Junior League and the Women's College of the University of North Carolina resulted in an amibitious program at the Pixie Playhouse on the Greensboro campus; with a new full-time director and a full season of plays, it became one of the outstanding theatres for children in the country. Renamed The Theatre for Young People (TYP) (q.v.), it was one of the first of its kind to combine educational and theatrical components on a regular, ongoing basis. Washington, D.C., with a new sponsoring organization called Mimes and Masks for Youth, the Dallas Theatre Center (q.v.), and the Honolulu Theatre for Youth (q.v.) also reported extensive programs reaching thousands of children annually.

Professional Theatre for Children

The fifties and sixties also brought increasing numbers of professional productions for child audiences. Three of the oldest companies, described earlier, were still in operation, while a number of new companies appeared. Most of the latter were small touring groups who were sponsored by Junior Leagues, PTAs, and community councils. Although some companies operated independently, doing their own booking, the majority were handled by two theatrical agencies specializing in children's entertainment. These agencies were Briggs Management (q.v.), and Haynes Management, both located in New York City. Records of their business during these years thus become a reliable source of information as to the availability and magnitude of professional activity. Puppetry, which does not fall within the scope of this book, was also popular and was often booked as a less expensive attraction in a series along with theatre, dance, music, and film.

Clare Tree Major Productions, America's oldest professional theatre for children, closed its doors in 1954 when its founder died. Major was not a member of The Children's Theatre Association of America (then called the Children's Theatre Conference); nevertheless, she helped to develop a young audience and in this regard contibuted immeasurably to the movement. She offered only traditional material, traditionally staged, to the end of her life, but her objectives were the same as those of the educators and community leaders who made up the bulk of the membership of the CTC.

The Phoenix was a well-known Off-Broadway theatre in New York City; however, during the years 1960 and 1962 it played matinees regularly for school audiences at reduced prices through an arrangement with the board of education. The Portable Phoenix, a small educational unit, later took assembly length adaptations of longer plays to schools. Fine professional actors in plays that in some instances had had successful runs on Broadway brought the best dramatic fare to young people during the sixties. Although not children's theatre per se, it was a carefully planned extension of the program, offered for young audiences.

In addition to entertainment designed specifically for children, there were two productions of *Peter Pan* in the fifties. The first, in which Jean Arthur and Boris Karloff starred, with music composed by Leonard Bernstein, was received enthusiastically. The second was the famous Mary Martin production in 1955, a musical version of the play, which, although the score was described as disappointing, enjoyed a four-month run.

Summary

The unprecedented expansion of all dramatic activities during the fifties and sixties was documented in *A Directory of Children's Theatres in the United States*, edited by Jed H. Davis of the University of Kansas and published by AETA in 1968. It listed 701 educational, community, and professional groups that produced one or more plays for children annually, and the total number may have been considerably larger. Some groups did not announce their founding, particularly the community theatres that gradually added plays for young audiences to their season's lists. Some, encouraged by the demand, shifted from offering an occasional production for children to offering a season of four to six productions. Others dropped programs without public announcement, or suspended activities, never to resume. Still others responded that they gave plays, though their offerings may have consisted of a single play or pageant as a seasonal celebration.

The most outstanding developments of the period were the proliferation of small professional companies and the new government funding programs. The latter made possible large-scale enterprises that enabled thousands of children to experience live theatre for the first time. They also encouraged cooperative planning by producers and sponsors. The Equity contract for actors in children's theatre at the end of the sixties legitimized some companies and destroyed others incapable of meeting the higher salaries and benefits required by the union. By 1970 the numbers were down, but the quality had gone up. Television also played a part in the growth and decline of children's entertainment as young audiences came to expect technical virtuosity of directors and performers. That, plus the higher fees that companies were forced to charge, caused many parents to settle for the small screen at home. Thus changing conditions led to changing practices, which a survey of the seventies and eighties reveals.

NEW DIRECTIONS: 1970–1985

Whereas expansion of children's theatre activities had taken place in all parts of the country during the fifties and sixties, a sharp reduction in the number of professional companies became evident in the seventies and eighties. The new Equity contract for actors in children's theatre forced higher salaries, affecting both union and nonunion companies. New groups were suddenly faced with problems their predecessors had not encountered: higher production costs and a need for imaginative programs that were markedly different from any already in existence. In order to succeed, it was necessary to capture the attention of sponsors. Producers had two choices: to follow a successful trend and try to improve on it, or to strike out in a new direction, risking failure in the hope of achieving success. Both strategies worked, though not in all cases and not always well enough to create a strong ongoing program. The result, however, was more experimentation in content and form than had taken place in the entire history of the children's theatre movement and more touring productions from the college and university drama departments.

Another new element was added which affected both professional and amateur groups. With subsidies and grants now available, proposal writing became an important skill for producers. No commercial children's theatre company could hope to survive on its box office revenue if adequate salaries were to be paid. Without salaries comparable to those paid to professionals in related fields, the constant turnover in actors was too great for the development of an ensemble. As a corollary to higher salaries, there were correspondingly higher fees for sponsors. Meanwhile, inflation was causing production costs to escalate. What had once been low budget entertainment was rapidly becoming high priced business. If a producer could manage to secure several small grants (grants were invariably small, hence the need for obtaining more than one), he or she could plan the next season with a degree of confidence. The budgetary problems were never solved, however, though they were sometimes relieved. Grants tended to be given for the development of innovative programs, new works, or work for new populations, not for meeting ordinary operational expenses. One exception, however, was made. Whereas the National Endowment for the Arts had established a policy of funding only new projects and not contributing to a company's ongoing operational costs, it established a new category in 1984. Under this new category called Ongoing Ensembles, some selected professional companies of nationally recognized quality have been given grants in order to sustain a group of actors, playwrights, directors, and designers over a long period of time. These grants strengthen the ensemble and also help in the writing and production of new works and in the training of new writers, actors, directors, and technicians. The producer's job ceased to be that of artistic director exclusively, if, indeed, he or she directed at all; it was rather that of public relations/fund-raiser. In some cases a special fund-raiser was hired, but this meant an added expense that few companies could afford. In many ways commercial theatre for children had come of age. It had faced the hard reality that it could not be self-supporting, and in order to survive, it had to adopt new business methods as well as produce a better product. Television had educated young viewers to expect the finest performance skills and elaborate production techniques; to compete, live theatre had to prove that it possessed another and more important dimension.

Not only the commercial theatre but the community and educational theatres were affected by these changes. Discerning sponsors, who had seen excellent productions at showcases and conventions, were no longer satisfied with mediocre work and, as a result, the cry "quality children's theatre" was heard across the land. Committees were established to preview touring groups before any contracts were signed. In some cities a consortium of local organizations and agencies was established to pool finances and critical judgment and thus bring in the best entertainment they could find. Instead of playing at only one school, a company could appear at several in the same town. This has proved to be an effective method, for it benefits both producer and sponsor. The consortium is able to pay higher fees, while touring companies can cut their travel expenses by remaining in one location for a week or more, often giving workshops following performances rather than booking a series of one-day stands in different towns.

National Organizations

Although a number of national organizations were interested in children's theatre, the two that dominated the field were The Children's Theatre Association of America and the Junior League. Others, such as the Parent-Teacher Association, the American Community Theatre Association, and the National Recreational Association, were supportive. In 1983 the Children's Book Council of New York held a national conference at which, for the first time, there was a panel discussion of plays as children's literature. The interest was spreading to other areas as a result of the expansion in the sixties and seventies.

Of the national organizations, however, The Children's Theatre Association of America (CTAA) continued to gain strength as it gathered members. Many directors of commercial companies had joined its ranks, and virtually all of the educational groups and many of the community theatre groups were represented in it. National conventions, regional conferences, and local meetings offered members opportunities to see interesting and new productions, to take part in panel discussions, and to hear speakers from both the professional stage and related areas such as education, psychology, anthropology, and literature. By the mid-eighties the CTAA had more than one-thousand members, though probably there were additional persons active on the local level.

In the seventies CTAA initiated two new projects relating to the improvement of children's theatre. One was the Winifred Ward Scholarship Committee, founded for the dual purposes of honoring the memory of this pioneer in the field and preparing future practitioners to carry on her work. With $1 million as a goal, a fund-raising campaign was launched and the first scholarship was awarded in 1978. Subcommittees for the certification of graduate drama/theatre departments and scholar selection were appointed. By 1985 eight scholars had been selected for graduate study in children's theatre and creative drama in a qualifying program. Theatre programs could apply for consideration, and departments could be dropped when their child drama programs failed to meet the standards of the organization or were phased out. Hence the work of the subcommittees was ongoing. It was hoped from the beginning that not only would the amount of the scholarship be increased (which it was in 1983) but that in time there might be enough money to assist two or more Ward Scholars.

The second project was launched by the Professional Children's Theatre Presenters and Producers Committee and took the form of a National Showcase, staged for the first time in 1979 in Chicago. This showcase is held every spring in a different city and follows a format similar to PACT (Producers Association of Children's Theatre) in New York. Presenters offer excerpts of plays for sponsors who come from varying distances to preview new productions for the following season. In 1984, sixteen companies from the United States and Canada showed work at the Detroit Institute of Arts.

ASSITEJ, originally a committee of CTAA, became an independent international organization of professional theatres and theatre professionals in 1981 and was henceforth officially called ASSITEJ/USA, Inc. The goals of the organization were to support the best in children's theatre, to create cultural understanding through the arts, and to promote international good will by sharing work and ideas. With a congress held in a different country every three years, ASSITEJ members were traveling and seeing more theatre produced by foreign groups than ever before. Except for the 1984 congress in Moscow, the United States has sent one or two companies to every meeting.

In 1982 Judith Kase-Polisini organized a series of symposia on child drama to take place at five different locations during the years 1983–1986. Speakers from other disciplines including psychology, anthropology, and education were invited to present papers during a two-day conference, with the respondents from CTAA. The symposia were held at Harvard in 1983; at the Ontario Institute for Studies in Education in Toronto in 1983; at the University of Texas at Austin in 1984; at Arizona State University in 1985; and at Rutgers in New Brunswick, New Jersey, in 1986. Attendance was limited to 200 CTAA members; however, the proceedings were recorded, and the first collection of papers was published by the University Press of America in 1985. This scholarly project was unique in the history of child drama and children's theatre in America.

A more traditional project is the awards ceremony that takes place each year during the national convention. By 1985 nine awards in a variety of categories were being presented to individuals or children's theatre companies nominated by members, with the final determinations made by the Awards Committee for the year. The descriptions of these awards indicate the areas deemed most important, and the contributions of recipients most valued by the members of the organization.

Jennie Heiden Award. Awarded for creative effectiveness and excellence in *professional* children's theatre. (Individuals as well as groups are eligible for this award.)

Zeta Phi Eta–Winifred Ward Award. Presented to a children's theatre which has attained a high quality of production and which has stimulated community interest in its endeavor. Nominees must have been in operation for at least one full year, but not more than four years. (Organizations may be nominated as often as possible within a four-year limit.)

Special Sara Spencer Award. This award acknowledges a long established children's theatre for meritorious achievement. To be eligible, a theatre must have been in operation for a minimum of seven years, as the thrust of this award is for proven, mature achievement.

Charlotte B. Chorpenning Cup. This award is given to a writer of outstanding plays for children. The playwright must be of national reputation.

Monte Meacham Award. Established as an award to a person or organization *outside* CTAA. The award is given for outstanding contributions to children's theatre.

Creative Drama for Human Awareness Award. Special recognition is given to a person or persons working in a creative drama program which does not lead to a production for an audience. Eligible recipients are: school programs K–12; Head Start; special education and the like; community drama or integrated arts programs; and programs in teacher training. The awards will usually go to younger people rather than those well known and widely recognized. (The key person rather than the organization will be recognized.)

CTAA Special Recognition Citation. Special recognition is given to individuals and/or groups which have established special programs, research projects, surveys, or experimental work in any of the forms of child drama.

Phi Beta Award. This is a grant-in-aid award established for a distinguished foreign visitor who enriches the lives of those involved in children's theatre by taking an *active* role in some aspect of the convention. The person is selected before the CTAA Awards Ceremony, and *expected* to be in attendance at the convention. Nominations can be made to the awards chair any time through Monday of the convention.

Campton Bell Award. Presented annually to an individual for a lifetime of outstanding contributions to the field of child drama.

Educational Theatre

Educational institutions continued to exert leadership through carefully planned drama/theatre curricula on both undergraduate and graduate levels. Lack of space prohibits lengthy descriptions of the variety of programs to be found throughout the country, but a few examples will indicate some of the successful ways in which departments were meeting student interests and needs in this area of drama/theatre education. The scope of the offerings, however, is revealed by the following figures: in 1970–1971 the *ATA Annual Directory* listed 1,600 institutions with theatre programs of some sort. These ranged from a few courses to programs offering graduate degrees.

A survey of college and university programs offering courses in child drama and/or children's theatre productions was made at Arizona State University in 1982. The results of this survey were published in the January issue of *Children's Theatre Review*. The general overview was as follows:

Responses were received from all fifty states and included reports from 116 junior colleges and 406 four-year colleges. Combining responses from both kinds of institutions, tallies of the different kinds of activities and programs are: schools that do no work in child drama (113); schools that do productions only (122); schools with courses and no productions (30); schools that present introductory classes in child drama as well as children's theatre productions (176); schools with no declared emphasis in the field but with course offerings of beginning and advanced classes plus strong production programs (30); schools with a declared emphasis in child drama at the undergraduate level (18); schools with a declared major or emphasis in the field at the graduate level (26); and schools with a graduate degree in education with a child drama emphasis (7).[19]

The most comprehensive programs in child drama were those qualifying for Winifred Ward Scholars. In 1985, they were located at the following universities.

Adelphi University
Arizona State University
California State University at Northridge
Eastern Michigan University
Emerson College
Empire State Institute for the Performing Arts
Hunter College

Illinois State University (Normal)
New York University
Pennsylvania State University
University of Hawaii at Manoa
University of Kansas
University of North Carolina (Greensboro)
University of North Iowa (Cedar Falls)
University of Texas (Austin)
University of Utah
University of Wisconsin (Madison)
Virginia Tech (Virginia Polytechnic Institute and State University)

The trend toward better theatre for children became increasingly evident as more universities scheduled plays on a regular basis as a part of their season's offerings. Taking the children's productions on the road following the campus performances became popular, particularly in areas where no other theatre for young people existed. In this way hundreds of children in rural and suburban neighborhoods were introduced to the theatre; this practice has proved to be good public relations as well as a contribution to the cultural life of the communities.

The University of Texas at Austin has a strong program that offers children's theatre as a major attraction, often featuring the premiere of a new Aurand Harris script. Courses include creative drama, children's theatre, and playwriting for young audiences. Coleman A. Jennings, chairman of the department, has brought Aurand Harris on campus nearly every spring quarter for a number of years to teach playwriting. From one to three Theatre for Youth (q.v.) productions are offered each year. In addition to the public performances, Jennings reported in 1984 that more than 6,000 Austin Independent School District students saw at least one production. Founded in 1938 as a separate department of the College of Fine Arts with a faculty of only four members, it is today one of the largest departments in the country and offers the M.A., Ph.D., and M.F.A. degrees. Jennings' particular interest in children's theatre has helped this area to grow along with the other departmental concentrations.

New York University, one of the institutions on the list approved for Winifred Ward Scholars, developed quite a different program including, as an option, substantial graduate study abroad. Initiated in the early seventies, a summer program on the campus of Bretton Hall College of Education in Yorkshire attracts students from all parts of the United States. Those who are accepted must take twelve credits of work in a summer and may return for a second or third summer. In England students have an opportunity to study with a variety of experts in all areas of drama and theatre, but there is special emphasis on TIE (theatre in education). Meanwhile, courses are also available on the New York campus. One of the outcomes of the Study Abroad program was the founding of CAT (q.v.) (Creative Arts Team), a professional TIE company attached to the university. CAT also offers opportunities for experiential learning on both graduate and undergraduate levels through an internship program.

The Empire State Institute for the Performing Arts (q.v.) has a totally different structure and modus operandi, though there are surface similarities. The first state mandated theatre for children in the United States, it was established in the seventies under the direction of Patricia Snyder.

Different from all of the other programs cited is The Children's Theatre Company (q.v.) and School of Minneapolis. In 1975, with financial support from the community, an impressive new theatre within the Minneapolis arts complex was constructed for drama/theatre activities. Classes for children and youth as well as a full season of productions for young audiences are held in this model building. By the eighties another feature was added: a fully accredited school with the arts at the core of the curriculum.

Arizona State University features, among other activities, an extensive touring schedule each spring. Two goals are stated: to introduce children to quality theatre and to present plays that will enrich the school curriculum. Because of the rich mix of populations in Arizona, shows from the Indian tribal, Mexican, and Anglo heritages are included. The University of Hawaii (q.v.) and the Honolulu Theatre for Youth (q.v.), with another heterogeneous population, make use of the indigenous material that is available with what are reported to be exciting results.

At Howard University (q.v.) in Washington, D.C., the focus is on the projection of positive black images on stage. Kelsey Collie, the director, consciously presents the black experience so that all audiences may derive educational and entertainment benefits from artistically sound productions. Folktales as well as documentaries are included in a format that emphasizes total theatre: development of a piece, emphasis on both visual aspects and movement, and the use of the theatre as a learning medium.

There is wide variation in programs because they have developed according to the interests and needs of the students, faculty preparation and interests, and the geographic location of the institution. For example, the University of Hawaii has developed along quite different lines from the University of North Carolina, as has Eastern Michigan University from Emerson College in Boston. Some programs stress creative drama; others, children's theatre; still others, a commitment to touring and community service. The superiority of a program lies in the quality of its work rather than the number of courses it offers, though, of course, there must be enough to meet the minimal standards established by ATA/CTAA.

Playwriting with Young People

Before leaving the educational theatre, mention must be made of yet another dimension that appeared in the eighties. This was playwriting. While it does not fall precisely under the rubric of children's theatre, it is so closely related that it warrants inclusion. Two examples shall be given.

In 1979 members of the Dramatists' Guild saw the work of a young Englishman, Gerald Chapman, at the Royal Court Theatre in London. They were so impressed with his ability to stimulate playwriting among young people that they engaged him to come to the United States to launch a similar program here. This was known as the Young Playwrights' Festival. Through workshops with elementary and high school students as well as teachers in the New York metropolitan area, playwriting was introduced, and an extraordinary number of scripts were submitted for consideration in a contest held in the spring. An unusual aspect of this competition was that staged readings and/or full productions were given the winning scripts by professional actors under the auspices of the Circle Repertory Company in New York. In 1981, the first year of the project, 732 scripts from thirty-five states were submitted. In 1982, 655 scripts from forty-five states were submitted, and in 1983, 1,160 from all fifty states. The plays were professionally reviewed and described in the New York papers as both an interesting project and an indication of the youthful talent in the land.

Meanwhile, Aurand Harris, the American children's playwright, was also conducting workshops but in quite different ways. He was invited for residencies lasting from a week to four months, during which time he taught playwriting to elementary school children and to college students. No productions of the students' work were given, but writing skills were taught through the medium of drama. Both men are highly successful in an area that heretofore has not received emphasis, except as a part of script development. But playwriting as a way of teaching written communication and self-expression belongs to this period of innovative programs and new directions.

Drama Kaleidoscope was established in Seattle in 1982 as a new concept in child drama. It is not a performing company but rather is a training program designed to bring together people who work with children in educational and recreational situations. The program provides workshop opportunities to develop and share skills in the use of drama to enhance learning. Drama Kaleidoscope is composed of three workshop options: (1) Creating the Performance; (2) Building Drama into the Curriculum; (3) Using Drama with Special Populations. Drama Kaleidoscope is also a resource and referral service for contacting drama specialists. The staff is a team of highly qualified and experienced professionals sponsored by The Children's Theatre Association of America, Region IX. It is available throughout the school year. Workshop schedules are adapted to suit individual requirements.

Kaleidoscope is based on the belief that drama is a fundamental process which allows for deep physical, mental, and emotional involvement, thus creating a positive environment for learning. As a social interactive experience, it fosters the spirit of play.

Community Theatre

Community centers, once the hub of children's dramatic activities, continued their support, though in somewhat different ways. The first and most usual were classes taught by highly qualified leaders in an effort to augment school curricula and offer children an alternative to the streets. Where budgets for the arts had been cut, the community center might increase its offerings to provide after-school and Saturday classes in acting, improvisation, mime, and dance for children and teenagers. Second, plays for young people were popular activities, performed either by adult actors or by combined casts of children and adults. Third, school and community cooperation improved on all levels: elementary, secondary, and college/university. Finally, as practical implementation of the second and third parts of the program, bussing audiences to the theatre and taking plays to outlying communities and to handicapped populations were being done on a much larger scale.

While many of the little theatres of the twenties and thirties had long since folded or changed directions, some regional theatres gathered strength. Indeed, a number of them had become professional, offering good entertainment, even challenging Broadway in quality of material, ensemble work through steady employment of actors, and expanded community services. An educational component was also often an important aspect. In some cases the community theatre booked in professional companies with reputations for offering plays of outstanding quality. While the occasional play for children still took place, the trend was toward a more comprehensive program of which theatre for children was a part. The following are examples of typical community theatres of the eighties.

They fall into three clearly defined categories: the large regional centers; the small civic centers; and ethnic groups. There are only a few in the first category; best known among them are the John F. Kennedy Center for the Performing Arts (q.v.) in Washington, D.C.; Lincoln Center (q.v.) in New York; the Children's Theatre Company (q.v.) of Minneapolis; and the Performing Arts Council Music Center of Los Angeles County. Also large and very active, however, are the Midland Community Theatre of Texas (q.v.); the Honolulu Theatre for Youth (q.v.); and The Nebraska Theatre Caravan (q.v.), the professional wing of the Omaha Community Playhouse. The playhouse is the largest community theatre in the nation and the home of the future Henry Fonda Center.

Lincoln Center in New York does not yet have as extensive a program as the Kennedy Center, but the Lincoln Center Institute does offer some services to the community. Artists who go into the schools, special performances of opera and dance for school children, and workshops for teachers and students are among the features recently developed. There are plans for further expansion when staff and budget permit.

Learning about Learning in San Antonio is quite a different type of operation, serving educational purposes rather than entertainment. It is described in a book by Jearnine Wagner and Kitty Baker entitled *A Place for Ideas— Our Theatre* (1978). Concerned with an interdisciplinary approach to the arts, Learning about Learning represents one of the new directions taken in the latter part of the century.

As to the smaller community and civic theatres, the Detroit Institute of Arts has already been cited as an active center with a full program of events for young people. A season's schedule lists such categories as Specials, Puppets, Musicals and Plays, and Films. A 1,200-seat theatre in a beautiful facility has grown in popularity and importance in the Detroit community; director Michael Miners' efforts have been strengthened by the length of his tenure, thus adding continuity to an ambitious enterprise.

Wichita, Kansas, today boasts a charming 487-seat theatre built exclusively for children. This represents thirty years of work on the part of Irene Vickers Baker, founder and director, and a supportive community. The building was dedicated in 1971 with Helen Hayes performing. The Troupers take plays into area schools once a week during the school year in addition to the regular performances in the theatre.

The Honolulu Theatre for Youth has a long history in the sense that the Honolulu Community Theatre is reported to be the second oldest in the nation. Theatre was introduced to the Islands by touring companies on their way to Asia and Australia. The first performing hall, the Royal Hawaiian, was erected in 1834; the second was an opera house, built somewhat later. Growth was slow because the missionaries condemned the theatre, whereas the Oriental population rarely set foot in either building. When the latter did attend performances, it was to see an occasional Chinese or Japanese program. The present theatre, founded in 1955, is the major cultural resource dedicated to young people of the Islands and their families. It is today a professional theatre, revealing once again the trend toward commercial status when a community enterprise becomes so successful that the demands are too great to be filled by part-time amateur actors.

The Emmy Gifford Theatre in Omaha and the Seattle Children's Theatre (q.v.), formerly Poncho, are two other community theatres that developed active programs in the seventies. The Emmy Gifford Children's Theatre (q.v.) is a well-known institution named for a dedicated member of the CTAA during the fifties and sixties. The Seattle Theatre, under the Department of Parks and Recreation of Seattle, has its own resident company of professional performers. A typical season of plays in Seattle includes both traditional and new scripts. The company is noted for its high standards and good work, and it was seen at conventions of ATA and recognized with awards.

As to the third category, ethnic theatre, there are not as many as one might expect to find in a pluralistic society. Those that do exist are located in areas with large populations of particular ethnic groups interested in preserving their culture. As they have not been well funded, few have grown into strong, effective organizations. Nevertheless, there are some that must be cited, and there are undoubtedly a number of others that have operated sporadically with little or no publicity.

Oldest in this category is black theatre, with the Karamu of Cleveland as the best known example. Described above for its work in the 1920s, Karamu is still in existence, but its children's theatre became less active in the seventies and eighties than it had been in the preceding decades.

The Black Theatre Alliance with headquarters in New York is a nonprofit service organization of black theatre and dance companies. It offers many services to its constituency, including the publication of a newsletter and a national theatre resource directory. While few of the companies (most of which are located in the New York area) offer work specifically for children, many of the programs are of interest to the family. One of the best known of these groups is the Harlem Children's Theatre (q.v.), founded in 1971. Here the performers are children, ranging in age from eight to eighteen.

The Billie Holiday Theatre for Young Folk (q.v.) is located in Brooklyn, New York; here quality plays, dance groups, and puppet shows are offered for child audiences on weekends at reasonably low prices. One very successful group is the Inner City Ensemble (q.v.) of New Jersey, which has worked with teenagers since 1973.

Teatro Doble (q.v.), a program of Back Alley Theatre, Inc., of Washington, D.C., announced plays in Spanish and English. While in New York the Don Quijote Experimental Children's Theatre, Inc. (q.v.), also began its performances for American and Hispanic youth.

This is by no means a comprehensive picture of ethnic theatre. Other groups perform plays occasionally, some of which are designed for children. Because they are done on such an irregular basis, however, they are not cited; the theatres described above have been in operation for a number of years, presenting plays for children on a more or less regular basis, and are therefore illustrative of this genre.

Professional Theatre

The number of professional theatres for children did not increase in the seventies and eighties, though, as stated earlier, the quality improved. A few of the well-known early companies continued operation, and a few new companies appeared. In reviewing the period three productions that many persons will recall (though none of the three was produced with children in mind) were *The Wiz, Peter Pan,* and *Annie.* They are mentioned only because there were many children in attendance at all performances; however, the Broadway theatre had become so expensive by the eighties that it was accessible only to young people whose families were well off and to recipients of complimentary tickets. In 1983 Erick Hawkins presented a program of dance for children's audiences, taking nine dancers and eight musicians on tour. Hawkins represented a major figure in the field of dance who was deliberately appealing to a new audience; however, this did not develop into an ongoing program.

One group that took off from an entirely different base was The Magic Carpet Company (q.v.) of San Francisco. A group of young professional actors, it solicited stories written by children and used them as material for plays. Magic Carpet was awarded the 1976 Winifred Ward Award by CTAA for its high standard of work and innovative concept. Subsequent touring engagements included workshops for teachers and students. In using children's writing, it forecast an interest that was later to appear as playwriting projects with children.

Among the better known professional companies that were founded or expanded their activities during this period were the Paper Bag Players (q.v.), The Magic Carpet Company, Children's Theatre International (q.v.), the Empire State Institute for the Performing Arts (q.v.), Maximillion Productions, Inc. (q.v.), PART (now Theatreworks/USA [q.v.]), the Little Theatre of the Deaf (q.v.), Periwinkle Productions (q.v.), Adventure Theatre (q.v.), the Children's Theatre Company of Minneapolis (q.v.), Metro Theatre Circus (q.v.), the Prince Street Players (q.v.), the Sheffield Ensemble Theatre (q.v.), and the Looking Glass Theatre (q.v.). Some professional companies shone brightly for a few seasons, then closed their doors; others are still in existence with little change or expansion. Perhaps the most accurate way of assessing the quality of the contemporary groups is to view the selections made for the CTAA Annual Spring Showcase during a five-year period. Productions for the showcase are screened during the year and some ten or twelve are chosen. The following companies were represented each year beginning in 1979.

1979	Archaesus Productions, Inc. (q.v.)
	Blue Apple Players (q.v.)
	Bob Brown Marionettes
	Chicago Moving Company
	The Everyman Players (q.v.)
	The Imaginary Theatre Company (q.v.)
	The Lovelace Theatre
	The Melikin Puppet Theatre
	Metro Theatre Circus (q.v.)
	Southern Educational Theatre
	Spanish Dances in Concert
	Stage One: The Louisville Children's Theatre (q.v.)
	Theatre 5
	Theatre of Youth Company (q.v.)
	The Truck, Inc.
	United Stage
1980	Albion Productions, Inc. (q.v.)
	Birmingham Children's Theatre (q.v.)
	Germantown Theatre Guild (q.v.)
	Jack Hill
	Hudson Vagabond Puppets
	Martin Kappel
	Looking Glass Theatre (q.v.)
	Loon and Heron Theatre (q.v.)
	Mermaid Theatre
	One Plus One
	Opera Theatre of Syracuse
	Danny Orleans, Magician
	Palisades Theatre Company
	Paper Bag Players (q.v.)
	Performing Arts Repertory Theatre Foundation, Inc. (PART) (q.v.)
	The Pocket Mime Theatre
	Story Theatre Productions, Inc. (q.v.)
	Theatre Beyond Words
	Theatre Sans Fil
1981	Arete Mime Troupe
	Asolo Touring Theatre (q.v.)
	Bits n' Pieces Puppet Theatre
	Das Puppenspiel Puppet Theatre, Inc.
	James Donlon (Steorra Enterprises)
	Kaleidoscope Theatre Productions
	Lynda Martha Dance Company
	Mime Musica
	The Nebraska Theatre Caravan (q.v.)
	Qwindo's Window

Roadside Theatre (q.v.) (Appalshop, Inc.)
Starry Night Puppet Theatre, Inc.
The Truck, Inc.
The Twelfth Night Repertory Company (q.v.)
The Umbrella Players (Alliance Theatre Company [q.v.])
Vagabond Marionettes

1982   Archaesus Productions, Inc. (q.v.)
Chicago Chamber Brass
Child's Play Touring Theatre (q.v.)
Emerson Stage (q.v.)
Ishangi Family Dancers (q.v.)
Lampoon Puppettheatre
Metro Theatre Circus (q.v.)
Omnibus
Robert Orth & Maria Lagios
Performing Arts Repertory Theatre (PART) (q.v.)
Rosenshontz
Theatre Beyond Words
Theatre Sans Fil
A Two Ring Circus (q.v.)
Underground Railway
United Mime Workers (q.v.)

1983   Joan Ballenger & Associates
Bravo Artist Management, Inc.
California Young People's Theatre (q.v.)
Child's Play Touring Theatre (q.v.)
Das Puppenspiel Puppet Theatre, Inc.
Emerson Stage (q.v.)
Green Thumb Theatre for Young People
Hallary Dworet Artist Management
Herrick Marionettes
Imago
Kolmar-Luth Entertainment, Inc.
Mermaid Theatre

1984   ArtReach Touring Theatre (q.v.)
Jerry Brodey
The Broque Opera Company (q.v.)
California Young People's Theatre
Green Thumb Theatre for Young People
Hippodrome Theatre-in-Education (q.v.)
The Melikin Puppet Theatre
Metro Theatre Circus
The No-Elephant Circus (q.v.)
Danny Orleans
Prince Street Players (q.v.)
Rod Rodgers Dance Company (q.v.)
Les Sortileges, Inc.
Stage One (q.v.)

  Theatre de la Marmaille
  United Stage

1985 Fairmount Theatre of the Deaf (q.v.)
  Gemini
  Green Grass Cloggers
  Green Thumb Theatre for Young People
  Hippodrome Theatre-in-Education (q.v.)
  The John F. Kennedy Center Programs for Children and Youth
   (q.v.)
  Dan Kamin
  Moebius
  The Nebraska Theatre Caravan (q.v.)
  Nubian Theatre Company
  Pascual Olivera and Angela del Moral
  St. Louis Children's Theatre
  Sharon, Lois & Bram
  Theatre de la Marmaille
  Theatre l'Arriere-Scene
  Theatre Passe Muraille
  Umbrella Players

  A number of names appearing on the showcase lists are not included in the profiles in Part Two. This is because they do not meet the criteria of five years in operation, or fifty performances a year. Canadian companies, of which there were several in 1984 and 1985, are not included. It is interesting to note, however, that there is a growing exchange between Canada and the United States. With Toronto, the ATA convention site in 1985, this apparent trend is continuing.

  Puppet and dance companies have been excluded from the profiles, although they appear on the showcase lists. Where a company performed more than one time, it is listed each time.

  The PACT Showcase, also held in March, represents a different type of organization. It is presented by the Producers Association for Children's Theatre (PACT), a group of New York Equity companies who present current offerings available for booking the following season. Familiar companies with new work continued to attract sponsors in the eighties. The first PACT Showcase was held in 1968, after it was given up as a regional project of The Children's Theatre Association of America. The members of PACT, being an association, have been more or less consistent in presenting their work. They are:

The Traveling Playhouse (q.v.)
Producers Association (q.v.)
Fanfare Productions (Fanfare Theatre Ensemble) (q.v.)
Paper Bag Players (q.v.)
The National Theatre Company

Maximillion Productions (q.v.)
Theatreworks/USA (formerly PART) (q.v.)
Gingerbread Players and Jack (q.v.)

Puppet companies have been omitted from the PACT list.

Summary

Any summary of the years 1970–1985 must recognize a number of trends, revealing some striking differences between this period and those preceding it. The sixties, with its challenges to tradition and its questioning of values, brought changes to the arts and education. Children's theatre, which occupied a unique position in both areas, was therefore affected in two ways: in its content and in its form.

Some of the most conspicuous changes that took place as a result of the impact of the sixties and the intrusion of television into our lives were:

1. Improvisational performances, peaking in the seventies and diminishing in popularity in the eighties.
2. Improved performance skills.
3. Episodic programs and revues rather than straight dramatic plays with traditional story lines.
4. Continuing popularity of the musical.
5. The addition of educational components in the offerings of commercial companies.
6. Deliberate use of interracial casts.
7. Uniform costumes and simple sets rather than fully costumed and mounted productions.
8. The blurring of lines between community and professional theatres, as the former began hiring well-trained performers for a season's employment.
9. A dependence on new funding sources. While this practice began in the sixties, it was taken for granted by the seventies, thus making proposal writing and fund-raising as important for children's theatre as for adult theatre.

Among the innovative ideas that emerged during these years were:

1. The appearance of the large cultural centers like the Kennedy and Lincoln centers as sponsors of theatre for children.
2. The use of Theatre-in-Education (TIE) in American theatre for young people.
3. The introduction of themes once taboo in children's theatre.
4. The combining of live actors and puppets in the same performance.
5. The appearance of bilingual companies.
6. Drama/theatre as therapy. (While this is not always children's theatre in the traditional sense, such companies as The Rainbow Company Children's Theatre (q.v.) and Imagination Theatre (q.v.) force a recognition of a broader view than had been taken previously.

7. A new commitment to young people on the part of some adult theatres, specifically those in Hartford, Connecticut, and Milwaukee, Wisconsin.

Time may reveal other trends that began during these years to which we are still too close to see clearly.

A POSTSCRIPT

Many of the problems that have plagued children's theatre since the beginning still exist, though there are indications that some of the more troublesome are being relieved. Lack of money has been the most crucial; after government funding programs were established in the sixties and more private foundations became involved in the arts, the situation improved. Some companies were strengthened with this assistance, whereas others were lost in a more highly competitive market. The result has been a decline in the number of professional companies, but those that survived have demonstrated superior performance skills and more sophisticated business and marketing methods.

The National Endowment for the Arts, founded in 1965 with a budget of $2.5 million, has grown from six to sixteen programs with a proportionate increase in staff and a budget of $163 million in 1985. While it contributes less than 5 percent of all monies on the arts in the United States, it is still the largest backer. Children's theatre is only one of the areas to which the endowment contributes, but its importance lies in the fact that it is recognized and that is an encouragement for matching funds.

Under frequent attack on the one side for its promotion of entertainment rather than education, and on the other side for giving support to the arts at all, the endowment has managed to survive through four administrations and six congresses. It has also expanded to all areas of the country, including rural as well as urban and suburban areas. Frank Hodsoll, chairman at the time of this writing, is described in the *New York Times* (November 10, 1985) as vigorous in his review of the panelists' recommendation and in his denial of partisan politics in the endowment's decisions. "What we've done essentially," says Hodsoll, "is to make it easier for institutions and creative individuals to pursue their art. More important, we symbolize the Federal government's recognition of culture in this country as an aspect of national health."[20]

Community theatre, different in structure and leadership from its historic counterpart, is still guided by many of the original objectives. Educational theatre early on differentiated between creative drama and children's theatre but in recent years has sometimes combined the two forms in participatory plays. Also, a more democratic theatre has emerged in our recognition of the handicapped and our new ethnic populations. Mixed casts show young viewers that just as theatre exists *for* all people, it can be created *by* all people, regardless of race, ethnicity, or sex. Recognition of theatre as a potent educational tool has brought more theatre into the schools. No longer is it regarded as a treat or frill but rather as an effective way of learning. Many professional, community, and educational companies now develop teacher packets to enrich and extend the experience.

Six national organizations have played a significant part in the growth and development of children's theatre in America: The Drama League of America, the Association of Junior Leagues of America, the Federal Theatre, The American Theatre Association, The Children's Theatre Association of America, and ASSITEJ. Whereas the early enterprises sprang up and functioned independently, today there is a growing tendency toward coordinating community efforts.

Strong influences from abroad have affected the content and goals of theatre, demonstrating what can be done with sufficient funding, talent, and commitment. Most encouraging is the change in public sentiment. The arts are no longer regarded as frills to be enjoyed by the few after other more important needs are satisfied. The Rockefeller Report, *Coming to Our Senses*, revealed a new attitude in America, even though it has not yet been implemented across the nation.

As in every previous time and place, theatre is an organic part of human society, and the value it has for a society varies according to the social and political conditions of the period. For the scholar a study of the theatre is an important way to discover ideas and values prevalent at a particular time. Children's theatre, paradoxically, tells us more about the adult than it does about the child because it is the adult who creates and sponsors it. There may, therefore, be a discrepancy between the interests of young spectators and what the adult assumes their interests are or should be. The liberation of subject matter and experimentation with form that began in the sixties attacked these assumptions, and this has resulted in some of the most striking changes that have taken place in the entire history of the movement.

Finally, responsible for introducing these new themes and forms is the children's theatre playwright. Whereas in the early years of the movement, plays were written by social workers and classroom teachers, and then by children's theatre enthusiasts who may or may not have had a grounding in the performing arts, there is today a growing number of playwrights whose skill, imagination, and preparation for this branch of theatre are affecting material available to producers. No longer must directors write their own plays or settle for adaptations of fairy tales. While the latter are still in plentiful supply, there are other plays from which to choose: some based on contemporary themes; some written in new forms; still others involving the audience in the action. These new playwrights take their work seriously, believing it to be an artistic challenge and a social responsibility, with the result that a number of fine scripts are appearing every season.

Because the script is the foundation on which a production rests, the emergence of the children's theatre playwright as a force is one of the most important developments in the history of the movement. With a strong script, a good production, and vastly improved performance skills, children's theatre in America may yet attain the level of respect and recognition that it enjoys abroad; it may become a branch of the American theatre and an art form in its own right with a multiplicity of styles designed to meet the particular interests and needs of its audience. Although we do not yet have dramatic critics writing on a regular basis, it is hoped that as the product improves, these practitioners will appear, to cast a professional eye on an art form that has finally come into its own.

NOTES

1. Max Shohet, "Scrapbook of WPA Children's Theatre" (New York: The New York Public Library Theatre Collection). Miscellaneous collection of clippings, letters, press releases, mimeographed questionnaires, and research files.

2. Katherine Camp Mayhew and Anna Camp Edwards, *The Dewey School* (New York: Appleton Century, 1936), p. 466.

3. Alice Minnie Herts, *The Children's Educational Theatre* (New York: Harper and Brothers, 1911), p. 5.

4. Winifred Ward, *Theatre for Children* (New Orleans: Anchorage Press, 1958), p. 48.

5. Mary Eleanor Ciaccio, *Prologue to Production* (New York: Association of Junior Leagues of America, 1951), p. 5.

6. "Children's Theatre at the University of Tulsa," *The Playground*, Vol. 22 (March 1928), pp. 697–98.

7. Constance D'Arcy Mackay, *Children's Theatre and Plays* (New York: D. Appleton Century Company, 1927), p. 168.

8. Wyatt Jones, "The Junior League Story," *Town and Country*, Vol. 110 (August 1956), p. 88.

9. The Association of Junior Leagues of America, "Children's Theatre and Puppetry Statistics," November 1956.

10. Hallie Flanagan, *Arena* (New York: Duell, Sloan and Pierce Co., 1940), p. 200.

11. Burdette Fitzgerald, "Children's Theatre Conference," *Players Magazine*, Vol. 24 (December 1947), p. 64.

12. Sara Shakow, "Children's Theatre in a Changing World," mimeographed copy in ANTA files, Washington, D.C.

13. Webb Waldron, "Children's Delight," *Reader's Digest*, Vol. 34 (January 1939), p. 33.

14. Mimeographed material from Junior Programs, Inc., files.

15. *Children's Theatre Conference Newsletter*, Vol. 5 (October 1955), p. 7.

16. *Children's Theatre Conference Newsletter*, Vol. 6 (March 1953), p. 2.

17. Nellie McCaslin, *Theatre for Children in the United States: A History* (Norman: University of Oklahoma Press, 1971), p. 210.

18. *Pacesetters in Innovation* (Washington, D.C.: Government Printing Office, 1966).

19. Lin Wright and Rosemarie Willenbrink, "Child Drama 1982: A Survey of College and University Programs in the United States," *Children's Theatre Review*, Vol. 32, No. 1 (January 1983), p. 4.

20. Grace Glueck, "A Federal Benefactor of the Arts Comes of Age," *The New York Times*, November 10, 1985, Section 2, pp. 1, 29.

1. The Heckscher Theatre in New York City, showing the Willy Pogany murals, 1922. (Courtesy of Billy Rose Theatre Collection. The New York Public Library at Lincoln Center. Astor, Lenox and Tilden Foundation.)

2. The Palo Alto Children's Theatre. (Courtesy of Patricia Briggs.)

3. Alice Minnie Herts. (Courtesy of Billy Rose Theatre Collection. The New York Public Library at Lincoln Center. Astor, Lenox and Tilden Foundation.)

4. Winifred Ward. (Photograph by Eugene L. Ray, courtesy of Hazel Easton.)

5. Aurand Harris, often called "America's most produced children's playwright." (Courtesy of Aurand Harris.)

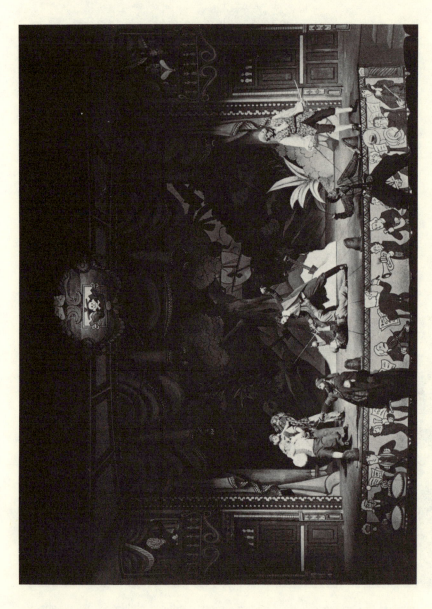

6. A scene from *Treasure Island* by Aurand Harris, produced by the Theatre for Young People at the University of North Carolina at Greensboro. (Courtesy of Tom Bohm.)

7. A scene from *The Magician's Nephew* by Aurand Harris, directed by Coleman Jennings, produced by the University of Texas at Austin. (Photograph by Alan Smith.)

8. Mary Martin in *Peter Pan*, 1955. (Courtesy of Billy Rose Theatre Collection. The New York Public Library at Lincoln Center. Astor, Lenox and Tilden Foundation.)

9. Maude Adams in *Peter Pan*, 1905. (Courtesy of Billy Rose Theatre Collection. The New York Public Library at Lincoln Center. Astor, Lenox and Tilden Foundation.)

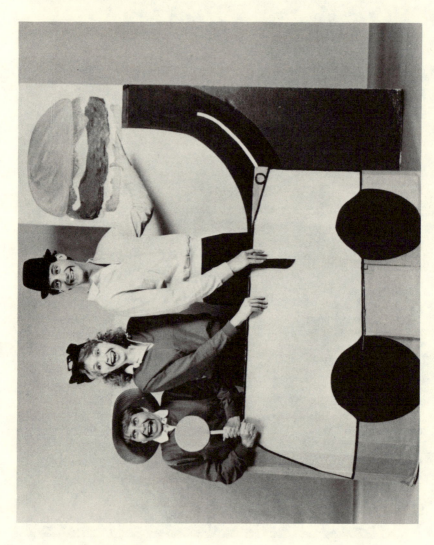

10. The Paper Bag Players of New York, production of *Everybody! Everybody!*. (Photograph by Martha Swope, courtesy of Judith Martin.)

11. *The Revolt of the Beavers*, presented by New York City's Federal Theatre for Children, 1937. (Courtesy of Billy Rose Theatre Collection. The New York Public Library at Lincoln Center. Astor, Lenox and Tilden Foundation.)

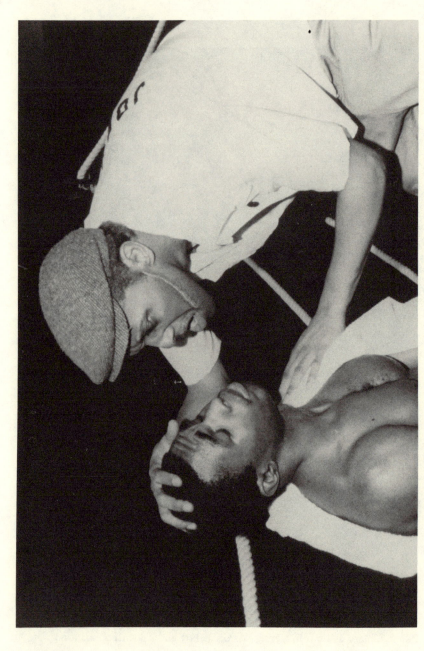

12. A scene from *Joe Louis: The Brown Bomber* by the Creative Arts Team of New York University, 1982. (Courtesy of Lynda Zimmerman.)

13. *Hansel and Gretel*, a production by the Nashville Academy Theatre.

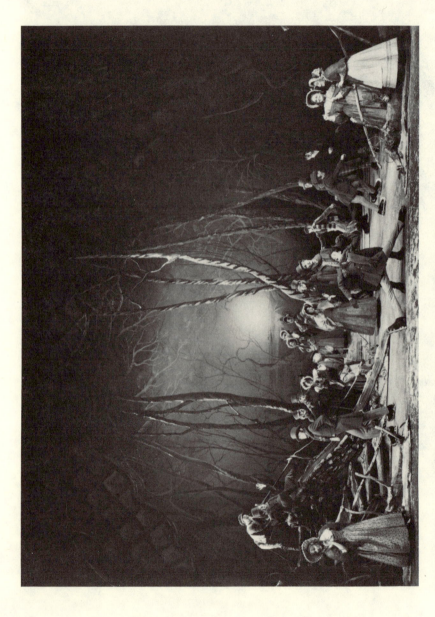

14. The Minneapolis Children's Theatre Company, production of *Mr. Pickwick's Christmas*, 1982-1983 season. (Courtesy of the Children's Theatre Company and School.)

15. A scene from *Play to Win*, which won the 1984 Audelco Award for "best writing of a new show by black authors for the noncommercial theatre." (Courtesy of THEATRE-WORKS/USA.)

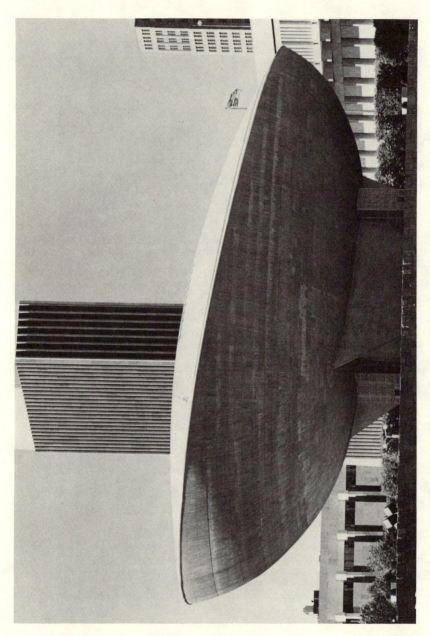

16. "The Egg," home of the Empire State Institute for the Performing Arts in Albany, New York. (Courtesy of NYS Office of General Services/Donald Doremus.)

PART TWO

Profiles of Children's Theatres and Children's Theatre Associations and Organizations, Past and Present

A

ACADEMY THEATRE FOR YOUTH
Address: 1137 Peachtree St., NE, Atlanta, GA 30309
Founding date: 1961

The Academy Theatre for Youth was founded in 1961 by Frank Wittow. By 1978, according to the CTAA *Directory of Children's Theatre in the United States*, it was offering 212 performances a year and was described as educational/professional theatre, with adult actors as performers. Productions took place both in the home theatre and on tour. The success of the enterprise may be seen in its move to expanded quarters with a program that today includes a series of four plays a season for grades K–7; one play for grades 8–12; a school of the performing arts for young people from age nine through seventeen; and an Artists-in-Schools touring and resident program.

Plays for the younger audience are based on folk material and children's classics rather than the traditional fairy tales. Participatory theatre techniques are employed to deepen the child's experience. For the older audience, original scripts, based on issues relevant to the adolescent, are offered. For example, drugs, family problems, alienation, and peer pressure are among the themes that teenagers face. Presented on stage, plays of this kind give young people an opportunity to identify with the protagonist yet maintain sufficient distance from the problem to explore it and consider alternative solutions. Other Academy Theatre productions are made available to high school students; these include plays for the adult audience offered on the main stage or in the First Stage New Play Series. During the holidays Dickens' *A Christmas Carol* is a traditional offering, renewed annually for family audiences.

The Academy Theatre School gives classes in a variety of theatre techniques for both avocational enjoyment and vocational training. The Artists-in-Schools program offers both half-day and full-day packages, combining one or two performances of a play, followed by workshops for students. Again, audience participation is encouraged to enhance the experience. Like most companies today, Academy Theatre for Youth prepares study guides for teachers and sponsors. Funding for the many activities it provides comes from federal, state, and city agencies, as well as tuition and gate receipts.

THE ACTOR'S TRUNK COMPANY
Address: 3928 Spurhill Dr., Bloomfield Hills, MI 48013
Founding date: 1971

The Actor's Trunk Company was founded by Henry K. Martin in Detroit, Michigan, as a touring theatre with programs designed expressly for children. Three years later The Actor's Trunk Company of Canada was founded in Toronto, Ontario. The companies offer two programs, one for younger audiences and the other for high school students. They are described in the brochures as follows:

1. A program that features classic fairy tales. The emphasis is placed on audience participation and the production is designed to stimulate the imaginations of children from four through ten years of age. Two plays are mounted each year and are presented in schools, shopping centers, and theatres. Scripts are written by Henry K. Martin with a teachers' supplement designed by Dr. Sue Ann Martin, who is director of the School of Dramatic Art at the University of Windsor in Windsor, Canada.
2. The second program is entitled *Shakespeare for Youth*; it is an hour-long adaptation of a Shakespearean play and is presented at theatres only. Recommended ages for these productions are eleven through fifteen. One production is mounted each year and it plays to an audience exceeding 25,000. All plays are adapted and directed by Henry K. Martin.

Graduates of the Windsor School of Dramatic Art are frequently hired by Martin, whose success can be measured by an expanding schedule of performances and praise from reviewers. Future plans include plays by Canadian playwrights and a bilingual troupe to tour eastern Ontario and Quebec. A unique aspect of the company is that it does not have government assistance or grants from cultural organizations. It survives on its box office but is able to keep ticket prices within a reasonable price range for children.

ADRIENNE MORRISON'S CHILDREN'S PLAYERS
Address: New York, New York
Founding date: 1930. Closed in 1930s.

This company of adult actors first appeared in 1930 in New York. Carefully selected plays were staged at the 92nd Street "Y" on Friday afternoons, with six plays in the series. Each play ran for one month. The company was established by Adrienne Morrison, a professional actress, to provide the best dramatic literature in the best possible productions. High praise was given the players in newspapers of the period; however, there are no records of productions after 1932.

ADVENTURE THEATRE
Address: Glen Echo Park, Glen Echo, MD 20768
Founding date: 1952

The old Penny Arcade of the Glen Echo Amusement Park was transformed into a permanent home for Adventure Theatre, a nonprofit organization of professional and amateur members skilled in directing, acting, and producing theatre for young audiences. It has always presented a wide variety of shows drawn from traditional fairy tales, folk legends, and ballads.

Adventure Theatre has seven performing divisions:

1. The Weekend Division, which gives plays in the Glen Echo Theatre.
2. The Matinee Division, giving similar plays for young people in the Glen Echo Theatre.
3. The In-School Players, who troupe to elementary schools in the area.
4. The Puppet Division, which presents shows involving live actors and puppets.
5. The Picture Book Players, who give benefit performances in the theatre for very young children.
6. The Education Division, which sponsors workshops and classes for teenagers and adults.
7. The Video Division, the newest group, which tapes shows for the use of directors and publicity purposes and which is also doing experimental work.

All groups perform in the Glen Echo Theatre except for the In-School Players, who operate exclusively in the schools. Adventure Theatre works cooperatively with the park, which sponsors and advertises productions.

Helen Avery, well known in children's theatre, was producer and director of Adventure Theatre until 1984, when she retired to devote her time to writing children's plays. Flora Atkin, a well-known children's playwright, has been associated with Adventure Theatre for many years, supplying the several divisions with a wide variety of new scripts, many of which have been published. Both Flora Atkin and Helen Avery have the distinction of winning the Chorpenning Award for Playwriting from the CTAA.

AKRON CHILDREN'S THEATRE
Address: 565 W. Tuscarawas, Barberton, OH 44203
Founding date: 1973

The Akron Children's Theatre is a professional adult company that performs plays both in its own theatre and on tour. It is a nonprofit company, dedicated to the goal of bringing theatre of fine quality to all children and thereby uplifting values and taste in entertainment. School children are bussed into the theatre during school hours, and performances are given for the public over weekends. The touring company travels throughout the state of Ohio and is sponsored by schools and community organizations. Simple sets make it possible for actors to perform in almost any venue.

Titles are generally well known: *Hansel and Gretel*, *Nightingale*, *Young Abe Lincoln*, *Pocohontas*, and *Mr. Scrooge* are among the most popular. Although teachers' packets are available, the stories are usually classics that can be enjoyed without special preparation. Elaborate costumes and careful attention to details are characteristics of the Akron group. The Children's Theatre offers three summer productions and three educational performances, and operates a year-round theatre school with an apprentice program for serious students. The touring company is a separate group, but together the entire company plays to as many as 65,000 children a year.

ALASKA JUNIOR THEATRE
Address: 2047 Duke Drive, Anchorage, AK 99504
Founding date: 1980

The stated purpose of Alaska Junior Theatre is to bring the excitement of live theatre to children in Anchorage and neighboring communities. It is a nonprofit organization managed by volunteers. Not a producing company, Alaska Junior Theatre imports works by such groups as the Seattle Mime Theatre, The Puk Puppet Theatre of Japan, The Children's Theatre Company (q.v.) of Minneapolis, and the Paper Bag Players (q.v.) of New York.

In 1984 Alaska Junior Theatre was given a Special Recognition Citation by The Children's Theatre Association of America. This award is given for establishing special programs of experimental works, distinctive contributions, and meritorious service for the betterment of child drama in America. Alaska Junior Theatre reached 16,000–18,000 children, parents, and teachers in that year.

ALBION PRODUCTIONS, INC.
Address: Southfield, MI
Founding date: 1975. No longer in operation.

Albion Productions, Inc., later known as Presentation Plus: Communications Resources, reported up to 110 performances a season in the 1978 CTAA *Directory of Children's Theatre in the United States.* By the mid-eighties, however, the company was no longer in production.

ALICE LIDDELL THEATRE COMPANY
Address: Chicago, Illinois
Founding date: 1971. Closed in 1980.

The Alice Liddell Theatre Company of Chicago was founded by David Child, whose interests and background included both theatre and psychology. With participation theatre as a particular thrust, he had several implicit, if not explicit, goals. The first was to entertain; the second, to educate; and the third, to move the audience/participants to action. Programs were planned for several age levels from very young children to upper elementary grades.

In a brochure issued in the 1973–1974 season, Child stated that he took stories from children's literature, hoping to instill pride in the children from whose cultural heritage the stories came and to create an interest in learning more about other cultures in the remaining children. He sought to broaden the horizons of older students to view theatre as an enjoyable experience to be carried over into adult life. By keeping costumes and scenery to a minimum, he hoped to expand the imagination. Finally, he wanted to help children adapt and act out stories on their own. His goal was not to provide lessons in creative drama; rather, it was to offer a program that would involve the audience more than the traditional play by being less "free form" than a creative drama session. Audiences were limited to one hundred and in some cases to sixty. Programs for junior and senior high schools dealt with historical documentary drama and included both participation and discussion. The Alice Liddell Theatre Company went into schools, community centers, and hospitals; workshops for teachers of the gifted were a special feature.

THE ALLIANCE THEATRE COMPANY/ATLANTA CHILDREN'S THEATRE
Address: 1280 Peachtree St., NE, Atlanta, GA 30309
Founding date: 1931

The Atlanta Children's Theatre continues as a leading professional theatre company in the nation, producing work of high artistic quality based on sound financial growth. It fosters and demonstrates its belief in the theatre as an art form and is prepared to engage and challenge audiences of divergent tastes and background. Performances are given in Georgia and the southeastern region.

For schools, the company provides material that is an extension of the prescribed curriculum. This enables the classroom teacher to maximize the enrichment experience. Workshops are offered, if desired, in the classroom following the assembly program. The company offers up to 340 performances a season.

This service is provided by the Umbrella Players, the educational arm of the Atlanta Children's Theatre. Special performances are also offered for the hearing impaired, which indicates the company's ability to keep abreast of current interests and needs. The original purpose of the Atlanta Children's Theatre, the children's branch of The Alliance Theatre Company, was entertainment, offered both on Saturdays and during the week. This program was augmented by high school matinees of plays appropriate for young adults and, in the seventies, the educational programs and workshops on tour in the schools. Workshops following performances are a half hour in length and are based on the productions the children have just seen. Recent play titles include *The Emperor's New Clothes*, *The Pirates of Penzance*, *The Adventures of Tom Sawyer*, and *The Prince and the Pauper* on the main stage, and *Tales from Hans Christian Andersen*, *Tales of Rat Alley*, *Dinosaur*, and *The Land Between*, designed for touring. Currently, the theatre gives 180 main-stage and 167 touring performances a season. Fred Chappell, artistic director, is an active member of CTAA.

The Alliance Theatre has drawn many well-known performers, such as George Voskovic, Paul Winfield, and Jane Alexander, and has also experimented in children's theatre with life-size puppets. Its theatre school is said to be one of the South's leading conservatories for actors.

THE ALMOST FREE THEATRE OF THE GERMANTOWN THEATRE GUILD

Address: 4821 Germantown Avenue, Philadelphia, PA 19144
Founding date: 1968

The Germantown Theatre Guild was founded in 1932 as a nonprofit theatre company of adult professional actors and technicians. The Almost Free Theatre was the children's branch of the guild, founded in 1968. Its prime purpose has been to equalize cultural opportunities for all young people and to give them early exposure to an art form to enrich their educational and social development. Programming was designed to bring young people and adults from diverse economic, ethnic, and racial backgrounds together. The theatre promotes interracial participation in all aspects of its productions, while achieving a balance of professionalism and theatrical creativity. The company presents original plays, classics, musicals, puppetry, and mime. The name, Almost Free, refers to the necessity of charging a small admission fee to performances that had always been free.

The "Little Theatre," a converted eighteenth-century carriage house with a seating capacity of 125, is the home of the Germantown Theatre Guild. Large productions are performed in the John B. Kelly School Theatre, especially designed for the guild's use. The theatre tours schools, libraries, community centers, day camps, hospitals, and other organizations. By touring for child audiences, the guild not only offers a rich experience but also hopes to develop an audience for the future.

Creative dramatics classes for children and acting classes for teenagers and adults are given. These range from early discovery of the creative process to advanced work for the professional performer. Classes also are offered in puppetry, mime, playwriting, and directing. In 1985 there was a complete reorganization of the theatre. As of July 1, 1985, the Germantown Theatre Guild and the Annenberg Center, University of Pennsylvania, merged to become the Philadelphia Theatre Caravan. Administrative offices are located in the Annenberg Center, while actual productions continue to take place in the Germantown Theatre Guild's Little Theatre. Stated goals of the Philadelphia Theatre Caravan are as follows: to develop a permanent theatre program in schools, libraries, and community centers in Philadelphia; to grow into a national training company; to commission new plays by established playwrights; to break new ground for writing plays for young audiences; and to develop a core of actors, teachers, and technicians who will perform, teach classes, and handle all technical aspects of production for youth theatre nationally.

AMERICAN ASSOCIATION OF THEATRE FOR YOUTH (AATY)

Address: Theatre Arts Department, Virginia Polytechnic Institute and State University, Blacksburg, VA 24061
Founding date: 1986

When The Children's Theatre Association of America (q.v.) was dissolved along with the parent organization, The American Theatre Association (ATA) (q.v.), in the spring of 1986, a committee of current and former officers quickly moved to incorporate independently under a different name, thus founding a new organization. Along with the name change came a change of address from Washington, D.C., to a university location. It was thought that, regardless of what eventually became of the ATA, the children's division must continue operations and should be able to survive given office space in a university theatre department. While AATY may conceivably become a part of a new federation of drama organizations at some future date, reduced operating expenses and careful budgeting were planned to insure a sound basis for the continuance of past programs and projects.

When the annual convention of the ATA in August 1986 was cancelled, an educational theatre conference was held in its place under the sponsorship of New York University and Montclair State College. Meetings were held on the campus of New York University with most of the original program included. The stated goals of the new organization were distributed in mimeograph form on August 19 and accepted by those present. They were as follows:

1. To foster and encourage the highest possible standards of theatre produced for audiences of young people and creative drama conducted for participants.
2. To provide leadership in creative drama and theatre for youth in educational, community, and commercial settings throughout the country.
3. To promote research and publication in the field.
4. To make available services, publications, programs, meetings and other activities designed to further the purposes set forth in clause 1.
5. To maintain close cooperation and liaison with state, regional and national organizations with mutual interest in theatre for youth and drama in education.
6. To maintain close cooperation with organizations devoted to making known the human, social, cultural, and educational values of theatre and other art forms.

AMERICAN COMMUNITY THEATRE ASSOCIATION (ACTA)

Address: c/o Ginny Winsor, Omaha Community Playhouse, 6915 Cass St., Omaha, NE 68132
Founding date: 1959

The American Community Theatre Association (ACTA), one of the divisions of The American Theatre Association (q.v.), has always included theatre for children in its program. When the American Theatre Association ceased operation in the spring of 1986, ACTA reorganized and established a central office at the Omaha Community Playhouse and the program continued as before. Although primarily dedicated to furthering and improving dramatic activities in the communities of America, ACTA serves all levels; indeed, some of the finest children's plays in the country are done or sponsored by this division. Community theatre may be described as growing out of the interests and needs of the community rather than being imposed upon it. Its actors tend to be amateur, though directors, designers, and business managers are frequently paid salaries, particularly as programs become more extensive and demanding. Some community theatres have their own buildings; others offer their plays in high school auditoriums, grange halls, churches, or facilities provided by the community.

Since the sixties, grants from state arts councils have been available to community theatres, but major funding is usually provided by wealthy patrons, subscribers, local merchants, and civic organizations. Some community groups have develped into large, fully professional theatres, with elaborate facilities and companies of salaried actors. These are generally referred to as regional theatres, and qualify for the Equity LORT (League of Resident Theatres), contract, which recognizes their professional status but extends special privileges in view of their being located away from large urban centers.

The children's plays are sometimes performed by adult actors, amateur or professional; sometimes by older children; and sometimes by a combination of the two. While the child audience is rarely a major focus of the organization, it is an important area of interest, and it benefits from sharing both a well-managed box office to handle ticket sales and publicity and, if it is the policy, good adult actors. Whereas the quality of productions varies considerably among member groups, because ACTA is responsible for so much children's theatre in the United States it must be recognized as extremely important in the history and current status of this genre.

AMERICAN CONSERVATORY THEATRE (ACT)
Address: 450 Geary St., San Francisco, CA 94102
Founding date: 1970

The American Conservatory Theatre is primarily a drama school, although in the 1978 CTAA survey it reported 125 performances a season. ACT identifies itself today as "educational/professional"; both performers and instructors are professional.

Classes include creative drama, acting techniques, musical theatre, scene studies, voice and diction, and a Saturday workshop for advanced students. ACT offers a student matinee program and casts students from the Young Conservatory for its main-stage productions. It also facilitates the casting of children for outside organizations, television, film, and theatre. William Ball, the general director of ACT, was a keynote speaker for The American Children's Theatre Association (q.v.) at the national ATA convention in San Francisco in 1984.

AMERICAN LIVING HISTORY THEATRE (ALHT)
Address: P.O. Box 2677, Hollywood, CA 90028
Founding date: 1975

The American Living History Theatre is a professional Equity company with a roster of some forty performers and a schedule of twenty productions constantly available to the public. Productions range from one to six plays, and all use primary source material dealing with historical or literary characters and events. ALHT is a nonprofit corporation that offers educational entertainment.

AMERICAN THEATRE ARTS FOR YOUTH, INC. (ATAFY)
Address: 1511 Walnut St., Philadelphia, PA 19102
Founding date: 1971

American Theatre Arts for Youth, Inc., is a nonprofit production company founded by Laurie Wagman to provide children of all ages with high quality professional theatre and film. Program content is related to the curriculum and is designed for integration with formal classroom instruction. Study guides are prepared for all productions.

It is the conviction of ATAFY that theatre touches the senses on many levels; therefore, through the components of language, lights, space, time, and emotion, children and youth are enriched and their horizons broadened.

ATAFY has commissioned and produced twenty-seven original musicals, including a series of *Portraits in American History* and a series that explores the experience of growing up in an urban environment. It also presents a series of award-winning film classics. A further extension of its program is the publication *Media and Methods*, a magazine of the teaching technologies. This includes a wide range of subjects at all grade levels and, while focusing on the language arts, now extends its coverage to all disciplines.

THE AMERICAN THEATRE ASSOCIATION (ATA)
Address: Washington, DC
Founding date: 1936. Closed 1986.

The American Theatre Association, founded in 1936, was the foremost professional association dedicated to the future of noncommercial theatre in the United States. ATA members represented every segment of the amateur and professional theatre: actors, directors, technicians, teachers, theatre enthusiasts. Through a variety of benefits—a theatre/education placement service, award-winning publications, reduced rates at the national convention, special programs and competitions—the American Theatre Association offered its members unique opportunities for both professional development and personal involvement in the future of educational theatre in America. In 1984 there were over 7,000 members in ATA, including its five constituents: the American Community Theatre Association (ACTA) (q.v.), the Army Theatre Arts Association (ATAA), The Children's Theatre Assocation of America (CTAA) (q.v.), the Secondary School Theatre Association (SSTA), and the University and College Theatre Association (UCTA).

Each division had its own journal published quarterly, and all members received *Theatre News* monthly, a newspaper containing news items and short articles. Divisional journals, on the other hand, carried longer articles, research, book reviews, and items of interest to their particular membership. The national office of ATA in Washington had an executive director and staff available to all of the divisions. Financial problems, which had plagued the organization for several years, finally forced its closure in the spring of 1986.

The nine regions that made up ATA are as follows:

Region I: Maine, Vermont, New Hampshire, Connecticut, Massachusetts, Rhode Island

Region II: New York, Pennsylvania, New Jersey, Maryland, Delaware, District of Columbia

Region III: Ohio, Indiana, Michigan, Wisconsin, Illinois

Region IV: Virginia, W. Virginia, Tennessee, Kentucky, N. Carolina, S. Carolina,
   Georgia, Florida, Mississippi, Alabama
Region V: Minnesota, Iowa, Missouri, N. Dakota, S. Dakota, Nebraska, Kansas
Region VI: Oklahoma, Arkansas, Louisiana, Texas, New Mexico
Region VII: Idaho, Montana, Wyoming, Colorado, Utah
Region VIII: California, Arizona, Hawaii, Nevada
Region IX: Oregon, Washington, Alaska

   Some states have associations which were affiliated with The American
Theatre Association. The New England Theatre was actually Region I
of ATA, but the following were state affiliates. They represent all areas
of theatre, most of which include children's theatre in their conferences,
services, and festivals. They represent another source of information
and may be reached through state arts councils.

Alabama Theatre League
Arizona Communication & Theatre Association
Conference on Arkansas Theatre
California Educational Theatre Association
Colorado Drama & Speech Association
Delaware Theatre Association
Florida Theatre Conference
Georgia Theatre Conference
Illinois Theatre Association
Indiana Theatre Association
Association of Kansas Theatre
Kentucky Theatre Association
Theatres of Louisiana
Michigan Theatre Association
Mississippi Theatre Association
Speech and Theatre Association of Missouri
Nebraska Theatre Association
New Mexico Theatre Association
North Carolina Theatre Conference
Ohio Theatre Alliance
Oklahoma Theatre Federation
Theatre Association of Pennsylvania
South Carolina Theatre Association
South Dakota Theatre Association
Tennessee Theatre Association
Texas Theatre Council
Utah Theatre Association
Virginia Theatre Conference
Washington Association of Theatre Artists
West Virginia Theatre Conference
Wisconsin Theatre Association
Mid-Atlantic Chapter of ATA (MACATA)
Southern California Educational Theatre Association (SCETA)

ARCHAESUS PRODUCTIONS, INC.
Address: 9613 Windcroft Way, Rockville, MD 20854
Founding date: 1973

Archaesus performed widely for nearly a decade on the East Coast and in the Midwest. The company was composed of professional actor-dancers and was financed by government and private funds. During its most active years it offered six productions and over 400 performances a season. It also offered classes for children. Originally based in Washington, D.C., it was later managed by a New York agent. Today it is known as the Gary Young Mime Theatre (q.v.).

ARIZONA STATE UNIVERSITY CHILDREN'S THEATRE
Address: Arizona State University, Tempe, AZ 85281
Founding date: 1963

Child drama has been taught at Arizona State since 1962. It is now a major area of departmental emphasis. Formal classes and practical experiences are offered in creative drama, theatre for young audiences, puppetry, theatre games, storytelling, playwriting for children, and research in child drama. These specialized courses are supplemented by offerings in the related arts, elementary education, child development, philosophy of education, and special education. In addition, candidates for all degrees in child drama are required to develop competency in dramatic literature, speech, acting, and stagecraft. Creative activity highlights the child drama program at Arizona State University as well as production work for young audiences and on-site training and evaluation.

Two major productions are staged each year as part of the University Theatre season. In the fall semester a fully mounted play for young audiences is staged on campus. In the spring semester a tour show is given thirty to forty performances in local schools. Puppet shows are also produced on campus and taken to local libraries and schools. The Imagination Corporation, a series of Saturday morning theatre and creative drama experiences for the young, is a regular outlet for the work of student actors, directors, designers, playwrights, and teachers. Ample opportunity exists for performing and teaching in local schools and recreation programs. Work with special populations is also encouraged.

Available degree programs are: B.F.A. in child drama, B.F.A. in theatre education, M.A. in theatre, and M.F.A. in child drama. The department is on the approved list for Winifred Ward Scholars. Professor Lin Wright, one of the program directors, is a past president of The Children's Theatre Association of America (q.v.). The CTAA has designated Arizona State University as the official repository for archival materials of the association and for special collections.

ARKANSAS ARTS CENTER CHILDREN'S THEATRE
Address: P.O. Box 2137, Little Rock, AR 72203
Founding date: 1972

By the end of the seventies the Arkansas Arts Center Children's Theatre was termed the largest professional performing organization of its kind in the state. It took its material from classical and contemporary children's literature, producing six main-stage productions, four touring productions, and two dance concerts each season. In addition, the summer Theatre Academy was designed to be a rigorous, challenging, and educational enterprise for students of high school age. Working with professionals in the field, they could learn both theatre principles and their application to the creation of an original musical.

The stated objective is to offer young people and their families the best possible theatre experiences. The emphasis from the beginning has been on performance and theatre skills, with added concern for the self-respect gained from the development of these skills.

ART INSTITUTE OF CHICAGO. *See* GOODMAN SCHOOL CHILDREN'S THEATRE.

ARTREACH TOURING THEATRE
Address: 3936 Millsbrae Ave., Cincinnati, OH 45209
Founding date: 1976

The ArtReach Touring Theatre, formerly the American Repertory Theatre of Cincinnati, offers a variety of theatrical experiences including audience participation, children's classical literature, and literary and cultural subjects. An emphasis is placed on new works for young people in order to explore the real-life concerns and situations of today's children. Scripts deal with family relationships, adolescent responsibility, death, the fears and frustrations of growing up. Performers have discovered that even young children can respond maturely to these subjects and develop a rapport with actors who handle them in a noncondescending way.

Recently ArtReach has been booked to capacity, performing over 400 times to audiences of over 120,000. As a result of its successful programming, it received the 1983 Zeta Phi Eta Award, presented by The Children's Theatre Association of America (q.v.) for the "best emerging children's theatre in the United States." This honor enabled the company to expand to include a nationwide tour. Services include residencies and workshops following performances.

Titles of productions range from the traditional (*The Emperor's New Clothes* and *The Mark Twain Show*) to *Haunted Houses*, a piece that explores the problems that haunt four friends as they explore a haunted house; *Blue Horses*, a peek into the imaginative world of children, their dreams and wishes; and *Dreamstuff*, a revue including scenes from plays by Thornton Wilder, Eugene O'Neill, Tennessee Williams, and others. Programs are designed for both elementary school and high school audiences.

ARTS ALASKA, INC.
Address: 325 East Third Ave., Suite 400, Anchorage, AK 99501
Founding date: 1960s

Arts Alaska is a statewide nonprofit arts management and service corporation funded in part by grants from the Alaska State Council on the Arts and the National Endowment for the Arts, and by contributions from individuals and businesses. It manages a Performing Arts Touring Program and an Artists-in-Schools Program, making professional artists available to communities throughout Alaska. Outreach services such as workshops, master classes, and residencies are also offered by the performing artists.

Through the Artists-in-Schools Program, students in grades K–12 are exposed to a variety of artists and art forms. In addition to theatre, music, dance, and puppetry are popular offerings.

ASOLO TOURING THEATRE (ATT)
Address: P.O. Drawer E, Sarasota, FL 33578
Founding date: 1971

Asolo Touring Theatre's goal is to present productions of the highest quality to young people in order to give them the excitement of live, professional theatre. Each year, ATT mounts three productions, each geared in style and substance to a different age group: K–grade 3; grades 4–8; and grades 9–12. The elementary school play is developed improvisationally by the company from a fairy or folk tale and performed in the round to a maximum of 250 children, who are encouraged to participate and interact with the actors; the middle school show is usually based on an issue of importance to young teenagers and presented in a standard proscenium style; and the high school show (which is sometimes performed for public audiences) is a classic play or an adaptation of classic literature.

ATT conducts workshops for teachers that include: Play Readiness, which helps teachers prepare students for the productions; Rehearsal Techniques for secondary school drama teachers; and Creative Dramatics for elementary school teachers. Actors also present post-show workshops to students, which include "meet the actor," creative dramatics, and acting skills.

ATT is committed to the development of what it considers challenging new scripts for young audiences and over the past few years has commissioned and produced four new plays. It presents 220 performances each season.

ASSITEJ (International Association of Theatres for Children and Young People)

Address of ASSITEJ/USA: Nancy Staub, 2311 Connecticut Ave., #501, Washington, DC 20008
Founding date: 1964

This world organization was founded at a meeting in England with thirty-three countries attending. At that time it became a committee of the Children's Theatre Conference. The committee has since become ASSITEJ/USA, a separate and independent organization of theatre professionals and professional theatres concerned with quality theatre for children, young people, and families. A congress is held every three years in a different country, which delegates from all member countries are invited to attend. There are now thirty-six member countries.

In June 1984, ASSITEJ/USA and the Louisiana World's Fair presented a World Festival of Theatre for Young Audiences in New Orleans as a special feature. Some 165 stage productions recommended by national theatre organizations and critics were viewed, and fifteen companies were selected to perform. Of the fifteen, four were from the United States: Theatreworks/USA (q.v.) (formerly PART), Sheffield Ensemble Company of Biloxi (*see* Sheffield Ensemble Theatre [q.v.]), the Honolulu Theatre for Youth (q.v.), and The Children's Theatre Company (q.v.) of Minneapolis. In addition, a World Theatre Symposium for theatre artists, scholars, and teachers was held as a special feature. Through ASSITEJ, Americans are able to experience the children's theatre of other countries (many of which show their respect for the arts through generous government subsidies) and to read about activities in different parts of the world in reports, journals, and newsletters.

ASSOCIATION INTERNATIONALE DU THEATRE POUR L'ENFANCE ET LA JEUNESSE. *See* ASSITEJ.

THE ASSOCIATION OF JUNIOR LEAGUES OF AMERICA

Address: 825 Third Ave., New York, NY 10022
Founding date of dramatic activities for children: 1912

The Junior League, a volunteer service organization composed of young women, has had and continues to have a commitment to theatre for children. As early as 1912 league members were working in settlement houses and hospitals, telling stories and guiding children in story-acting and puppetry. By the twenties they were also producing elaborate plays in which league members performed. This aspect of their work spread throughout the United States over the next fifty years, not only in the larger cities but also in rural areas and suburban communities. Many children's theatres were begun by league members.

In the seventies the league continued its interest in children's theatre with sponsorship rather than performance as its focus. Some leagues still gave plays, but the trend was toward joining the consortium or local community theatre in order to bring in the best available touring companies. A report in 1970 called attention to some of the more significant developments. The Atlanta Children's Theatre, spearheaded by the Junior League of Atlanta, was the first resident professional company for children in the United States. The Junior League of Minneapolis commissioned a study of resources and needs in the area and a long-range developmental plan. The presentation of the plan resulted in the establishment of an arts council by a steering committee of the league and the community. In Oakland, California, the league was involved in a project to bring live theatre of superior quality to high schools in low-income areas and to provide an orientation program for teachers.

In San Diego pupils in grades 7–12 were enabled to attend performances of the Shakespeare Festival. The league of St. Louis worked with the Title III MECA Project in an administrative capacity to take plays to the schools and to conduct workshops in improvisations for teachers. It also provided some financial aid for the program. MECA, the Metropolitan Educational Center in the Arts, supplemented and enriched existing educational programs in the arts in both elementary and secondary schools. Weekly museum trips, attending theatre performances, and classes in the dramatic arts for teachers were features of this program which received federal funds for the three-year period 1967 to 1970.

The Junior League of Pittsburgh reported the establishment of an ambitious cultural program for children in elementary schools. In Springfield, Illinois, the Junior League established an arts council, which was turned over to community leadership in 1970. A great variety of programs was made possible under league sponsorship for thousands of boys and girls throughout the country during this period. The emphasis on serving the disadvantaged continued but on a larger scale than at any other time in Junior League history. The league today works with community organizations rather than as a separate entity, and its services over the years can scarcely be overstated.

ATLANTA CHILDREN'S THEATRE. *See* THE ALLIANCE THEATRE COMPANY/ATLANTA CHILDREN'S THEATRE.

AUBURN CIVIC THEATRE, INC.
Address: P.O. Box 506, Auburn, NY 13021
Founding date: 1958

The Auburn Civic Theatre, originally known as the Auburn Children's Theatre, has been active since 1958. The 1978 survey of children's theatres in America conducted by a committee of The Children's Theatre Association of America (q.v.) stated that Auburn offered as many as 700 performances a season; growth since then has increased its activities and standing in the field. Today the program falls clearly in the category of educational theatre, professionally presented.

In 1980 the Auburn Merry-Go-Round Playhouse was established by Edward Sayles, producing director, to extend its goals of community service and artistry. This resulted in its being the largest regional professional theatre in central New York dedicated to innovative presentation and emphasis on literary quality of plays. Within five years from its inception the Merry-Go-Round Playhouse was reported to be reaching the greatest number of young people in the area, and providing programs for the Institutes for the Arts in Education in the four major regions of upstate New York.

The Merry-Go-Round Playhouse also operates a large summer program, in addition to its fall and winter touring program and in-school service. Recent titles of plays given in Auburn and on the road are *Alice in Wonderland* and *The Lion, the Witch, and the Wardrobe*. Actors perform with minimal scenery and properties, handling the latter themselves as needed. Brochures for the theatre list its objectives as follows: to promote spontaneous reaction and interaction between audience and story characters; to provide the means for exploring the literary form through dramatizing it; to assist students in their ability to visualize literature; and to guide students in participatory theatre in social studies. The Merry-Go-Round Playhouse has received two community service awards for its "Outstanding Contribution to the Cultural Climate of the State" (publicity release, 1986).

B

THE BARTER THEATRE
Address: Abingdon, VA 24210
Founding date: 1932

The Barter Theatre was not a children's theatre, but the fact that it early recognized a need for the performing arts for children and offered many programs that could be considered "family theatre" warrants its inclusion here. It was reported to have been the first state subsidized theatre in the United States and was founded by Robert Porterfield, who became a well-known figure in regional theatre in this country.

As its name implies, seats could be purchased with produce from local farms. Although the majority of patrons later paid the box office price, a jar of beans, a smoked ham, or a bunch of flowers made it a sound business venture in the Depression years. The Barter Theatre had the largest professional company in continuous operation outside New York City; it had a training school for young actors, and, in addition to an extensive season, an annual tour to hundreds of towns in the rural South. The repertory included classics and contemporary plays in an effort to offer a cross section of the world's best drama to the community. Children's plays were introduced in its expansion program in 1961. Five or six productions were given annually, with five performances a week during the summer season. Equity actors offered a varied program of fantasy, historical, and modern plays to hundreds of children who would otherwise have no opportunity to see them. It is still in existence.

BIJOU THEATRICAL ACADEMY
Address: 803 Gay St., SW, Box 1746, Knoxville, TN 37901
Founding date: 1979

Built in 1908, the Bijou Theatre, the home of the Bijou Theatrical Academy, is considered one of the handsomest theatres in the South. It has served as a legitimate theatre, a vaudeville house, a movie theatre, and at one time as a used car lot. In 1973 it was suggested that the Bijou be torn down, but the building was saved by Knoxville Heritage, a local restoration group. Today, it is an active performing arts center, in which many community groups perform and drama classes are held. The calendar events list four shows a season for children, of which two shows tour. Titles of plays for the 1984–1985 season include *Tarradiddle Tales*, *Your World or Mine*, *The Hobbit*, and the musical, *Oliver*.

The Bijou Theatrical Academy was formed in 1979 to offer instruction in the performing arts. Improvisation, mime, musical theatre, and creative drama are taught as regular courses, whereas students interested in technical theatre are given responsibilities on major productions. The following titles were announced for the 1985–1986 season: *Wiley and the Hairy Man*; *Mime, Magic and More*; and *The Best Christmas Pageant Ever*. These suggest the variety of their repertory.

BILLIE HOLIDAY THEATRE FOR LITTLE FOLK AND BUBBLE GUM PLAYERS
Address: 1368 Fulton St., Brooklyn, NY 11216
Founding date: 1972

The Billie Holiday Theatre is a sponsoring agency, which brings the performing arts to children in the community. Plays, puppet shows, and dance and musical programs are among the many offerings. There is an emphasis on African and Caribbean arts and performers. Tickets are low-priced, and there are a number of programs especially designed for very young audiences. The company belongs to the Black Theatre Alliance and is well publicized in the New York metropolitan area.

BINGHAMTON CHILDREN'S THEATRE COUNCIL
Address: Binghamton, NY
Founding date: 1938

The Binghamton Children's Theatre Council was established to bring live entertainment to the children of the city and to supplement the work of the schools. A group of parents and interested citizens banded together in 1937 as an outgrowth of preliminary work done in the area by the Junior League. Gloria Chandler, the league consultant at the time, urged the council to make it a community-wide effort. This was done and the result was representation from the Board of Education, the PTA, the American Association of University Women (AAUW), the Junior League, and two local women's clubs. Much of the work was carried on through the public schools, and the programs were given in the junior high school auditorium.

The success of the first year was encouragement for launching a second. By obtaining strong community cooperation, the project soon developed into a popular civic institution. In fact, a description of its work was later written by four members of the council and compiled by Mrs. Reah Stanley Drake, who made the document available as both a record and a guide for other groups wishing to enrich the lives of the children of their communities in the same way.

Binghamton has continued to be one of the most active sponsors of junior entertainment in the state. Every year several companies are brought to the children of the city.

BIRMINGHAM CHILDREN'S THEATRE
Address: P.O. Box 1362, Birmingham, AL 35201
Founding date: 1945

The Birmingham Children's Theatre has been creating live theatrical performances for hundreds of thousands of young people since the mid-forties, and today the theatre, which is a nonprofit corporation, is recognized as one of the oldest, largest, and most successful organizations of its type in the state of Alabama. Including professional actors, it has a staff of full-time and part-time employees, plus volunteers. Ticket prices are low, and the company tours as well as playing in the home theatre.

The Birmingham Children's Theatre gives three productions a year with approximately 150 performances in the home theatre and 45 touring engagements. Like many other theatres for young audiences, it was originally sponsored by the Junior League and was called Birmingham Junior Program. In 1965 it became a separate organization. Plays were performed first in a local high school and later in the Highland Park Recreational Center. A fire in 1970 destroyed the center, again causing the Birmingham Children's Theatre to find a new home. Four years later, board members, community volunteers, and employees began moving the theatre into its present location. James Rye, who joined the organization in 1978, has been instrumental in building it into a successful enterprise, now operating ten months of the year. In addition to plays, special programs, including opera for children, were introduced in the 1984–1985 season. Since 1982 The Conservatory of Fine and Performing Arts and the theatre have worked together. In addition, Birmingham Southern College offers classes in creative drama in conjunction with the Children's Theatre. Thus the original goal of the program has been maintained while new services have been added to meet the interests and needs of the city.

BLACK ARTS WEST THEATRE UNLIMITED
Address: Seattle, WA
Founding date: 1970s. Closed.

Black Arts West Theatre was the only black professional company between Alaska and Los Angeles and west of the Rockies in the seventies.

Its productions embraced all facets of performing arts: dance, drama, and music. The theatre offered complete training in all of these areas. Black Arts West also maintained a complete children's theatre program and offered touring children's productions. To entertain and enlighten the young were the goals of this West Coast theatre company. According to the Washington State Arts commission, the theatre received state funding during the seventies but by the mid-eighties was no longer in existence.

BLACK HAWK CHILDREN'S THEATRE (WATERLOO COMMU-NITY PLAYHOUSE)
Address: Box 433, Waterloo, IA 50704
Founding date: 1962

The Waterloo Community Playhouse, winner of the 1983 Iowa Award for Distinguished Service to the Arts, is one of the oldest, largest, and most successful community theatres in the country. In addition to offering a full season of plays for adult audiences, it also provides a series of plays for children and young people. All work is done by volunteers with open auditions for actors.

The history of the Black Hawk Children's Theatre began in 1962 when the Recreation Commission began productions. There was no set schedule or organization, however, until 1965, when discussion between the Junior League and the Recreation Commission resulted in a contract, including:

1. The hiring of a drama specialist for children's theatre and drama classes.
2. The specific financial contribution of the Junior League to the project.
3. A board which would be drawn from the PTA, schools, library, and Junior League.

In 1965 the Black Hawk County Children's Theatre became a corporation. Theatre activities were expanded during the next few years with more productions and additional classes for children. In the fall of 1982 a full education program was introduced for preschool through adult groups. The wide choice of classes at both Waterloo and Cedar Falls locations included: Creative Play for the youngest children (ages three–five); Creative Drama for K–grade 3; Improvisation for grades 4–6; Acting for junior and senior high school students; Dance for Musical Theatre for ages ten–fifteen; Puppetry for grades 3–6; Recital Classes; and Story Theatre for K–2. All classes are taught by experienced teachers of the Waterloo Community Playhouse.

Black Hawk plays tend to be traditional. The 1984–1985 list, for example, included *Tom Sawyer*, *Pinocchio*, *The Best Christmas Pageant Ever*,

Charlotte's Web, The Owl and the Pussy Cat (presented by the Metro Theatre Circus [q.v.] of St. Louis), and an adaptation of Frank Stockton's story, *The Griffin and Minor Canon.*

BLUE APPLE PLAYERS
Address: P.O. Box 4261, Louisville, KY 40204
Founding date: 1976

The Blue Apple Players, formed by Paul Lenzi and his wife, Geraldine Ann Snyder, have created a number of productions for children that are not only entertaining but are designed to contain educational messages as well. During performances the actors encourage audience participation and welcome questions. The Blue Apple repertoire includes musical versions of such well-known tales as *Pinocchio, Johnny Appleseed, The City Mouse and the Country Mouse,* and *The Ugly Duckling.* They have also written and dealt with sensitive issues such as death. In 1984 the company was awarded a $10,000 commission by Jefferson County to create and produce a musical concerned with the sexually exploited child. *No More Secrets,* the musical, was scheduled to open the 1984–1985 season. Other musicals dealing with serious subject matter have included immigration through Ellis Island at the turn of the century, attitudes toward the elderly, conservation, prejudice, and death.

Blue Apple Players is one of Kentucky's largest and best known theatres for young people. It performs for over 160,000 students each season. Shows are all original musicals designed for touring in schools and arts centers. The company also presents a regular season at its home theatre located in a renovated turn-of-the-century bakery, Bakery Square. It has performed in a variety of venues from Kennedy Center for the Performing Arts to the Desert Inn in Las Vegas. Set and costume designs are an important component of the company's work and are created by Geraldine Ann Snyder, cofounder of the company.

THE BOSTON CHILDREN'S THEATRE
Address: 791 Hammond St., Chestnut Hill, MA 02167
Founding date: 1951

This theatre company was founded in 1951 by the Community Recreation Service of Boston, which absorbed the administrative cost of the theatre. Both training and productions were stressed as part of the recreational and cultural offering of the city. Creative dramatics and acting classes for children from age eight to fourteen met once a week under the guidance of the director and assistant director. About 125 boys and girls were registered regularly for three-month terms. These children were cast, and five plays were produced within a season, with about three performances of each play produced in the New England Mutual Hall. Children were also given an opportunity to assist backstage.

Personnel, from the director to ticket sellers, were employed. Admission to plays was kept in a popular price range to encourage child audiences. The repertoire selected by the director was approved by a committee of prominent citizens. A summer "Stagemobile" was inaugurated in 1953 to take plays to sponsors in the Boston area. The success of the first summer caused this to be a regular adjunct to the winter program.

Still in existence, The Boston Children's Theatre is considered professional and educational. It has responded to community interests and needs, and to these ends has varied its program over the years since its founding. For example, the 1985–1986 series of plays includes a traditional production of *Cinderella*; a favorite modern story dramatized for the stage, *Pippi Longstocking*; and a fast-moving musical version of *Oliver Twist*. Workshops are offered in two comprehensive terms rather than in the former three shorter terms in order to improve the quality of the training. Musical theatre, stage combat, and an acting class for hearing impaired students are among the added workshops.

BOSTON YOUTH THEATRE (BYT)
Address: 93 Summer St., Boston, MA 02110
Founding date: 1978

Boston Youth Theatre is a nonprofit, interracial company organized by former high school teacher, Elaine Koury, in response to the needs of inner city young people. Productions focus on their concerns and fears as well as providing a showcase for those who seek a professional career on the stage. The first production in 1978, *Night Excursion*, was greeted with enthusiasm by critics and neighborhood audiences alike.

Actors ranging in age from the mid-teens to the mid-twenties play in shows conceived and developed by the artistic director and the players. All productions are musicals featuring dance, song, improvisation, rap sessions, and fantastic costumes or simple uniforms, depending on the style of the program. Described as energetic and fresh, the company eschews traditional titles in favor of original content. Some of the titles have been: *I Am Boston, Z'Appenin, Inner City Energy, Xax, The Game, Just Desserts, The Survival Cycle,* and *The Best Kept Secret.* Audiences for BYT productions have grown from 300 in its first season to over 50,000 in 1985–1986. For 1987 two main-stage productions, two educational plays for schools, a six-week tour of schools in the area, and a television special are planned. Unlike many socially conscious groups of adult professionals, BYT continues its policy of casting inner city young people and young adults to whom the content of the plays is relevant.

THE BRIDGE

Address: 90 North Main Street, West Hartford, CT 06107
Founding date: 1978

"Looking In" (officially known as The Bridge) is a family life theatre group comprised of teenagers from the greater Hartford area who present a series of improvisational role plays around a wide variety of issues confronting today's adolescents. The purpose of the progam is to serve as a catalyst for discussion of teenage problems. The scenes depict situations of adolescent relationships, parent-child conflicts, peer pressure and acceptance, and external pressures. The program is designed to heighten adult awareness of young people's problems and encourages young people to make informed, responsible decisions affecting their lives.

"Looking In" was begun in 1978 to fill a need for innovative methods of allowing young people access to information about themselves and the rest of society in the area of interpersonal relationships. It is funded by a grant from the Connecticut Department of Human Resources. It is available to perform throughout Connecticut and elsewhere, with travel expenses paid by the requesting group.

BRIGGS MANAGEMENT

Address: New York, New York
Founding date: 1948. Closed in 1981.

Briggs Management was the principal agency handling professional theatre for children for thirty-three years. Frances Schram, the director, not only carried out the usual functions of promotion, contractual agreements, bookings, and scheduling of tours, she also offered help and guidance to young groups and companies of high quality, which she described as having something to share. She was interested in supporting the serious artist dedicated to performing for children and to that end worked hard to promote the best talent she could find during the years she was in business. Among the attractions she handled were the Paper Bag Players (q.v.), Tony Montanaro, Percival Borde (dancer), The Traveling Playhouse (q.v.), Children's World Theatre (q.v.), John Begg (ballet), and a number of puppet companies.

It was Schram's conviction that until or unless children's theatre was subsidized, the uphill struggle for existence would continue, resulting inevitably in poor quality or failure to survive. It was not until the establishment of state arts councils and government funding agencies for the arts in the sixties and more generous contributions from private foundations that her conviction proved true. Today there are fewer companies performing for children than there were in the seventies. Those that we have are better prepared and charge higher fees. Many belong to Actors' Equity, and a career in children's theatre is a reality.

Although Briggs Management has closed and Schram has officially retired, her interest in this branch of the American theatre remains keen, and her critical judgment is still sought. Schram was always active in The Children's Theatre Association of America (q.v.) on both the regional and national level. While Briggs Management was not a producing company, the fact that Schram handled so many of the finest theatre and puppet companies playing for young people for so many years qualifies it for inclusion here.

BRIGHAM YOUNG UNIVERSITY'S WHITTLIN' WHISTLIN' BRIGADE

Address: Brigham Young University Theatre and Cinematic Arts Department, Provo, UT 84602
Founding date: 1974

The Children's Theatre of Brigham Young University is one of the largest and best known in the West. It offers seven productions a year for youth audiences both in the university theatre and on tour in the community. Although the department is committed to educational theatre, it is also interested in the presentation of new scripts and states that stimulating theatre as well as entertainment is a priority. Elaborate and beautiful production is a hallmark of the work at Brigham Young.

In 1983 the university sent a company to the Sibenik Festival of the Child in Yugoslavia. Performed in English for multilanguage audiences there and in several other sites in Europe, *The Patches of Oz* showed what American children's theatre can be. Harold Oaks, the director, was active in The Children's Theatre Association of America (q.v.) on both the regional and national level. His students give over one hundred performances a year. The program is included among institutions approved for Winifred Ward Scholars.

THE BROQUE OPERA COMPANY

Address: 216 E. 82 St., #19, New York, NY 10028
Founding date: 1976

The Broque Opera Company presents the classic folk and fairy tales in a vivid modern style. A company of fifteen singers and dancers brings the old stories to the stage with music, elaborate costumes, and original choreography and direction. In addition to appearances at schools and community centers in more than twenty states, the company has performed at the Kennedy Center in Washington, D.C., New York's Town Hall, and the Detroit Institute of Arts. In 1981 the company's *The Ring of the Fettuccines* was presented by Kraft Music Hall on CBS Cable. The touring season runs from October to May, and productions are advertised for children six to twelve.

BURBAGE THEATRE FOR CHILDREN

Address: Century City Playhouse, 10508 W. Pico Boulevard, Los Angeles, CA 90064
Founding date: 1973

The Burbage Theatre for Children performs every Saturday afternoon in its home theatre, the Century City Playhouse in West Los Angeles. It also gives special performances both at the theatre and at other sites in the city and the surrounding area as they are booked. In 1980 the Burbage Theatre for Children toured twenty California cities under a grant from the California Arts Council, and the summers of 1981 and 1982 found the group performing at Los Angeles city parks and recreation centers under a grant from the Cultural Affairs Department of the city of Los Angeles.

The Burbage Theatre for Children is a professional group of actors and educators with specialized training in creative drama. Its unique program of participatory plays and creative drama workshops has been entertaining children in Southern California since 1973. More than a children's theatre, all plays and workshops are designed to assist children in the development and acquisition of social values and concepts. It has performed in schools and camps as well as community centers. A recent touring grant enabled the company to expand its program to encompass the entire state of California.

The ensemble is named in honor of Richard Burbage, a Shakespearean actor who lived in England from the time of his birth in 1567 until his death in 1619. Popular by the age of twenty, Burbage was the first actor to play the roles of Richard II, Romeo, Henry V, Hamlet, Macbeth, Othello, and Lear.

The company's concern for the social and cultural problems of young people today has resulted in a series of sociodrama workshops. These were developed in consultation with administrators and teachers, who helped to identify specific problems. Through structured improvisations children are helped to express themselves at the close of each workshop by sharing their feelings and revelations about their experiences. Thus Burbage is engaged in a three-way program: performance for children, creative drama with children, and sociodrama to help children better deal with their problems.

BURGER KING TOURING COMPANY. *See* COCONUT GROVE PLAYHOUSE/BURGER KING TOURING COMPANY.

C

CAIN PARK CHILDREN'S THEATRE
Address: Cleveland Heights, OH
Founding date: 1941. Closed in 1950.

Cain Park Children's Theatre was an outgrowth of Cain Park Theatre, a highly successful project that began activities in 1934 under the leadership of Dina Rees Evans, a teacher at Cleveland Heights High School. "Doc" Evans, as she was known, had a dream of a community theatre that would include a civic theatre, a high school drama club, and a summer theatre offering both adult plays and plays for children. Actually, classes in creative drama preceded the children's productions. According to Evans, this happened because in 1939 municipal funds could not be used to pay actors but could be used to pay teachers. By having actors who could teach classes in acting, puppetry, movement, and creative drama, the adult staff was strengthened and a program for children and teenagers was created.

A civic theatre and a high school drama club operating year round came first. It was not until 1938 that summer productions were given in a spacious amphitheatre built in a ravine of a wooded area of Cleveland Heights. With excess building supplies donated by the city, trees and shrubbery given by John D. Rockefeller, and WPA labor supplemented by local volunteer help, a parksite was cleared and landscaped to accommodate an open-air auditorium seating 3,000. Two years later a special pavilion with 400 seats was built for the children's productions. The park was named for Mayor Frank C. Cain, and the children's pavilion for his wife, Alma. Kenneth Graham, later to become well known in educational theatre and a president of The American Theatre Association (q.v.), headed the children's classes. By 1945 there were eleven teachers, whose specialties included creative drama, puppetry, and choral speaking and rhythms. The children's plays were performed by adult actors with appropriate parts (children's roles) taken by older children. Among the most popular titles were *Racketty Packetty House, Tom Sawyer, Peter Pan, Mr. Popper's Penguins, The Wizard of Oz, The Doctor in Spite of Himself,* and *The Shoemaker and the Elves.* Gilbert and Sullivan operettas were favorites with family audiences. *Babes in Toyland* included one hundred boys and girls in its cast, but this was unusual.

Throughout the forties the Cain Park Theatre was a popular attraction for Clevelanders. It weathered the war years, the loss of actors to the armed services, and difficulties in obtaining supplies; however, Evans' retirement in 1949, severe budgetary problems, poor weather conditions, and a shortened season brought changes by the end of the decade. After only a handful of productions were mounted in the fifties, the amphitheatre was abandoned in the sixties. An effort to revive the project in the mid-seventies led to the installation of a sound system for musicals in 1980, and what was hoped would be a new beginning. The subtitle of the book *Cain Park Theatre: The Halcyon Years* by Dina Rees Evans refers to the period in which the children's theatre was an active component.

CALIFORNIA STATE UNIVERSITY AT NORTHRIDGE
Address: Northridge, CA 91330
Founding date: 1956

The Theatre Department at California State University at Northridge is well known for the high quality of its children's productions and academic program. Its plays have been featured at regional and national conferences of The Children's Theatre Association of America (q.v.) and the retired director (also chairperson of the Department of Theatre), Mary Jane Evans, has long been active in the organization.

The department offers a master of arts degree in theatre with an emphasis on creative drama and theatre for young audiences. Courses in creative drama, including fieldwork experience, theatre for young audiences, and speech/drama activities in classroom and community settings are available, as are independent studies in child drama. A seminar in child drama is required, as is a thesis or thesis project. Two productions for young audiences are part of each year's major season. Both play to public audiences on campus, and one tours the metropolitan Los Angeles area; the other schedules school-time performances for bussed-in audiences. The summer Teenage Drama workshop offers opportunities to teach and direct in its season of four plays for young audiences.

California State at Northridge is on the list of university theatre departments approved for Winifred Ward Scholars. Evans is a Fellow of The American Theatre Association (q.v.) and coauthor with Jed Davis of the college textbook *Theatre, Children and Youth,* published by Anchorage Press in 1982.

CALIFORNIA YOUNG PEOPLE'S THEATRE (CYPT)
Address: 6840 Chiala Lane, San Jose, CA 95129
Founding date: 1976

This is one of the most active and best known of western children's theatre companies. It has grown since its founding in 1976 from a small group to a full-time professional company offering ten productions a season with 400 performances, including those presented at the home theatre and those on tour. California Young People's Theatre is available for touring four months of the year throughout the United States and Canada. Among its educational services are paid internships in acting, design, directing, and business; in-house workshops; and residencies.

The goal of CYPT is to bring the art of the theatre to young spectators and their families and, in so doing, help them develop a greater appreciation, enjoyment, and understanding of this art form. The company has been described as young and dynamic. It is staffed full-time by nineteen professionals, who come from all parts of the United States. The superiority of its work is widely recognized; productions have been invited to the Kennedy Center in Washington and to international festivals in Edmonton and Winnipeg, Canada. CYPT presents traditional titles but also offers new plays by recognized children's theatre playwrights such as Brian Kral, Gayle Cornelison (executive director of CYPT), and the Paper Bag Players (q.v.). The repertory includes plays for both younger and older children. For instance, *The Miracle Worker* and *A Midsummer Night's Dream* appear in a schedule that also lists *The Tales of Br'er Rabbit*, *The Nightingale*, and *Hansel and Gretel*. Cornelison has been active in The Children's Theatre Assocation of America (q.v.) for many years and was chairman of the 1978 Directory Committee. In 1984 CYPT hosted Pre-Convention day, a significant occasion in that it represented the fortieth anniversary of the first gathering of children's theatre leaders at Northwestern University; it was this meeting, called at the invitation of Winifred Ward, that led to the establishment of the Children's Theatre Association of America. The two productions presented on that occasion were *Most Valuable Player*, by the touring company, and *The Greeks: The Quest of Perseus*, performed by children. In October 1984, *Most Valuable Player* began a national tour, which was highlighted by a week's residency at the John F. Kennedy Center in Washington, D.C.

CASA MAÑANA PLAYHOUSE
Address: P.O. Box 9054, Ft. Worth, TX 76107
Founding date: 1962

During the nearly twenty-five years since its founding, Casa Mañana has developed a professional children's theatre company, a touring program that includes ninety independent school districts, various private and parochial schools and numerous day-care and kindergarten centers within a 300-mile radius of Ft. Worth, and a theatre school. A typical season at the Casa Mañana Playhouse includes such titles as *The Wizard of Oz*, *The Adventures of Br'er Rabbit*, *Babes in Toyland*, *The Willie Tree*, *Beauty and the Beast*, *Jack and the Beanstalk*, *Cinderella*, and *Pinocchio*. Productions are geared to a wide age range, providing some plays for younger children and some for older. Its arena style theatre has 1,800 seats, but all are within forty-five feet of the stage. Performances are given on Friday evenings and Saturday afternoons throughout the school year. Touring plays are given in school time.

The curriculum of the Theatre School is designed to develop and improve the student's concentration, imagination, body movement, voice, and speech. Under the direction of professional teachers, students are offered an opportunity to develop poise and self-confidence through self-expression or to lay the foundation of a career in the theatre. A full-scale production is presented at the end of the spring semester with every student performing on the Casa Mañana stage.

A summer workshop for children completes the year's program. Classes for preschool aged children and children in grades 1–3 focus on creative drama, whereas children in grades 3–5 learn the basic disciplines of acting through work on improvisation, body, and speech. Children in grades 6–8 explore the excitement of learning the performing aspects of theatre. Here voice and diction, characterization, and improvisation are included in the workshops. Although children do not appear in Casa Mañana Playhouse productions as part of their studies, they are encouraged to audition for shows requiring young actors.

CELEBRATION MIME THEATRE
Address: 50 Danforth St., Portland, ME 04101
Founding date: 1972

Mime became popular with audiences of all ages during the sixties. One artist who began playing to children and later to college students and adults was Tony Montanaro. In the seventies he moved his studio from New York to Maine, curtailing his formerly numerous performances and workshops so that he could open a school and have time to create new works. He and his company have continued to be highly regarded among mime artists in this country, though his personal appearances are now rare.

Today Celebration Mime Theatre defines itself as a center for the exploration and development of the art of mime and improvisation. It encourages individuals to develop their own style of performance. The results of its work are expressed in two major vehicles: the touring Celebration company of nine performers and the resident school. Performances are held in the Theatre of Fantasy in Portland, described in the company's brochure as "Portland's newest and best little theatre." Seating only eighty persons, it provides an intimate setting for an art form that ranges from vaudeville to delicate portrayals of the insect world, and from commedia dell'arte to detailed realistic studies of contemporary life. Other companies also perform in this space, which enhances work that can best be enjoyed at close range.

Montanaro's performers must be skilled in juggling, acrobatic movement, and sounds that suggest insects, animals, and mechanical equipment.

CENTRAL HIGH SCHOOL PERFORMING ARTS CENTER
Address: 275 North Lexington Parkway, St. Paul, MN 55104
Founding date: 1970

The St. Paul schools began a system of arts centers in 1970 as an aid to integration. Although several other schools have absorbed programs similar to Central's, the wide range of facilities and studies of Central made it an example of what such programs can offer. In addition to teaching classes, faculty are professionally active in the arts. A new theatre, television studios, music room, and dance studio are among the facilities that enable the school to offer classes and perform plays. Students work on scene study and improvisation but, unlike most high school programs, much time is devoted to the development of original material. Some of the plays that are developed in this way deal with subject matter appropriate for young audiences. These pieces stress problems and concerns of children and urge discussion following the presentation. Although the St. Paul students work with many different kinds of material, they make a definite effort to appeal to children.

CENTRAL WASHINGTON UNIVERSITY
Address: Ellensburg, WA 98926
Founding date: 1970

The Drama Department at Central Washington University provides extensive work in child drama and children's theatre for college students, and runs, in addition, a school for children in the arts. Courses for children include creative drama, puppetry, and theatre skills. Central has a long history of productions for adults and children; designed for the latter have been such well-known titles as *The Land of the Dragon*, *The Wizard of Oz*, *The Brave Little Tailor*, and *A Christmas Carol*.

Two well-equipped theatres are available for productions and experimental works. Besides the campus performances, "Theatre-Go-Round" tours children's plays in the area annually. The 1978 Children's Theatre Association of America survey reported 200 performances a year. Offerings have expanded since then, making Central Washington one of the better known departments in the West.

CERT (Community Experimental Repertory Theatre, Inc.)
Address: 12 Vassar Street, Poughkeepsie, NY 12601
Founding date: 1974

The Community Experimental Repertory Theatre was formed in December 1974 by public spirited citizens who believed that live theatre should be a part of every child's learning experience.

CERT became incorporated and established a nonprofit, tax exempt status. A touring theatre company was developed, specializing in educational theatre. Performances were presented in elementary, junior, and senior high schools. Workshops were conducted by teacher/artists prior to the performance, in each classroom of the school. Students are involved in every aspect of the play production. Consequently, an educated student views the play the following day.

Word of the value of the CERT program soon spread to districts outside of Poughkeepsie, and CERT began touring in a wider area. Ten years later CERT was touring in three states: New York, Connecticut, and New Jersey.

A School of Theatre was developed offering classes in creative dramatics, improvisation, beginning and advanced acting, and scene study. Children begin at four years of age to explore the world of imagination through dramatic play. The school enrolls young people from seven to seventeen.

Family theatre was another addition to the CERT program. Four productions are presented in the historic Vassar Institute in Poughkeepsie. Children, young people, and adults come together to experience theatre as performers and audience members. Plays range from dramatizations of classic folk and fairy tales to *The Arkansaw Bear*, *A Toby Show*, *The Miracle Worker*, and *The Effect of Gamma Rays on Man-in-the-Moon Marigolds*.

CHAMBER THEATRE PRODUCTIONS, INC.
Address: 739 Boylston St., Boston, MA 02116
Founding date: 1977

Chamber Theatre is a professional touring company. It represents a return to a traditional view of theatre, where the actor is the most important element. Productions are simple, and offerings are selected to reach a broad range of audiences. Some of the current shows are *Great Expectations* by Charles Dickens, *Sketches of Mark Twain* as well as stories by Mark Twain, and *Tell Tale Poe*, a play based on the last hours of the writer's life.

This company gives workshops for students from the eighth grade through high school and for teachers and professional actors. They differ from most workshops in that they cover a wider area of interests, including basic technical theatre, careers in the theatre, the adaptation of literature to the stage, and voice and movement for the actor.

CHARACTERS UNLIMITED
Address: New York, NY
Founding date: 1950. Closed in 1955.

Characters Unlimited was originally a one-man show organized by Jim Powell. It soon expanded into a small troupe who accepted touring engagements in the New York area. In response to requests from organizations outside the city, Characters Unlimited became a producing company that traveled throughout the country. Flexibility was the hallmark, however, and its shows were often carried by hand to such venues as the *New York Times* Book Fair, the Metropolitan Museum of Art, and the Brooklyn Institute of Arts and Sciences. It offered variety programs rather than straight drama. In 1955 Powell was killed in the same automobile accident that claimed the life of Monte Meacham, director of Children's World Theatre (q.v.). Unable to reorganize, the company was forced to disband and close.

THE CHILDREN'S CENTRE FOR CREATIVE ARTS (CCCA), ADELPHI UNIVERSITY
Address: Adelphi University, Garden City, NY 11530
Founding date: 1937. Closed 1985.

The Children's Centre for Creative Arts was founded in 1937 under the name Adelphi Children's Theatre (ACT) by Grace Stanistreet, who directed it until her retirement in 1977. The focus of the theatre differed from others of the period in that it stressed an integrated arts experience for the education of both child and college student rather than participation in theatre alone. Its goals were to serve the child by providing workshops in both performing and visual arts; to give the college student a laboratory for experience with children; and to function as a community service by providing speakers, conferences, information, and touring productions for elementary school children throughout western Long Island. These various services developed and expanded over the years according to community needs, but the basic philosophy remained unchanged.

Weekly classes in dramatic arts at the college and in a public school in Cedarhurst, an extension of the children's theatre, served the interest of area children, while the needs of college students preparing for teaching were recognized. An opportunity to participate in the program while taking education courses correlated arts experience with the students' major interest. Class activity resulted in performances shared within the educational program. In 1968 the project was reorganized and the name changed to The Children's Centre for Creative Arts, Adelphi University. Stanistreet continued to direct the program, although it had become autonomous and no longer produced plays for child audiences. The center was however, based on the belief that growth, could be achieved when the individual expressed himself freely. In the center the arts were used as a language to achieve this freedom effectively. The center was dedicated to helping students of every age to see meaning and to comprehend experience so that they could take part in improving the quality of living. In this program, where the arts were used for developmental purposes, the child had the opportunity to relate to persons of all ages because of the participation of teachers, college and high school students, and, on occasion, parents and grandparents. In fact, Grace Stanistreet was one of the first to recognize the value of intergenerational participation in workshops.

Saturday morning children's classes were a unique offering of the center. The program is conducted for two hours. The first half hour was devoted to meeting together for the purpose of sharing ideas. Children, college students, and teachers took an active part at this time. Then the groups separated and each group had two workshop periods. For several consecutive weeks one group would divide its morning with a class in acting and a class in music; another group might have a class in dance and a class in acting; another, a class in painting and a class in puppetry. At regular intervals a new combination of classes would begin for each group, with different teachers. It took an entire season for a participant to experience every art form and every teacher. Decreased interest in the arts and the popularity of computer science caused the phasing out of this unique program.

THE CHILDREN'S CIVIC THEATRE OF CHICAGO
Address: Chicago, IL
Founding date: 1917. Closed.

Also called the Municipal Pier Theatre, this theatre company was put together in 1917 by three founding agencies, namely, the Drama League of Chicago, the Civic Music Association, and the Mothers' Drama Club of the Municipal Pier. Specific activities for children were added in the summer of 1918. These activities included choral classes, storytelling, pantomime, play rehearsals, and folk and interpretive dancing. An article entitled "The Children's Civic Theatre of Chicago," appearing in *Drama*, vol. 17 (October 1926), p. 12, stated its purpose to be: "1. To give inspirational direction through dramatic play, music, and dance; 2. To stimulate the imagination and to open avenues more beautiful than are to be found in the city streets."

Several hundred children, including many from the large immigrant community, attended these classes, with the figure for the weekly programs being as high as 3,000–6,000. This was one of the earliest centers for drama and theatre for children in the United States. In 1922 the junior work at the Pier was incorporated as The Children's Civic Theatre of Chicago, Inc., Bertha L. Iles, director, and it was given credit as being the only children's civic theatre in the world.

THE CHILDREN'S EDUCATIONAL THEATRE
Address: Educational Alliance, New York, NY
Founding date: 1903. Closed in 1909.

The Children's Educational Theatre was the first significant theatre for children in America; therefore the founding date of 1903 became the birth date of the movement. The founder was a social worker named Alice Minnie Herts, who, unlike the majority of pioneers in the movement, had a definite educational policy governing the choice of plays for young audiences, performance skills of actors, and quality of stage production. She established a budget in terms of the institution and its audience and maintained high standards during the six years of the theatre's existence. While it lasted for only a short time, The Children's Educational Theatre more than fulfilled its promise. It was reported to have been an excellent enterprise and became a model for other communities to follow.

As for the Educational Alliance, it had been established to teach the English language and American ways to Russian and Polish immigrants in the neighborhood. Herts saw theatre as an attractive means of fulfilling that purpose. Moreover, she wanted to offer better quality plays than those she saw being performed at the Educational Alliance or by local professional companies. The result was The Children's Educational Theatre. Her objectives, in addition to those stated above, were to meet the social needs of the community by providing them with a place to gather, and, as stated in *Children's Theatre Conference Newsletter* 5 (October 1955), p. 7, to "help people create an ideal from within rather than to impose one on them from without." It is interesting that these have been among the goals of children's theatre and creative drama programs throughout their history, though they are ranked in importance according to the priorities of the producing groups and the situations in which the programs were established.

The Children's Educational Theatre opened with a production of *The Tempest* in October 1903. To teach classes and conduct rehearsals, Herts hired Emma Sheridan Fry, whose experience as an instructor at Franklin Sargent's American Academy of Dramatic Art and on the stage brought professional expertise to the project. The success of the production, judging from the sale of 1,000 copies of the play in the neighborhood in the weeks preceding the opening and the enthusiastic audience response, was proof of Herts' good judgment in launching the project and in her choice of vehicle. *Ingomar*, *As You Like It*, and *The Forest Ring* followed, all of which were greeted with similar enthusiasm. The next season opened with *The Little Princess* by Frances Hodgson Burnett. One of the most popular plays presented by The Children's Educational Theatre was Samuel Clemens' *The Prince and the Pauper*; Clemens' interest in the project resulted in his being asked to serve on the board, an invitation he accepted.

Touring performances around the city, a move to larger quarters, and a distinguished governing board, however, did not manage to attract the funds necessary to meet the mounting expenses. As a result, six years later, The Children's Educational Theatre was forced to close its doors. Within the next two years, however, it was reactivated as The Education Players, adhering to the original principles but operating under different management. Performers were adults; children no longer took part but were members of the audience exclusively. One criticism that was leveled at the first company was that by using children on stage, it was exploiting them. This criticism was to be heard many times in the history of children's theatre when young children performed in public. In the case of The Children's Educational Theatre, however, it was deliberately used to educate, improve social relationships, and develop aesthetic appreciation.

No other theatre of the period attracted so much attention or was described in as much detail as The Children's Educational Theatre and its successor, the Education Players. Constance D'Arcy Mackay, a writer of the period whose interests included children's theatre, observed an interesting by-product: for the first time, plays for public elementary schools were being written and some of them published. The importance of The Children's Educational Theatre lay in the following: it was the first organized theatre for children in this country, and it adhered to a clear policy of education for both members and audience. This included a dual emphasis on literature and production.

CHILDREN'S EXPERIMENTAL THEATRE OF BALTIMORE
Address: Baltimore, MD
Founding date: 1943. Closed 1966.

One of the early, highly successful theatres for children was the Children's Experimental Theatre of Baltimore, directed by Isabel Burger. Burger had taught creative drama classes at Johns Hopkins University prior to the founding of the theatre in 1943. While the classes were part of a laboratory for teachers, the parents of the participating children were so enthusiastic about Burger's work that eighty of them became charter members of the theatre when it was officially opened. The project developed rapidly with four public productions a year in addition to classes for children. Some performances were given at the art museum in Baltimore and others at the Vagabond Theatre, the name of the building in which the activities took place. Teacher training continued in the new quarters with additional lectures, demonstrations, and classes in leadership techniques as a result of the publicity and interest in Burger's work.

In 1948 the burgeoning enrollment required new quarters. A century-old carriage house was chosen, though it was another year before the necessary renovation was completed and the facility made ready for occupancy. It was at that time, September 1949, that the Charter of Corporation was amended and the new official name changed to the Children's Theatre Association. Further expansion led to a suburban branch in Catonsville with Clare Babb, a member of Burger's staff, in charge. The schedule of four plays a year continued, although the demand for tickets often extended the run. Burger's pioneering work included extensive travel in the United States and abroad; the writing of a popular textbook on creative drama, *Creative Play Acting*; and, after her retirement, two other books: *Creative Drama in Religious Education* and *Creative Drama for Senior Adults*. At the 1984 ATA Convention Burger received the Campton Bell Award for "A Lifetime of Outstanding Contributions to the Field of Child Drama."

THE CHILDREN'S MUSEUM—RUTH ALLISON LILLY THEATRE
Address: P.O. Box 3000, Indianapolis, IN 46206
Founding date: 1976

The Ruth Allison Lilly Theatre was established in 1976 when the present building for the museum was completed. The stage is a three-quarter round thrust, and the house seats 350 persons. Lilly Theatre is used by the museum staff for a variety of programs, including a film series, lectures, classes, and special events. The community also uses the theatre through rental of the facility, or sponsorship of programs in cooperation with the museum. Primarily, however, the theatre is a touring house into which are booked professional and semi-professional touring companies in a variety of art forms. The spring season operates from the end of January through the end of April. The summer season consists of three one-week residencies by national touring companies, and the fall season completes the year, operating from September until the end of November or early December.

Two programs in the spring and two in the fall are designed especially for preschool age children. One of these programs each season is produced in the museum. The theatre is also responsible for the museum Show Wagon, a trailer stage, which tours three new shows to fairs and festivals each summer. The goal of all of the seasons is to provide quality performing arts for young people. There is an attempt to tie some, if not all, of the shows each season into museum exhibits and events. For example, in the spring of 1985, a dance company with a piece on children's imagination was engaged. It performed on the opening day of an exhibit called "Dream Makers," which had to do with artistic expression of children's dreams. The Lilly Theatre is important in that it attempts to provide top quality experiences in the arts for young people; those experiences are said to be growing richer as they enhance and are enhanced by the other activities of the museum.

CHILDREN'S MUSICAL THEATRE, INC.
Address: P.O. Box 657, Mobile, AL 36601
Founding date: 1974

The Children's Musical Theatre, Inc., was listed in the 1978 CTAA directory as offering 150 performances a year. Today the number has doubled and the company has become fully professional. The thrust of the organization is to present live musical theatre to audiences of children who otherwise would probably have no opportunity to see them. In addition, members of the company offer classes and workshops on tour and provide summer performances in the park in Mobile. The three productions a year tend to be traditional. Some recent titles are *Pinocchio*, *Wild Pecos Bill*, *The Enchantment of Don Quixote, Is That a Fact?*, and *The Jumping-Off Place*. The fact that the productions are all musical differentiates this group from the majority of children's theatres, which often add music to plays or present an occasional musical.

The company was organized as an affiliate of the Mobile Opera Workshop of Mobile but became a separate entity in 1977. It has received the support of the city's recreation department and is a funded member of the Allied Arts Council of Mobile and the Alabama State Council on the Arts and Humanities. Musical puppetry was added in the 1980–1981 season for preschool, kindergarten, and early elementary grade children. The relative ease with which puppets can be transported has made it possible for the musical theatre to perform in shopping malls and areas too small to accommodate a full-fledged production.

THE CHILDREN'S REPERTORY THEATRE COMPANY
Address: 3707 Garrett Rd., Drexel Hill, PA 19026
Founding date: 1977

The Children's Repertory Theatre Company is a full-time adult professional touring company. It has performed in schools, parks, shopping malls, community centers, libraries, museums, and camps. It accommodates itself to places where there are no theatre facilities as well as to places where there are stages. It is the belief of the company that future appreciation is the result of early experience in the arts, therefore attention is paid to choice of script and production. Since its inception it has played to thousands of children in Pennsylvania, the Delaware valley, and the tri-state area. The company currently has four shows in repertory.

During the past six years The Children's Repertory Theatre Company has been supported in part by the Pennsylvania Council on the Arts, the

Camden County Cultural and Heritage Commission, Intermediate Unit No. 19, and various private foundations. It has appeared at conferences of the Theatre Association of Pennsylvania.

CHILDREN'S REPERTORY THEATRE OF SAN FRANCISCO STATE UNIVERSITY

Address: Theatre Arts Department, 1600 Holloway Ave., San Francisco, CA 94132
Founding date: No official date, but activities began as early as 1910.

The Children's Repertory Theatre of San Francisco State University was an early company dedicated to the concept of educational theatre. Although the university has had a long history of dramatic activities for children and young people, the present thrust of the program is a combination of theatrical performance and work in the classrooms by the actors/teachers. Workshops are part of the regular program, and teacher workshops are also given in order to educate teachers in the use of process oriented drama. Study guides provide for preplanning and follow-up activities.

Performances can be done in all-purpose rooms, gymnasiums, or any large open area. Scripts range from cut versions of Shakespeare to traditional fairy tales as well as participatory theatre and curriculum oriented material. *See also* San Francisco State College Theatre.

THE CHILDREN'S THEATRE ASSOCIATION OF AMERICA (CTAA)

Address: Washington, D.C.
Founding date: 1952 (originally known as the Children's Theatre Conference). Closed in 1986.

The Children's Theatre Association of America, a division of The American Theatre Association (ATA) (q.v.), was the professional organization for children's drama and theatre in the United States between the years 1952 and 1986. Its members included professors, teachers, students, playwrights, and individuals dedicated to the development of creative drama as an educational tool; producers of theatre for children; and institutions in which children's plays were produced. Like the ATA, it was composed of nine regions, all of which had regional officers and planned regional meetings. Once a year all divisions of ATA met together at a national convention, held in a different geographic area each year. By 1986 there were over 1,000 members of the children's theatre division. Members received *Theatre News*, a monthly newspaper that gave information on upcoming events, news items, and short articles of interest to the entire membership; and *Children's Theatre Review*, a journal published quarterly. The latter carried longer articles of particular interest to persons working in this area, book reviews, and research on child drama and young people's theatre.

Many regions had their own newsletters and directories of children's theatres in member states. The division also published several books available for sale to nonmembers as well as members. *Give Them Roots and Wings,* coedited by Dorothy Schwartz and Dorothy Aldrich, is a handbook on creative drama for elementary school teachers; originally published by the organization, it was reissued in 1986 by Anchorage Press. Other CTAA publications include bibliographies on creative drama and children's theatre, religious drama for children, and reports on symposia held during the years 1983–1986. Work with handicapped children was an area of interest of many members, and was also included in programs of regional and national conferences. Awards were presented for outstanding contributions to the field in all areas cited. Because leaders came from educational, community, and professional theatre, membership was diverse.

An account of the founding of this organization is given in Part One. When The American Theatre Association closed in 1986, the children's theatre division reformed as the American Association of Theatre for Youth, a separate and independent organization.

CHILDREN'S THEATRE BOARD, INC.
Address: 610 Coliseum Drive, Winston-Salem, NC 27106
Founding date: 1941

The Children's Theatre Board of Winston-Salem is one of the oldest in the country. In its forty-fifth season it reported eighty-eight performances of nine plays for over 40,000 students, parents, and teachers in one season. The Children's Theatre Board is a sponsoring organization that brings professional entertainment to the children of Winston-Salem. The program is comprehensive and includes:

Children's Theatre—For kindergarten through grade 2. A series of three professional shows per year. A variety including fairy tales, puppets, mime, stories from other cultures, dance, and music.

Adventure Theatre—For grades 3 through 5. A series of three professional productions chosen to enhance the interest and appreciation of all forms of theatre—musicals, classics, biographies, opera, plus those that were introduced at the Children's Theatre level.

Theatre Series (Middle/High School)—For grades 6 and up. A series of three professional productions building upon the student's earlier experiences and adding new and more challenging theatre material. This series aims to encourage a more mature appreciation of the arts.

In-School Performances—One show from any series given at a school in the auditorium, cafetorium or gymnatorium.

All entertainment is previewed or commissioned. This assures quality shows appropriate for the audiences. Background information and study guides are available, if desired, for all programs. Except for in-school performances, all productions take place at the Arts Council Theatre.

THE CHILDREN'S THEATRE COMPANY (CTC)
Address: 2400 Third Ave. South, Minneapolis, MN 55404
Founding date: 1961

The Children's Theatre Company is a leading children's theatre organization in the United States. It was founded by John Clark Donahue, who remained its artistic director until 1984. The CTC is dedicated to providing theatre of the highest artistic quality for young people and their families, while offering unique opportunities in education and technical and performing arts training for the interested student.

The two programs, performance and theatre education, mutually support and energize one another. The company has provided nationally recognized theatre for twenty-five years. Over many years theatre training programs were offered, but in recent years a full-time school with the arts at the core of the curriculum was opened to meet the special academic needs of talented young people. Upon graduation, students completing the program were prepared for any field of further study, whether in the arts or in other subject areas. The school was accredited by the North Central Association of Colleges and Schools; it closed its doors in 1985.

The institution is one of the few in the United States with its own well-equipped theatre building. Visitors to the theatre are impressed with the visual beauty of the productions. Movement and acting are stressed in a concern for the totality. According to a report in the 1981 *ASSITEJ Newsletter*, there had been sixty-four new adaptations and translations of existing tales and thirty completely original plays since its first season in 1965. This was a total of ninety-four theatre pieces in sixteen years created by the company for child and/or mixed audiences. Such statistics indicate a strong commitment to the development of its own script material.

CHILDREN'S THEATRE CONFERENCE. *See* THE CHILDREN'S THEATRE ASSOCIATION OF AMERICA (CTAA).

CHILDREN'S THEATRE FESTIVAL
Address: University of Houston, University Park, Houston, TX 77004
Founding date: 1978

The Children's Theatre Festival is a summer enterprise that reaches hundreds of children during the months of June through August. There are four productions per season in a proscenium setting. Apprenticeships and paid internships are an added feature. Productions include both classics and traditional plays; titles in recent years have included *The Sleeping Beauty*, *The Little Match Girl*, *The Wizard of Oz*, and *Little Red Riding Hood*.

THE CHILDREN'S THEATRE GUILD OF NEW ORLEANS
Address: New Orleans, LA
Founding date: 1924. No longer in existence.

A self-supporting company from its start, this historic organization was reported to maintain a program of good entertainment for young people. At the same time it trained grade school and high school students in the art of play production. It embraced a plan that combined the good qualities of professional theatre, student training for the stage, and the school program. The staff was composed of professional adults, while the actors were children.

The Children's Theatre Guild was a precursor in an area which was subsequently to have strong and well-supported programs in the performing arts for children. It has been closed for some time, prior to the establishment of the state arts councils.

CHILDREN'S THEATRE INTERNATIONAL
Address: New York, NY
Founding date: 1961. Closed in 1979.

This company was established in 1961 in New York under the direction of Vera Stilling and William Schill, both of whom had been active in children's theatre prior to that date. As the name suggests, the emphasis was on material from different ethnic backgrounds from around the world. Visual beauty was an important element of the productions. Plays toured to schools and were popular well into the seventies. A professional cast offered traditional stories with great care lavished on the production. Children's Theatre International was seen regularly on the showcase held at The 92nd Street "Y" (q.v.) every spring during the sixties and early seventies. By the late seventies the company had suspended operation.

THE CHILDREN'S THEATRE OF EVANSTON
Address: Evanston, IL 60201
Founding date: 1925

Founded by Winifred Ward, a Northwestern University professor and pioneer in child drama, The Children's Theatre of Evanston was established to provide worthwhile plays for boys and girls of the North Shore of Chicago. Children in the seventh and eighth grades were cast in the parts of young characters, while university students played adult roles, thus creating close cooperation between the Northwestern students and the public schools. Originally four plays were produced a year and were given on Saturday mornings and afternoons. These plays were presented in public school auditoriums rather than at the Northwestern University theatre, making them as accessible as possible to children of Evanston and the North Shore.

For six decades The Evanston Children's Theatre was an outstanding example of good theatre for young audiences and a model for other groups with a similar structure. The plays were generally traditional and were staged traditionally. In contrast to many performing groups in recent years, costumes and mounting were lavish, for it was the conviction of Ward and her colleagues that children should experience visual beauty and color as well as good literature on the stage. In 1971 the theatre was subject to severe financial cutbacks and the once model program was drastically reduced.

After 1971 the theatre continued on a reduced basis for three more years under the sponsorship of the public schools. Local schools furnished rehearsal, performance, office, and shop space, while funds were raised privately. The university continued to furnish two graduate assistants for production work as well as adult cast members. At the end of the three years a Comprehensive Employment and Training Act (CETA) grant was procured and the theatre office was moved to Kendall College in Evanston. The name had been changed in the sixties to Theatre 65 and registered as a nonprofit organization at that time.

The current operation at Northwestern, established in 1979, is called Northwestern University Children's Theatre and Northwestern University Tour Company. The program consists of one main-stage show per season, one summer festival presentation, a winter tour (twenty performances), and three participation productions on tour in the spring (fifteen performances).

Creative drama, which had been introduced by Winifred Ward in the twenties and taught in all of the elementary schools of Evanston along with art and music, had been phased out during the seventies, but it was restored and is now a part of the curricula of all grades, K–8 and junior high school.

The Evanston theatre was an illustration of what can be done when university, public schools, and community all work together. This was one of Ward's major contributions to the field; the other two were a theory of creative drama and the founding of The Children's Theatre Association of America (q.v.).

THE CHILDREN'S THEATRE OF GARY
Address: Gary, IN
Founding date: Early 1920s. Closed.

The Children's Theatre of Gary emerged in the early 1920s with the establishment of the "Work, Study, Play System" in the city. The school

hours began at 8:15 A.M. and ran until 4 P.M. because the superintend-
ent, Dr. William Wirt, felt the need of giving the immigrant children of
Gary music, art, shop, and theatre in addition to an inclusive education.
This was the origin of a unique Auditorium system, which was inaugurated by his wife, Mildred Harter Wirt. Every child from the first
grade through high school was enrolled for an hour a week in Auditorium. Groups of children were taken from the Auditorium for periods
of five weeks to prepare plays or programs for presentation to the rest
of the students in the audience. The classroom teachers provided the
material for these programs, and the actual training was handled by
specialists. Informal discussions, criticism, poetry, and choral speech
were also part of the work.

The teachers who worked backstage directed the class plays with the
high school students. Rehearsals were held after school as well as during
Auditorium periods. Many of the plays were for children, who came
from all of the elementary schools of Gary to see them. As Gary grew,
the problems changed. After Dr. Wirt's death his wife continued with
the Auditorium system. By 1964, however, budget cuts eliminated Auditorium for the first five grades, and within the next few years changing
conditions caused the cessation of activities for the upper grades. This
innovative program, while not a children's theatre in the conventional
sense, was well known at the time and was often cited for its comprehensive plan and community service. The name of Mildred Harter Wirt
was often mentioned along with Winifred Ward and Charlotte Chorpenning, who were pioneering in the Chicago area during this period.

CHILDREN'S THEATRE OF RICHMOND, VIRGINIA
Address: 6317 Mallory Dr., Richmond, VA 23226
Founding date: 1942

This theatre company evolved from a small organization with several
community groups contributing to its efforts. While as early as the mid-
twenties there were accounts of high school students giving plays for
children under the sponsorship of the recreation department of the city,
it was not until 1942 that a strong and lasting children's theatre program
was established. The first plays were offered through the efforts of a
consortium consisting of the Parent-Teacher Association, the Junior League of Richmond, Miller and Rhoades department store, the Musicians
Club, and the Virginia Museum of Fine Arts. So popular were the productions that in 1962 an independent board was created to assume responsibility for an expanded program. The Junior League discontinued
the puppet shows it had been giving, as plans were made to bring in a
director for the entire season. In 1966 this took place, and under his
direction the children's theatre increased the number of its productions
and added trouping throughout the state. Three years later the Rich-

mond, Fredericksburg, and Potomac Railroad offered the use of an old repair shop for a theatre workshop.

In the early eighties, sensitive to the changing needs of the city, the leaders of the theatre shifted their focus and reorganized as an educational theatre. A small touring company now goes out to the schools with programs geared to grades K–8. Plays are generally of a participatory nature, often presenting local legends and stories that tie into the school curriculum. Main-stage productions are still given, however, as are puppet shows, but entertainment is no longer the major thrust of the Children's Theatre of Richmond. While new young leadership has made significant changes in the organization, it remains committed to its original purpose of community service and high standards.

CHILDREN'S THEATRE OF TERRE HAUTE
Address: The New Theatre, 540 N. 7th St., Terre Haute, IN 47803
Founding date: 1936

In November 1936 a group of twelve women met to formulate a plan for establishing a children's theatre in Terre Haute. Realizing the value of such a project, they set out to interest others in what is known today as the Children's Theatre of Terre Haute, Inc. The purpose of the organization was to encourage and develop in the child appreciation and dramatic talent for the theatre. The plays presented in the first season were *The Wizard of Oz* and *Treasure Island*, and they were given in the Woodrow Wilson Auditorium and the old Hippodrome Theatre. The following year Indiana State Teachers College (now Indiana State University) and the public school systems of Terre Haute and Vigo County expressed a desire to become affiliated with the organization. Since the aim of the children's theatre was to encourage self-expression in children, the founders believed that sponsorship by the schools would prove valuable, and the proposal for a cooperative association was accepted.

Lillian Decker Masters of the college was director and her husband, Robert Masters, wrote many of the scripts. In 1947 the university assumed responsibility for the production of the plays, while the membership continued to handle ticket sales. A touring program, arena as well as proscenium productions, and creative drama workshops indicate the changes that were taking place during the next decades. In 1977 a new alliance was formed by the Children's Theatre of Terre Haute, Indiana State University, and St. Mary-of-the-Woods College for the purpose of producing a season of plays in the community and sponsoring The Peppermint Stick Players (q.v.), founded by the two academic institutions in 1970. Today the theatre is not only for children but offers an opportunity for college students to have direct contact in most levels of production. By 1984–1985 plays were given in The New Theatre, especially designed and built for the Children's Theatre of Terre Haute.

THE CHILDREN'S THEATRE OF THE WEST
Address: Sacramento, CA
Founding date: 1949. Closed.

This professional group was established during the early fifties. While Wilma Murphey was producer and manager, Burdette Fitzgerald, a well-known educator specializing in theatre for young people at San Francisco State College, directed the productions. Based in Sacramento, the company toured through California, Oregon, Washington, Montana, Idaho, Texas, Nevada, New Mexico, Arizona, Wyoming, and Colorado. Advance bookings were made with local organizations like the Parent-Teacher Association and schools. The cast members were young graduates from western schools who wished to go into professional theatre, teaching, or recreation work with children. In the mid-fifties the company played to 1,400 at San Francisco State College and to about 10,000 regularly during a season's tour.

Production titles tended to be familiar and traditional: *The Emperor's New Clothes*, *The Bremen Town Musicians*, *Johnny Appleseed*, and *The Sorcerer's Apprentice*. Special attention was given to costumes and mounting, an important consideration in the opinion of the director. The company was not well known outside the area, but it was popular and successful in the region it covered. By the seventies there was no further record of its work.

THE CHILDREN'S THEATRE OF TULSA
Address: Tulsa, OK
Founding date: 1926. Closed.

Established as a gift from the University of Tulsa, this theatre set forth its aims as acquainting the younger generation with the inspiration as well as the fun that drama offers, and showing, through productions, that worthwhile plays bring beauty into all people's lives. The college students worked directly with the children who enrolled for the Saturday morning laboratory. This way, both adults and children were learning together the values and techniques of play production. In addition to the scheduled performances, Christmas and Easter plays were taken to various churches in the community. Four hundred children enrolled in the first season, and the number increased in succeeding semesters. The Children's Theatre of Tulsa is important historically, for it was one of the early organizations involving community and educational resources. It was not listed in the 1968 or 1978 CTAA directories.

CHILDREN'S WORLD THEATRE
Address: New York, NY
Founding date: 1947. Closed in 1955.

"One of the brightest hopes of the children's theatre in America has been a very fine professional company, the Children's World Theatre."

This statement was made by Sara Spencer, publisher of the Children's Theatre Press, in 1955, the year in which the director, Monte Meacham, was killed in an accident and the company was dissolved. The six founding members established a nonprofit corporation to create a permanent repertory theatre for children using all adult professional actors. Its fundamental purpose was stated to be arousing children's imagination through active entertainment; inspiring with the best in movement, speech, art, and music; and increasing their understanding of other national cultures and customs. High praise for the quality of material and performance was given from the beginning as the company performed in New York and on tour up and down the East Coast and through the Middle West.

CHILD'S PLAY TOURING THEATRE, INC.
Address: 2835 W. Logan Blvd., Chicago, IL 60647
Founding date: 1979

Child's Play is a full-time, professional theatre company that performs stories and poems written by children. Over 250 shows and 200 workshops a year are given by a company of four adult actors. A typical program consists of plays, songs, and dances adapted from submissions by children. Each performance includes from seven to twelve original plays, songs, and dances, of which from one to four are by children in the school being visited. Works by both elementary and high school students are read and performed; the most successful entries are put in the program segment called "New Voices" and become part of the company's permanent repertory.

The work of the younger writers is called "Everything under the Rainbow"; that of the older students is called "Changes," and reflects some of the common problems that trouble adolescents. Motivating children and young people to write creatively is the major goal of the Child's Play Touring Theatre. The four actor/teachers are experienced in helping young writers to find subject matter, organize their ideas, and begin to write. In addition, they introduce children to the scenario form, through which they express themselves. The initial step is improvisation of the situation, and the last step is the performance of the scenario in a classroom workshop. Here children join company members in performing their own plays.

As the work of the Child's Play company became known, bookings increased and programs occasionally appeared on area television. In 1982 it was one of sixteen U.S. and Canadian troupes selected to perform on the CTAA Showcase in Milwaukee. The following year the company was invited to represent the United States at two international theatre festivals at Wolf Trap National Farm Park for the Performing Arts and in Windsor, Canada. In 1984 it received a grant from the Illinois Arts

Council to support a full-time managing director and was recognized for its artistic excellence by the National Endowment for the Arts.

Teachers are given guidelines to assist classes in preparing manuscripts for submission. Although the material is solicited from schools and the primary goal is written communication, the company describes itself as educational theatre. Performances are given in parks, museums, libraries, and community centers as well as in school auditoriums and gymnasiums.

CHILDSPLAY, INC.
Address: Box 517, Tempe, AZ 85281
Founding date: 1977

Childsplay, Inc., is a theatre dedicated to issues and themes of contemporary relevance to children. The material is developed improvisationally by the resident company of actor/teachers and musicians. All shows are designed for touring and require the presence of the audience to create what the company calls "whole" theatrical experience. Workshops are available for both students and teachers, and engagements may be requested the year around. Childsplay serves the Southwest. The company is completely professional.

CITY CENTER YOUNG PEOPLE'S THEATRE
Address: New York, NY
Founding date: 1969. Closed in 1979.

Young People's Theatre of New York City was formed by Marjorie Sigley at the City Center as a theatre in education, patterned after the British model. Rather than presenting either entertainment or traditional plays, the programs consisted of three parts: observation, participation, and presentation. In Part I the audience saw a forty-minute presentation by a professional company with original music and environments. This presentation was designed to stimulate the imagination and involve spectators in the theatrical experience.

Following the presentation, the audience was divided into work groups of about twenty-five children each. Every group had its own rehearsal room, separated from the others. Together, the group discussed what they had seen and how they wanted to solve the problem presented, develop the form, or interpret through improvisation some aspect of Part I. For Part III the audience reassembled in the theatre space and each group showed what it had planned, discussed, or improvised. The program utilized the tools of the theatrical medium—characterization, story creation, dramatization, and improvisation—in the teaching/learning situation.

Financial problems caused the city of New York to close City Center, thus removing the space that made possible this unusual concept of theatre for children. The company continued for a season, offering youth services and teacher workshops, but it was impossible to continue operation without a central location that offered space for both presentation and participation.

THE CITY THEATRE COMPANY
Address: University of Pittsburgh, B39 Cathedral of Learning, Pittsburgh, PA 15260
Founding date: 1974

The City Theatre Company is a professional theatre in residence at the University of Pittsburgh dedicated to producing both modern and classic plays by American writers. In addition to the four main-stage productions in its New City theatre, the company engages in an extensive touring program that reaches over western Pennsylvania and the tri-state area. City Theatre touring shows range from original and imaginative short plays for children of all ages to elaborate full-length plays for adults. The children's performances are sponsored by the Gateway to Music program, which is a chapter of Young Audiences, Inc. (q.v.). Over 200 performances are given annually in schools, parks, hospitals, and prisons.

The City Theatre Company was originally known as the City Players but changed its name in 1979. It tours to approximately 35,000 school children every year and falls, of course, in the category of educational theatre for young audiences.

CIVIC CHILDREN'S THEATRE OF YOUNGSTOWN (CCTY)
Address: 600 Playhouse Lane, Youngstown, OH 44511
Founding date: 1952

The Children's Theatre was formed as part of the Junior League of Youngstown's Children's Theatre Committee. It was incorporated in 1955 with the following purposes: to foster the interest of children in cultural arts through participation in plays, workshops, and classes; to produce the best possible theatre for children with high standards of technical production and direction; to produce plays that are ethically sound; to make the experience for the adult and youthful volunteer as creative and enriching as possible; and to utilize theatre as a cultural catalyst.

During the 1983–1984 season it performed to nearly 20,000 school children during school days. Public performances brought an average of 1,000 other children. Plays have included such children's classics as *Raggedy Ann and Andy, Charlotte's Web, Simple Simon, Merlin's Tale of Arthur's Magic Sword, Little Women, The Emperor's New Clothes,* and *The Brave Little Tailor.*

The Civic Children's Theatre offers classes for children three-and-a-half through twelve. They include preschool creative play, creative drama, preparation for the stage, and basic acting. Classes are under the supervision of its educational director, Veronica Gibbs. Basic classes are offered in five six-week sessions, beginning in mid-September and ending in mid-May. Additional specialized and advanced classes are scheduled throughout the year. In addition to the home-based classes at the Youngstown Playhouse and in Warren, Ohio, CCTY will arrange special after-school classes during the week for schools that are interested.

In recent years CCTY touring performances have been sponsored by Girl Scout, Boy Scout, and Campfire troops, Parent-Teacher Organizations, Rotary and Kiwanis Clubs, festivals, fairs, church groups, and a variety of other organizations. CCTY holds open auditions for all its productions. In general, it is the policy to use actors and crew personnel around the fourth and fifth grade level; however, casting requirements vary with each production, and occasionally younger children are needed. Programs are made possible with the support of the Ohio Arts Council.

CLARE TREE MAJOR PRODUCTIONS (THRESHOLD PLAYERS)
Address: New York, NY
Founding date: 1923. Closed in 1954.

The Clare Tree Major Children's Theatre was one of the oldest and longest lived companies in this country. The founder and director, Clare Tree Major, was educated as an actress in England and performed there until she came to the United States in 1916. She was first associated with the Washington Square Players, which later became the Theatre Guild; however, an interest in entertainment for young people and an ability to organize and direct actors led her to establish a professional company. In 1922 she had approached the New York Association of Teachers of English regarding an expansion of offerings to include material for high school students. Approval led to plays of literary quality coordinated with the high school curriculum. This is reported to have been the first time that a professional theatre worked with the schools on plays selected by teachers.

Further expansion of her program included tours of her children's plays by 1931. These plays were presented in schools and community centers and were generally her own dramatizations of classic folk and fairy tales as well as favorite stories such as *Little Women* and *Hans Brinker*. Major believed that children should experience plays of literary worth, beautifully mounted. She stressed also the use of international material in order to promote an interest in the culture of other peoples and an apreciation of the theatre as an art form.

By 1940 Clare Tree Major was traveling from coast to coast. Her company had tripled, with a repertory of six plays for sponsors booking a series. The success of her company was proved by many return engagements, performances of classics on college campuses, and the establishment of a school for actors in Pleasantville, New York. Summer classes for teachers were also conducted by Major and her staff. The fact that she directed the company herself with little administrative assistance, however, led to the closing of the theatre and school with her death in 1954. She did not belong to The Children's Theatre Association of America (q.v.) or any other major organization during the more than twenty-five years the company was in operation. Many actors later employed by other children's theatre companies got their start with Clare Tree Major, and one doctoral study has been written about her and her company.

THE CLEVELAND PLAY HOUSE. *See* THE CURTAIN PULLERS OF THE CLEVELAND PLAY HOUSE.

CLIMB, INC.
Address: 529 Jackson, Suite 227, St. Paul, MN 55101
Founding date: 1975
   CLIMB, Inc., is unique in its artistic approach and in the diversity of the audiences it serves. It spends months training professional actors in the CLIMB philosophy, organizational structure, and relationship to the audience. This includes work in improvisation, scripting, sensitivity to disabling conditions, and sharpening the ability to adjust to the interests of particular groups. CLIMB differs from most other theatre companies that play for children in that it begins with the audience rather than the play. Then it creates a piece around that audience's interests and needs. The result is an improvisationally evolved script, incorporating traditional theatre, creative drama, and participation. In serving the disabled, it differs significantly from the usual and meets a need in a new and effective way.

COCONUT GROVE PLAYHOUSE/BURGER KING TOURING COMPANY
Address: P.O. Box 616, Miami, FL 33133
Founding date: 1979
   The Burger King Touring Company is the official outreach program of the Coconut Grove Playhouse, a state theatre of Florida. It has been in existence since 1979 and has been bilingual and multicultural since 1981. The program commissions original scripts that reflect the multicultural composition of Miami. Original music and lyrics are also commissioned. The company travels to schools, libraries, parks, and recreational facilities throughout the state of Florida and the southeast-

ern states. Produced by the Coconut Grove Playhouse, plays are funded by the Burger King Corporation; the Dade County School Board, the Dade County Council of Arts and Sciences; the state of Florida, Department of State, Division of Cultural Affairs; the State Theatre Board; and the National Endowment for the Arts. The thrust of the program includes entertainment, education, and social consciousness.

THE COLORADO CARAVAN
Address: The University of Colorado, Boulder, Department of Theatre and Dance, 201 University Theatre, Boulder, CO 80309
Founding date: 1972

The Colorado Caravan started as a touring company, providing plays and giving workshops for groups of different ages and circumstances. Although The Colorado Caravan has never identified itself as a children's theatre company, most of its work has been with children from K–grade 6. The thrust of the work has been to perform in the round, involving the youngsters as closely as possible; to simplify the production techniques so as to make active use of the imagination; and to follow up performances with workshops aimed at personal development rather than teaching theatre techniques. In a typical season about one hundred performances of the children's play are given for the benefit of some 30,000 boys and girls in every section of the state of Colorado. No community is considered too small or too remote for touring, but the Caravan does not go outside the state. In 1983 it toured to some fifty communities. Well over 200 performances in a season were reported at the end of the seventies.

Some of the shows given by the Caravan have been *Hidden Treasure* (a program for young children), *The Bear* and *The Marriage Proposal* (Chekhov), *The Importance of Being Earnest*, and *Dance Caravan*.

The Colorado Caravan is now an integral part of the B.F.A. theatre performance degree and a senior year requirement for the theatre performance degree.

COLUMBUS JUNIOR THEATRE OF THE ARTS (CJTA)
Address: 115 West Main St., Columbus, OH 43215
Founding date: 1963

The Columbus Junior Theatre of the Arts is an educational and community theatre whose stated purpose is to provide opportunities in the dramatic arts for children and youth in the greater Columbus area. While other groups now offer either children's performances or classes, CJTA remains the only theatre in central Ohio devoted entirely to youth and the only theatre in Ohio teaching, facilitating workshops, performing, producing, and presenting plays for youth. CJTA was founded and incorporated in 1963. Classes in creative drama, the art of theatre, and scene study are among course offerings. In 1966 it purchased the current building on Main Street and in 1967 formed The Curtain Callers, a volunteer support group focusing on presenting professional children's theatre. In 1971 the Adult Trouping Company began in-school performances with volunteer actors from the community.

Cultural Arts Day began in 1979; it involved professional performances at the Ohio Theatre combined with visits to other cultural institutions by school children. Satellite preschool classes were also introduced in that year. In 1980 professional touring was made accessible to the handicapped. A year later a part-time development director was hired and a middle school summer program was initiated. In 1983 CJTA co-taught a production class for teens with Players' Theatre of Columbus and a scriptwriting project was begun with the Columbus public schools. In the same year a summer program for teens was initiated; this included a class in commedia dell'arte and a fully produced in-house production.

With a large full-time and part-time staff, CJTA in the fall of 1983 added several professional actors to perform in a newly organized professional touring company. This company performs in public and private schools in the area and conducts workshops when requested.

COMMUNITY THEATRE OF DULUTH
Address: Duluth, MN
Founding date: 1911

A little theatre which early in the century incorporated dramatic activities for children was the Community Theatre of Duluth, Minnesota. It was established in 1911 and by 1914 had its own little playhouse. While the children's branch was not firmly organized until the twenties, the Duluth Playhouse was one of the first of the community theatres to recognize this need, hence it belongs to the earliest period of children's theatre history.

Although there is still community theatre in Duluth, the children's branch, described above, is no longer reported as active.

CONTINENTAL THEATRE COMPANY
Address: Manhattan, KS
Founding date: The mid-1960s. Closed in 1976.

The concept behind the founding of the Continental Theatre Company was somewhat different from others of the sixties and seventies in that its home was a state university. The name was considered representative of the company's willingness to perform wherever an audience assembled. The Continental Theatre Company promised to travel to any location that requested a production and to play for audiences of all ages, although children's theatre was an important component.

Basic to its artistic policy was the conviction that professional and university theatres could be strengthened through integration. Company members were encouraged to remain for a long period of time in order to achieve ensemble, whereas students might complete undergraduate and graduate degrees while working with the company. Founder Wesley Van Tassel came to the project with a background in both theatre and education. This was one of the first professional companies to be sponsored by a university.

The company moved to Wichita in 1975 and closed its doors permanently in 1976.

CRATES N' COMPANY
Address: 1200 Kennedy Blvd., Apt. 44, Bayonne, NJ 07002
Founding date: 1978

Some multicolored crates, four young actors, creative energy, and a love of theatre are the basic ingredients of Crates n' Company, a children's repertory ensemble dedicated to a fresh new approach to children's theatre. Performers present theatre in a way that is both entertaining and educational. They act, sing, and dance as they combine learning with the art of the theatre in order to help children gain an appreciation of others as well as a better understanding of themselves. The repertory consists of programs for kindergarten through third grade and fourth through eighth grades. Original works are created from script to performance. They are assisted by professional costumers, choreographers, technicians, and a consultant in educational psychology. Crates n' Company offers 210 performances a year.

CREATIVE ARTS TEAM (CAT)
Address: 715 Broadway, New York, NY 10003
Founding date: 1973

The Creative Arts Team is the resident educational theatre company at New York University. Composed of professional actor/teachers, the team has pioneered a combination of original theatre performances and participatory drama workshops on social and curricular issues. While not a children's theatre in the traditional sense, CAT deals with issues important to children. Conflict resolution through drama, drama for students with special needs, reading support projects, and workshops for teachers are among their offerings. Based in New York, the company works in the area and on tour and has been the recipient of numerous awards and honors.

The founders of the team, Lynda Zimmerman and Jim Mirrione, have remained with it from the beginning, which accounts for its stability and singleness of purpose. With a background in educational theatre at New York University and summers at Bretton Hall in England, where they studied the philosophy and techniques of TIE (theatre in education), they built an organization through which programs are developed and presented in a fresh and challenging way. CAT's aim has never been merely to entertain but rather to make audiences think, feel, and act. Although there are other companies in the United States that describe themselves as TIE, the Creative Arts Team was the first and has remained faithful to its stated purpose.

Some of the team's programs have dealt with racial discrimination (*The Brown Bomber*, based on *The Life of Joe Louis*, and *Rosa Parks—The Back of the Bus*); child abuse (*I Never Told Anybody*); energy (*Watt Went Wrong?*); lack of communication (*The Tower of Babble*); strip mining (*Appalachia*); and the New York City transportation system (*Stop the Subway—I Want to Get On!*). In addition to the presentation of problems and conflict resolution, the team has carried out a successful reading support project for the schools and is a member of the New York City Board of Education program, Arts Partners.

CREATIVE ARTS THEATRE AND SCHOOL (CATS)

Address: 1100 W. Randol Mill Rd., Arlington, TX 76012
Founding date: 1977

Creative Arts Theatre and School, or CATS, is unique among children's theatres today in that performers are all young people, enrolled in a performing arts school. The school offers both education in the arts and family entertainment. CATS gives after-school classes in creative drama, acting, ballet, tap dance, musical theatre, and technical theatre during the school year, and hosts a series of seven shows for family audiences. During the summer CATS has a daytime schedule of classes designed to give performing experience to the more advanced actors, and daily exercise to help dancers keep fit.

While the school is nonprofit and does not discriminate against applicants on the basis of race, color, or national or ethnic origin, it offers a special two-week "Summerstars Program" for the gifted and talented. Instructors are all trained in their special disciplines and are experienced in teaching on all age levels from four years to eighteen. Productions are traditional; recent titles popular with family audiences include *Raggedy Ann and Andy*, *The Legend of Sleepy Hollow*, *Winnie the Pooh and Friends*, *The Emperor's New Clothes*, *Charlotte's Web*, and *Cinderella*.

CREATIVE THEATRE FOR CHILDREN, INC.

Address: 30 North Van Brunt St., Englewood, NJ 07631
Founding date: 1976

Creative Theatre for Children, Inc., is a nonprofit organization employing adult actors in plays for child audiences. On occasion it employs Equity union members and is currently in the process of receiving Equity recognition. The company was founded to bring plays of high quality to the area; it specializes in traditional children's classics such as *Snow White*, *Mary Poppins*, *The Wizard of Oz*, *Hansel and Gretel*, and *Pinocchio*, and in the 1985–1986 season presented a shortened version of *Annie*.

The company prepares study/color booklets for each production; these are directed primarily toward bilingual, handicapped, and very young children. A playwriting contest is held for children of the intermediate grades, and for each play a design contest is held. In addition, there are classes in creative drama for children six to twelve years of age, and backstage tours for older children. Plays are given in both the home setting and in area schools. Although a high standard of entertainment is the primary goal, an educational emphasis is considered an important element. Thousands of children are served by the company each season.

CREATIVE THEATRE UNLIMITED
Address: 33 Mercer St., Princeton, NJ 08540
Founding date: 1969

Creative Theatre Unlimited is a nonprofit organization dedicated to nurturing creativity in children and encouraging self-expression through creative drama and the related arts. Its program has three prongs: after-school classes for younger children; touring performances by a troupe presenting original participatory plays for audiences of children; and workshops and residencies in schools, libraries, and community centers for children and professionals.

Literature, history, nature study, and drama are included in the classwork. Actors in the performing troupe must be able to sing and dance as well as act. The troupe works primarily in the state of New Jersey. Creative Theatre Unlimited is housed in the basement of a church, where classes and rehearsals are held. Performances dealing with local history or environment are often given on the actual sites where the action occurred.

CROSSWALK THEATRE OF YOUNG AUDIENCES OF MASSACHUSETTS, INC.
Address: 201 Huron Ave., Cambridge, MA 02138
Founding date: 1978

Crosswalk Theatre is unique in its dual emphases: bilingual presentations and theatre for retarded, hearing impaired, and disturbed children. Plays are also given for nonhandicapped audiences, but the players are equipped to work with these special groups. The staff consists of ten professional actors and educators: five actors, one musician, one understudy, two dance/drama educators, and one artistic director. All the performing arts may be incorporated in one production, which is presented through repetition of sound, color, image, and theme. When a play is presented in both Spanish and English or in sign language and English, it is largely nonverbal.

The company is available throughout the year and travels primarily in New England.

THE CURTAIN PULLERS OF THE CLEVELAND PLAY HOUSE
Address: Cleveland, OH 44106
Founding date: 1933

The children's activities of this outstanding regional theatre began in the thirties. They started with an experimental series of plays performed for children. By the end of the decade the group had grown from 100 to 500; the audiences, from 500 to 5,000; and the series of productions, from three to seven a season. Members of the company received free weekly lessons in acting with the opportunity of auditioning for parts in public performances. While the Cleveland Play House has always focused on the adult theatre, it has not ignored the value of children's entertainment. The activity has fluctuated over the years since the thirties, however, as a result of changing administrative policies and new directors. In the seventies the name was changed to Youtheatre.

Today there is a renewed effort to establish more and better theatre for children at the Play House. In the early eighties playwright Aurand Harris was brought in to direct his own plays as special Christmas holiday productions. In 1985 the name of the group was changed back to The Curtain Pullers.

D

DALLAS THEATRE CENTER TEEN-CHILDREN'S THEATRE (TCT)

Address: 3636 Turtle Creek, Dallas, TX 75219
Founding date: 1959

A producing and teaching organization, the Teen-Children's Theatre was founded in 1959 and subsequently became allied with the graduate school of Trinity University and the Dallas Theatre Center. The stated aims of the TCT are the development of young actors and the enlightenment of young audiences. Theatre classes are divided into four categories, as follows:

1. Creative Theatre for children aged three to seven. Classes include story-acting, music, movement, and the visual arts.
2. Children's Theatre for children aged eight to twelve. In these classes participants are introduced to all kinds of theatre, including celebrations, rituals, and activities relating to the Egyptian, Greek, Roman, and medieval theatres.
3. Teen Theatre for young people aged thirteen to eighteen. Classes focus on acting styles for classical and contemporary drama, including improvisational theatre.
4. Musical Theatre for children and youth aged eight to eighteen. Participants explore this form of theatre through the study of musical history.

A spring festival of plays is presented by the students from all four categories with as many as thirty productions offered annually free of charge to the public. As an extension of the classes, students may audition for productions offered by the center's three professional companies. These include The Encore Company (grades 9–12), The Junior Encore Company (grades 6–8), and The Summer Magic Players (grades 7–12). Teenagers accepted by The Encore Company and The Summer Magic Players are given an opportunity to work with professional actors, designers, and directors.

The Young People's Series presents four productions during the winter season at the Dallas Theatre Center, the Dealy Recreation Center, and the Bathouse Cultural Center. During the summer months productions are toured to the six city parks. Producer/director Synthia Rogers has been associated with the Dallas Theatre Center for twenty years and has led the TCT for the past ten years, during which period the program has grown in size and scope.

DAN KAMIN
Address: Harlequin Enterprises, 604 St. Clair St., Pittsburgh, PA 15206
Founding date: 1970

Dan Kamin is a mime who performs for children, college students, and family audiences. Although much of his work is humorous, there is a serious dimension, which may be responsible for his appeal to classes in education, psychology, and therapy. He gives workshops and accepts one- and two-day residencies on college campuses, teaching master classes in drama and dance as well as mime. Kamin offers special programs for elementary schools; these may be straight performances or a combination of talk and illusion. Programs for school assemblies include *The Pantomime Man* and *The Return of the Pantomime Man* (a follow-up program). Seven programs for young audiences are given in connection with symphony orchestras; these include *The Story of Babar, Carnival of the Animals,* Maurice Ravel's *Mother Goose, Peter and the Wolf, The Nutcracker, Young People's Guide to the Orchestra,* and *The Pantomime Man and the Lollipop Lady.* In the last one, Kamin works with Kate Young, a singer and actress; this program combines orchestra, mime, storytelling, and audience participation. He reports over 150 performances a year, most of them for children.

DAVENPORT JUNIOR THEATRE
Address: P.O. Box 130, Davenport, IA 52805
Founding date: 1951

Davenport Junior Theatre is a year-round community children's theatre. The accent of the program is on personal growth, a spirit of cooperation, a sense of belonging, and the acceptance of responsibility in all phases of the program. The focus is not on the classes and performance themselves, but on how each individual child can grow through time.

The program operates as part of the city of Davenport's Park and Recreation Department, but support is provided by a group of volunteers who sell tickets, accompany children arriving by bus, and help raise funds for needed capital expenditures.

The Junior Theatre program is not only children's theatre performed by children for other children and adults, but has an apprentice program where a paid high school crew designs and constructs the costumes, set, and props. These young people learn all aspects of production including sound, lighting, and makeup. Theatre in the Quad-Cities (Davenport, Rock Island, Moline and E. Moline) comes alive as children relate to and perform for other children.

Four full-length plays are presented each year to children from fifty elementary schools throughout the Quad-Cities. Plays performed in recent years include *The Wizard of Oz, Magic Horn, The Unwicked Witch, Aladdin and His Wonderful Lamp, Daniel Boone, Jack and the Beanstalk, Imagine That, The Beeple, The Butterfly That Blushed,* and *The Emperor's New Clothes.* Total audience participation for 1983 was 43,247.

More than seventy free performances of ten different productions are held in the area parks during the summer. A self-contained twenty-six foot show wagon travels with casts to each location where children are gathered to participate. The show wagon assures that all students enrolled in classes get a chance to perform. In 1983 approximately 7,000 youngsters viewed the show wagon performances.

A special clown called "Show Time Pal" gives guidance to the Junior Theatre audiences by teaching theatre manners and etiquette, giving story background and development, and leading exercise and song sessions.

Junior Theatre participates in seminars, conferences, and workshops throughout the Midwest. The University of Iowa gives college credit for its students who intern with Junior Theatre. The first Iowa Arts Council Grant awarded in Scott County went to Junior Theatre for a show tour of the state.

DE PAUL GOODMAN SCHOOL OF DRAMA. *See* GOODMAN THEATRE FOR CHILDREN.

DENVER CENTER THEATRE COMPANY
Address: 1050 13th St., Denver, CO 80204
Founding date: 1979

At one time the Denver Center Theatre Company presented an Equity School Tour in the Rocky Mountain region of Colorado and Wyoming. The professional troupe offered plays and musicals to junior and senior high school students. Workshops were available and could be tailored to fit the curriculum or special interests of the students. In addition, discussions followed the performance if workshops could not be scheduled. The center reports no children's theatre plays offered by the eighties.

DETROIT RECREATION DEPARTMENT THEATRE
Address: 735 Randolph, Detroit, MI 48226
Founding date: 1963

The Detroit Recreation Department offers an extensive program in the performing arts for and with young people. Shirley Harbin, the director, is active in both community and educational theatre as well as currently chairing the local chapter of Young Audiences of Michigan. This is a national organization that sponsors live programs and provides administrative support and artistic consultation to thirty-eight chapters across the country. Performing arts classes are offered by the Detroit Recreation Department and include creative drama for ages seven to eleven, performance for ages seven to seventeen, and stage movement for ages seven to seventeen.

In addition, Young Audiences sponsors over twenty professional ensembles, who offer performance-demonstrations, classroom workshops, and in-service teacher training sessions. These include instrumental and vocal music, theatre, dance, and creative writing workshops.

Also, in addition to the regular winter season, the Recreation Department offers a summer arts festival. In 1984 the Chene Park Summer Arts Festival presented programs of music, theatre, and puppets on Wednesdays, Fridays, Saturdays, and special Sundays during the summer months. Five new pieces of sculpture were also installed in the park that year with support from the National Endowment for the Arts, the Detroit Council for the Arts, the Michigan Council for the Arts, and the Michigan Foundation for the Arts. The newsletter *Recreation Renaissance* brings information about performances, trips, and classes to the people of Detroit. Though not strictly for children, the program in its totality reaches thousands of area children and includes them in its many programs for the family. The relationship between the Detroit Recreation Department Theatre and Young Audiences of Michigan is an example of the way in which a municipal organization and a national association work together. *See also* Young Audiences, Inc.

THE DETROIT YOUTHEATRE
Address: The Detroit Institute of Arts, 5200 Woodward Ave., Detroit, MI 48202
Founding date: 1968

Detroit Youtheatre is a series presentation within the Performing Arts Department of the Detroit Institute of Arts, providing young people and their families, clubs, and schools the opportunity to view live theatre designed specifically for their age groups and interests.

A typical season of attractions includes dance, plays, musicals, and puppet shows. While the aim is entertainment, the material is carefully selected, and the performers are experienced professionals. The institution has a large, solid following in the city of Detroit. The director of Youtheatre, Michael Miners, was an active participant in The Children's Theatre Association of America (q.v.), and he travels widely in his search for new and interesting material. Over 500 performances a year are listed, including touring engagements. Emphasis is on a varied season, and fine performance skills are a hallmark. The Prince Street Players (q.v.), originally a New York company, are now based at the Detroit Institute of Arts.

DON QUIJOTE EXPERIMENTAL CHILDREN'S THEATRE, INC.
Address: 484 West 43 St., New York, NY 10036, and P.O. Box 112, Times Square Station, New York, NY 10108
Founding date: 1974

The Don Quijote Experimental Children's Theatre is a nonprofit organization located in New York. It takes its name from the fanciful character created by the Spanish novelist Cervantes. Don Quijote appeals to our ideals. He is the firm believer in generosity and kindness. He is the optimist in the face of malice and misfortune. He is the poet and artist who encourages us to dream, to feel that anything is possible in our lives, and that the world is within our grasp. With this philosophy as its base, the company offers a bilingual show; actors perform in both Spanish and English in order to meet the needs of the new large ethnic populations of the city.

The company performs regularly throughout the metropolitan New York area in elementary and junior high schools, community and daycare centers, libraries, museums, parks, and hospitals. It has been supported in part by local government agencies and corporations, and it tours the Northeast as well as the New York metropolitan area.

THE DRAMA LEAGUE OF AMERICA
Address: Evanston, IL
Founding date: 1910. Closed in 1931.

The Drama League of America was founded in Evanston, Illinois, in 1910. While children's theatre was not a primary interest, it emphasized the best in dramatic literature on every level and included among its projects a Junior Department under the direction of Cora Mel Patten. The children's leagues were important community centers in many large cities, however, serving as sites for the plays and pageants that were popular with child audiences in those years. Among the founders of the league were professional theatre persons, playwrights, laymen interested in bringing the arts to their communities, and university professors. Percy Mackaye, a playwright, was particularly enthusiastic about the pageant as an art form and saw this grassroots movement as a way of promoting original works on regional subject matter. He was highly critical of Broadway for exploiting theatre for private gain, and of the schools for their failure to include it in their curricula. He believed that only through the communities of America would we be able to achieve an art form worthy of the name.

In addition to establishing centers in towns throughout the country, the league published a magazine, *Drama*, which carried information about theatre activities as well as scholarly and critical articles. Contributions by Walter Pritchard Eaton, George Pierce Baker, and Barrett Clark indicated the interest of educators in this burgeoning new movement. The league also published an index of plays for children in 1915. It was the first volume of its kind to appear. In order to serve the needs of the schools and social centers more effectively, the Educational Drama League was organized in 1913. Its goal was to promote dramatic activities in schools and settlement houses. Constance D'Arcy Mackay, who was an ardent member of the organization and a keen observer of the scene, reported that there were twenty-five clubs and three classes in story-acting after only one year. The Boston league during the same period of time had acquired 2,300 dedicated members. In the Middle West the league was particularly strong; children's theatre advocate Winifred Ward was among the large number of educators who joined its ranks.

Playgrounds and recreation centers were also recipients of the league's stimulation and support. While much of this latter activity was unorganized and spontaneous, *The Playground* and *Recreation* carried accounts of noteworthy amateur theatre. Other periodicals and newspapers of the twenties reported swelling numbers of community theatres as a result of the league's influence. Children's theatre was considered sufficiently important to be included as a topic of discussion at conferences.

The league's program and sphere of influence grew during the decade of the twenties, therefore it comes as a surprise that all activities were terminated in 1931. According to Mrs. A. Starr Best, one of the founders of the organization and its first president, it had served the public in a number of important ways. It had stressed the need for better plays than the commercial theatre was producing and, in so doing, had educated audiences to demand them. It had helped little theatres and children's theatre to initiate projects; and it had published a magazine. With these goals met, its job was done and it was no longer necessary to continue as an organization. The activities of the league spanned two decades and were intertwined with those of a variety of educational and community institutions throughout the United States. Viewed in a historical context, it is apparent that the extent and intent of its contributions can scarcely be overemphasized. In *Theatre for Children* (New Orleans: Anchorage Press, 1958), p. 23, Winifred Ward said of it, "In the awakening of general interest and dissemination of knowledge concerning children's plays, the Drama League of America deserves highest credit."

E

EAST BAY CHILDREN'S THEATRE, INC.
Address: 3612 Webster St., Oakland, CA 94609
Founding date: 1932

One of the oldest in the country, the East Bay Children's Theatre has held to the same objectives for over fifty years. The company tours to the public schools in two counties where the student bodies are primarily underprivileged. Approximately forty free performances are given each year. In addition to the free performances, East Bay travels to small towns outside the metropolitan area for special performances. Throughout the season, it is seen by approximately 10,000 children. The plays are musical, and the stories are taken from children's classics; scores and book are always original.

EAST-WEST FUSION THEATRE
Address: P.O. Box 141, Sharon, CT 06069
Founding date: 1975

East-West Fusion Theatre was founded in 1975 as Kings and Couriers and was reorganized and renamed in 1983. The company performs the year around, offering fifty or more performances representing both new Western plays on international themes and Asian plays and stories. The repertory for both adults and children's audiences includes nine productions and over twenty-five short plays and dance programs. The group claims to be the first permanent, professional theatre in the United States devoted to "fusion of the arts" and has as its goal the creation of a truly international theatre. Artists and scholars from many countries have been brought to the center in Sharon and to the campus of Vassar College, where East-West Fusion Theatre was the resident summer theatre in 1983 and 1984.

The advisory board includes faculty members from Vassar College, the University of Hawaii, Tufts University, Michigan State University, the University of California in Los Angeles, and the University of Wisconsin; faculty disciplines include anthropolgy, drama, Asian theatre, and dance. Performances combine acting, dance, music, mime, puppetry, and masks, and are staged as authentically as possible. All performances are in English, though the works are based on the cultures of China, India, Bali, Java, Japan, and the Pacific Islands.

A special educational component named "Sights and Sounds of Asia and the Pacific" features lectures, workshops, exhibits, and teaching materials. All programs are of educational value, however, in that they present the old traditions of countries that are little known to American children. The company has toured eleven states from the East Coast to the Middle West and as far west as California, although most performances are given in local schools and colleges. Among the titles in the 1985–1986 repertory are *Animal Tales of India*, *East Meets West*, *Japanese Comedies*, *The Ramayana*, and *Sights and Sounds*, which is actually a series of programs drawn from the collections of the center. It is taught by scholars and theatre professionals and is offered at all levels. Audiences are invited to participate in movement, voice, puppet, mask, and costume workshops, through which they gain insight into other cultures, where the arts are not isolated experiences but are a part of everyone's daily life.

EAST WEST PLAYERS
Address: 4424 Santa Monica Boulevard, Los Angeles, CA 90029
Founding date: 1965

The East West Players were established as a nonprofit educational and performing arts company. They depart somewhat from all the traditional Hollywood formulas, for the company shapes new and compelling images of its own and addresses a variety of problems connected with the Asian/Pacific American community and the art of theatre.

The initial guiding philosophy of the East West Players was, according to its 1985 brochure:

To establish a medium through which Asian/Pacifics could create a truer and more meaningful place for themselves in the American theatre;
To offer opportunities for professional writers to experiment and develop;
To serve the Asian/Pacific American community as an integral part, the expression and preservation of its cultural life, and perhaps most importantly,
To bridge cultural understanding between East and West through the performing arts.

EASTERN MICHIGAN UNIVERSITY THEATRE OF THE YOUNG (TOY)
Address: Ypsilanti, MI 48197
Founding date: 1963

Eastern Michigan University has one of the nation's leading drama/theatre programs for the young. In addition to serving students of widely varying interests, it has expanded its program to include both the Master of Arts and the Master of Fine Arts degree in this area of theatre. A program within the Department of Communication and Theatre Arts, it has officially represented Michigan at the Great Lakes Theatre Festival, has been designated United States Resource Center for Drama in Education by the International Amateur Theatre Association (IATA), and is certified as one of the universities in which Winifred Ward Scholars can pursue graduate study. The curriculum includes courses preparing students for careers in teaching, community theatre, telecommunications, recreational, social service, and religious work, in which drama/theatre is relevant.

TOY began in 1963–1964 and has offered full-scale stagings of such plays as *The Trial of Tom Sawyer*, *Don Quixote of La Mancha*, and *Canterbury Tales*. Productions are given on the stage of the Quirk Theatre on campus and on tour. The Little Theatre of the Young and the Caravan TOY tour schools, libraries, and hospitals with original, intimate performances. Here they may introduce story theatre, bringing children such great literature as Aesop's fables, folk tales of many lands, Charles Dickens, and the poetry of Carl Sandburg. Often combining music and movement with the spoken word, the Little Theatre of the Young reaches thousands of youngsters a year, many of whom would otherwise never experience live theatre. In addition, a ten-performance run in the home theatre plays to audiences totaling over 4,000 a season. The children's productions are on the regular season ticket and also include special school-time performances. TOY experiments with innovative forms designed to heighten audience involvement. It makes a concentrated effort to reach and serve disadvantaged areas, both urban and rural, and to provide experiences mixing ages and cultures in ways that foster understanding and the sense of human kinship.

Virginia Glasgow Koste, one of the directors of TOY, is a playwright and author of the book *Dramatic Play: Preparation for Life*, published in 1978 by Anchorage Press. She is active in The Children's Theatre Association of America (q.v.), serving on committees and appearing on programs at national conventions and conferences.

EDWIN STRAWBRIDGE THEATRE FOR CHILDREN
Address: New York, NY
Founding date: 1940. Closed in the late 1950s.

Edwin Strawbridge was a dancer who had been with Junior Programs, Inc. (q.v.), until 1937. Three years later he established his own company and began touring in 1940. The popularity of his work and the professionalism of his performers made it necessary for him to expand his schedule, until by 1954 he had made eighteen trips across the country, playing to audiences totaling 4 million. The preceding year (1953) Strawbridge joined Actors' Equity, thus becoming the first producer of children's theatre to take this step. Thirty years later nearly all of the leading companies were Equity members, which meant better salaries for the actors, better working conditions, superior performance skills and, as a result, higher fees for sponsors. While this cut down the number of small touring companies, it proved beneficial to the children's theatre movement in the long run, in that actors were able to remain with companies for a longer time and produce better quality work as a result. Whereas ensemble work was difficult to achieve when performers were forced to seek employment outside or leave the theatre altogether, it became a reality when a living wage and desirable conditions were assured. For this alone, Strawbridge may be given credit; union membership was a step forward in that it represented a growing professionalism in an area of theatre that had been primarily amateur.

Strawbridge was also affiliated with the Children's Theatre Conference (later The Children's Theatre Association of America [q.v.]), and at the summer conference at Adelphi University in 1953, both performed and hosted an al fresco supper on the lawn of his Mt. Kisco, New York, estate. The company terminated activities in the late fifties, but the Junior Programs and Strawbridge contributions were to be viewed both at the time and in the perspective of history as having advanced the movement and its image.

EMERSON COLLEGE CHILDREN'S THEATRE
Address: 100 Beacon St., Boston, MA 02116
Founding date: 1920

Imogene Hogle's work in putting on plays for children during her senior year at Emerson College led to the founding of a children's theatre within the college in 1920. It was an extracurricular venture that grew into a well-established part of the Emerson program at the time. Although most of the plays given were well-known classics, occasionally new scripts by faculty members and students in playwriting classes were produced. The program of a monthly play performed on Saturday afternoons often had repeat performances by popular demand. All phases of play production were offered in the Emerson dramatic workshop. Titles of plays included *Master Skylark, Aladdin, Alice Through the Looking Glass, Damon and Pythias*, and other children's classics.

Emerson College Children's Theatre is one of the oldest theatres for children in America. The Emerson College students are still carrying on the tradition but in modern terms. Since 1969 Emerson College Youtheatre has offered children and young people the opportunity to enjoy the excitement of both contemporary and traditional theatre. It offers an in-depth theatre arts program in theatre instruction and performance for young people in grades 7–12, and an innovative integrated arts program encompassing a broad range of art forms for children in grades K–6.

The goal of the Emerson Youtheatre today is to bring students of varying backgrounds, ages, and abilities together to work on projects that allow each individual to thrive in a supportive atmosphere. Emerson College is on the list of approved institutions for Winifred Ward Scholars. TIE (theatre in education) is an important component of the work offered for students majoring in drama/theatre education. Summer productions often take place off campus in parks and historic locations. *Canon Fields*, an original script, was presented and videotaped in Concord in the summer of 1982. Other original scripts based on social issues and curricular topics are developed by students in the theatre program under faculty supervison for local schools. Outreach programs have always been a major thrust of the Emerson College Theatre.

EMERSON COLLEGE YOUTHEATRE. *See* EMERSON COLLEGE CHILDREN'S THEATRE.

EMERSON STAGE. *See* EMERSON COLLEGE CHILDREN'S THEATRE.

EMMY GIFFORD CHILDREN'S THEATRE
Address: 3504 Center Street, Omaha, NE 68105
Founding date: 1949

The Emmy Gifford Children's Theatre, Nebraska's first professional performing arts center dedicated entirely to children and their families, celebrated its thirty-fifth year of operation in 1984. Founded in 1949 by the Junior League and seventeen local civic organizations, the theatre was originally known as the Omaha Junior Theatre. In 1981 the board of directors changed the name to honor Emmy Gifford, the theatre's first president, for both her original service and her continued dedication to the theatre's growth and development.

For the first twenty-five years the theatre staged its productions in various locations in the city. In 1975, however, the theatre found a permanent home. A building was purchased and additional space was constructed for rehearsal rooms, offices, a costume shop, and a scenery construction dock. The theatre has developed into one of the most highly respected arts organizations in the Midwest. Today its membership numbers 1,500 families and its budget exceeds a quarter of a million dollars annually. It has produced one videotape, *The Little Match Girl*, which is being distributed both nationally and internationally, and it is in the process of producing another. The Emmy Gifford Children's Theatre has grown from one full-time employee (the director) to ten full-time employees, including five actor/teachers.

Each season five fully staged plays are produced. Each production is performed a minimum of twenty-six times to school children and subscription members, and to the general public on weekends. A theatre school offers three semesters of instruction in theatre crafts, dance, and acting, including a summer session. Touring solo performances take place throughout the year, going to schools, colleges, churches, and other organizations. As an Outreach Program response to community requests, the theatre writes original plays that speak to particular concerns, such as chemical dependency, child abuse, and so on. Production titles during the regular season have included *Little House on the Prairie, Peter Pan, The Revenge of Baba Yaga, The Hobbit, The Diary of Anne Frank*, and other children's and young people's classics.

The Nebraska Touring Program is sponsored by the Nebraska Arts Council. Future plans and goals include more plays for the family, new scripts as well as favorite children's stories, an increase in the core company of actors, an enlarged school and institute program, a studio theatre, and more videotapes of productions. The original goal of "the best possible children's theatre" continues to be the top priority, according to Nancy Duncan, the executive director, and Bill Kirk, the artistic director of the theatre.

EMPIRE STATE INSTITUTE FOR THE PERFORMING ARTS (ESIPA)
Address: Empire State Plaza, Albany, NY 12223
Founding date: 1976

The Empire State Institute for the Performing Arts was the first state mandated theatre for children in this country. It was established in the seventies under the direction of Patricia Snyder of the State University of New York in Albany. Housed in the "Egg," a magnificent facility designed for both large- and small-scale productions with generous work areas, rehearsal and classroom space, the institute sends companies on tour throughout New York State and offers workshops and in-service training for teachers.

The ESIPA program focuses on top quality theatrical productions for the widest possible family audiences. By combining high professional and artistic standards with a dedication to educational and community involvement, its productions are aimed at fostering a knowledge and appreciation of performing artists and their art. Since 1982, when the present program was officially established, ESIPA has gained wide recognition. It is firmly committed to the development of young audiences and the presentation of new artistic works.

ESIPA continues to maintain its basic belief that the arts should be integrated into the school curriculum. To that end it now includes in its program seminars, educational and community in-service master classes with visiting artists, critics' and playwrights' forums open to the public, an extensive touring and school residency program, and an internship program for adult students. A monthly bulletin announces coming attractions at the Egg and on tour. ESIPA offers one hundred performances a season.

Patricia Snyder's involvement on the international level led to the 1972 world congress of ASSITEJ (q.v.) in Albany and to several appearances of the company outside the United States. Two highly acclaimed tours to the Soviet Union and a performance at the world congress in Lyons, France, in 1981 gave the Empire State Institute for the Performing Arts worldwide exposure, making it one of the best known and most highly respected children's theatres in America by the eighties.

EQUITY LIBRARY CHILDREN'S THEATRE
Address: W. 103 St. and Riverside Drive, New York, NY 10025
Founding date: 1955. Operations suspended by the seventies.

The Equity Library Theatre was a project established in 1955 by a New York Public Library system and Actors' Equity Association in 1943 and incorporated in 1949. Its primary purpose was to provide professional actors with an opportunity to perform when they were not employed and, in so doing, to bring live theatre to the people of the city at low cost for tickets. The shows were originally presented in the branch libraries, but the need for a permanent base led to the establishment of a headquarters first at the Lenox Hill Playhouse, and in 1961 to its present location on Riverside Drive.

In 1955 Equity Library Children's Theatre was added. The National Council for the Living Theatre, the League of New York Theatres, and the Theatre Guild provided support. Full-length children's plays were produced with sets and costumes designed by professional scenic artists and costumers. During the sixties a short-lived program called Equity Community Theatre was formed as a result of the success of the project. It offered four shows a year to communities in the metropolitan area. Entitled Scrapbook Productions, these were assembly-length plays consisting of scenes from classics. They introduced thousands of high school students to dramatic literature from Shakespeare to O'Neill during the few years it was in existence.

Although Equity Library had stopped producing plays for child and teen-age audiences by the seventies, it offered some of the best scripts available at the time and was interested in staging new, more experimental work. One of the plays first seen by Equity Library Children's Theatre audiences was Joanna Kraus' *The Ice Wolf*, a play that has since been published and widely produced throughout the United States. Equity Library Theatre still offers eight major productions each season and may consider resuming the children's plays at some future date.

THE EVERYMAN PLAYERS, INC.
Address: 4621 St. Charles Avenue, New Orleans, LA 70115
Founding date: 1959. Activities suspended after 1981.

The Everyman Players, originally under the direction of Orlin and Irene Corey of Shreveport, Louisiana, attracted wide attention in the sixties for a variety of reasons. First among them was an adherence to classical material for the entire family rather than to the standard children's fare. Second was a high standard of performance, and third was Irene Corey's extraordinary costume and makeup designs. The latter have been described as "unique," "beautiful," and "visually exciting." They may be seen in her book, *The Masque of Reality*, lavishly illustrated and printed by Anchorage Press. Both content and style differed markedly from anything seen on the American stage prior to their appearance, and there is still no company that has attempted to imitate their work.

The Coreys were also in demand for many years as lecturers and workshop leaders and frequently spent several weeks in one place so as to accept workshop engagements while performing evenings. They were often identified as leaders in the area of religious drama, a reputation not undeserved, for *The Book of Job* and *The Pilgrim's Progress* were among the most popular works in their repertoire. Since the mid-seventies, when Orlin Corey purchased the Anchorage Press and moved to New Orleans, the Everyman Players have been less active and have attempted some innovative work of a different sort. Two recent productions have been *The Butterfly*, a fantasy for any age level, and a program based on nursery rhymes that was visually so beautiful that it could hold an audience older than the content would suggest. Orlin Corey has been president of The Children's Theatre Association of America (q.v.) and is active in ASSITEJ (q.v.). In 1984 he handled local arrangements for the children's theatre offerings at the World's Fair held in New Orleans. He has presented his own company in Europe at ASSITEJ meetings and privately by invitation on numerous occasions.

F

FAIRMOUNT THEATRE OF THE DEAF
Address: 1925 Coventry Rd., Cleveland Heights, OH 44118
Founding date: 1975

This acting company includes four hearing actors and four deaf actors in addition to the artistic director and company interpreter. A technical director and his assistant also travel with the group. The goal of the theatre is the development of a form that incorporates the expressive use of sign language and is simultaneously understood by both deaf and hearing audiences. Productions include a varied and well-balanced repertory of productions ranging from the contemporary to the classic, and frequently original work is performed. Each year one production is selected for touring; the basis for choice is its universal appeal to a wide age range. Among past productions were Saint-Exupéry's *The Little Prince*, Molière's *The Doctor in Spite of Himself*, *Beauty and the Beast*, Tennessee Williams' *The Glass Menagerie*, and an original musical entitled *Alice in Deafinity*.

The company also offers classes, demonstrations, and workshops for middle school and secondary school students interested in the learning processes of the hearing impaired. Master classes in mime, sign language, and improvisation are also available with fully staged performances of a classic one-act play as a culmination. Residencies are offered and may be of various lengths. By 1980 the Ohio Arts Council was listed as a sponsor. The Fairmount Theatre of the Deaf has performed for the Ohio Theatre Alliance as well as for other groups both in and outside the state. In 1983 the group performed in Czechoslovakia; in 1984 in Jordan; and plans are being made for further travels in Europe and the Middle East.

FANFARE PRODUCTIONS (FANFARE THEATRE ENSEMBLE)
Address: 102 E. 4th St., New York, NY 10003
Founding date: 1970

Fanfare Productions began in 1970, but when, in 1973, it became a not-for-profit corporation, the name was changed to Fanfare Theatre Ensemble. It was based on the principles that theatre for young people cannot be educational without being entertaining and that it must be as good as any other kind of theatre. Since its inception it has mounted over twenty productions, each emphasizing adaptations, as faithful as possible, of the best-loved fairy tales and classic children's stories. Performers are actor/singers, all of whom have had extensive professional experience in Broadway and Off-Broadway productions. Hundreds of performances a year are offered on tours nationwide. Staging is important to Fanfare, which uses professional designers for scenery and costumes.

The company has been seen on the New York PACT Showcase on numerous occasions. It represents the small touring company, offering musical theatre for schools and community centers. Titles of shows include the following: *Alice Through the Looking Glass*, *Beauty and the Beast*, *A Connecticut Yankee in King Arthur's Court*, *East of the Sun and West of the Moon*, *Hansel and Gretel*, *Huckleberry Finn*, *The Legend of Sleepy Hollow*, *Sleeping Beauty*, *Young Robinson Crusoe*, and many others equally familiar.

FARGO MOORHEAD COMMUNITY THEATRE
Address: P.O. Box 644, Fargo, ND 58107
Founding date: 1946

The Fargo Moorhead Community Theatre was founded for the purposes of maintaining and operating a community theatre in the city of Fargo, North Dakota, as an institute for the teaching and study of the dramatic arts and for other philanthropic and educational uses. From 1946 to 1976 the theatre organization functioned in rented spaces in both Fargo, North Dakota, and Moorhead, Minnesota. It was then that the Emma K. Herbst Playhouse was completed and became the permanent home of the Fargo Moorhead Community Theatre. The theatre stages seven productions a year for adults and children. Five plays are presented for adult audiences and two for the youth theatre component, Prairie Theatre for Young People. This is an educational program for children in grades 1–12.

The theatre has grown from one full-time staff member to a current level of five full-time and three part-time employees. In line with this expansion of personnel are plans for a new wing. The addition will include a children's theatre stage, handicapped access restrooms, scene and costume shops, and administrative offices. Children's productions of the past have included *Scrooge*, *Snow White*, and other familiar and favorite children's classics.

THE FEDERAL THEATRE FOR CHILDREN
Address: Various cities throughout the United States
Founding date: 1936. Terminated in 1939.

Children's theatre was one branch of the WPA Federal Theatre project, which was established and funded by the United States government between the years 1936 and 1939. Its children's plays were given in the following cities: New York, New York; Gary, Indiana; Los Angeles, California; Seattle, Washington; New Haven, Connecticut; Portland, Oregon; Cleveland, Ohio; Denver, Colorado; and Tampa, Florida. While the Federal Theatre was a relief measure designed primarily to help unemployed actors, it was also successful as public entertainment, and it introduced many communities to the concept and value of children's theatre. Age level programming was practiced, and a number of plays were written to meet the special needs of the companies and their audiences.

Research was done as to appropriate plays for children and young people; this included ticket prices, times of performance, and audience analysis (reactions to plays). Unfortunately, in spite of the acknowledged success of the project, the Federal Theatre was terminated after only three years by an act of Congress. Some of the children's theatres that were established at this time, however, were continued under community sponsorship and given different names. Also, some of the actors, directors, and playwrights continued to work in this area of theatre. Thus the work continued, though under different conditions and auspices.

Among the plays produced by The Federal Theatre for Children during these three years were *The Emperor's New Clothes, The Revolt of the Beavers, Expedition to the North Pole, Winnie the Pooh, Little Black Sambo, Hansel and Gretel, Pinocchio, Rip Van Winkle, Br'er Rabbit and Tar Baby, Night Beat,* and a children's revue entitled *Mother Goose Goes to Town.* Although there was criticism of *The Revolt of the Beavers* as being Communist inspired, the variety of titles above indicates an interest in traditional scripts, folk and fairy tales, modern stories, and different forms and styles. The Federal Theatre for Children's long-range plans, on which it had already embarked, included much more than production, however, as the following list of projects from Max Shohet's "Scrapbook of Children's Theatre" in the New York Public Library Theatre Collection shows:

1. Research—to determine the best times for performances and the most suitable admission charges.
2. Promotional Problems—to get the cooperation of school principals in taking children to the plays.
3. Repertory Problems—to find appropriate plays for presentation.
4. Audience Analysis—to determine the reactions of children to the plays.
5. Caravan Theatre—to take plays out to the parks during the summer.

6. Festivals—to present Christmas Festivals during Christmas week.
7. Dance Project Production—to introduce dance as entertainment to audiences of children.
8. Theatre for Youth—to attempt to set up theatre for high school students.
9. Community Drama Division—to send out dramatic directors to settlements and neighborhood centers.

While the short life of the theatre precluded the accomplishment of all of these projects, a start was made, and future groups with similar goals have tried to pursue at least a few of them, albeit on a smaller scale.

FIREBIRD THEATRE COMPANY
Address: 6128 Romaine St., Hollywood, CA 90038
Founding date: 1977

Firebird Theatre Company is a professional group of ten actors and musicians who average 200 performances a year. A nonprofit organization, it specializes in original adaptations of myths, folktales, and classical plays for young audiences. Plays involve dance, music, ethnic costumes, and the use of masks. Although most performances take place in primary and secondary schools, they are also given in museums, libraries, art centers, and community theatres.

Some of the plays in the repertory have been a Kabuki version of *The Fisherman and His Wife*; *The Gallant Tailor*, set in sixteenth-century Persia; an original play about the Chamash Indians of California; Oscar Wilde's *The Happy Prince*; Sophocles' *Antigone*; and a Guatemalan myth, *A Journey to Xibalha*. Preceding the performance the company demonstrates the style of the play to the audience, and after the play there is a follow-up session for those who are interested.

The company offers workshops in theatre games and improvisations. Funding is provided by the National Endowment for the Arts, the California Arts Council, the Cultural Affairs Department of the city of Los Angeles, various corporations, private donations, and income from school performances and workshops.

THE FIRST ALL CHILDREN'S THEATRE
Address: New York, NY
Founding date: 1969. Closed in 1985.

The First All Children's Theatre was established by Maridee Stein in 1969. A resident company, it also toured a repertory of traditional plays and children's classics. While professional adult actors performed leading roles, children took part in productions, with auditions held periodically throughout the season. By 1980 there were two companies: the Mini Players and the Teen Company. Membership involved an understanding by both child and family of the seriousness of a commitment to the theatre.

The stated primary purpose of the group was to produce theatre of top professional quality including both performance and visual effects. It was one of the few children's theatres to have its own theatre and studio for rehearsals and classes. Unlike the majority of children's theatres, The First All Children's Theatre did not belong to The Children's Theatre Association of America (q.v.), nor was it affiliated with any community or educational institution. It closed down in January 1985. While it was never well known outside the New York area, it had a following among parents and children pursuing an acting career, and a local reputation for visual beauty and an emphasis on performance techniques.

FIRST NIGHT, INC.

Address: 739 Boylston St., Boston, MA 02116

Founding date: 1976

First Night is not a children's theatre, but it is included here because theatre for young audiences is an important aspect of its program. It came into existence as a way of providing a community-wide celebration of New Year's Eve through the performing arts. The founding goals were to bring the city, suburban, and neighborhood communities of Boston together for a joint celebration. Between 1976 and 1984 First Night grew from a local event into a significant national festival attracting out-of-state visitors to Boston at New Year's time. Its audiences increased from the original 60,000 to 200,000 by 1983.

The celebration takes place in Boston's Back Bay. Among the thirty-six indoor sites are fourteen historic churches. Many of the area's landmark theatres, concert halls, and cultural centers are venues for every variety of the performing arts, as are the streets, sidewalks, and plazas. "Countdown to New Year's" begins with a children's festival in the afternoon. A procession of giant puppets and costumed artists and musicians leads the audience to the Boston Common. Evening brings over one hundred continuous performances of dance, music, mime, storytelling, theatre, poetry, multimedia and cultural programs featuring many of the region's artists. Midnight fireworks over the Boston Harbor conclude the celebration.

In 1984 there were 135 performances at thirty-six indoor locations consisting of the children's festival, performances for the elderly in residential houses, and a participatory procession as well as indoor/outdoor presentations.

FLINT YOUTHEATRE
Address: 924 East Sixth St., Flint, MI 48503
Founding date: 1958

Flint Youtheatre is a community theatre with several components. It includes classes and workshops offering drama, stagecraft, mime, music, and dance for both children and adults; local productions; professional productions; and Artists-in-the-Schools.

Local productions include opportunities for beginning students to share their drama skills with an invited audience, as well as plays performed and staged at Flint's Bower Theatre. Among the latter have been such well-known titles as *Wiley and the Hairy Man, The Princess and the Ogre, Noah's Flood,* and *Charlotte's Web.* The Ten O'Clock Players are a touring group who go to elementary schools. Life Theatre presents experimental dramas based on social themes, and Rovin' Mimes is a mime group that operates out of the theatre.

An integral part of Flint Youtheatre is its program of sponsored professional productions for young audiences. These are selected from throughout the United States and Canada and have included the Paper Bag Players (q.v.), Metro Theatre Circus (q.v.), Theatre-Beyond-Words, the Prince Street Players (q.v.), and Theatreworks/USA. With its various services, Flint Youtheatre is said to reach over 40,000 children and adults annually. It is a program of the board of education with funding from local foundations, the Junior League, and the state legislature through The Detroit Youtheatre (q.v.).

THE FLOATING HOSPITAL CHILDREN'S THEATRE
Address: 275 Madison Ave., New York, NY 10016
Founding date: 1978

The Floating Hospital Children's Theatre is a unique enterprise. It offers a variety of productions, ranging from musicals for the entertainment of the audience to programs on health education. Programs are original and designed to raise consciousness, promote better health habits, and also be a source of enjoyment. In addition to performances for visiting classes on board the Floating Hospital ship, the troupe also visits schools and is available for special events. Titles of plays include *The Choice Is Yours,* in which the theme is the dangers of smoking; *General Mineral's Musical Medicine Show,* a comedy that explores nature's elixir to good health; and *Dear Diary,* a dramatic piece dealing with the subject of teenage alcohol abuse.

FLORIDA STATE UNIVERSITY CHILDREN'S THEATRE
Address: Tallahassee, FL 32306
Founding date: 1969

A unique children's theatre was established at Florida State University in the sixties. Certain features characterized the program. The first was the age of the audience (five to eight); the second was an emphasis on improvisational drama; and the third was experiential training for college students interested in this area of theatre education. These experimental features were successful in all respects. Brian Way's participatory approach to children's theatre encouraged young audiences to become actively engaged in the plays by taking part vocally, physically, and verbally, often creating portions of the plot. Children were offered an opportunity to use their imagination, from the acceptance of an "invisible" property man to becoming partners in the production. Director Moses Goldberg, for many years an active member of The Children's Theatre Association of America (q.v.) and of ASSITEJ (q.v.), is an advocate of age level programming as well as participatory theatre. Under his leadership the program grew, and the university was awarded a grant from the Florida State Fine Arts Council in 1970–1971 in support of this innovative project.

One important aspect of the program was the development of an extensive touring schedule with the Asolo State Theatre in Sarasota. Advanced students were enabled to spend a quarter off campus each year in order to perform in schools throughout Florida. The actors received college credit for this professional touring experience, in addition to salary and travel expenses. In spite of the success of the program, there were problems, and it was phased out in 1978. Funding and administrative problems were given as reasons. Also, the fact that the university and the Asolo Theatre are some 300 miles apart presented difficulties in maintaining the strong affiliation built by Goldberg and his immediate successors. Goldberg is now director of Stage One: The Louisville Children's Theatre (q.v.). Both graduate and undergraduate work in theatre and child drama are still offered but on a limited basis. *See also* Asolo Touring Theatre.

FORT LAUDERDALE CHILDREN'S THEATRE
Address: 640 N. Andress Ave., Fort Lauderdale, FL 33311
Founding date: 1960

Fort Lauderdale Children's Theatre was established as a community resource for young people in 1960. The founders purchased a warehouse in the downtown area and transformed it into a well-equipped little theatre seating 140. It was the first not-for-profit organization in the country to be housed in its own facility. Each year since then the theatre has presented two productions featuring plays *for* children *by* children. Many performances of these two plays are given during a season. In addition, the theatre mounts trouping shows, offers workshops for teachers, and participates regularly in regional and state conferences.

A season's activities today include such major productions as *The Wiz-*

311 *ard of Oz, Tom Sawyer, A Christmas Carol, The Legend of Sleepy Hollow,*
312 *Androcles and the Lion,* and *Babes in Toyland.* A list of productions given
313 during the past twenty-five years shows a variety of children's classics,
314 musicals, melodramas, and modern plays among the attractions.
315   The Studio Troupers are a group of students who perform locally at
316 schools, libraries, festivals, and fairs between November and April. On
317 Friday nights there are Showcase Performances, demonstrating class
318 work in progress. Fort Lauderdale Children's Theatre students also use
319 video cameras in their classes. The Instructional Television Center for
320 the Broward County school system and the state of Florida work closely
321 with students in making these tapes and films available to teachers. Other
322 community services include seminars, lectures, panel discussions, and a
323 guest artist series, which are open to the public.
324   Classes for students from age three to eighteen are held after school
325 during the academic year; play rehearsals take place on Saturdays. A
326 six-week summer theatre, offering a wide range of classes, and a summer
327 touring show have become popular additions to the schedule. Adult
328 mime classes, begun in the summer, are now a part of the winter pro-
329 gram. Finally, the popularity of the project led to the establishment of
330 a satellite program in Sunrise, Florida, in 1985, with requests for similar
331 programs in several other nearby towns.
332

FORT WAYNE YOUTHEATRE
333 Address: Att. Harvey Cocks, Director, 303 East Main St., Fort Wayne,
335 IN 46802
336 Founding date: 1935
337   Fort Wayne Youtheatre is one of the oldest continuously operating
338 children's theatres in the United States. A committee of citizens, ap-
339 pointed by the president of the Old Fort Players in 1934, first organized
340 drama classes for children and a year later presented its first major
341 production, *The Steadfast Tin Soldier*, with a cast of seventy-five children.
342 During the next few years the classes expanded and the public perform-
343 ances were augmented by professional outside shows of high quality. By
344 1941 full season membership in the Youtheatre was available at prices
345 low enough to make admission possible for all children. In 1947 the
346 Majestic Theatre, where the children's plays were given, was pronounced
347 unsafe by the fire marshal, and for the next ten years the children's
348 theatre had no home. Performances were given in rented halls and school
349 auditoriums.
350   In 1957 the children's theatre returned to the Civic Theatre's new
351 home, the former Palace Theatre. This move enabled the committee to
352 reestablish classes in creative drama and embellish productions with the
353 elaborate mounting that had been abandoned during the years in which
354 the children's theatre had no home base. The sixties and seventies saw

14

growth and development of work in Fort Wayne and on tour. It was during this time that the name Youtheatre was adopted. This was done in an effort to emphasize the fact that productions and training included high school as well as elementary school youngsters. New scripts were sought, and performances were added for school bookings during school hours. The first production in the new Performing Arts Center took place in 1975. The Golden Year celebration for fifty years of public service featured a new play written and directed by Aurand Harris, in the 1983–1984 season.

FOURTH WALL REPERTORY, INC.
Address: Truck and Warehouse Theatre, 79 E. 4th St., New York, NY 10003
Founding date: 1974

The Fourth Wall Repertory, founded in 1974, plays children's theatre all year long. Every week, Saturday and Sunday matinees bring contemporary children's musicals to its stage. Also, shows travel throughout the greater New York area to perform at day-care centers, hospitals, community centers, public schools, and street fairs. Its own old shool busses are in constant use, traveling into the community to bring classes to the Truck and Warehouse Theatre for special weekday performances.

Shows include some familiar titles, but they are performed in new and original ways. As an example, the company offers a rock musical entitled *Toto and the Wizard of Wall Street*. This is a New York City adventure story filled with humor and magic that takes Dorothy and Toto on a subway ride in a re-creation of the city subway to find help for themselves and their schoolmates. Past children's productions include *Captain Boogie and the Kids from Mars*, which ran for four seasons, *The King of the Entire World*, and *Alice in Wonderland*.

Fourth Wall productions have been shown on cable and network television and have been featured on WOR-TV's "The Apple Polishers," a series about people and events that serve the New York City community.

FULLER YOUNG PEOPLE'S THEATRE (FYPT)
Address: 4800 Grand Ave., South, Minneapolis, MN 55409
Founding date: 1977

The Fuller Young People's Theatre was founded to provide children of the twin cities (Minneapolis and St. Paul) with hands-on experience in the performing arts. Classes in dance, drama, voice, and mime are an integral part of the program and, when requested, master classes in dance, mime, improvisation, stage fencing and combat, make-up, musical comedy techniques, voice, and classical drama can be arranged for schools. Children participate in the four major productions offered each year as well as in the workshop and summer touring plays.

The FYPT is a nonprofit organization, designed for children of all social and economic levels, not as training for the professional stage but as a means of giving participants an opportunity to grow through self-expression, to learn discipline through the arts, and to discover personal values through literature and the experience of working with others. Fuller receives its support from various private foundations, the Minneapolis Park and Recreation Board, the Minneapolis public schools, and the Minnesota Arts Commission.

More than sixty performances a year are offered, counting main-stage, workshop, and touring productions. In 1982 the theatre went abroad, taking a repertory of three different productions of world classics to children's audiences in the London metropolitan area. In 1983 FYPT offered *Peace Child*, a project of the Peace Child Foundation, thus indicating a commitment to world peace. Unlike the majority of children's theatres today, a FYPT brochure states as its goal "to produce the richest, most rewarding theatrical experience *for* children, *by* children."

FULTON OPERA HOUSE—THEATRE FOR YOUNG AUDIENCES
Address: P.O. Box 1865, 12 N. Prince St., Lancaster, PA 17603
Founding date: 1977

The Fulton Opera House is one of the oldest continuously operating theatre in the United States; it is a professional performing arts center serving audiences in central Pennsylvania. Its productions for young audiences are performed by a company of four full-time and seven part-time professional actors. Although subscribing to some of the goals of children's theatre companies, Kathleen Collins, its artistic director, holds certain others to be important. These are the encouragement of new works, works that speak of a region and make use of its history; of actors who want to work in the regional theatre and who regard young people's theatre as just as important as the adult counterpart; and of dramas that are appropriate for all ages, or family theatre. In addition to staged plays, she hopes to develop a program that will include staged readings of new works, playwriting competitions, classes in different areas of theatre, and workshops.

The Fulton Opera House—Theatre for Young Audiences performs both in the home theatre bulding and on tour, where the majority of its performances are given. Government and private grants have helped this relatively young company to get started, and during its short existence it has demonstrated its ability to meet its goals and work toward new ones. On a typical nine-week tour to schools, libraries, community centers, and churches the theatre company serves approximately 26,000 children. At its home base, the 900-seat Fulton Opera House, performs for almost 18,000 young people annually, 2,100 of whom are subscribers. In 1984 two tour plays saw 106 performances between the end of February and the end of April. As part of this outreach program it also offers creative drama and theatre arts workshops. Through these and more intensive classes at the Fulton, 2,500 young people were reached last year. In the 1984–1985 season Barbara Robinson's *The Best Christmas Ever*, Suzan Zeder's new play, *Mother Hicks*, and *The 'Write' Stuff*, a play of poetry by the children of central Pennsylvania, were produced.

G

GARY YOUNG MIME THEATRE (formerly Archaesus Productions, Inc.)
Address: 9613 Windcroft Way, Rockville, MD 20854
Founding date: 1973

Archaesus, a professional dance/mime company, was formed in 1973 in Washington, D.C. It performed extensively in elementary schools, high schools, and colleges in the area. Now known as the Gary Young Mime Theatre, it also gives in-service courses for teachers and workshops for both children and adults, and is available for residencies. In addition to giving dance/mime programs, the performers are equipped to work in subject areas as a teaching medium. The company has performed and taught at the Smithsonian on many occasions.

Shows are available year-round and explore up to six styles of mime with music, audience participation plus nonmime acting and dialogue. Subjects range from the concrete to the fantastic. *See also* Archaesus Productions, Inc.

GEORGE STREET PLAYHOUSE CHILDREN'S THEATRE
Address: George Street Playhouse, 414 George St., New Brunswick, NJ 08901
Founding date: 1974

A professional company of actors is in residence at the playhouse but is also available for touring on request. Entertainment is the stated primary objective, and interaction with the children's audience is a frequently used approach. Folk and fairy tales and young people's classics comprise the material.

GERMANTOWN THEATRE GUILD. *See* THE ALMOST FREE THE-
ATRE OF THE GERMANTOWN THEATRE GUILD.

GEVA ON TOUR
Address: 168 Clinton Ave., South, Rochester, NY 14604
Founding date: early 1970s

GeVa on Tour is a professional touring company whose major purpose
is the presentation of curricular-related material to school audiences.
For example, its 1979–1980 season included a classic tale that was also
signed for deaf audiences, as well as an original dramatization of Iroquois
Indian legends. Previous attractions included traditional children's fairy
tales and original pieces.

The company does both a preparatory and a follow-up session with
the audience, in which participatory theatre, creative drama, theatre
games, and improvisation may be a part. The intent of the follow-up
workshops is to extend and enrich the experience, and the activities are
directly related to the material of the play that has just been seen. Workshops for teachers are available on request. Study guides and bibliographies are prepared so that programs may become a part of the
curriculum rather than being special, unrelated frills or treats. GeVa on
Tour's original sponsor for listing was the Theatre Program of the National Endowment for the Arts. It is available during the school year
and was established to serve the Rochester area and surrounding
country.

GINGERBREAD PLAYERS AND JACK
Address: 36–05 88th St., Jackson Heights, NY 11372
Founding date: 1964

The Gingerbread Players and Jack first came to the attention of sponsors at the PACT children's theatre showcase in New York in the early
sixties. A young professional company, it was primarily concerned with
mounting shows that were lavish in costume and design and theatrical
rather than educational in thrust. The company's stated aim was to raise
the standards of children's theatre in order to develop the taste and
appetite of young audiences for the living stage. In addition to bringing
old and familiar tales to life, the company hoped to bring new insights
and imagination to the production. The accent was on human relationships and situations that would offer guidelines for children to follow
when confronted with the problems of growing up. The company continued to be traditional rather than innovative, theatrical rather than
educational, and was popular with sponsors seeking this type of children's entertainment.

The Gingerbread Players and Jack is an Equity company and a charter
member of PACT.

GOODMAN THEATRE FOR CHILDREN

Address: De Paul University, 804 W. Belden, Chicago, IL 60614–3214

Founding date: 1937

The Goodman Theatre for Children was one of the first to be established in the United States. Although there is some controversy as to the actual founding date, there are references to dramatic activities in the twenties, and a successful opening play was described in newspapers of the period. The children's plays became a permanent adjunct of the Goodman Theatre, however, after a successful season in 1925. The actors and technical staff were the apprentices, adult students at the Goodman. The popularity of the plays led in time to a second performance on Saturdays; both performances were said to be attended by capacity audiences of children of all ages. While the Goodman could be described as a community theatre, since it emphasized the presentation of worthwhile plays for local audiences of children, the fact that it was maintained by a school of the theatre rather than a community playhouse places it more appropriately in the category of educational theatre.

The Goodman auditorium, in which children's plays were presented, was beautiful and well equipped. It was located in the heart of the city as part of the complex including the Art Institute of Chicago. Both the good work that was done and the ideal location were factors in its survival through the Depression, the war years, inflation, and the competition of other theatre groups in the area.

One name associated with the Goodman Theatre for Children in the early years was Charlotte Chorpenning, a children's playwright and the first to set down specific guidelines for this genre of literature. Chorpenning taught playwriting at Northwestern University, but many of her scripts were given their first production at the Goodman. Indeed, her work is still widely used today, and it has been only recently that writers of children's plays have departed from her rules. Much of her work consisted of adaptations of familiar folk and fairy tales and children's classic stories, which also became the repertory of the theatre. Traditional titles, traditionally and elaborately produced, were the hallmark of the Goodman Theatre for Children.

Despite the popularity and success of the children's productions for decades, the theatre's connection with the Art Institute of Chicago was dissolved in 1978. The children's theatre became a part of De Paul University, and its name was changed accordingly to the De Paul Goodman School of Drama. Bella Itkin, for many years head of the children's work, now teaches acting at De Paul and directs plays for adult audiences. Carol Delk was named head of the children's theatre, which is now called the Theatre School Playworks. Shows are given at the First Chicago Center, a small auditorium in the First National Bank. Saturday and weekday performances are offered.

The Theatre School is now fully accredited with an enrollment of 211 undergraduates and graduate students from thirty-seven states. Faculty represent both the academic and professional theatre areas in a conservatory program. Two hundred public performances of three productions a season are given for children's audiences, with many more performances presented as part of the student training process within the school. Objectives of the Theatre School are twofold: to provide practical experience for students and to provide exciting theatre for young audiences in the Chicago area.

GRACE PRICE PRODUCTIONS
Address: Pittsburgh, PA
Founding date: 1934. Closed in the 1960s.

This company was founded in 1934 in Pittsburgh. Grace Price, a former professional actress and resident of Pittsburgh, had gathered together a company of actors as early as 1930. Her company toured sixty-seven towns within a hundred-mile radius of Pittsburgh. Return engagements, as well as new engagements, made Grace Price Productions the best known children's theatre company in the area for many years. In the repertory were familiar children's classics and new scripts, a policy that brought the group numerous original manuscripts for experimental productions. The company closed in the early sixties.

THE GREAT AMERICAN CHILDREN'S THEATRE COMPANY
Address: P.O. Box 92123, Milwaukee, WI 53202
Founding date: 1975

The Great American Children's Theatre Company produces a number of large-scale professional attractions for young audiences each season. It is described in its brochure as educational, based on the belief that theatre must "stimulate imaginations and assist the young person in his/her development from passive spectator to active participant." The company does not offer classes and employs adult performers.

Within the past ten years more than 875,000 children and adults from southeastern Wisconsin have attended the company's performances at the Pabst Theatre, Milwaukee Performing Arts Center, and at the Madison Civic Center. In that season they expanded their touring program to include Green Bay. Support comes from foundations, private donors, and box office receipts. Current play titles suggest that the material offered by the company appeals to audiences of all ages: *Toby Tyler*, a new musical; and *The Lion in Love*, performed by the National Theatre of the Deaf.

THE GREAT INTERPLANETARY SOAPBOX REVIVAL
Address: 6 Pine St., Wakefield, RI 02879
Founding date: 1978

The Great Interplanetary Soapbox Revival offers a unique blend of entertainment patterned after the medicine shows and vaudeville acts that were popular in the United States in the early part of the twentieth century. Jokes, riddles, juggling acts, music, comedy routines, dance, and audience participation are all included in a format designed for children of all ages. While the main objective is entertainment, the content of the show gives young audiences an insight into some of the customs and styles of the past. The two performers bring a background in mime, clowning, dance, and storytelling, as well as teaching experience on elementary school and college levels, to their performance.

Shows are given in schools and libraries throughout New England and Canada and are available for non-English speaking children as well. Workshops and residencies of varied lengths are also offered; study guides for teachers are sent on request.

THE GREEN MOUNTAIN GUILD, INC.
Address: White River Junction, VT 05001
Founding date: 1971

The Green Mountain Guild is a not-for-profit regional touring company that has been operating continuously since 1971. The touring company is supported, in part, by a grant from the National Endowment for the Arts in Washington, D.C., a federal agency.

Produced and directed by the guild, a company of actors weaves words, song, dance, and pantomime into a unique story theatre format. The group can play in any open space (they require a sixteen-foot-square performing area, with the children seated on three sides) or any traditional stage space.

The purpose is to bring professional theatre into city and rural schools in a way that fits the school day schedule. All of their shows are original scripts (many with music) based on well-known fables, tales, and stories. They are presented in a story theatre format by four or five actors and a stage manager. All shows are forty-five to fifty minutes long and require little more than hand props and sometimes a bi- or tri-fold unit.

GREENVILLE FINE ARTS CENTER
Address: 1613 W. Washington Rd., Greenville, SC 29609
Founding date: 1974

Categorizing itself as an educational theatre, the Greenville Fine Arts Center reported forty to sixty performances for children a season in 1978. Performers were listed as teenagers, who prepared two productions a year; these productions were toured as well as given in the home theatre. Regular classes were a part of the community program serving the Greenville area.

THE GROWING STAGE
Address: P.O. Box 132, Chester, NJ 07930
Founding date: 1982

The Growing Stage is a professional Equity company offering plays for children. It is composed of adult performers whose stated objective is to provide quality theatre for young audiences. Its 1983 season indicates the variety of material it chooses to produce: *Nightingale, Wiley and the Hairy Man, Cinderella, Hans Christian Andersen, The Masque of Beauty and the Beast,* and *The Belle of Amherst.* Some of these are musicals, and the last title would obviously appeal to adults and older children. The company has featured plays by some of America's outstanding children's playwrights, among them Aurand Harris and Suzan Zeder.

The Growing Stage is available throughout New Jersey and adjoining states from September to June. It offers, in addition to performances, in-house workshops in acting and creative drama.

GRUMBLING GRYPHONS
Address: c/o Leslie Elias, Rt. 4, Mountain Rd., Brookfield, CT 06804
Founding date: 1980

Grumbling Gryphons is a traveling children's theatre troupe that performs a variety of shows in schools, libraries, museums, hospitals, and parks throughout the tri-state and New England areas. Shows include myths, legends, and fairy tales drawn from many countries around the world. By taking part in productions, children discover that fun and learning go hand in hand. Shows motivate them to act, sing, dance, and learn about the world around them. According to the actors, some of the questions that come up in a Grumbling Gryphon show are: "Where did fire originate?" "What are children of other lands like?" "How did the seasons come to be?"

The shows are described in the brochure as "a feast for the senses—including a colorful array of masks, costumes and scenery." Original songs are accompanied by a collection of musical instruments, many old or unfamiliar to American audiences today. Some of the titles of Grumbling Gryphon plays are *The Snow Queen, The Dragon's Tale, Trickster Tales,* and *The Myth of Persephone.* In the last, masks, songs, and chorus are included as part of the traditional Greek style of performance. Children are directly involved in movement and singing activities. *Trickster Tales* was developed in cooperation with the American Indian Archaeological Institute in Washington, Connecticut, and premiered there for Founders Day.

Grumbling Gryphons also offers a broad spectrum of educational and artistic workshops for children of all ages. Each member of the troupe is an experienced teacher and performer. In-school, after-school, and weekend workshops are given in creative drama, dance, music, mask-making, puppetry, juggling, and children's literature. The troupe is a member of ConnTours (Connecticut Commission on the Arts Touring Program) and TAPCO (Travelling Artists and Performers Company). It has been the recipient of various grants including several from the Danbury Cultural Commission.

H

HARLEM CHILDREN'S THEATRE
Address: 420 W. 42 St., New York, NY 10036
Founding date: 1971

The Harlem Children's Theatre Company was formed as a professional multiethnic children's theatre whose members range in age from seven to eighteen. Its stated goal was to provide excellent performing arts training for the children of New York City and to offer young people the benefit of theatre experience both as participants and spectators. Harlem Children's Theatre tours to cooperating cultural centers, churches, and schools, and interacts with all racial, ethnic, and economic classes of the city under the artistic direction of Aduke Aremu.

Aduke Aremu has written all the plays for the company and has directed for the Billie Holiday Theatre (q.v.) in Brooklyn. She was the recipient of the Producer of the Year Award and the Audelco Award in 1974; she also won the Woman of the Year Award of the Afro-Caribbean Theatre in 1975.

Since then the Harlem Children's Theatre has toured out of the city and abroad. A highlight for the twelve young people who were able to go was an African tour in 1977. Although theatre as an aesthetic experience is the primary goal of the directors, there is a strong social consciousness and motivation to perform as well.

HARWICH JUNIOR THEATRE
Address: Harwich, MA
Founding date: 1951

A different type of venture was launched on Cape Cod in the fifties, the Harwich Junior Theatre. Said to be the first "straw hat" theatre for children in America, it was held to a high standard of production under the leadership of Betty Bobp, who is still involved, though retired, and has invited such well-known guest directors as Aurand Harris, George

Latshaw, and Helen Avery. By the eighties, Harwich Junior Theatre had become a year-round resource, operating in new and expanded quarters. Unlike the majority of children's theatres located in resort areas, it was established for the sole purpose of bringing good entertainment to young people and not as an adjunct to an adult operation. Good literature, artistically produced, is an aim, with classes in the performing arts as an added component.

THE HECKSCHER CHILDREN'S THEATRE
Address: 1 E. 104 St., New York, NY 10029
Founding date: 1922

The Heckscher Children's Theatre was opened in 1922 on upper Fifth Avenue at 104th Street in New York City. It was an immediate sensation both as a showplace and as an example of a high standard of entertainment for young people. Unlike the majority of children's theatres of the period, The Heckscher Theatre was part of a foundation rather than an offshoot of an adult community theatre or settlement house. Constance D'Arcy Mackay titled an article about the theatre published in the February 1924 issue of *Drama* magazine "The Most Beautiful Children's Theatre in the World."

August Heckscher, a New York philanthropist, provided the funds to build a well-equipped structure with an auditorium decorated in blue, cream, and gold, with beautiful fairy tale murals designed by Willy Pogany. In addition to the stage, dressing rooms, and spacious backstage areas, it included a gym, swimming pool, club rooms, manual training workshop, and indoor play space. For several years the Heckscher served the children of the city as a model cultural center.

The first production in November 1922 was a program of scenes taken from the Pogany murals; these included *The Pied Piper, Cinderella,* and *The Sleeping Beauty.* Performers were children from age seven to seventeen who attended the Professional Children's School. The second production in December of the same year was *The Snow Queen.* The director was Bertram Hauser, a professional director and educator who believed, as did Heckscher, that children's theatre should teach actors and audiences alike the value of the theatre as an art form in addition to enjoyment of the experience.

In 1929 further progress was made with the establishment of a stock company performing regularly for children's audiences under the direction of Ashley Miller. Saturday matinees were apparently successful financially, but with the deepening depression the operation was suspended, never to be resumed. The building has continued to be used, however, though never again exclusively for children's theatre. For one or two seasons it was the base for the New York Shakespeare Festival which, incidentally, was patronized by high school groups who were brought to see productions. Today the space is used for a variety of social services, including an occasional program by or for children. As a children's theatre, it no longer exists; as a used and usable building, it remains.

HEDGEROW THEATRE
Address: Rose Valley Road, Wallingford, PA 19086
Founding date: 1975

Hedgerow Theatre is one of the oldest and best known regional playhouses in America. Founded in 1923 by Jasper Deeter, it offered plays for adult audiences exclusively until 1975. In that year the first children's shows were added. Titles represent traditional stories and children's classics such as *Charlotte's Web* and *Winnie the Pooh*. A fire in the early eighties destroyed the theatre building, including all records of the history and development of the institution. At present, therefore, the children's plays are presented on Saturdays and Sundays in a neighboring facility, and on weekdays in schools. The touring program runs from November through May. Restoration of the building is under way and, while fewer than fifty performances a season are offered for young audiences at the present time, the conditions limiting further expansion are understandable. A record of children's theatre in America would be incomplete if it neglected mention of the contribution of this old and respected institution.

HEIGHTS YOUTH THEATRE
Address: 2155 Miramar Blvd., Cleveland Heights, OH 44118
Founding date: 1958

Heights Youth Theatre does approximately six major productions a year. There are 300 students enrolled in the twenty-three classes in five communities of Cleveland's East Side. Eighteen teachers handle theatre classes for children from kindergarten to age twelve. One hundred and fifty performances a season were reported in 1978, and there are more today.

Open auditions are held for each show, but only children enrolled in the classes can be in the productions. Titles of plays given by the Heights Youth Theatre include only well-known fairy tales. Performances are given every Saturday afternoon from October through May. At the present time Heights Youth Theatre is a for-profit organization, but it is sponsored by the Cleveland Heights and University Heights departments of community services. It falls in the category of educational theatre.

THE HENRY STREET SETTLEMENT
Address: Lower East Side, New York, NY
Founding date: 1915

Although there had been informal dramatic activities at Henry Street before 1910, it was soon after this date that festivals and dramatic programs began to appear with some regularity. Lillian Wald, the director of The Henry Street Settlement, believed in the value of the performing arts for children and encouraged both participation and the production of appropriate plays for young audiences. Like Alice Minnie Herts and Jane Addams, she adhered to high standards and firmly endorsed the social values that a strong drama/theatre program held for the people of the neighborhood. Classes in dance and drama were offered for children by volunteers as part of an after-school program of activities. In 1915 the Neighborhood Playhouse was built through the interest and generosity of Alice and Irene Lewisohn and Rita Wallach Morganthau, wealthy New Yorkers who had been among the most ardent volunteers. The playhouse was affiliated with The Henry Street Settlement until 1927, when it moved uptown.

After the move of the Neighborhood Playhouse the little theatre building on Grand Street was christened the Henry Street Playhouse and continued to serve the needs of a changing community. Productions for both adult and child audiences were given here, some of which originated in the settlement, whereas others were brought in by outside producing companies. In 1965 the theatre was renamed the Harry DeJur Henry Street Settlement Playhouse as a result of a large contribution made to insure the continuation of its services to the community. In 1975 a spacious new facility was officially opened adjacent to the playhouse. This was the Louis Abrams Arts for Living Center, which incorporated all of the arts under one roof. One program that should be mentioned, although it did not offer plays specifically for children, was the New Federal Theatre, founded in 1970. It was dedicated to the work of minority playwrights, whose plays were given production in the various auditoriums, depending on suitability and the availability of space. Occasionally appropriate plays were given for family audiences at special matinees; however, the thrust of the New Federal Theatre has never been to offer plays for young people. *See also* The Henry Street Settlement, Louis Abrams Arts for Living Center.

THE HENRY STREET SETTLEMENT, LOUIS ABRAMS ARTS FOR LIVING CENTER
Address: 466 Grand Street, New York, NY 10002
Founding date: 1975

An institution that has been sensitive to the interests and needs of the neighborhood, The Henry Street Settlement has made changes and added new programs throughout the years. Today it offers an extensive arts program under the name of the Louis Abrams Arts for Living Center. It includes American Jewish theatre, an Arts-in-Education Program, dance classes, acting classes, classes in music and the visual arts, family theatre, Latino theatre, a playwrights' reading workshop, theatre for adults, and writing workshops. Classes are taught on all levels: children, teens, adults, and seniors. The Arts-in-Education Program works with the public schools, bringing children to the center as well as going to schools and working with students in the classroom. Plays and programs are sponsored, but very few are produced at the center today.

The Henry Street Settlement, Louis Abrams Arts for Living Center is a busy place. Although today it does not offer children's theatre in the traditional sense, it is included here in view of its rich offerings for young people and its continuation of a historic commitment to the arts. *See also* The Henry Street Settlement.

HIPPODROME THEATRE-IN-EDUCATION
Address: 25 S.E. 2nd Place, Gainesville, FL 32601
Founding date: 1973

Following the tradition of the Hippodrome Theatre in bringing the best of contemporary plays and productions to the stage, the Theatre-in-Education company was founded to produce original theatre pieces for young audiences. It explores relevant themes in a variety of styles rather than presenting plays in a traditional manner. Hippodrome is available for touring engagements through several adjoining states during most of the year. Educational services such as workshops and internships can be arranged.

As an example of Hippodrome's work, the show *Signposts* was developed in 1981 in honor of the National Year of the Handicapped. *Signposts* explores some of the communication problems that exist between the deaf and the hearing worker. Hippodrome's Theatre-in-Education company does not offer traditional plays, and many of its programs are of interest to family and adult audiences as well as to young people.

HONOLULU THEATRE FOR YOUTH
Address: P.O. Box 3257, Honolulu, HI 96801
Founding date: 1955

According to the brochure issued in the year of its twenty-fifth anniversary, the theatre in 1955 was the property of a select few. Although Honolulu laid claim to having the second oldest community theatre in the nation, only the Honolulu Community Theatre and the University of Hawaii presented plays on a regular basis. Theatre as we know it was introduced to Honolulu by touring companies on their way to Asia or Australia. The first auditorium in Hawaii was the Royal Hawaiian Theatre, built in 1834. It was patronized by the *alii* (royalty) and upper class Caucasians. Most of the programs were musical and included cantatas, operettas, and variety shows.

The second playhouse, the Hawaii Opera House, was built across from the Lolani Palace. The other part of the population, the growing number of Oriental families, rarely stepped inside the halls of the Western theatres or attended the amateur productions given in churches and homes. Their dramatic entertainment consisted of occasional Chinese or Japanese touring programs offered at the Chinese theatre. In order to build new audiences and meet the needs of children, the Honolulu Theatre for Youth was founded. It was established as an adjunct to the city parks department. By the end of the sixties it was Hawaii's largest theatre. Its touring program reached nearly 73,000 children during the 1969–1970 season and, in spite of having no permanent theatre building, it won national and state awards. Today it is considered to be one of the finest theatres for young people in the nation. Plays are chosen for both their entertainment and educational value. According to the theatre's brochure, "Each play contains something the child must reach toward to understand, something which challenges his intellect and causes him to grow."

Honolulu Theatre for Youth is made possible by the efforts and interest of citizens of the community, business people, professional actors, and university students; in brief, it is a community effort which serves children in a wide area. The Junior Theatre Workshop for children from ages seven to fifteen and teachers' materials further augment the program. Financial support comes from many quarters including government, foundations, the Parks Department, and private contributions.

According to its brochures, the Honolulu Theatre for Youth aims to stimulate the imagination; develop communication and expressive skills; maintain a high standard of entertainment; create appreciation of the art of the theatre; broaden intercultural understanding; and allow "every child to recognize within himself the qualities of a hero." By the late seventies, 250 performances a year were being given; and by the mid-eighties the Honolulu Theatre for Youth was enjoying a national reputation for creative work of the highest quality. Its 1984–1985 season included the following six productions: *To Kill a Mockingbird, East of the Sun and West of the Moon, Raven the Hungry, The Code Breaker, Tears of Joy* (a special guest presentation using puppets), and *The Best Christmas Pageant Ever*. This varied bill demonstrates both the diversity and the concern for a wide age range that is characteristic of the Honolulu Theatre for Youth. It has received from The American Theatre Association (q.v.) the Winifred Ward Award for a children's theatre that has attained excellence and has been in operation for at least one full year but not more than four years, and the Jennie Heiden Award for professional excellence in children's theatre, two of the highest honors the organization gives.

THE HOUSE OF PLAY
Address: Washington, DC
Founding date: 1915. Closed.

In Washington, D.C., more than one center for children's entertainment was operating before the twenties. The most formally organized was The House of Play, a regular little theatre for boys and girls. It was opened in 1915 and was run under the auspices of the Drama League of the city. Its program of plays was directed exclusively to children and young people. Conducted as a recreation center, The House of Play was open on Saturday with trained leaders guiding activities. Its primary objective was the social development of the participants rather than excellence of performance. It is important historically as one of the earliest theatres with a trained staff and a definite point of view as to the role drama can play in the life of the participants.

HOWARD UNIVERSITY CHILDREN'S THEATRE
Address: Washington, DC 20059
Founding date: 1973

The Howard University Children's Theatre performs on a regular basis in the Washington area, though occasionally it accepts outside engagements and is frequently seen at regional theatre conferences. As a student group, it places emphasis on the education of both participant and audience. As a black group, however, there is an additional emphasis: black theatre of high quality, which includes both African folktales and contemporary themes relating to the life of this minority. The company rarely offers more than fifty performances a year, but it maintains stability and enjoys a fine reputation for the consistent quality of its work and its adherence to its stated goals. Director Kelsey Collie has worked with the group from the beginning. He was active in The Children's Theatre Association of America (q.v.), and his students have performed frequently at both regional and national meetings. While the theatre belongs in the category of educational theatre, its service to the D.C. area places it just as appropriately in the category of community theatre.

HULL HOUSE
Address: Chicago, IL
Founding date: early 1900s

Under the guidance of Jane Addams, there were dramatic arts programs for both adults and children at Hull House soon after the turn of the century. By 1930 there was a history of six dramatic clubs and a well-equipped, 500-seat little theatre for productions. Both classics and traditional children's stories were included in the repertory. Like the majority of settlement houses, Hull House has maintained a program in the arts as well as other activities, but it is important to the early history of children's theatre because of the emphasis theatre was given and the influence it was said to have had on other community centers in the nation.

The extent to which theatre for children has been offered has depended on the needs and interests of a changing neighborhood and the interests and skills of the staff.

I

THE ILLUSTRATED THEATRE

Address: 802 Madison St., 3R, Evanston, IL 60202
Founding date: 1982

The Illustrated Theatre is a theatre-in-education company staffed by seven actor/teachers, all of whom are experienced educators and Equity members. Their respective backgrounds include extensive work in the Chicago area, California, the O'Neill Theatre in Connecticut, and Stratford-upon-Avon in England. The objectives of the company are to introduce children to story theatre, movement, and mime; to show the different ways that stories can be told; and to give children an opportunity to practice the various techniques they have just seen on the stage. Mask-making and its uses are an important part of the performance and the workshop experience.

The company sends out curriculum materials to teachers in advance of the engagement and provides an evaluation tailored to the situation following the workshop. Shows are geared to specific grade levels. For example, *CREATE* (K–8) stands for Conflict Resolution: The Educationally Active Theatre Experience. In a series of humorous vignettes, conflict resolution techniques are explored. *Push Back the Desks* (K–8) includes story theatre, mask work, and figuration mime. *Macbeth* (grades 9–12) shows actors in roles from the play, with a workshop in speaking Shakespearean verse, and a study of life in Elizabethan England. *A Child's Christmas in Wales* (all ages) brings Dylan Thomas' work to the stage; a poetry workshop follows the performance. The company maintains a repertory that includes commedia dell'arte, the classics, and original new material.

THE IMAGINARY THEATRE COMPANY (ITC)

Address: P.O. Box 28030, St. Louis, MO 63119
Founding date: 1973

The Imaginary Theatre Company is the touring arm of the Repertory Theatre of St. Louis. It performs without sets, props, or costumes, relying instead on collective creative abilities to bring folktales, ballads, poetry, plays, and stories to life. As modern storytellers, ITC members take advantage of the wealth of literary resources at their fingertips. By focusing upon the language, ceremony, and imagination inherent in its sources, ITC attempts to develop a theatre style that is a stimulus to the imagination. A forty-five to sixty-minute production, providing specific choices for elementary school children, high school students, and adults, is available for two months in the fall and during January and February.

Workshops are also offered for groups of twenty-five to thirty. The three different types of workshops are theatre games, improvisational performance techniques and story theatre. In the late seventies the Imaginary Theatre Company was offering 150 performances a season. The dual thrust of the program is education and entertainment. In its commitment to bringing great literature (Edgar Allan Poe, the Brothers Grimm, Aesop's fables, Shakespeare, etc.) to life, ITC tours its original story theatre productions and workshops on improvisational techniques throughout the state of Missouri and parts of Illinois.

IMAGINATION THEATRE, INC.

Address: 5875 N. Lincoln Ave., Chicago, IL 60659
Founding date: 1966

Imagination Theatre, Inc., has gone far beyond its original purpose of performing plays with and for children. It was founded in 1966 by a group of elementary school teachers who developed what was at the time a unique idea in children's educational theatre. A creative drama workshop presented in the form of a play, it was called Imagination Theatre. Based on the concept of total involvement and participation of the audience, the children in actuality became the playmakers. The goal of Imagination Theatre was to show children how they could become playmakers every day by using the tools within themselves.

Over the years Imagination Theatre evolved into an organization with three companies and a series of programs. Responding to the city of Chicago's needs, it began work for and with the handicapped and the elderly. Today the children's theatre component has been subsumed by these other areas, thus Imagination Theatre today places its highest priority on the therapeutic aspect of drama, with educational and aesthetic objectives occupying a lower rank. Its success in meeting community needs is attested by the fact that over 1,200 performances a year are given and numerous prestigious awards have been presented to the company. Because children are included in the special education classes it serves, Imagination Theatre still qualifies as a special kind of children's theatre.

Eunice Joffe, the founder, was the director until 1985. Her background includes a degree in childhood education as well as experience in special education, professional theatre, and radio and television in Chicago, in addition to public school teaching. In 1984 she was presented with the Human Awareness Award by The Children's Theatre Association of America (q.v.) for her work in theatre for groups least likely to be included in the more conventional forms available to other populations.

IMPROVISATIONAL THEATRE PROJECT (ITP)
Address: Mark Taper Forum, 135 North Grand Ave., Los Angeles, CA 90012
Founding date: 1971

The Improvisational Theatre Project is the Mark Taper Forum's theatre for young people. It was founded with the help of the National Endowment for the Arts in 1971. Each year ITP tours to schools and community centers throughout Los Angeles County. The company also performs on occasion on the main stage of the Mark Taper Forum, at the Taper LAB, and at Taper, TOO; and it has appeared at the Kennedy Center, the Denver and Scottsdale centers for the performing arts, and at various locations throughout the state of California. Originally under the direction of Wallace Chappell, it has had several directors and is now operating under the leadership of Peter Brosius. The present thrust of the company is new work, developed through research and improvisation. ITP plays are centered around specific themes and concerns of the young people for whom they are performed.

A review of all the seasons since the founding of ITP reveals some familiar titles but many more new ones. The 1984–1985 spring tour lists *A Family Portrait*, a popular play of the preceding season, for grades 1–6. Another favorite, *School Talk*, was presented for junior and senior high school students. In 1981–1982, however, *A Christmas Carol* was given in repertory with *Holiday Pudding* and *Guns*. Plays are adapted and set to music when they are not developed by the company. ITP has been cited for its sensitivity to the problems and interests of young people today and for its dedication to confronting those problems through a dynamic theatre approach. Plays are designed to stimulate thinking and feeling and to offer a starting place for educators on all levels. Teachers' guides are available for classroom use.

IN SCHOOL PLAYERS OF ADVENTURE THEATRE
Address: c/o Adventure Theatre, Glen Echo Park, Glen Echo, MD 20768
Founding date: 1969. *See* Adventure Theatre. In School Players is a component of Adventure Theatre.

INDIANAPOLIS JUNIOR CIVIC THEATRE
Address: 1200 West 38th St., Indianapolis, IN 46208
Founding date: 1929

The Civic Theatre of Indianapolis is one of the oldest community theatres in the country. Relocated and renamed, it has continued to serve the city, expanding its services and attracting new and wider audiences. In the early years the children's plays were under the supervision of a chairperson chosen for each individual play. While the organization has changed considerably since then, the junior theatre has remained an important component. An average of four plays during a season presented on Saturday mornings and afternoons was the practice in the early years.

By the eighties, however, the program had gradually expanded to include workshops as well as productions for children. For grades 1–3, they are designed to introduce the theatre to the young child as a place to discover, create, and express himself. At the intermediate level, children are offered puppetry and creative drama. Design, construction, creative writing, and performance are all a part of the puppetry class, whereas creative drama includes dance, movement, and improvisation. Sixth graders experience many different forms of self-expression: athletics, music, dance, dramatics, mime, and hands-on technical instruction. Junior and senior high school students take voice, dance, tech, theatre history, audition, costume, makeup, and performance.

Plays are generally traditional, including in recent years such favorites as *Snow White*, *Treasure Island*, and a program of Italian folktales.

INNER CITY ENSEMBLE
Address: 128 Ward St., Paterson, NJ 07505
Founding date: 1973

Based on the premise that the performing arts, when taught as a therapeutic process, can help to develop the adolescent's self-image, confidence, and sense of personal worth, the Inner City Ensemble began with a rehabilitative focus. This focus still exists, though the youthful group of black and Hispanic performers has also been extremely successful artistically. The process employed by director Ralph Gomez has developed skilled actors and dancers who, in turn, have created a product that attracts attention and praise. Workshops in drama, music, dance, arts, and crafts engage the interest of a large number of children in need of after-school activities but not yet ready for public performance.

Through the workshops they develop an awareness of self and others; they learn the discipline of the theatre and a sense of responsibility for team work; and, in time, they improve their skills to the point where they are ready for public performance. When there are openings in the

Ensemble Theatre and Dance Company they are filled by qualified students. All applicants, either from the workshop classes or from outside, must audition. The companies perform throughout New Jersey but have been seen in other parts of the United States and abroad. What would have been described as a community-educational enterprise ten years ago can add the word "professional" today.

INTERPLAY PRODUCTIONS
Address: Box 1595, Georgetown University, Washington, DC 20057
Founding date: 1975. Suspended operations in 1980.

InterPlay Productions was founded in 1975 to bring environmental theatre productions to schools in northern Virginia. Its first presentation was *Creation of the World*, written by Donn B. Murphy of Georgetown University for presentation at the 1970 convention of The American Theatre Association (q.v.). Subsequently, over a four-year period, Murphy and Kathleen Barry, of Barry Associates, coauthored four other audience involvement plays.

The five pieces were presented in successive summers at Wolf Trap Farm for the Performing Arts. Each play was given ninety performances in an outdoor tented pavilion erected for the purpose. A scenic backdrop and the pavilion floor were redesigned for the show each year, as were elaborate props, magic tricks, special effects, and costumes. The presentations were: 1975—*Creation of the World*; 1976—*Creation of a Nation*; 1977—*Happy Landings*; 1978—*The Curious Computer from Planet Z*; and 1979—*The Magic Falcon*.

Groups of up to 250 children and adults attended each performance, and all participated under the guidance of Barry and Murphy. A cast of seven young performers distributed hand props, masks, hats, and costume pieces to the audience, and, to assist the guest participants, operated as role models and gave live instructions. In various productions cast members also roller-skated, unicycled, skate-boarded, did gymnastics, tap danced, and sawed one of their number in two. Audience participants moved about almost continuously during the shows. Their "performance" was implemented by a prerecorded tape of dialogue, sound effects, music, and directions to the audience/performers.

After the fifth summer, Murphy and Barry felt that they had carried these performances to their logical limit. They then turned their energies to other activities at the National Theatre, a Broadway-type booking house in Washington, D.C. Murphy became president and executive director of the theatre, and Barry became director of children's programming and showcase productions.

THE ISHANGI FAMILY DANCERS
Address: c/o OYO House, 1388 Bedford Ave., Brooklyn, NY 11216
Founding date: 1965

The Ishangi Family Dancers offer a program that includes music, storytelling, and acting as well as African dance. Through it the folklore, religious rites, and customs of Africa come to life for audiences ranging in age from five to seventeen. Older students and adults respond to the authenticity and technical skill of the performers. Ishangi, the leader of the family, prepares the audience for the program with explanations of each segment as it occurs. He introduces the members of the family, all of whom take part in one way or another, depending on their age and experience. Exotic costumes, textiles, jewelry, and household objects are displayed on the stage, making the visual aspect of the production as important as the performance.

The movements of the dances are explained by Ishangi, who also translates the songs and demonstrates the use of the drums and other instruments that are played. The objectives of The Ishangi Family Dancers are twofold: to offer an artistic performance to children, and to provide a picture of Africa through an understanding of its culture. While they do not present a play in the conventional sense, the Ishangi family maintains unity in its selection of material and over the years has achieved an ensemble spirit through working and living together. In 1980 The Ishangi Family Dancers were awarded the United Nations World Peace Medal for outstanding work in the arts, communications, and education, and furthering the understanding of the importance of culture. The family has been seen in concert halls, schools, churches, and on university campuses. Although most of their performances are geared to children, they could be classified as family entertainment equally well. The adult members of the company are available for lectures and workshops; the age level and ability of the participants determine the content of any particular class.

J

J. P. NIGHTINGALE
Address: 7830 Oso Avenue, Canoga Park, CA 91306
Founding date: 1974

This company originated in San Jose, California, as an offshoot of a trio who toured the state with shows that included storytelling, pantomime, improvisation, live music, and audience participation. Pamela Wood, one member of the trio, decided, after a highly successful period of four years, to separate from the group and form her own company. The other two members of the trio made the same decision, one of them remaining in San Jose, and the other going to San Bernardino (later moving to West Virginia). The company is designated as educational/professional; it offers four productions a season for at least 300 performances.

THE JACK AND JILL PLAYERS
Address: Chicago, IL
Founding date: 1925. Closed in the 1960s.

This private children's theatre school is of historical importance, for it was founded at the same time as the Goodman School Children's Theatre (q.v.) and The Children's Theatre of Evanston (q.v.). Its structure was different from the other two, however, and it served a different interest. It was planned for children ranging in age from three to eighteen. After giving performances at the Jack and Jill Playhouse, the company toured the Chicago metropolitan area. Since the emphasis was on the touring engagements, scenery and costumes were designed to facilitate the technical production. That it survived for more than forty years meant that the company was financially stable, with a sound organization as a private theatre school. In spite of the fact that instruction took place, it could be designated as a community theatre. It closed its doors in the mid-sixties.

JACK TALES TOURING THEATRE TROUPE
Address: Ferrum College, Ferrum, VA 24088
Founding date: 1975

An example of an innovative and highly imaginative program is the one developed at Ferrum College in southwest Virginia. Rex Stephenson, chairman of the theatre department, began work with a group of students and a personal interest in the local folklore known as the "Jack Tales." These stories from the Blue Ridge Mountains, which had been handed down through an oral tradition, appealed to Stephenson as having dramatic possibilities. Through group process short plays were developed, and programs that included several of the tales began touring local schools. The success of the programs led to further touring engagements to old age homes, community centers, churches, and veterans' hospitals. Thus the stories that came from the mountain people were given back to them in dramatic form.

Although the troupe uses other kinds of material, particularly for its adult audiences, the Jack Tales continue to provide rich content for audiences of all ages, and the simply staged short plays have proven a successful format. They have been featured at regional and national meetings of The Children's Theatre Association of America (q.v.). In 1983 a new theatre was erected on campus; although not built for the exclusive use of the theatre department, it was designed to accommodate the Jack Tale players and the school audiences who were bussed in to performances. Teachers' materials and study guides are developed by Stephenson to extend the experience beyond the performance, and an introduction to mountain music using homemade instruments further enhances it. A summer theatre featuring local history, dramatized by Stephenson, offers another dimension to the contribution made by a small college to a community remote from professional stage. Moreover, Ferrum is unique in its use of natural resources—content of plays, format, and, on occasion, the actual spots where historic events took place. The Ferrum program is a prime example of the kind of innovation that was taking place during the late seventies and early eighties. Also, like many others, it was reinforced by funds from government and local sources.

JEWISH REPERTORY THEATRE FOR YOUNG AUDIENCES
Address: Board of Jewish Education, Inc., 426 W. 58 St., New York, NY 10019
Founding date: 1983

Although the Jewish Repertory Theatre was only founded in the early eighties, the fact that its founder and director, Joyce Klein, had been involved in educational theatre for over a decade, and that Jewish theatre for young people has been an important part of the New York theatre scene for many years qualifies it for inclusion. It is a touring company dedicated to the presentation of children's plays that draw from the Jewish tradition and speak to the contemporary Jewish child. Two separate programs, designed for ages nine to twelve and thirteen to sixteen, are available for booking; in the 1983–1984 season alone the theatre gave one hundred performances of the musical *Jerusalem*. The goals of the company are simply stated: to visit the past; to understand the present; and to enrich the future of students and their parents through theatre that opens the window to Judaism. The Jewish Repertory Theatre is an Equity company specializing in religious material.

THE JOHN F. KENNEDY CENTER PROGRAMS FOR CHILDREN AND YOUTH

Address: Alliance for Arts Education, The John F. Kennedy Center, Washington, DC 20566
Founding date: 1976

The Kennedy Center inaugurated its Programs for Children and Youth in 1976, the year of its first major festival, "Imagination Celebration." The staff of the Education Department works with children's theatre producers and the public to bring the best possible programs to the national capital. All programs presented at the Kennedy Center have accompanying materials for teachers. In addition, the staff under the direction of Jack Kukuk and Carole Huggins Sullivan have developed a Discovery Experience Series of resource books in the performing arts for young people. Furthermore, the participation of handicapped persons is welcomed, and special arrangements can easily be made for them. "Imagination Celebration" takes place in the spring; added outreach "Celebrations" are located in selected cities around the country.

By the mid-eighties many children's theatre groups, both professional and educational, had been seen at the Kennedy Center as a result of the support and interest extended to them by the staff. Bulletins issued by the Education Department announce as many as twenty performances or productions a season. Free performances for school groups make this a unique resource. On any day of the week one may see school busses lined up in front of the center for the morning or afternoon showings. This is an example of the way in which one large cultural center serves an area. Because of its location in the capital, the programs are also seen by many persons from outside the Washington metropolitan area; and as a stated policy, the center invites companies from different parts of the country to perform. At the present time it is a sponsoring agency, though it welcomes conferences and meetings on the arts for children as well as assuming an active role in the furthering of theatre for young spectators in America. On several occasions the premieres of new works have been shown as main-stage productions. In general, however, the children's programs take place in an open playing space upstairs. ASSITEJ (q.v.) and American Theatre Association (q.v.) meetings have been held in the center on many occasions.

JUNIOR ENTERTAINMENT, INC., OF DENVER
Address: Denver, CO
Founding date: 1943. Closed.

This organization, founded in 1943, concentrated on the procurement of the best live entertainment for children of all ages. It enlisted the cooperation of civic and educational institutions that included the Denver public schools, the Denver Symphony Orchestra, the Denver Art Museum, the Parent-Teacher Association, and the Junior League, with the University of Denver as its strongest ally. Junior Entertainment, Inc., offered professional and nonprofessional entertainment for which 2,000 season tickets were sold annually.

JUNIOR PROGRAMS, INC.
Address: New York, NY
Founding date: 1936. Terminated in 1943.

Junior Programs, Inc., was a short-lived though highly praised enterprise in the late thirties and early forties. The founder was Dorothy McFadden, a civic-minded woman in Maplewood, New Jersey, whose concern for good children's entertainment began when her own children were of school age. Her search for material led her first to active participation in the community's effort to book better assembly plays than the schools had offered heretofore. She learned that while the field was limited, more was available than her committee had been aware of. Realizing that she could accomplish something for all children if she extended her efforts, she established an organization that sponsored the best theatre she could find.

The success of this enterprise led her before long to the next step: production. Though her background was not in theatre, her taste and judgment were apparently good, and her energy was limitless. Just as she had sought and found quality in the attractions she booked, she sought and found quality in directors, performers, scene designers, and public relations personnel. The result, according to all reports at the time, was an exceptional company. The material was first-rate and the performances professional in every respect. Within the next few years she expanded the organization to include ballet and opera companies as well as theatre. All three received high praise from the National Council of Parents and Teachers and the Child Study Association of America. An article in *Reader's Digest* in April 1940 entitled "The Miracle ... That Is Children's Theatre" brought Junior Programs to the attention of the general public from coast to coast.

McFadden's stated goals were to make available to every child, rich or poor, productions by the finest adult artists in America; to educate the parents and the community in general as to the need for wholesome entertainment for every child and to provide it at the lowest possible cost; and to continue to act as a clearing house for children's programs. In short, her aim was to raise standards of all offerings for children in the entertainment field. This was an ambitious goal, but for the brief existence of Junior Programs, Inc., it was apparently met.

In 1943, however, trouble came from an unexpected source. The war caused a sudden shortage of gasoline, curtailing the extensive cross-country tours. In addition, many of McFadden's performers were drafted into the army, a much more serious obstacle, for it prevented any thought of continuing the New York engagements as well. And so Junior Programs suspended operations, as it turned out, permanently. When the war was over, the actors and dancers had scattered, and the activities of the company were never resumed. Thus a children's theatre that had begun so brilliantly came to an abrupt end. It was reported that 4 million children saw Junior Programs offerings during the seven years it existed. It stands today as a high point, however, in the history of a branch of the American theatre that had consistently been distinguished for its good intentions but rarely for the excellence of its work.

JUNIOR PROGRAMS OF CALIFORNIA, INC.
Address: P.O. Box 24572, Los Angeles, CA 90024
Founding date: 1955

Junior Programs of California is the outgrowth of Los Angeles Junior Programs, which was founded in 1955 by Dorothy Allen, wife of UCLA's chancellor, Raymond Allen. It was the first such group in Southern California to present theatre for children on a continuing basis, and it enjoyed almost immediate popularity and success. This led to the formation of other similar programs, established to serve outlying communities. Junior Programs of California thus became the official parent organization of which each of the following is a part: Los Angeles Junior Programs, Junior Programs of Long Beach, San Gabriel Junior Programs, Santa Monica Junior Programs, Culver City Junior Programs, and La Mirada Junior Programs.

Junior Programs of California is a sponsoring organization rather than a producing company, and all productions for all of its components are booked through its office. With subscription series as its operating policy, it is able to handle much of the administrative work and budgets for all of the programs comprising it. Both group and individual ticket sales are available, in addition to season subscriptions. Unlike many children's series, its plays are directed to audiences between the ages of six and nine; no child under six is admitted. Volunteer committees preview attractions, most of which are traditional children's classics. Los Angeles Junior Programs usually offers six different productions a season, which are given during weekends. The other programs under the "umbrella" organization present five or six productions, depending on community interest and support. Its stability is attributed to sound business practices, good theatre, and excellent volunteer help.

THE JUNIOR REPERTORY THEATRE OF MINNEAPOLIS
Address: Minneapolis, MN
Founding date: 1929. Closed.

This was an early community group formed by Elizabeth Hartzell. The first venture of its kind in Minneapolis, it met with an enthusiastic response from both children and adults. The plays that were presented were ambitious, including, for example, *The Taming of the Shrew* and *Peter Pan*. Minneapolis has proved hospitable to theatre for children, perhaps because of this early exposure to fine literature and a clear emphasis on appropriate plays and performances for the young spectator. The Junior Repertory Theatre is historically important in a survey of the children's theatre movement.

JUST AROUND THE CORNER COMPANY
Address: P.O. Box 1130, Brookline, MA 02146
Founding date: 1976

The Just Around the Corner Company describes itself as a multiethnic theatre dedicated to fostering young people's active and creative participation in high quality theatre experiences. These are designed to illuminate a variety of cultures, social isues, and other areas of human concern. To this end, the group tours original plays, which generally involve audience participation in which children are invited to perform along with the professional adult actors. The audience, consisting of no more than 150 children, is divided into five groups, who are prepared for their participation in workshops conducted by the actors prior to the performance.

Just Around the Corner is available for residencies in which creative drama, improvisation, and theatre in education techniques are included. It gives over 200 performances a year.

K

KALEIDOSCOPE DANCERS

Address: New York University, Dance Department of SEHNAP, New York, NY 10003

Founding date: 1974

The Kaleidoscope Dancers performing group is a professional adult company so theatrical in its presentation that it belongs under the children's theatre umbrella as well as the field of dance. Colorful costumes and frequent use of a story line capture and hold the attention of young spectators, and nearly all of the numbers on any given program can be related to some area of the curriculum. Audiences learn about other cultures through dance, experience new ways of approaching classroom studies, and gain an appreciation of dance as an art form.

Workshops for teachers as well as for children are available. The group performs in schools, hospitals, community centers, and museums as well as occasionally at the university. There is a Kaleidoscope student group also, some of whose members may, on graduation, audition for the adult performing group when there are vacancies.

In the summer of 1985 the Kaleidoscope Dancers were invited to perform at the Festival of the Arts for Children in Sibenik, Yugoslavia. This was the only company from the United States that was represented at the Festival that year.

KALEIDOSCOPE PLAYERS

Address: California State University, Theatre Department, Fullerton, CA 92634

Founding date: 1959

Theatre for children has been a part of the program at California State University, Fullerton, since its founding; in 1976, however, the first full-time specialist in children's theatre was hired. Courses in creative drama and children's theatre are offered on both undergraduate and graduate levels. The production program centers on the Kaleidoscope Players, who tour from February through May. Two weekends of the tour are devoted to appearances in the Arena Theatre on campus as part of the main-stage season. Kaleidoscope has performed at the Southern California Theatre Festival for Young Audiences each year since 1977.

The focus is on new plays rather than older, more familiar scripts. The list since 1976 includes *Gypsy Cat and the Magic Boots*, adapted by Ronald D. Wood from Brian Way's *Puss in Boots*; *The Magic Toy*; *Mr. Grump and the Clown*; *The Ugly Duckling*; *Androcles and the Lion* and *The Arkansaw Bear* by Aurand Harris; and *The Humble King* by Yellow Brick Road Shows (q.v.).

KARAMU HOUSE CHILDREN'S THEATRE
Address: 2355 E. 89 St., Cleveland, OH 44106
Founding date: 1918

This is one of the few early children's theatres in America still in existence. Unlike most community and civic theatres, Karamu was not an outgrowth of an adult theatre but preceded it. The founder/directors, Rowena and Russell Jelliffe, were social workers who went to Cleveland in 1915 to direct the small Negro settlement house. Realizing the appeal and social values of theatre, they began the children's work during their first years there, and they based the first plays on stories the neighborhood children brought with them from the South. The enterprise was so successful that Karamu became known not only throughout America but internationally as an arts center. By the thirties it became necessary to expand into new quarters that offered more space for backstage operation, rehearsal rooms, and audience. While the level of interest and activities has fluctuated for more than sixty-five years, Karamu has never ceased to offer plays and classes in drama and dance for young people. It was the first black theatre in America and one of the very few theatres to have continued operation for so long a period of time.

KIDS FOR KIDS PRODUCTIONS, INC.
Address: P.O. Box 222, Lake Grove, NY 11755
Founding date: 1977

Kids for Kids is one of the few theatres for children in which children perform under the direction of a staff of professional adults. It is primarily an educationally oriented organization with classes in all areas of theatre for a wide range of ages. Creative drama, puppetry, mime, and movement are available to the seven- to ten-year-olds; classes in acting, speech, voice, dance, circus arts, and production are offered for older children and teenagers. An active student at the arts center participates in both workshops and performances with poise, self-confidence, and skills as goals.

Special programs, summer programs, a weekend workshop series, master classes and touring are all part of the total offerings of the organization. In addition, a sociodrama workshop for teenagers is a unique feature. It is occasionally available as a demonstration for conferences of education and community leaders. Main-stage productions, roadshows, and touring engagements add up to eighty-five performances a year. The group is funded by the New York State Council on the Arts as a semi-professional children's theatre.

K.I.D.S. REPERTORY THEATRE (later renamed Poormen's Riches)
Address: P.O Box 1462, Madison, WI 53701
Founding date: 1975
K.I.D.S. Repertory Theatre is a regional professional theatre for children based in Madison, Wisconsin, but touring throughout the Midwest and Northwest. Performing well-known children's stories adapted to the stage and holding workshops were the objectives at the time of its founding. In addition to standard works, however, there was an interest in the creation of contemporary drama and original musicals and revues for high school age children. Audience participation is included as an effective technique for reaching younger children.

Like the majority of professional companies, K.I.D.S. aims to present the highest quality theatre for young people who may never have been exposed to living actors in plays written and performed expressly for them. Residencies in schools are another way of reaching young people and helping teachers and children to understand the theatre arts and encourage further participation in them.

Productions for 1983 illustrate the type of shows K.I.D.S. offers: *Hansel and Gretel, Jumpin' Beings, Butterscotch Adaptations, The Back Porch Revue,* and *The Student Guide to the Universe.* The company is available from October through May.

THE KING-COIT SCHOOL OF ACTING AND DESIGN
Address: New York, NY
Founding date: 1923. Closed in 1958
The King-Coit School of Acting and Design differed from all other children's theatres of the period as, indeed, it differs from groups today. The school was established in 1923 by Edith King and Dorothy Coit in New York City as an afternoon and weekend studio for children from kindergarten to high school. The work for the year consisted of a single piece of classic literature, around which the activities were centered. The children were first familiarized with the story, then they studied various aspects of the period. In their art classes with King the children worked

on costume and scene designs, some of which were later used in the mounting of the play. In their classes with Coit they worked on speech, movement, dramatization of the plot, and character development. The emphasis was described by the two teachers as being on creativity, though technical excellence was stressed and apparently achieved; every account of the work made mention of it.

At the end of the year a production of the play or story was given in a midtown theatre or hotel. Professional lighting experts and scene builders constructed and lighted the productions under the supervision of Coit and King. Audiences were adults and included members of the children's families and friends. The two or three performances were among the publicized social events of the spring. There has been controversy as to how many of the ideas were actually the children's and how many were imposed on them by the teachers. Some of the children who took part in the productions are still living in New York, and they recall the experience vividly, most of them with enthusiasm. How creative it actually was is impossible to determine, but there was agreement that the results were beautiful, and photographs of the children in their costumes posed before the scenery bear out this judgment.

The plays given by the King-Coit School were different from those given by other groups, with the exception of *The Tempest. Kai Khosru, Aucassin and Nicolette, The Story of Theseus, The Rose and the Ring, The Image of Artemis*, and *The Golden Cage* (from the poems of William Blake) were some of the most popular productions. The school gave its last performance in 1958 and then closed its doors permanently. An unusual opportunity was afforded persons interested in the King-Coit School in 1979, however, when an exhibition of photographs, prompt books, costumes, and pieces of scenery was mounted in the Performing Arts Library of Lincoln Center in New York. This exhibit was arranged by Ellen Rodman, whose doctoral study at New York University was "The King-Coit School and Children's Theatre." It attracted great attention because it was the first time that present-day practitioners were able to see the extraordinary visual effects of the productions and from them get a sense of the philosophy and achievements of the directors.

KITCHEN SINK MIME THEATRE
Address: P.O. Box 1124, Portsmouth, NH 03801
Founding date: 1977

Kitchen Sink Mime Theatre consists of two professional mimes, Dennis McLaughlin and Genevieve Aichele. Kitchen Sink has a varied repertoire from which pieces are chosen according to the size and general response of the audience. School programs are forty-five to fifty minutes in length and are geared to specific grade levels: K–3, 4–6, 7–9, and 10–12. Performances include the following: (1) Introduction to the art of mime, its history, and (especially for older grades) some of the different forms of mime technique. This is done through explanation and specific demonstration. (2) Comic and dramatic mime stories—silent or with musical background. Some are based on classical themes, others use more modern techniques and ideas. (3) Poetry interpreted through mime, movement, and vocal and sound effects.

Kitchen Sink Mime Theatre offers workshops in mime, theatre movement, basic acting techniques, and chamber theatre (interpretation of literature through mime and drama). These workshops can be geared to any grade level and are lecture/demonstration or process oriented depending on the number of participants. Teacher workshops are also available in the above areas, as well as in the use of dramatic techniques in education. The company is available for preplanning and follow-up sessions with teachers. It is also prepared to perform for handicapped audiences of all kinds, especially performing for the deaf. Kitchen Sink is available year-round. The touring range covers the entire United States.

In 1983 Kitchen Sink created *Heart on a Sleeve,* a production designed for school-age children and their families. Joining McLaughlin and Aichele is Pat Spalding, a storyteller and puppeteer who has entertained audiences with her performance of *Ha' Penny Story Theatre* since the early seventies. *Heart on a Sleeve* is an original script derived from historical pantomime, using three "zanni" characters of the commedia dell'arte.

Kitchen Sink has appeared at the New England Theatre Conference, the University of Massachusetts, and the University of New Hampshire. On occasion it gives workshops at its studio in Portsmouth.

KNICKERTY KNOCKERTY PLAYERS
Address: Pittsburgh, PA
Founding date: 1950. Closed.

Based in Pittsburgh, this touring theatre company played for audiences in the United States and in six foreign countries during the fifties and sixties. It was composed of adults, and a premiere of each production was given at the Pittsburgh Miniature Playhouse. Margot Frye, formerly of Grace Price Productions (q.v.), produced, and Madge Miller directed. The group played a full season five days a week, including performances in schools during school time. Literary quality and careful production were stressed with the help of an advisory board of educators, writers, and civic leaders. The company is no longer in existence.

L

LAND OF OZ
Address: Banner Elk, NC
Founding date: 1969. Closed.

The Land of Oz was a community theatre that reported 960 performances a year in 1978. Although a successful enterprise in its first decade,
it had apparently ceased operation by the early eighties; the North Carolina State Arts Council has no record of activities after that time.

THE LEARNING THEATRE
Address: 88 Broadway, Paterson, NJ 07505
Founding date: 1972

The Learning Theatre regards its performances not as ends or cul-
minating experiences but rather as beginnings. Programs are a place for
children to develop their imagination, both during the performance and
afterward at home or in the classroom. Plays use folklore and legendary
material as well as contemporary situations, thus offering substance and
an opportunity for thought and decision-making.

The company tries to reach audiences that have little access to formal
theatre. For that reason it is committed to touring. Technical requirements are limited so as to fit all facilities and conditions. In the 1984–
1985 season The Learning Theatre was in residence at the Paterson
Museum as part of a tri-museum consortium under a National Endowment for the Humanities grant. A new show, *Children of the Mills*, was
produced as part of the educational outreach. This show did not tour,
however, in order to allow more time for work in depth. Normally over
one hundred touring performances a season are reported.

As a way of involving children in the performance, audience participation is employed. The company believes that children, unlike adults,
view their experience as participants (or participant/spectators) as being
a part of their life—not as something that happened on a stage but as

something that they lived through and so have made a part of themselves. At The Learning Theatre, children are given an opportunity to explore the power of human imagination. In order to achieve this goal, all plays are written and directed by the ensemble.

LIBRARY THEATRE, INC.
Address: 1314 Eye St., NW, Washington, DC 20005
Founding date: 1971

Library Theatre, Inc., was founded as a nonprofit educational and professional company specializing in programs for children. It began with a single program called *Books Alive,* which is still a major activity. *Books Alive* is a fifty-minute musical that has as its purpose the stimulation of reading. Stories are introduced through the format of the program. Each year new stories are included so that the company may return to the same school annually yet offer new works. The five actors appear in costume, carrying with them scenery and properties.

A second program is *Summer Storybuilders.* This was developed to meet the needs of children during the summer months. Using the *Books Alive* format, *Summer Storybuilders* concentrates on motivating children to use their local public libraries. Actors perform in branch libraries throughout the metropolitan area. In 1981 Library Theatre opened a media department, which specializes in educational films, slides, and videotapes designed for elementary school children. These are used by teachers in the classroom. Library Theatre also publishes educational materials including teachers' guides filled with performance-related activities, bibliographical material, song sheets, and relevant games; a newsletter; and scripts. It has also produced programs for Washington television.

LILLY THEATRE. *See* THE CHILDREN'S MUSEUM—LILLY THEATRE.

LINCOLN CENTER INSTITUTE
Address: 140 W. 65 St., New York, NY 10023
Founding date: 1975

The Lincoln Center Institute describes itself as a partnership program linking the cultural resources of an arts organization to the educational resources of a school. The institute and school districts work together to develop programs in aesthetic education, preparing young people to better understand dance, music, drama, and the visual arts and to be able to determine what kinds of artistic expression they wish to make a part of their lives. Currently, this partnership involves 187 schools in forty-two districts in the metropolitan area.

Districts work with the institute in developing a long-range educational program in sites selected by the district, and share in the financial cost of the program. In addition, districts and schools provide the needed administrative support for teachers so that they can include aesthetic education in the curriculum, both in the planning stage and in classroom implementation. In 1984 more than 700 teachers of English, social studies, and languages and specialists in other areas, as well as elementary school classroom teachers, were involved. Typically, a student participates in about twenty-five classes, of which half are conducted by the classroom teacher alone and half in association with an institute teaching-artist. In addition, students attend two to four dance, music, and drama performances either in their schools or at Lincoln Center. These are performed by the finest artists in the city.

Lincoln Center does not offer children's theatre in the traditional sense but rather includes all of the performing arts in its program and, in addition, gives opportunities for young people to see such visual artists at work as the scene designer and other backstage personnel. Beautiful facilities and a growing interest in this aspect of its work indicate that the Lincoln Center Institute and Lincoln Center will in time become an outstanding example of what can be done in a large regional center.

LITTLE FLAGS THEATRE
Address: 22 Sunset St., Roxbury, MA 02120
Founding date: 1974

Little Flags Theatre is an intergenerational theatre with a major emphasis on the cultural education of the young. Our multiethnic heritage is used as material for actors and musicians, who perform and teach young people how to create plays of their own. They are taught how to use material from their own lives and to express their creative work through puppets, which they learn to make, and through music of their own composition. Basically, Little Flags is dedicated to the production of plays about history and to presenting them for audiences not usually served by the commercial theatre. It strives to build entertainment that clarifies life experience for working people. Performances are given in working-class neighborhoods, union halls, community centers, old age homes, prisons, and schools throughout Massachusetts.

One musical production is given each season, and a repertory of four major and four shorter works is maintained. Among their educational services are the following: apprenticeships in all areas, internships, workshops for all ages, professional training, residencies in schools, and theatre in education for elementary groups and high school. Little Flags is available from September to May. Titles of 1983 productions indicate the thrust of the company: *To the People, Step in Time, From Our Lives, Improvisatours, Troubadours, Little Colt,* and *Chief Joseph.* Many of these were written or adapted by the director, Maxine Klein, and James Oestenreich, the music and education director for the company. Some are geared to elementary school and others to high school, but all are deemed appropriate to the audiences they serve. Little Flags is a professional Equity company.

LITTLE MIAMI THEATRE WORKS
Address: P.O Box 248, West Liberty, OH 43357
Founding date: 1978

Little Miami Theatre Works takes its name from the Little Miami River, which flows through southern Ohio. Is is a full-time professional company whose dramas are based on local history and legends. Using everyday stories as well as more dramatic material, the players develop plays and programs about that part of the Midwest. Actors and musicians work together to broaden appreciation of a common heritage and to give children a live theatre experience. How people lived at an earlier time in Ohio's rural and small town communities forms the basis for humor, understanding, and images of the past.

Performances are given in schools, museums, theatres, parks and grange halls throughout the region; settings are so simple that a stage is unnecessary. Teachers' kits precede appearances in schools, and workshops are available following performances. Little Miami Theatre Works uses a grassroots approach that is described as imaginative in concept and warm in appreciation. The four performers sing, play simple instruments, dance, and tell stories as well as offering longer pieces for both children and family audiences.

THE LITTLE PALM THEATRE FOR YOUNG AUDIENCES
Address: Florida Academy and Theatre Enterprises, Inc., P.O. Box 1682, Boca Raton, FL 33429
Founding date: 1978

The Little Palm Theatre for Young Audiences offers over fifty performances a year of nine different shows for children. It is a community theatre under the aegis of The Florida Academy and Theatre Enterprises, Inc., and performs in the Royal Palm Dinner Theatre facility. Occasional touring engagements take the company to neighboring towns, but in general Little Palm serves the Boca Raton community. A recent addition to the program has been a theatre training wing for both young people and adults. An experienced professional faculty offer classes in all areas. One of the traditional attractions is an annual production of *Amahl and the Night Visitors* every December. Little Palm's long-range goal is the development of a professional children's theatre company and a drama school with an expanded curriculum for young performers. Funding is sought to enable the management to make the shift from community to professional theatre and training school.

LITTLE PEOPLE PRODUCTIONS
Address: 226 W. 78 St., Suite B-A, New York, NY 10024
Founding date: 1968

Little People Productions evolved out of years of performing Christmas industrials in the West. The company is now based in New York but has given productions in Chicago, Los Angeles, and Portland, with tours to ten other states for corporations such as Kodak and IBM. These productions inspired the creation of over thirty original musicals for children, both seasonal and nonseasonal in content. Tours take place between August and June.

The five performers offer both variations on traditional stories and original scripts based on contemporary concerns of young people. An example of the latter is *Multiple Choice*, the story of a school dropout. Plays for younger children bear such titles as *The Peppermint Bear and the Magic Jingle Bells*, *Benny and the Easter Bunny*, and *It's My Birthday*. Fanciful costumes and an emphasis on seasonal material characterize the work of Little People Productions.

LITTLE RED WAGON CARAVAN
Address: Theatre Resources for Youth, Theatre & Communication Department, University of New Hampshire, Durham, NH 03824
Founding date: 1966

The Little Red Wagon Caravan was listed in the 1978 CTAA directory as offering 1,000 performances a year. *See also* Theatre Resources for Youth.

LITTLE THEATRE OF THE DEAF
Address: 305 Great Neck Road, Waterford, CT 06385
Founding date: 1970

This group made its debut in 1968 as a component of the acclaimed National Theatre of the Deaf, a project of the Eugene O'Neill Foundation in Connecticut. It was first seen in the small experimental theatre at Lincoln Center in New York. Poetry, stories, mime, and narrative were combined in a new and original concept of theatre for children. Performers are deaf actors, but audiences are composed of both hearing and nonhearing children. Although the company received critical acclaim at the time, it has never attempted to perform on a regular basis, but it must be mentioned because of its artistic merit and the fact that it stimulated activity by, for, and with this heretofore neglected population. It has toured Australia, Scandinavia, England, India, and the West Indies, and is given credit for encouraging the signing of plays by other companies.

LIVING STAGE THEATRE COMPANY
Address: 6th and Maine Ave., SW, Washington, DC 20024
Founding date: 1964

The Living Stage, a venture of Washington's Arena Stage, has played an active role in theatre for children and youth since the early sixties. Among its many offerings are performances by professional adult actors, teacher training classes, improvisational theatre workshops, educational consultants for theatres, schools, and museums, and a touring program. The last feature was added in 1968. In 1972 the Washington summer and fall schedule was followed by a seven-week tour in Boston under the auspices of Boston University.

The aim of the Living Stage from the beginning has been to make theatre a relevant, intense, personal experience for children. To accomplish this end, it deliberately eschewed the artifices of theatre that serve to separate the play from the audience and keep the spectator at a distance. Living Stage works in ordinary rooms, preferably without furniture, because the actors and audience need to move. One hears Living Stage before one sees it; music floods the area, and the first thing one sees is people dancing. The actors encourage the audience to move, touch, shout, sing, and dance, and imperceptibly the action begins. Living Stage is designed to exalt the creativity of the audience, unlike other theatres, which are designed to let the audience see the creativity of the actors and the playwright.

Robert Alexander, the director, found in the early years of the theatre that children of every background were concerned about the same things: family, school, sex, drugs, human relations, and social problems. A nonprofit cultural institution, Living Stage has been funded from the beginning by private and government grants as well as its tour fees.

The company has moved several times since outgrowing its original space at Arena Theatre. In 1984 it moved again to a new venue, once the location of the old Club Bali. According to Alexander, this is the perfect choice for a permanent home for the Living Stage.

THE LONG WHARF ACCESS THEATRE COMPANY
Address: New Haven, CT 06511
Founding date: 1965

The Long Wharf Theatre's extension program for children was one of several outreach programs that sprang up in the sixties. Particularly concerned with inner city children, Long Wharf geared its first plays to the four- to eleven-year-old level but soon extended the program to include audiences up to fourteen years of age. High school students came next, but rather than producing plays specifically for them, selected adult plays were offered.

Meanwhile, a touring group was going into the ghettos with apprentices assisting on a work/study basis. The goals of the program were to provide good quality entertainment and aesthetic education for the audience as well as training in performance skills for the actors, thus demonstrating some of the values of theatre for all persons involved. Within the next ten years, The Long Wharf Theatre expanded its services to include more school districts. It worked closely with teachers to relate plays to the curriculum wherever possible and so motivate learning. The Ford Foundation, Community Progress, Inc., the New Haven Board of Education, and The Long Wharf Theatre were all responsible for developing a program that differed from many others of the period in its preparatory and follow-up activities. This has become standard practice among both professional and educational groups, but Long Wharf was a pioneer in the setting up of appropriate activities to enrich and extend the theatre experience for young audiences. By the early eighties the program had changed. Long Wharf no longer offered a season of plays specifically devoted to young people. It did, however, maintain a school tour program and a series of educational forums for high school students. It occasionally still offers a production suited to children's interests.

LOOKING GLASS THEATRE
Address: The Casino, Roger Williams Park, Providence, RI 02907
Founding date: 1962

Looking Glass Theatre is a touring theatre for children that performs in schools, libraries, and community centers throughout the state of Rhode Island. Founded over twenty-five years ago, the Looking Glass Theatre combines improvisational techniques with audience participation. It was begun and has remained dedicated to the concept of theatre in education. Its actor/teachers have also taught classes at the University of Rhode Island and in local public schools. The development of new scripts interests it members, who perform in the round, working with the audience before and often following a performance.

Other educational and community services have included a series of creative drama sessions in public libraries, aesthetic education, a special Saturday series for special and economically disadvantaged children, and participation in the various events offered at the Casino. Programs are designed for two grade levels: 1–3 and 4–7. Over 300 performances a year are given on an average. Members of the company are schooled in both education and theatre. Occasionally scripts by writers outside the group are produced, but they follow the same format: theatre in education, in which the audience takes an active role. The key to Looking Glass productions, according to the company manager, is the fact that the children are an integral part of the performance. Funding for this not-for-profit professional company comes from the National Endowment for the Arts, the Rhode Island State Council for the Arts, and performance fees.

LOOKING IN. *See* THE BRIDGE.

LOON AND HERON THEATRE
Address: 194 Boylston St., Brookline, MA 02146
Founding date: 1978

The Loon and Heron Theatre is a professional touring company offering a comprehensive program of theatre, dance, and music designed to stimulate a child's interest and participation in the performing arts. Highly acclaimed for its lively, spirited productions and colorful sets, costumes, and puppets, the company has performed and given workshops for schools, colleges, community groups, and special needs institutions throughout New England. During the 1980–1981 season the Loon and Heron launched its first international tour, visiting eight states, Canada, and Korea.

The Loon and Heron Theatre offers:

Five productions in repertory (programs to fit any audience and performing space).

Educational programs (preparatory and/or follow-up workshops to tour with all productions. These include both special needs and mainstreamed classrooms. Residencies incorporate a combination of performances and workshops and are designed to meet the particular needs of a sponsor).

Curriculum packets and study guides.

Unique programs for groups with special needs (sign language, special productions for children with a wide range of disabilities, and an in-service training workshop for teachers which presents techniques that they can use along with exercises designed to demystify handicapping conditions and to aid awareness and understanding of disabilities).

Past productions have included *Baby and the Bear*, a visual rather than verbal play for younger children; *Grunion the Grouch*, which dealt with overcoming disabilities; and *In a Pickle*, which featured a tactile set for the visually impaired and won a Special Recognition Citation from The Children's Theatre Association of America (q.v.). In 1982 the National Committee on the Arts for the Handicapped recognized the work of the company by naming Loon and Heron a Model Site. The Shakespeare's Players Series is designed to introduce high school students to Shakespearean plays. Loon and Heron claims to be Boston's most comprehensive children's theatre program, performing for audiences from kindergarten age through high school.

LOUISVILLE CHILDREN'S THEATRE. *See* STAGE ONE.

M

THE MAD HATTERS
Address: Hunter College, Department of Theatre and Film, 695 Park Ave., New York, NY 10021
Founding date: 1979

During the forties and early fifties Hunter College sponsored an active program of children's drama. Charlotte Perry, who later retired, not only developed a program of creative drama and children's theatre, but contributed new scripts, one of which was given a premiere production at the Perry Mansfield School of Theatre in Colorado. This was *The Cockney Cats*, later produced at Hunter College.

The current program in child drama is offered by the Department of Theatre and Film and includes courses in creative drama, creative drama in the community, theatre for youth, and children's theatre lab. The company of actors called The Mad Hatters comes from the theatre lab. This troupe began in 1979 under the direction of Professor Patricia Sternberg and presents a production every spring at the Hunter College Little Theatre. Original scripts are presented at the college and on tour for elementary schools in Manhattan and the Bronx.

On the graduate level Hunter offers a master's degree in developmental drama. Courses include creative drama, drama leadership techniques, developmental drama for special populations, sociodrama, theatre for youth, and theatre in education. The Hunter program is certified for Winifred Ward Scholars.

MAE DESMOND'S COMPANY
Address: Philadelphia, PA
Founding date: 1941. Closed.

Founded in 1941 in Philadelphia, this company toured the East, North, and Middle West. It began with a series of six plays presented at the Philadelphia Town Hall. The company suspended activities for two years during the war. It resumed production on a touring basis with four new titles added to the repertoire in the late forties. The company is no longer in operation, although there were some performances in the Philadelphia area in the early fifties.

THE MAGIC CARPET PLAY COMPANY
Address: 304 Balboa St., San Francisco, CA 94118
Founding date: 1972

The Magic Carpet Play Company of San Francisco is a company of eight professional actors in the vanguard of contemporary theatre for young people. Awarded the 1976 Winifred Ward Award for their work in children's theatre, The Magic Carpet Play Company has also been recognized by numerous other professional and educational organizations throughout California and across the country. It is at home playing for any age audience, whether it be for an elementary school or a university, on the street or on the concert stage. Magic Carpet developed out of a group of actors in transition from traditional forms of theatre. They discarded sets, props, costumes, and all preconceptions of theatre for children. Having studied ballet, music, mime, and improvisation, they were able to embark on a new form of theatre involving the other performing arts.

A special feature of the company is its use of material sent to them by children. *Kids' Writes* is the title of a collection of original and unedited work written by children. Stories, thoughts, and poems are selected from students of various ages and cultural and economic backgrounds who have seen The Magic Carpet Play Company. By the end of the seventies the company was reporting as many as 250 performances a season composed entirely of children's work. It accepts residencies in schools, working directly with children in the classroom, stimulating creative writing and participation in creative drama. The actors' use of jumpsuits in lieu of representational costumes further places the emphasis on the creation of script rather than theatrical production. James Mairs, the artistic director was the founder of The Magic Carpet Play Company and has remained with it. In 1982 a videotape was made of *Kids' Writes*.

THE MAINE ACTING COMPANY (MAC)
Address: Performing Arts Center, 113 Lisbon St., Lewiston, ME 04240
Founding date: 1978

The Maine Acting Company is a professional resident and touring company offering plays for both adults and children. In its new home, opened in 1985 in downtown Lewiston, a season of six productions was announced, in addition to hundreds of touring performances throughout New England. These performances are given in elementary and high schools, offering such titles as *The Lion, the Witch and the Wardrobe*, a play based on a C. S. Lewis classic story; *Snap Shots*, an original script; and *Stage Fright—Stories of the Macabre*. The company also performs on college campuses where one-day or week-long residencies are available. These workshops include play production, improvisation, makeup, voice production, and character movement. The two instructors and founders have backgrounds in college teaching in addition to professional stage experience.

With the new space now in use, classes in the performing arts are planned for the future. The Maine Acting Company is a nonprofit organization designed to offer intimate and challenging theatre, which embraces classical, modern, and innovative forms of drama.

MARK TAPER FORUM. *See* IMPROVISATIONAL THEATRE PROJECT.

MAXIMILLION PRODUCTIONS, INC.
Address: 98 Riverside Dr., New York, NY 10024
Founding date: 1962

Maximillion Productions was founded in the early sixties by Max Traktman and Peggy Simon. Their style was unique for the period and has been described variously as lively, original, and "camp." Modern scripts, most of them written by Peggy Simon, have predominated in Maximillion Productions, with music as an important element. Maximillion bore little resemblance to other children's theatre of the sixties, but it has had a following because of its humor, originality, and performance skill. Indeed, a high standard of technical competence is a hallmark, though the overall content and style have remained controversial. The thrust of the company is entertainment with a stated aim to encourage young theatre-goers to create their own plays.

Maximillion is an Equity ensemble that has presented a wide variety of programs in its repertory of more than thirty productions. These include the following originals: *Absolutely Time, Gabriel Ghost, Sam Stiller: Private Eye*, and *Are There Alligators in the Sewers of the City of New York?* The repertory also carries classic fairy tales such as *Aladdin, Sleeping Beauty*, and *The Stone Age*. Its Information Series presents revues such as *This Was America*, a musical dealing with American history; *The Playmakers*, which deals with the making of a play; and *The Fireman's Revue*, a lively musical with a message about firefighting and the history of the fire department. While an educational aspect may be present, Maximillion Productions are always first of all entertaining. They appear regularly on the New York PACT spring showcase.

MEMPHIS CHILDREN'S THEATRE

Address: 2599 Avery, Memphis, TN 38112
Founding date: 1951

The Memphis Park Commission's Children's Theatre, founded in 1951 by Lucille Ewing, is dedicated to the philosophy of "children doing theatre for children by children." Not only is this one of the oldest theatres for children in the country, it has adhered to a point of view not shared by many in the field. Memphis Children's Theatre features six shows in its regular season today. Two of these shows are designed for children under the age of twelve, and two are designed for those over twelve. Its 1984–1985 season announced *Harvey, Babes in Toyland, Antigone,* and *Heidi.*

In addition to its regular season, Memphis offers a summer repertoire called the Lucille Ewing Youth Festival. In 1984 the summer season opened with *Tom Sawyer* and followed it with *Raggedy Ann and Andy* and *The Matchmaker.* The theatre falls into the triple categories of educational/ community/professional.

A unique feature is the inclusion of playwriting by students in second through eighth grades, and directing for students aged fifteen to eighteen. Winning plays are seen on the Young Playwrights' Showcase, and youthful directors are given an opportunity to direct some of the plays. Classes in creative movement, ballet, tap, and jazz are offered, as well as creative drama, mime, and character creation. Instructors are adults, many of whom have a professional theatre background, but the stated purpose of theatre for children and by children is practiced in this popular and extensive program.

MERRY-GO-ROUNDERS

Address: New York, NY
Founding date: 1956. Closed in the mid–1970s.

The Merry-Go-Rounders was established at the New York YM and YWHA in 1956. Directed by Bonnie Bird and supervised by Doris Humphrey, it attracted attention for its professionalism and unique format. Like The Traveling Playhouse (q.v.), it always gave some performances in the "Y" auditorium, but the majority were given on tour. While it could more properly be described as a dance company, the dramatic character of the performance placed it just as appropriately in the area of children's theatre. Merry-Go-Rounders was very successful for a number of years and was well received by audiences; however, it did not survive beyond the early seventies, when financial problems caused it to refocus on a more educational goal and cut the number of dancers down to a very small performing group. A move to New Jersey shifted its touring program to fewer performances in local schools.

A hallmark of Merry-Go-Rounders was the "Magic Mechanic," who acted as narrator or emcee. He involved the audience in some limited participation as a warm-up and set the tone for the performance. Costumes were an extremely important element of every production; colorful, beautifully designed, and changed for each number, they made a memorable aesthetic contribution to the overall effect. The elaborate staging and costuming even after the reduction of performances were reported to have made the Merry-Go-Rounders too expensive to compete in an expanding market and shifting format. By the mid-seventies it had ceased operation entirely.

THE MERRY MIMES
Address: New York, NY
Founding date: 1958. Closed by 1970.

Blanche Marvin's Merry Mimes performed regularly Off-Broadway in New York in the late fifties and early sixties. Located in lower Manhattan in the small Off-Broadway Cricket Theatre, the group emphasized style and new ways of presenting familiar materials. The director's belief in physical comfort, charm, and cleanliness made the Cricket's 200-seat theatre ideal, as all the children could see and hear well. The Merry Mimes adhered to a program of weekend performances; it had no touring program and was completely professional. By the end of the sixties Blanche Marvin, the founder and artistic director, had closed the theatre.

THE MERRY WANDERERS
Address: New York, NY
Founding date: 1954. Closed in 1964.

The Merry Wanderers Children's Theatre of New York opened in 1954. It played for several seasons as both a resident and a touring company. Under the direction of Gian Pace and David Dunham, the group offered children's classics by a professional cast. Pace's background as a dancer led to an emphasis on movement, although the group performed plays and worked in the theatre tradition.

MESA YOUTHEATRE
Address: Mesa Cultural Program, P.O. Box 1466, 155 North Center, Mesa, AZ 85201
Founding date: 1976

The Mesa Youtheatre was founded by a group of public spirited citizens with the help of the city in order to bring suitable plays to the children of Mesa. In addition to regularly scheduled productions, there is a schedule of classes for children of all ages and special one-day workshops with great artists throughout the year. A professional administrative and teaching staff handles the program with a volunteer support group to make sets, sew costumes, and assume responsibility for the house during performances. The goals of providing quality entertainment for young people and increasing opportunities for participation were realized during the first five years. The three productions selected for the 1985 season, for example, included *Winnie the Pooh, The Pigman,* and *Androcles and the Lion,* with Poko Puppets as an added attraction. Graduate students from Arizona State University's theatre department are frequently involved in the Youtheatre program.

METRO THEATRE CIRCUS
Address: P.O. Box 28098, St. Louis, MO 63119
Founding date: 1973

A not-for-profit corporation, Metro Theatre Circus has performed in St. Louis, throughout the Midwest, and from coast to coast since 1973. Words, music, dance, and mime are woven together into professional productions that entertain and instruct. The repertory ranges from modern works to a Renaissance masque with original scripts and musical scores. Colorful visual effects are as much a part of the presentation as lively movement and choreography and a distinctive performance style.

Residencies, classroom sessions, and adult workshops are available and are taught by experienced professional leaders. More than 200 performances are given every season. Founders John and Phyllis Weil held high standards for the company, which today is managed by Carol Evans, Kim Bozark, and Janice Feater, with a staff of six professional performers and four collaborating artists. The company has won high praise, including the Winifred Ward Award for a children's theatre that has attained excellence and has been in operation for at least one full year but not more than four years, the Jennie Heiden Award for excellence in professional children's theatre, and selection for a national tour for Imagination Celebration '82 (John F. Kennedy Center for the Performing Arts). Originality of scripts, music, and choreography, good performance skills, and lively color are hallmarks of the Metro Theatre Circus.

MIDLAND COMMUNITY THEATRE OF TEXAS
Address: 2000 Wadley, Midland, TX 79705
Founding date: 1946

Organized in the mid-forties, the Midland Community Theatre grew through the years from a membership of 250 to 5,386 by 1984. Like many community theatres, the adult component came first, with the children's wing developing later as interest spread. Each season six adult and six children's plays are reported presented in a handsome new facility. An educational program was added and includes work designed for both adults and young people.

Midland's children's theatre, the Pickwick Players, observes an active schedule both winter and summer. In the summer of 1984, for instance, it announced beginning and advanced jazz dance classes, ballet, and improvisation; voice and diction; comedy techniques; technical theatre; and allied crafts. In addition, Pickwick Players offered a mini-Mummers show (the Mummers is the name of the adult acting group) and a West Texas premiere production of the Maurice Sendak–Carol King children's musical, *Really, Rosie!* Professional storytellers entertain children in the library as another feature, and puppets are an additional art form occasionally to be found at Midland.

Actors and backstage workers are unpaid volunteers guided by a full-time professional theatre staff.

MIDSUMMER MIME THEATRE
Address: 429 E. Vermont St., Indianapolis, IN 46202
Founding date: 1977

Midsummer Mime Theatre was founded in 1977 as a small children's theatre company with limited touring capacity. Since then it has expanded its touring and staff in order to accommodate the increased demand for its unusual programs. In the 1983–1984 season the company presented over 200 performances in schools and theatres throughout Indiana and the surrounding region.

Educational concepts such as creative problem solving and general subjects such as the importance of friendship and honesty are incorporated into the productions. The company provides the schools with a principal information package and an extensive study guide, which contain information about the history of mime, and projects for both before and after the performance. Midsummer Mime Theatre also presents workshops on silent communication skills, movement, masks, and makeup. Although each program uses traditional white face illusory mime extensively, the full color of the theatrical spectrum is explored through the use of clowning, masks, music, dialogue, sets, and props. The current repertory includes *Triple Images* (a three-act concert program for adults); *A Company of Fools* (a program patterned after traditional commedia dell'arte performance offered in the summer out of doors); and a children's series including *The Silent Treatment, Imagination Station*, and *Fibble's Fables* (entertainment recommended for grades K–8, with study guides provided. Midsummer Mime Theatre is a professonal nonprofit company.

MILWAUKEE IMAGINATION THEATRE (MIT)
Address: 5964 N. Lydell Ave., Whitefish Bay, WI 53217
Founding date: 1972

The Milwaukee Imagination Theatre was founded by Nancy Weiss-McQuide as a two-member company specializing in improvisation and mime. As the company grew, performance skills were expanded to include juggling, clowning, various forms of improvisational theatre, and special projects created by the group. Titles of projects created within the past few years are *Pirate Days*, *Christmas Magic*, *Fractured Fables*, *Bastille Days*, *Summerfest* (street characters and jugglers), and *Kinderkonzert*.

The members of MIT believe that the arts serve a more basic purpose than entertainment, however, and when correctly implemented can supplement reading, writing, and speech development, as well as creativity in educational settings. MIT performs and teaches at all levels. Many performances are given at festivals, fairs, and other community events, but the majority are given in the schools on the elementary and high school level. Weiss-McQuide has also served as artist-in-residence in some school districts. Her educational background in social welfare, education, and the theatre arts has enabled her to reach other populations, such as handicapped children, minority groups (mainly Spanish speaking children), and senior citizens.

Productions use some music and minimal properties to create a setting for the plays. They can, therefore, be performed in any space from streets to proscenium stages.

MUDHEAD MASKS
Address: Cambridge, MA
Founding date: 1972. Closed.

Mudhead Masks was a two-performer mask and mime theatre troupe incorporating classical mime, commedia dell'arte, and circus techniques in a performance which used Balinese masks. It was devoted to bringing good theatre to a cross section of spectators, particularly to those who may not have had an opportunity to see live theatre performances. Because of its use of mime, Mudhead Masks was able to reach children with hearing impairment as well as those with language backgrounds other than English.

Dedicated to the use of theatre as an educational medium, Mudhead Masks conducted workshops in various aspects of theatre techniques. Hour-long workshops in characterization and mask movement often followed performances. Workshops in movement, juggling, circus techniques, dance, yoga, and theatre in education were also available. These were generally participatory in nature and were offered to both students and teachers. Performers were experienced in the use of video and offered workshops in its use and performance.

Although the troupe was listed in the 1978 CTAA directory, there was no record of activity by the early 1980s, and it is now reported closed. The founder, Ron Jenkins, now freelances in the Boston area and teaches in the theatre department of Emerson College in Boston.

N

NASHVILLE ACADEMY THEATRE
Address: 724 2nd Ave. S., Nashville, TN 37210
Founding date: 1931

Nashville Academy Theatre initiated its first theatre activities in 1931. It is recognized as one of the oldest, largest, and most successful family theatres in the country. It has won numerous national and international awards and was the first to receive The Children's Theatre Association of America (q.v.) award for serving as a "national model of excellence."

In 1960, with the help of the Parks and Recreation Department, the Nashville Academy Theatre became the second children's theatre in the United States to have its own municipally funded building expressly designed for children's theatre production. A fully accredited theatre school was opened in 1970; it offers over twenty-five courses of study in a year-round academic program. Members of the company, who are qualified teachers, conduct classes for elementary, middle, and high school students as well as classes for adults. In 1974 the Nashville Academy Theatre had the distinction of being the first children's theatre to perform in the Eisenhower Theatre of the Kennedy Center for the Performing Arts in Washington, D.C. The company has toured through several European countries and in the summer of 1978 was awarded first prize at the International Maytime Festival in Ireland.

While it produces the best children's plays available, the company also has an interest in the development of new scripts; for example, fourteen original plays were recently produced on the Nashville Academy stage within a period of five years. Ann Stahlman Hill, a Nashville community leader who was one of the theatre's founders and supporters, has been instrumental in the remarkable growth of this cultural center. The newly renovated auditorium was named in her honor. More than 215 performances a year are reported, including those for children bussed into the theatre, and touring engagements. Five plays a year are regularly produced.

THE NATIONAL CHILDREN'S THEATRE ASSOCIATION
Address: P.O. Box 8044, Dallas, TX 75205
Founding date: 1958

The National Children's Theatre Association was founded in Dallas and performed primarily in the Middle West and West. Fisk Miles and his wife, Ruth Gilley Miles, had been booking agents for a number of years, and among their clients was Clare Tree Major. In 1955, following Major's death, they decided that the tradition she established must be carried on and that they were the ones who must do it. Two years later they established The National Children's Theatre Association in their own city of Dallas and toured from October to May, including in their repertory plays for children from kindergarten through the sixth grade. Good literature, beautifully costumed and mounted, was basic to their philosophy of theatre for young audiences just as it had been for Clare Tree Major. The company is still in existence and reports 135 performances a season.

NATIONAL COLLEGE OF EDUCATION CHILDREN'S THEATRE
Address: 2840 Sheridan Rd., Evanston, IL 60201
Founding date: Given as 1974; previous activities took place.

National College of Education has had a long history of children's theatre activities but it has undergone several changes. In the twenties plays based on children's favorite stories were written by Clara Belle Baker, then principal of the Children's Demonstration School, and produced by college students for neighborhood children. During this same period and continuing for several decades afterward, college students produced a spring festival, which, though not designed for children, attracted children because of its color, inclusion of all the performing arts, and appropriate content. In the forties and fifties plays for child audiences were produced on a regular basis both in the college auditorium and on tour to neighboring towns. In the seventies the activities underwent yet further revision, this time with a strong educational thrust, which the earlier programs did not emphasize. As a teacher education institution, National College is dedicated to the service of children rather than to the development of professional performers or the establishment of a theatre major.

The progressive philosophy of the college has consistently encouraged the arts for both the adult student and the child spectator, and has been open to change. Only sixty-four performances a season were reported in the 1978 survey taken by the Children's Theatre Association of America (q.v.). It is probable that the college will continue the tradition of innovative work with an emphasis on education rather than entertainment. Whereas the activities before the seventies did not stress education as the major goal, it was nevertheless implicit in choice of material, consideration of audience age level, student experience, and teamwork involved in theatre production and performance.

THE NATIONAL JUNIOR THEATRE OF WASHINGTON, D.C.
Address: Washington, DC
Founding date: 1927. Closed in the early 1930s.

   This theatre company began activities in the twenties. Appropriate Broadway plays of good literary quality were presented instead of the usual children's scripts. Three years after the founding it had presented twenty-seven successful productions. The idea of selecting this type of drama was apparently novel for there are no reports of others like it. The theatre is of historical importance even though it apparently did not last long.

THE NEBRASKA THEATRE CARAVAN
Address: 6915 Cass St., Omaha, NE 68132
Founding date: 1975

   The Nebraska Theatre Caravan is the professional wing of the Omaha Community Playhouse, which is the largest community theatre in the country and the home of the future Henry Fonda Theatre Center. It is composed of professional artists and craftsmen who are dedicated to quality theatre and what they describe as worthwhile educational opportunities for young people. The Caravan promises productions for children as well as adults and a package of services that can be utilized and enjoyed by the entire community. This includes multiple school performances and workshops plus an evening's performance within a one-day residency engagement. Education is an integral part of the Caravan project. A detailed assortment of workshop outlines is included in each sponsor packet.

   In addition to such well-known titles as *The Night Thoreau Spent in Jail*, *Treasure Island*, and *Strider* are new scripts. By the end of its sixth season Caravan had performed in twenty different states throughout the Midwest. It is available for single engagements and residencies and/or funding assistance through the Nebraska Arts Council Touring Program, the Mid-America Arts Alliance Regional Touring Program, and its own agent.

NETTIE GREENLEAF'S CHILDREN'S THEATRE
Address: Boston, MA
Founding date: 1903. Closed in 1904.

This theatre was patterned after The Children's Educational Theatre (q.v.) in New York, but it was less ambitious in its program and was of short duration. Performers were drawn from the Dorothy Dix Home for Stage Children, and short plays rather than full-length productions were featured in the popular matinees for neighborhood children. The drastic new fire laws that were enforced at the time unfortunately caused the theatre to close down within a year of its founding, and it was never reopened. Its auspicious beginning qualifies it for mention in the history of the children's theatre movement.

THE NEW ENGLAND THEATRE GUILD FOR CHILDREN
Address: 12 Melville Ave., Boston, MA 02124
Founding date: 1955

The New England Theatre Guild for Children conducts one of the most extensive continuously operating touring seasons of educational theatre for elementary schools and youth organizations in Massachusetts. In 1983 more than 65,000 children saw and participated in 230 performances of classical children's literature incorporating original music and dance. Since its inception in 1955 The New England Theatre Guild has brought live theatre to approximately 450 schools and organizations. It has been able to keep the cost of performances low through support from the Massachusetts Council of the Arts and Humanities, corporations, private donors, and substantial donations of time from guild members.

Nine years and ten different productions later, more than 350,000 children and teenagers had seen and participated in their performances. In addition to schools and organizations, the guild has played benefit performances at the New England Aquarium, Summerthing (in Cambridge), the children's festival for the Boston Children's Hospital, Salem State College, and the conference for the Boston Association for the Education of Young People at Copley Plaza.

The mission of the guild has remained the same since its beginning—to adapt children's classics to forty-five-minute participation plays. The performers, all professionally trained actors with substantial acting credentials, portray several characters, singing and dancing in highly energetic performances.

The guild's children's productions include *Aesop's Fables*; *Pinocchio*; *The Great Grimm Brothers*; *The Pied Piper*; *Aladdin and His Lamp*; *Aesop's Fables, Going On*; *Andersen's Fairy Tales*; *Budulinek and Friends*; and *City Mouse and Country Mouse*.

NEW WESTERN ENERGY SHOW
Address: Helena, MT
Founding date: 1976. Closed in 1979.

The New Western Energy Show was begun in 1976 and continued in full operation through the year 1979. During the summer it performed for children and adults together but offered one show especially designed for young people. In the spring of 1977 the first school tour took place. After the performance, the actors went into classrooms and followed up the theme with discussion. In 1978 it took another fall school tour called *The Starship Parade*, and in 1979 it toured Indian reservations with *The Frog Does Not Drink Up the Pond in Which It Lives*. By the following year funding had become scarce and the troupe reorganized with only three actors and puppets. For two years the company gave puppet performances only in Montana and Utah. At the close of the 1981–1982 season all activities were terminated.

The New Western Energy Show was in the tradition of TIE (theatre in education) but was dedicated to a specific topic: the environment. It was created by AERO (Alternative Energy Resources Organization) as a way of spreading the word about alternative energy. With this traveling troupe of actors, writers, musicians, and technicians, energy-related musical theatre and exhibits of renewable energy devices and systems were taken to towns and cities throughout the Northwest. It was this thrust that distinguished the company from all other children's theatres of the period, though some did use the topic on occasion; they were not, however, environmental activists, as was AERO, which worked with state and federal agencies in a variety of programs, including the Energy Shows.

NEW WORLD THEATRE COMPANY
Address: Route 3, Box 191, Berkeley Springs, WV 25411
Founding date: 1976

The New World Theatre Company represents a contemporary trend in children's theatre: a program consisting of clowning and vaudeville acts, juggling, improvisation, storytelling, and magic tricks. The two performers develop their own pieces from many sources, including literature, legends, circus, and cinema. Their stated purpose is entertainment, although they do offer workshops in a variety of areas and are available for residencies. One such residency was a two-year invitation from the Theatre Project in Baltimore. In general, however, they are known as a touring ensemble, performing primarily in the South and the mid-Atlantic states. Their tours have also taken them across the United States and to Europe.

The *Hot and Cold Running Circus* is flexible enough to meet the requirements of every age level from a fifteen-minute performance for very young children to an hour and a half show for older audiences.

Easily assembled constumes and props make it possible for the pair to perform both indoors and out, on stage and in all-purpose rooms and gymnasiums. Workshops in vaudeville techniques, acting, and video are available for schools. The video workshop offers a "hands on" experience in creating, writing, casting, taping, and camera work. Sessions end with a screening of the students' projects. Teachers' guides and lecture/demonstrations prepare teachers in advance for the experience that the children will have and show ways in which the experience can be enhanced through orientation and follow-up sessions.

NEW YORK UNIVERSITY—PROGRAM IN EDUCATIONAL THEATRE

Address: New York University, Shimkin Hall, New York, NY 10003
Founding date: 1967

Theatre has been a feature of New York University's School of Education for several decades. In 1967, however, a special program was introduced that included drama and theatre for children and young people as well as plays for adults. Nancy and Lowell Swortzell were brought in to design a curriculum appropriate to the new direction that the department had taken. One of the characteristics of the Program in Educational Theatre has been its responsiveness to student interests and society's needs. For example, teacher education is offered to students interested in teaching on the elementary and high school levels. For those wanting to work in the community, other courses are available. The program brochure states that it offers

practical and theoretical training for a variety of careers in the theatre including basic and advanced study in all phases of theatre production, educational drama and theatre, theatre history, and dramatic literature. The program offers courses of study leading to the Bachelor of Science, Master of Arts, Doctor of Philosophy, and Doctor of Education degrees and is a part of the Department of Communications Arts and Sciences, which offers course work in all phases of communication study such as electronic media, deafness rehabilitation and many others.

A unique feature is a summer Study Abroad Program in England for graduate students. The purpose of this program is to provide directors, actors, teachers, university students, recreation leaders, librarians, and language and speech arts specialists with an opportunity for concentrated study and daily participation in the uses of drama in education. Students learn about theatre in education (TIE) by participating in it. In addition to classes at Bretton Hall College in Yorkshire, students work with youth in improvisation, street theatre, playground activities, story dramatization, and other techniques currently employed in British and American drama/theatre education.

Graduate studies in drama therapy are a recent addition, thus joining

New York University's programs in music, art, and dance therapies. A summer musical theatre workshop is another popular feature of the Program in Educational Theatre. The program is on the approved list of institutions for Winifred Ward Scholars and has had the distinction of having one of them in its doctoral program. The Creative Arts Team (CAT) (q.v.) was begun as a project in the Program in Educational Theatre. It has since become a professional company, autonomous but affiliated with the university. Although no longer a part of the program, it maintains a strong relationship, often teaching and giving demonstrations of TIE techniques.

THE 92ND STREET "Y"
Address: Lexington Ave. and E. 92nd Street, New York, NY 10028
Founding date: 1934 special arts programs introduced.

One of the most active institutions of its kind in the East has been the 92nd Street YM and YWHA of New York. From the early part of the twentieth century the "Y" showed an unusual interest in theatre for young people. It has consistently offered a wide variety of programs for persons of all ages, however, from nursery school children to senior citizens. Physical education, classes in the visual and performing arts, social events, poetry readings, and special programs have been carried on for several decades in its beautiful Manhattan facilities. Indeed, the Kaufman Concert Hall is considered one of the finest auditoriums in the city, and it is here that plays for children found a warm welcome, particularly during the fifties and sixties.

William Kolodney, for thirty-five years director of the Education Department of the "Y," was responsible for the programming. He appointed a Junior Entertainment Committee to preview productions and assist him in planning a varied season of quality entertainment for children and young people. Sensitive to the interests and needs of the audiences who frequented the "Y," Kolodney sponsored some of the finest artists and performing groups. Although the "Y" has always offered classes and clubs in acting and dance, it has primarily taken the role of sponsoring agent with a substantial budget and a loyal following. During the forties, fifties, and sixties the "Y" was home base for the Merry-Go-Rounders (q.v.), a dance company for children, and The Traveling Playhouse (q.v.), a theatre troupe for children. It offered regular performances of other performing groups and artists including John Ciardi, the poet; Fred Berk's Dances of Israel; Tom Glazer, the folksinger; and Peninah Schram, the storyteller. The Junior Drama Department of the "Y" always presented a spring play as a special event. In addition, the nationally known playwriting contest for children's plays established by Aline Bernstein in 1951 was conducted by the "Y" staff, and the award-winning play was first presented by The Traveling Playhouse in the Kaufman Concert Hall.

During its most active years the "Y" presented ten children's programs a season on Sunday afternoons at special subscription rates. Nearly twice as many additional entertainments for young people (nonsubscription events) were planned on selected dates throughout the season. In the sixties a summer program was added for children who were in the city or attending day camps in the area. After Kolodney's retirement in 1969 the emphases changed, and although children's plays continued to be offered, there were fewer of them. Nevertheless, the "Y" still hosted the annual PACT Showcase of professional entertainment for young people each spring, and some years it has booked the Paper Bag Players (q.v.) for several weeks of performances.

Today one still sees the school busses parked outside the building on weekdays, and after-school classes in the arts are popular. Whereas theatre once dominated the program, music now is given a high priority. The 92nd Street "Y" is a cultural institution which has had an enormous impact on the cultural life of the city and has been responsible for introducing new companies and promoting others in the interest of the best possible programs for children of the greater New York community.

THE NO-ELEPHANT CIRCUS
Address: 131 Purchase St., E43, Rye, NY 10580
Founding date: 1977

The No-Elephant Circus is a theatre company that was formed in 1977 by a group of students from the State University of New York at Purchase. The four-member troupe gives performances in the New York metropolitan area as well as offering educational programs in schools from the elementary to the college level.

Clowns mime, juggle, walk tightropes, eat fire, pedal unicycles, do magic tricks, and perform slapstick comedy, all at a nonstop pace. Through audience participation and interaction with circus professionals, children are provided with a behind-the-scenes look at the special world known as the circus. Music is a strong concern of the performers, however, and the company frequently works with major symphony orchestras. The No-Elephant Circus was the first circus troupe to be recognized by Actors' Equity Association.

NORTHWESTERN UNIVERSITY CHILDREN'S THEATRE AND NORTHWESTERN UNIVERSITY TOUR COMPANY. *See* THE CHILDREN'S THEATRE OF EVANSTON.

O

OFF CENTER THEATRE, INC.
Address: 136 West 18 St., New York, NY 10011
Founding date: 1968

Off Center Theatre performs 400 shows a year for children. Its programs are classical fairy tales, which instruct youngsters about contemporary morals tailored in the language of today. It does not produce political plays for children but rather offers the stories with which they are familiar and uses them to expand new ways of thinking about old issues.

The company has been reviewed by professional New York critics and is described as having a sense of humor, imagination, and a high level of acting. It is professional and is composed of all adults.

OKLAHOMA CITY UNIVERSITY (OCU)
Address: NW 23rd at North Blackweider, Oklahoma City, OK 73100
Founding date: 1960

OCU Children's Theatre and Let's Pretend Players, under the direction of Claire Jones, offer the following programs and workshops:

The Children's Theatre presents three plays by college actors for children each year. Two plays are proscenium style, one is arena style.

The Let's Pretend Players offer two plays each semester of arena style audience participation. These are given on-campus in the Children's Center for the Arts, or tour to schools, churches, and libraries. Generally there are two performances each Wednesday and one other during the week.

Creative Dramatics Workshops are offered each week during the fall and spring terms in twelve-week sessions. These are divided into three groups: Creative Dramatics—grades K–2; Creative Theatre—grades 3–6; Teen Acting Studio—grades 7–12. Students in the workshops are used in major productions and children's productions as required.

The Children's Theatre season program stresses the value of being a patron of the theatre. The popular "Spring Surprise!" is really a fourth production—a variety show—open only to season ticket holders. Both proscenium and arena productions provide broad experience of theatre.

OCU is noted for its Children's Theatre program, which is the oldest in continuous production and the most active in Oklahoma. Students can major in children's theatre through the graduate level. Audience participation "involvement dramas" are a particular specialty; production units tour the area regularly. Since 1966 the Let's Pretend Players have performed roughly eighty-five shows during a school year.

OLD GLOBE THEATRE
Address: Simon Edison Center for the Performing Arts, P.O. Box 2171, San Diego, CA 92112
Founding date: 1935

Old Globe Theatre states its goals to be the pursuit of excellence in the world of dramatic literature and art. It has long been committed to preserving and presenting the best in classical drama, be it Greek, Shakespearean, eighteenth-century French, or any other form of the living theatre that touches the great themes of thought and feeling.

Old Globe Educational Tours have been visiting schools in San Diego, Imperial, Riverside, and Orange counties since 1974, playing to over 500,000 students in that period of time. Their purpose is to introduce classical theatre to young people in an informal and entertaining way, involving them as directly as possible through language, music, mime, and student participation. The directors of the Old Globe believe Greek and Shakespearean plays to be as relevant to young people today as they were at the time they were written. In 1983–1984 the school tours took Homer's *Iliad* to student audiences in addition to continuing programs begun the preceding season—*Shakespeare from Page to Stage* and *Art to Art: A Unified Arts Experience*.

As a collaborative art, theatre is a melding of many allied and connected art forms. According to the theatre's brochure, "Live theatre stretches students to a greater comprehension of language and concepts while they are being entertained." Also held at the Old Globe is a theatre arts training program. Classes take place on Saturdays during the school year and in Camp Orbit, a theatre camp, during the summer. All classes are taught by members of the Old Globe staff and other theatre professionals; classes include voice, movement, and acting skills.

Free teachers' handbooks, backstage tours, and post-performance symposiums are available upon request. Adult entertainment is also offered at Old Globe from January to May.

OLD LOG THEATRE
Address: Box 250, Excelsior, MN 55331
Founding date: 1940

The Old Log Theatre is a resident stock company performing 52 weeks a year. It is the oldest continuously operating theatre in the United States. In 1960 the Old Log Theatre moved into a new, year-round building and has never been dark since. A number of company members have been with the organization for over thirty years. In addition to the regular schedule of plays, at the December holiday season a production for young audiences is also given. Ten performances a week are reported to be sold out during the four-week run, with audiences of 18,000 to 25,000 children in attendance. Though not a children's theatre, the fact that Old Log offers some plays for young spectators and many plays for family audiences qualifies it for inclusion in this volume.

THE OMAHA CHILDREN'S THEATRE
Address: Omaha, NE
Founding date: 1929. Closed.

This community enterprise under the auspices of the Omaha Community Playhouse was modeled after The King-Coit School of Acting and Design (q.v.) in New York. Through active participation, it promoted interest in the visual and performing arts. Monthly design competitions were open to children between the ages of five and fourteen and resulted in regular children's art exhibitions. Children assumed an important part in the total productions of the theatre company, for they not only acted but constructed their own sets. The theatre is of historical importance because of its early founding date and because it was inspired by The King-Coit School. Unlike those of its model, productions were traditional, including such titles as *Robin Hood, The Wizard of Oz, Treasure Island,* and *The Blue Bird.*

While The Omaha Children's Theatre apparently ceased operation (there is no record of activities in the sixties or seventies), the city has been hospitable to subsequent groups. The Emmy Gifford Children's Theatre (q.v.) in Omaha is an outstanding theatre providing both productions and classes in the dramatic arts for children of the city; its program is indicative of community interest and support for the performing arts for young people today.

OMAHA JUNIOR THEATRE CENTER. *See* EMMY GIFFORD CHILDREN'S THEATRE.

ON STAGE!
Address: P.O. Box 25365, Chicago, IL 60625
Founding date: 1974

On Stage! describes its program as being in two parts: live production of classic children's tales, and publication of playscripts. The primary thrust of the company is to produce high quality productions with professional production values so that children's audiences are exposed to theatre done in what they describe as a "complete" style rather than on an amateur basis. Within these perimeters the intention is not only to entertain but to educate audiences in positive social values. The secondary aim is to provide material for other theatres. A catalogue listing On Stage!'s published scripts is available on request.

OPEN CITY THEATRE COMPANY
Address: 360 Fortune St., Atlanta, GA 30312
Founding date: 1975

Founded at the time when many children's theatres with an educational thrust were being introduced, Open City described itself as educational, though performers were reported to be of all ages. A small company of actors and a technical director gave fifty touring performances of one production a season. Today, Open City's project CREATE provides participatory arts programs for children and high school students in which they can experience an art form by taking an active role in it.

Professional artists/teachers create and present informative and entertaining scripts on a wide variety of subjects appropriate to specific age levels. For example, *The Journey of Aru-Hito* is a colorful production using puppets and masks for grades K–4. *Private Places*, a piece dealing with child abuse, is available for grades 5–8. *Propaganda*, designed for grades 5–8 and 9–12, demonstrates the use of drama as a means of learning and building a better self-image. Some of the other programs deal with the Indian culture of Georgia, the immigrants from Europe to America, and well-known persons such as Sarah Bernhardt, Louisa May Alcott, Vincent Van Gogh, and Henri Matisse.

Performances are arranged through Young Audiences of Atlanta, and are comprised of the live performance, followed by workshops, discussions, and audience participation. Open City also offers training for teachers and other interested persons in creative drama, acting, storybook theatre, creative problem solving, puppetry, creative play, and movement. By the mid-eighties workshops outnumbered plays; while the number of touring performances remained approximately the same as a decade earlier, the company reported 800 to 1,000 a year.

OTHER THINGS AND COMPANY
Address: Dance Program, Center for the Arts, Oakland University, Rochester, MI 48063
Founding date: 1976

Other Things and Company is a professional troupe of dancers, singers, and musicians who perform a unique blend of music, dance, and mime for children. The ensemble tours schools, community centers, conventions, malls, and theatres to present an exciting and totally new form of entertainment for children. The company performs throughout the state of Michigan for audiences of all ages. Besides the performance, each member of the company is prepared to conduct classroom workshops in creative dance or music. Programs last fifty minutes and include some audience participation.

Other Things and Company is a resident company of the Dance Program at Oakland University.

P

THE PALO ALTO CHILDREN'S THEATRE
Address: 1305 Middlefield Rd., Palo Alto, CA 94301
Founding date: 1932

The Palo Alto Children's Theatre was established as part of the Palo Alto Community Center, which included recreational facilities, a public library, a museum, and a swimming pool. Although dramatic activities began in the early thirties, 1935 was the year that a beautiful, fully equipped building for the production of children's plays was erected. Unlike the majority of children's theatres, it operated year-round and had the distinction of being the only completely tax supported children's theatre in the country. The financial and operational structure has changed since then, but the theatre is still in existence and is a popular community resource. In 1972 it was host to The Children's Theatre Association of America (q.v.) preceding the annual American Theatre Association (q.v.) convention in San Francisco.

The seventies were busy years at the theatre, with classes, workshops, concerts, special events, outreach programs, conferences, and festivals. In addition, the theatre became part of the newly organized Arts and Sciences Department of the city. It hosted the first Northern California Children's Theatre Play Festival and participated in the Children's Theatre Association Festival in Marin County. Outreach and Summer Conservatory became two very important components of the program along with Children's Theatre Day. Productions of the seventies included *Snow White, The Lion, the Witch, and the Wardrobe, A Midsummer Night's Dream, The Hobbit, Pickwick, Minnie's Boys,* and *Godspell.* Some of the eighties plays included *Beauty and the Beast, Down in the Valley, Once upon a Mattress, The Importance of Being Earnest, Dracula, Pale Pink Dragon, The Wizard of Oz,* and *Joseph and the Amazing Technicolor Dreamcoat.* From the list, it is apparent that a typical season includes traditional plays, new titles, and plays for older audiences.

Currently the Palo Alto Children's Theatre staff teaches two of the Jordan Middle School drama classes at the theatre as part of the Jordan curriculum. The elementary portion of the Outreach Program has been formalized to include producing plays at school sites in cooperation with PTAs as an after-school opportunity for youngsters to experience children's theatre in a familiar surrounding. The adult acting troupe produces in-school plays that are designed to complement curriculum topics, values, and educational goals. The Palo Alto Children's Theatre Summer Conservatory, begun in 1976, has as its purpose the providing of intense training in theatre for young people. This includes acting, scene study, voice and diction, makeup, costume, technical theatre, movement, mime, music, fencing, history of the theatre, audition techniques, resume writing, advanced acting and directing, Shakespeare study, house management, stage management, and video.

In the summer of 1984 the summer stock experience was expanded by the formation of a company of twenty-six young people ranging in age from fourteen to twenty. They took part in *The Music Man*, *The Birds*, *Hello, Dolly!*, *Frankenstein*, and *The Pirates of Penzance*. The more than fifty years that have passed since its founding have seen growth and expansion of one of the best known and most successful children's theatres in the United States.

PAN ASIAN REPERTORY THEATRE
Address: 47 Great Jones St., New York, NY 10012
Founding date: 1977

Pan Asian Repertory Theatre is not a children's theatre in the traditional sense; however, it takes plays regularly into the public schools of the city, holds special student matinees, and tours productions to schools in other East Coast cities. As the only professional Asian American theatre in the East, it brings a new dimension to the lives of Western children as well as performing a service for the growing Asian community.

In 1973 a small group of Chinese artists began to give public performances at La Mama, an Off-Broadway theatre in Greenwich Village. The company presented both old and new plays, offered staged readings of new scripts, dramatized Chinese fables, and taught workshops in Eastern theatre techniques, including Peking opera, Kabuki, Noh, Indian theatre movement, and stage combat. In 1977 the group was incorporated and the name changed from the Chinese Theatre Group to the Pan Asian Repertory Theatre. Today the company has an Equity contract and consists of a full-time staff of four, a core of forty performers, and from seventy-five to a hundred additional actors, designers, technicians, and management personnel. While the plays were originally presented under the aegis of Ellen Stewart, the well-known director of La Mama, they are now under the artistic direction of Tisa Chang, whose aim is to build a respected theatre for Asian American artists and to bring cultural enrichment to the community. This goal includes special attention to the interests of young people, with performances at prices they and their schools can afford.

PAPER BAG PLAYERS
Address: 50 Riverside Dr., New York, NY 10024
Founding date: 1958

The Paper Bag Players are a group of performers who captured the attention of New Yorkers in 1958 and who have continued to draw critical acclaim in the United States and abroad ever since. Their inventive manipulation of simple props and their use of uniform garments, consisting of leotards with bits of costume added when needed, revealed an originality in format as well as in content. "The Bags," as they are known, are also unique in that they celebrated their twenty-fifth birthday in 1983 under the same leadership with which they began. Judith Martin, founder, director, and performer, has held to a single format and style consisting of mime, improvised dialogue, and dance, with original music composed for the skits, which are developed by the company. Her group of four performers and a composer/accompanist has stayed together with relatively few changes over a period of twenty-five years, as contrasted with other children's theatre companies. Hailed by some critics as the best children's theatre in America, the Paper Bag Players have been fortunate in getting sufficient funding to enable them to create new works and accept no more engagements than they can handle without jeopardizing their artistic standards. The result has been a consistently high quality of work and a distinctive performing style.

Amusing titles like *Group Soup*, *I Won't Take a Bath*, *Mama Got a Job*, *Getting Older*, and *Everybody, Everybody* are characteristic of their inventive, humorous approach. Skits have little relationship to each other, yet there is often an underlying theme and a satiric thrust. The company develops its own programs, eschewing as artistic policy the scripted play. Paper Bag Players productions appeal to young children but have a sophistication that many adults find delightful.

THE PARTICIPATION PLAYERS
Address: Manchester College, North Manchester, IN 46962
Founding date: 1978

The name of this touring children's theatre company, The Participation Players, reflects the type of plays performed. Founded by Professor Scott K. Strode in 1978, it receives funding from the Indiana Arts Commission, the Honeywell Foundation, the Shaw-Burkhardt-Brenner Foundation, and the Indiana Educational, Cultural, and Fine Arts Foundation. Plays offered between 1978 and 1985 were *Hansel and Gretel* by

Moses Goldberg (a participation version of the play), and *The Story Tellers*, *The Crossroads*, *The Sleeping Beauty*, and *The Opposites Machine*, all by Brian Way. The touring performances are limited to the month of January because of the college January term, which enables the student actors to give their entire time to the project.

THE PATCHWORK PLAYERS
Address: 1512 Columbia College Dr., Columbia, SC 29203
Founding date: 1980

The Patchwork Players is an adult professional company in residence at Columbia College. Some of the performances are offered on campus as part of the Gingerbread Theatre Series for children, with as many as 300 performances a year given on area tours. Begun in 1970, the Gingerbread Theatre is comprised of after-school classes in creative drama, a summer arts program for children and high school students, and the public presentation of plays for young audiences. The close collaboration between The Patchwork Players, the Gingerbread Theatre, and the college theatre department has resulted in a carefully designed curriculum in child drama for undergraduates, who are thus enabled to work with and observe children of all ages.

Catherine Eaker, founder of the Gingerbread Theatre, directs the program; Genie Eaker-Martin, her daughter and a graduate of the college, coordinates activities and directs The Patchwork Players. Many of the scripts are written by Catherine Eaker for specific age levels. Among the titles are *The Lost Prince* (based on *The Prince and the Pauper*), *Tales from Shakespeare* (selected scenes and sonnets with music), *The Tom Sawyer Sketchbook*, *Around the World with Jennifer, Gee!*, and *White Feather, the Indian Princess. A Medley of Mime*, created by Genie Eaker-Martin, is a program for all ages. Plays and programs include both adaptations of traditional tales and original scripts on social issues. Teaching materials are sent to schools in advance of performance dates to help teachers extend or use the plays in connection with classwork. The Patchwork Players' P-Nut Butter and Jelly Series is described as a total fine arts curriculum for kindergarten and primary children. Plays for this age group are *Little Red Riding Hood*, *The Snow Queen*, *The Magic Clock of Cuckoo*, and *The Red Shoes*. Through this program young children are introduced to the elements of the living theatre.

While there are other children's theatre companies in the state, The Patchwork Players is the largest; it is unique in its integration with the college theatre program and the community. It is on the approved list of the South Carolina Commission on the Arts, and it was selected for the Stage South Community Fair for 1982. The company has been invited to perform twice at the International Children's Theatre Festival at Wolf Trap.

PEEL AND SMITH (formerly Producers' Association)
Address: 2095 Broadway, New York, NY 10023
Founding date: 1960s

Peel and Smith is a management agency that includes children's shows among its attractions. It no longer produces entertainment but is an agency for such children's productions as *Maid Marian (and Robin Hood, Too)*, which is always followed by a short demonstration of stage combat techniques used in the performance. A study guide based on the play is sent out to schools in advance; this enables teachers to incorporate the play into their curricula. Folk Music for Young Folk, Green Grass Cloggers, and The Opera Express are other types of performing groups handled by Peel and Smith. *Starblast* is a new intergalactic musical space journey, described in the brochure as "encouraging resourcefulness and creative thinking" in young people.

PEGASUS PLAYERS. *See* YOUNG PEOPLE'S THEATRE ON TOUR.

PENNSYLVANIA STATE UNIVERSITY, DEPARTMENT OF THEATRE AND FILM
Address: 103 Arts Building, Pennsylvania State University, University Park, PA 16802
Founding date: 1965

This theatre, which at the end of the seventies boasted ninety performances a season, was less active by the mid-eighties. It was described in the 1978 CTAA survey as educational, with adults taking major roles. It is on the list of approved child drama programs for Winifred Ward Scholars, with a current emphasis on drama in education.

THE PENNY BRIDGE PLAYERS
Address: 81 Columbia Heights, Brooklyn, NY 11201
Founding date: 1976

The Penny Bridge Players is a nonprofit, adult, professional company performing for young audiences in New York's five boroughs. Founded in 1976 and home-based in Brooklyn Heights, The Penny Bridge Players is dedicated to producing what it considers to be the best possible live theatre for children at the lowest possible prices. All productions are originals—new scripts and new music; some plays are original adaptations of children's classics and fairy tales. The Penny Bridge Players was founded on the belief that fine children's theatre has a unique place in the growth and development of young imaginations. Recent productions include such titles as *Snow White and the Seven Dwarfs*, *Beauty and the Beast*, *The Purple Dragon*, and *Peter and the Wolf*.

The theatre operates both summer and winter in a facility seating just under 300. The company also tours. It offers over 150 performances a year.

THE PEOPLE'S LIGHT AND THEATRE COMPANY
Address: 39 Conestoga Road, Malvern, PA 19355
Founding date: 1974

The People's Light and Theatre Company is a nonprofit professional theatre that aims to bring entertainment of high quality to audiences in a relaxed country atmosphere. Among its offerings are plays for adults and children, prison tours, and a year-round theatre school. The original building at Strode's Mill seated only seventy persons, which, given the growing popularity of the plays, necessitated additional space located at Yellow Springs. In 1980 the theatre moved to Malvern, twenty-three miles northwest of Philadelphia, a move that provided additional rehearsal and playing space and made further expansion possible, although the company remains dedicated to the original aims of its founders: classical and contemporary plays, a resident ensemble of theatre artists, and an outreach program.

The People's Light and Theatre Company has attracted national attention through tours to Ford's Theatre in Washington and the Annenberg Center in Philadelphia, among other sites. The outreach and education programs include an extensive tour to elementary, middle, and high schools throughout the Greater Delaware Valley; an annual prison tour; classes in acting, writing, and design for both adults and children; "Winterfest" (puppet shows, a storytelling festival, and musical programs); free seminars on main-stage productions; student matinees, and internships for eighteen college and university students interested in theatre administration and production. Children's plays tend to be nontraditional and experimental.

PEPPERMINT PALACE COMMUNITY THEATRE
Address: 545 Vallombrosa Avenue, Chico, CA 95926
Founding date: 1974

Peppermint Palace Community Theatre is a theatre without a home. It uses recreation rooms and senior and junior high school stages for its performances. The main purpose of the group is to provide children with theatre experience, both as performers and as spectators. It offers drama classes for children six through twelve years of age and uses performers from twelve years of age through young adult. Younger children are cast in plays as needed. The theatre is nonprofit and has a ten-member board of directors.

There is an effort to balance the season with traditional tales, Broadway musicals, some serious drama, and new scripts. Altogether, Peppermint Palace offers ten plays a year.

THE PEPPERMINT PLAYERS
Address: New York, NY
Founding date: 1960. Closed in 1965.

This company, established in 1960, was popular with New York audiences until 1965, when it closed. Unlike the majority of professional groups of the period, The Peppermint Players was a resident company located at the Off-Broadway Martinique Theatre in Manhattan. It did not tour but performed weekends throughout the fall, winter, and spring. It specialized in musicals, with the following original versions of traditional stories in the repertory: *Jack and the Beanstalk, Pinocchio, Sleeping Beauty, Ali Baba,* and *The Emperor's New Clothes.* By the end of the decade more than 80,000 scores had been distributed. The repertory without the music was filmed and distributed in the United States, Canada, and Europe by McGraw-Hill Publishing Company.

Carole Schwartz Hyatt and Paul Libin, the coproducers, disbanded the group after five successful years, convinced that television and the new forms of technology were more relevant to children's interests and growth. While this point of view was expressed by other producers and some educators, it was debatable, and many companies changed their scripts and performance styles. Schwartz and Libin, however, preferred to leave the field rather than make alterations in a form of theatre they had created and found effective.

THE PEPPERMINT STICK PLAYERS
Address: St. Mary-of-the-Woods College, St. Mary-of-the-Woods, IN 47876
Founding date: 1970

The Peppermint Stick Players of St. Mary-of-the-Woods were formed in 1970 under the joint sponsorship of Indiana State University and St. Mary-of-the-Woods College, Terre Haute, who joined hands to provide unique support for this theatre for young audiences. Additional support from the Indiana Arts Commission provided the impetus for the first full-year tour in the 1976–1977 academic year.

By 1978 they were reporting up to 140 performances annually, including those in the home theatre and on tour. The Peppermint Stick Players have performed in Cleveland, Ohio, for the Region III conference of The American Theatre Association (q.v.), in Indianapolis at the Children's Museum, and for community sponsors through the Indiana Arts Commission.

Both traditional titles and new plays have been in their repertoire from the beginning. Among the latter, produced in 1978, was *Indiana Folktales*, a program with music and dance, based on folk material native to the state. The Peppermint Stick Players perform in the round, either outdoors or in all-purpose rooms, gyms, and libraries.

PERCIVAL BORDE AND COMPANY
Address: New York, NY
Founding date: 1960s. Closed in 1979.

An interest in racial and ethnic customs during the sixties brought a new kind of program to children's theatre different in form and content, often combining several arts in exciting ways. One of these was Percival Borde's *Drums of the Caribbean*, a dance/drama program that appealed to audiences of all ages, including even the youngest children. Drums, dance, song, and storytelling expressed the spirit of the island peoples. Colorful costumes and native drummers set Borde's programs apart, and they were sought for school assemblies as well as evening performances.

Borde's distinguished background on the professional stage and in U.S. universities brought a new dimension to children's theatre, further closing the gap between theatre and education in performances relevant to the times and superb in showmanship. African dance and plays based on indigenous subject matter followed. Borde's sudden death in 1979 brought the company to an abrupt end. It never reformed, but it has had a lasting influence through its stimulation of interest in ethnic material and in the dance/drama form as exciting theatre for young audiences.

PERFORMING ARTS FOUNDATION (PAF)
Address: Huntington, Long Island, NY
Founding date: 1966. Closed in 1981.

The Performing Arts Foundation was a unique resource for the educational and cultural communities of Long Island from the sixties until the early eighties. This large and successful enterprise had several components. A well-prepared staff offered courses designed to meet the needs of classroom, drama, and special education teachers. After-school and Saturday classes for children were offered in addition to a full season of plays for elementary and junior and senior high school audiences. Fully mounted productions were given on the PAF/McDonald proscenium stage, and the professional PAF touring troupe took participatory plays into the schools. Teacher guides were carefully prepared for curriculum related programs. PAF, in cooperation with Central Midwestern Regional Educational Laboratory (CEMREL), a nonprofit organization, was one of eleven aesthetic education learning centers in the nation.

The company was interested in trying out new scripts and in producing foreign plays as well as favorite and known titles. For nearly ten years PAF was an outstanding community/educational resource with desirable facilities, serving an area just far enough from Broadway and Off-Broadway to benefit from "twofers," student tickets and Theatre Development Fund (TDF) vouchers. The closing of the Performing Arts Foundation only a decade after its founding was as unexpected as it was unfortunate.

PERFORMING ARTS REPERTORY THEATRE (PART). *See* THE-ATREWORKS/USA.

PERIWINKLE PRODUCTIONS, INC.
Address: 19 Clinton Ave., Monticello, NY 12701
Founding date: 1963

This company, based in Monticello, is considered one of the New York producing companies. Since its founding in the early 1960s it has toured extensively throughout the East and Middle West, presenting plays and programs with an educational thrust. Sunna Rasch, the founder and producer, had a background in elementary education as well as in theatre, and her interest has always been children's theatre that related to or enriched the curriculum. While not a theatre in education company, it nevertheless preceded in philosophy and practice what many of the children's theatre companies have turned to in recent years. Study guides are an important part of every school presentation, with teacher and student workshops available either before or after the program. Although poetry was the first material used by Periwinkle, history, the problem of drugs, peer relationships, and folk and fairy tales have all been included among its later offerings. For its Bicentennial production, Periwinkle developed a musical, using as its narrative the history of the United States told through popular and patriotic music of each period. This production, *America Yes!*, has remained a favorite in its repertoire.

Periwinkle has received awards from The American Theatre Association (q.v.) and The Children's Theatre Association of America (q.v.), and it is frequently invited for return engagements to schools in which it has previously performed and led workshops. Its stated goals are to motivate self-expression, to stimulate intellectual curiosity, and to bridge the gap between entertainment and education. To these ends fresh new material is always used by the professional actors, who aim to inspire children to explore their own worlds after the final curtain of the play has gone down. A board of directors that includes educators, psychologists, and community theatre leaders offers guidance to the group, which is under the direction of its founder and artistic director, Sunna Rasch.

PHANTASY COMPANY
Address: P.O. Box 28247, San Jose, CA 95159
Founding date: 1975
See San Jose Repertory Phantasy Company.

PHILADELPHIA THEATRE CARAVAN
Address: Annenberg Center, 3680 Walnut Street, Philadelphia, PA
19104
Founding date: 1985
Although Philadelphia Theatre Caravan was founded in 1985, it qualifies for inclusion here because the founding date represents a merger of the Germantown Theatre Guild and the University of Pennsylvania's Annenberg Center. The emphasis of the Caravan is on programming for youth, with a touring schedule throughout the metropolitan area and to a variety of schools, libraries, and community centers in several adjoining states. Productions are also offered in the Germantown Theatre Guild's Little Theatre. The company is professional and is dedicated to developing theatre that excites the imagination and deals with concerns of young people today. Education and the performing arts are held as equal emphases in selecting program material and preparing stage presentations. The company commissions new works for children as well as bringing traditional plays and adaptations of children's classics to the stage.

An example of the latter is *The Nightingale* by Hans Christian Andersen. New works included *Sojourner*, a play based on the life of the abolitionist and advocate of women's rights, Sojourner Truth; *The Apple Tree*, a play with music, based on Mark Twain's story of creation; and *Lifeforms*, a collection of mime pieces for puppets that deals with the environment and the interdependency of life on this planet. The directors of the Annenberg Center plan to develop new theatre techniques and ways of reaching young audiences with high quality as a stated goal.

For the earlier history of this group, *see* The Almost Free Theatre of the Germantown Theatre Guild.

PHILADELPHIA YOUTH THEATRE (PYT)
Address: Society Hill Playhouse, 507 S. 8th St., Philadelphia, PA 19147
Founding date: 1971
The Society Hill Playhouse opened in 1960 as part of the regional theatre movement in the United States. The Philadelphia Youth Theatre, however, was not founded until the summer of 1971, but it has since grown in size and scope. Since its inception it has been a production oriented training program for teenagers, who present plays for both young adults and children. Participants cross all social, economic, and

racial barriers in a common interest: theatre. In 1974 the Philadelphia Youth Theatre became part of the Alternative Schools Network, Philadelphia School District. PYT operates within the Society Hill Playhouse, offering training in all aspects of theatre throughout the school year. Participating students receive academic credit toward high school graduation.

The purpose of the Philadelphia Youth Theatre has remained unchanged since its founding: to place emphasis on practical experience through which students may develop their talents, strengthen team work, learn respect for the disciplines of the theatre, and achieve a high standard of performance. Thousands of young people ranging in age from five to nineteen are reached by the Philadelphia Youth Theatre in its performance series each year. Not a children's theatre in the traditional sense, it is considered unique in its organization and relationship to the school system, while at the same time offering appropriate theatre to citywide audiences on the elementary and secondary school level.

THE PHOENIX LITTLE THEATRE
Address: 25 East Coronado Rd., Phoenix, AZ 85004
Founding date: 1981

The founding date of the children's wing of The Phoenix Little Theatre is difficult to determine because of the structural changes that have taken place since the opening of the theatre in 1920. From that date on there have been several children's wings, some of which produced plays on an irregular basis, though others have produced them regularly. In the late 1960s The Phoenix Children's Theatre became part of The Phoenix Little Theatre and, along with The Phoenix Musical Theatre, shared facilities at 25 E. Coronado Road. This merger apparently did not work out, and the two decided to become separate entities.

Shortly after the separation another wing was created, underwritten with Comprehensive Employment and Training Act (CETA) funds. It produced six shows a season for three years. In January 1981 a new wing for the children's productions at the Phoenix was formed, using adult actors. This was named The Cookie Company, and it produces four shows a year. Classic and new works are included in the schedule, and each year ends with a creative writing contest for local children. Winners have their works adapted for the stage by the company for its final production. Audience participation is encouraged, and titles of plays include familiar folk and fairy tales. *The Emperor's New Clothes*, *Peter and the Wolf*, and *The Reluctant Dragon* are typical of a season, with the original script as the fourth attraction.

PICCOLI JUNIOR THEATRE GUILD
Address: 1932 Second Ave., Seattle, WA 98101
Founding date: 1968

Piccoli Junior Theatre Guild has put on 114 productions in a little over fifteen years. It is a professional non-Equity company administered by a board of directors. It specializes in original plays and musicals for children aged four to seven. Piccoli also has a touring company, which plays in a number of states including Alaska.

In 1978 it was offering 186 performances a season in only one location. In 1985 it opened in two new locations in the Seattle area.

PICK-A-PACK PLAYERS
Address: Milwaukee, WI
Founding date: 1960. Closed in 1975.

The Pick-a-Pack Players began operation in 1960 under the auspices of the Milwaukee Repertory Theatre. There was little live theatre in the area at the time and no professional companies performing on a regular basis for children. The program was successful, and by the end of the first ten years director Edith Mahler reported a repertory of fourteen children's classics. Adult actors performed in most productions, though frequently children in the creative drama classes were cast in children's parts.

Today there are several other children's theatre groups in the Milwaukee area. Pick-a-Pack, by introducing activities, may be credited with having developed an audience for live theatre as an art form and for drama as a creative experience in the performing arts.

PICKLE FAMILY CIRCUS
Address: 400 Missouri St., San Francisco, CA 94107
Founding date: 1974

Since its founding in 1974 the Pickles have created a joyous family show based on circus and vaudeville traditions. The twenty-member touring company performs over 200 shows each year throughout the western states. The circus has developed a network of over fifty community-based sponsors who present the shows as fund-raisers for their organizations. The troupe also performed in England in 1981.

The idea of the Pickle Family Circus was conceived by Larry Pisoni (artistic director, performer, a.k.a. Lorenzo Pickle), grandson of a life-long vaudevillian and himself a seasoned performer of the streets, parks, fairs, and stage. In 1974, while working with the San Francisco Mime Troupe (q.v.), Larry joined forces with Peggy Snider (designer, technical director, performer) and founded the Pickle Family Circus. In 1975, with $4,000 borrowed for equipment and some of the first CETA arts funding in the country, the twenty-member group made its debut in San Francisco.

The Pickle Family Circus is a traditional one-ring variety show of tumblers, aerialists, jugglers, clowns, acrobats, and musicians. The variety show concept, one act after another, is a fast-paced ninety-minute presentation that combines traditional skills with elements of dance, drama, music, comedy, and character development.

THE PITTSBURGH PLAYHOUSE JUNIOR CHILDREN'S THEATRE

Address: 222 Craft Ave., Pittsburgh, PA 15213
Founding date: 1948

The Pittsburgh Playhouse has been involved in theatre for young audiences for thirty-six years. A branch of the well-known and established community theatre, it has been fortunate in having permanent facilities and other conveniences such as ample public parking sites and a box office. Subscription tickets are available as well as tickets for individual performances. In the 1984–1985 season five productions were announced; these included *The Frog Princess and the Witch*, *The Christmas Carol*, *The Brave Little Tailor*, *Hansel and Gretel*, and *The Emperor's Nightingale*. Material tends to be selected from familiar folk and fairy tales, staged traditionally.

In addition to the regularly scheduled performances at the playhouse, special grade school field trips may be arranged on specified dates. Performers are adult, and plays are designed to appeal to children in the elementary schools.

THE PIXIE JUDY TROUPE

Address: 8 E. 64 St., New York, NY 10021
Founding date: 1965

Pixie Judy, a professional touring company, was formed by Judith Ann Abrams in 1965 as an outgrowth of her interest in theatre for children. Abrams had previously worked on television and had produced and directed *The Magic Christmas Gift* for RKO General. Her *Wonderful World of Children* was seen by over 50,000 youngsters; it originated at the Kennedy Institute for Retarded Children. The Kennedy family's interest in her led to special performances for 18,000 mentally retarded children and the production of a special two-week benefit for the Willowbrook State School. She was also committed to working for inner city children who had never seen live theatre. This effort was furthered through cooperation with the Mayor's Office of Cultural Affairs in New York.

Abrams produced three shows for national television, one of which won the Best Programming Award of the Year, as well as three original cast albums for the Rodgers and Hammerstein Music Library. Like many other companies of the period, Pixie Judy shows featured musicals for children. Its *Littlest Circus* was performed at the White House in 1977 as a Christmas holiday program for the Carters.

THE PLAY GROUP
Address: Knoxville, TN 37916
Founding date:1970

The Play Group, a professional theatre company, employs, in addition to actors, a writer-in-residence, an artistic director, and a managing director. It performs a variety of plays for a variety of audiences: children, adults, the handicapped, and the economically disadvantaged. A major concern has been the development of new theatre that is accessible to local audiences and at the same time on the frontier of the theatre currently being produced in America. The Play Group repertory ranges from original children's plays to original plays for adults, from improvisational programs to adaptations of the work of well-known authors. *Tell Me a Story* was developed in the late seventies during a "Reading Is Fundamental" program. The company urges teachers to prepare their students for shows by reading stories and books from the school library and by creative writing. During the performance the children may tell their favorite stories to a member of The Play Group, who then relates it to the actors, who in turn improvise it for the audience.

The Play Group offers workshops in improvisation, storytelling, and writing for both students and teachers. Company members are also available for preplanning sessions and follow-up periods with the class. Touring has been primarily in the southeastern United States. Sponsorship has included the Educational Program of the National Endowment for the Arts.

THE PLAYERS' THEATRE OF NEW HAMPSHIRE
Address: Unknown; reported to be in Europe.
Founding date: 1967

The Players' Theatre differed from other companies performing for children in its choice and handling of classic plays that were rarely performed. Organized in 1967, within three years of its founding it had produced such titles as *The Devil and Daniel Webster*, *The Pranks of Scapin*, *The Story of a Soldier*, *The Headless Horseman*, and its own dramatization of Plato's law dialogue, *The Crito*. In fact, most of the scripts were original. Under the direction of Harvey Grossman, the company toured New England extensively, going to schools, colleges, and community centers. It received support from the New Hampshire Commission on the Arts and two Title III programs. The New England Theatre Conference presented it with an Achievement Award for pioneering work and high artistic standards. Mime, mask-playing, song, and dance were often aspects of imaginative nontraditional productions. The company has performed throughout Europe and is reported to have relocated in Belgium. The former agent for the company, Frances Schram, had no current address for The Players' Theatre but believes it may still be in existence.

PLAYMAKERS OF BATON ROUGE, INC.
Address: P.O. Box 4286, Baton Rouge, LA 70821
Founding date: 1982

While Playmakers does not meet the criterion of five years in operation, its record of 108 performances a year and sponsorship by the East Baton Rouge Parish School Board, the Louisiana Arts Council, and the National Endowment for the Arts give evidence of stability and belief in its future. Playmakers is a nonprofit professional adult company that performs for young audiences, tours to schools, organizes an annual summer neighborhood tour, issues a newsletter, and offers a subscription season of four programs, eight productions, and creative drama classes. Plays include both the traditional (*The Legend of Sleepy Hollow* and *The Tales of Br'er Rabbit*) and the avant garde (*The Tingalary Bird* and *Professor Filarsky's Miraculous Invention*). In 1985 the company listed 80 personnel, 170 volunteers, and total number of persons reached as just under 30,000.

PLAYMAKERS REPERTORY THEATRE
Address: Westchester County, NY
Founding date: 1969

In the seventies, the Playmakers Repertory Theatre of Westchester performed widely in Putnam and Rockland counties and in New York City. Players performed on any size stage or open area in an effort to make theatre come alive for children, rather than treating it as a formal and distanced art. Their programs were based on familiar themes; original songs, scripts, costumes, and sets were developed by the company. Active audience participation was encouraged so that each child might contribute to the production. The dynamics of cast-audience interaction provided children with an entertaining and stimulating experience.

Titles of plays were familiar but were not among the most frequently produced. They were, for example, *Indian Summer*, which celebrated the Bicentennial year with American Indian legends, music, and dance; *Bag O'Tales*, an original adaptation of the stories "Henny Penny," "The Golden Goose," and "Which Witch Is Which"; *Aesop's Fables*; and *Oft Told Tales*. Less well known than most of the East Coast groups, Playmakers received praise from educators and administrators of schools in which they performed. By 1980 there was no record of continuing activity.

PLEXUS MIME THEATRE
Address: 7904 Holstein St., #1, Takoma Park, MD 20952
Founding date: 1979

Plexus Mime Theatre offers a program described in its brochure as a "new form created by a network of interlacing parts. . . . Plexus reflects the ensemble's performance style, evolved through the meeting of popular classical and modern theatrical concepts." Its techniques are drawn from the commedia dell'arte, traditional mime, circus performance, and contemporary theatre. Masks are used in some of the acts, which otherwise have minimal technical requirements.

The three performers bring training in dance, music, mime, circus skills, and extensive professional experience to their work. They offer workshops in conjunction with performances to introduce children to the skills they have just seen on the stage. Plexus is appropriate for children of all ages and may also be considered family entertainment. Making use of the popular vignette format for the opening, titles include "Rollercoaster," "Only One Chair," and "Grumps," all suggestive of the contents or theme. The second part of the show is an extended skit that generally includes some audience participation. Programs as well as workshops are designed for specific age levels (K–6 and 7–12). Teacher preparation materials covering mime, clowning, and mask-making are sent to schools in advance.

PONCHO THEATRE
Address: Seattle Department of Parks and Recreation, 100 Dexter Avenue North, Seattle, WA 98109
Founding date: 1975
See Seattle Children's Theatre.

POORMEN'S RICHES. *See* K.I.D.S. REPERTORY THEATRE.

THE PORTLAND CHILDREN'S TRAILER THEATRE
Address: Portland, ME
Founding date: 1944. Closed.

A joint project of the Parks and Recreation Department of Portland and the Portland Children's Theatre, this trailer theatre was established in Portland, Maine, in 1944. With plans laid during the preceding year, its itinerary was carefully charted when it began traveling in the summer of 1944. Tuesday and Friday performances in the greater Portland area constituted the first season's engagements. The small stage was designed to rest on the floor of the trailer, opening into a platform with an apron in front and dressing rooms on the side. By 1948 a crew of fifteen, including actors, traveled throughout Portland, presenting performances of two plays to 20,000 children in playgrounds, housing projects, and parks. The trailer theatre was one of the features of the Children's Theatre Conference with its production in Central Park in New York City in 1949. Like many projects funded by recreation departments to meet current needs, the trailer theatre did not continue beyond the fifties.

THE PORTMANTEAU THEATRE
Address: New York, NY
Founding date: 1915. Closed by the 1920s.

The unique character of this theatre company was due to the simplicity of its set designs and its use of a portable stage, complete with lights and scenery, packed in ten lightweight boxes and carried as luggage by the ten players. This lent itself to a production which could be made ready in two hours' time and taken apart in less. Although the company was not organized primarily as a children's theatre, its repertoire included plays suitable for children written with an emphasis on fantasy rather than realistic adult drama. The philosophy of the company was to encourage young people to write their own plays and design and build their own scenery within the framework of the tiny portmanteau stage.

The founder, Stuart Walker, is known today for a number of one-act plays that are still produced and considered among the best short plays written for children. *Six Who Pass While the Lentils Boil* is probably the best known of his works. While The Portmanteau Theatre did not last long, it attracted attention in the New York area at the time and was a forerunner of the modern self-sufficient touring company with an educational objective and high standards regarding original scripts.

PRACTICAL CATS THEATRE COMPANY
Address: Anne Rosenthal/Ian Kramer, Soho Booking, 625 Broadway, 8th floor, New York, NY 10012
Founding date: 1980

Alice Eve Cohen is the performer and composer of children's programs offered under the name of Practical Cats Theatre Company. Her programs are varied in content but similar in their use of storytelling, acting, movement, puppets, music, and masks. A solo artist, she presents folktales and stories, many of which are unfamiliar to American children. She also creates pieces on contemporary social issues, examples of which are *The Owl Was the Baker's Daughter*, a piece on alienation; and *Without Heroes*, a play dealing with incest. Her work has been acclaimed by teachers, social workers, and administrators for its originality, artistry, and universality. Cohen has performed in the United States and abroad, on television and on radio, and has been a teaching artist on the faculty of the Lincoln Center Institute in New York City. The integration of many art forms in a single performance distinguishes her work from that of other solo performers.

PRAIRIE THEATRE FOR YOUNG PEOPLE. *See* FARGO MOORHEAD COMMUNITY THEATRE.

PRINCE STREET PLAYERS, LTD.
Address: 5200 Woodward Ave., Detroit, MI 48202
Founding date: 1965
In the mid-sixties New York audiences saw a brand new type of children's theatre in the Prince Street Players. Performing to a hard rock beat in mini-skirted costumes, Prince Street took traditional fairy tales and turned them into twentieth-century musicals reminiscent of the Broadway stage. Controversial though they were at the time, the performers had vitality and technical skill. In the late seventies they left New York for Detroit, which has been their home base since then. The Prince Street Players perform in the Detroit area and on tour. They are an example of a trend toward "camp" that characterizes some of the smaller professional touring companies.

Performers are professional adults whose primary objective is entertainment; to this end they use colorful costumes and employ elaborate, spectacular stage effects.

PRODUCERS' ASSOCIATION. *See* PEEL AND SMITH.

PROGRAMS FOR CHILDREN AND YOUTH
Address: AAE/Kennedy Center, Washington, DC 20566
Founding date: 1976
See The John F. Kennedy Center Programs for Children and Youth.

PROJECT DISCOVERY, TRINITY SQUARE REPERTORY COMPANY
Address: 201 Washington St., Providence, RI 02908
Founding date: 1966
Trinity Square Repertory Company launched its program for school children in 1966 after a two-year trial period. The original goals were to provide live theatre for secondary school students and to build an adult audience for the future. The success of the venture led to an expansion that included elementary school children as well. In addition to performances in Providence, the company carries on an extensive touring program throughout the state and in Massachusetts, Connecti-

cut, and as far away as Albany, New York. Special performances with a signer are given at the Rhode Island School for the Deaf.

During the first three years the program was funded by the United States Office of Education and the National Endowment for the Arts, and performances were given in the auditorium of the Rhode Island School of Design. Teachers and principals contributed names of plays they hoped the company would consider for production. In the 1969–1970 season, Trinity Rep had to assume responsibility for funding of the project. Since then grants have been obtained from the Rhode Island Council on the Arts and from the Ford, Mellon, and Rockefeller foundations, and more recently from the Rhode Island General Assembly Services to the Schools. Before each play portfolios of educational materials are sent to the schools; following selected performances, discussions with actors are held. Project Discovery performances are scheduled during regular school hours, whether given in school or in the theatre. Plays are classics and range from Shakespeare and Molière to modern American dramas.

PROJECT IMPACT
Address: 41 E. Center St., Midland Park, NJ 07432
Founding date: 1966

Project IMPACT is one of the few survivors of the original Title III funding in 1965. It is a nonprofit sponsoring organization serving both elementary and secondary school children in New Jersey. Printed materials state goals as follows:

1. To involve the student in the creative arts process.
2. To illuminate the need for and value of creating the proper environment for students to directly experience the world of the practicing professional artist—the discipline, the art form, and, particularly, the creative processes.
3. To utilize the arts as relevant and valuable tools for enrichment in all areas of study, expanding a child's perception, creativity, concentration, and confidence through interest and knowledge in the arts.
4. To instill and develop for the future the life-enhancing joy that continued experience of all the arts provides.

In the selection of programs, entertainment and substantive content are requirements. Since 1966 Project IMPACT has been providing subscription series of professional performing arts for young people. It also offers workshops in both the performing and visual arts to community organizations and educational institutions in the state. Teacher training workshops are an added feature, and in recent years it has expanded its services to include entertainment for populations with special needs. In 1984 its school population outreach was approximately 150,000 annually.

As a coordinating service for 150 sponsoring agents in New Jersey, Project IMPACT also raises funds in order to subsidize a portion of the cost for these sponsors. Where need is demonstrated, free performances can be arranged. The IMPACT series consists of appearances by three different companies annually, each of which is engaged for 150 performances. In addition to school audiences from K–12, the program serves community centers and general family audiences. Among recent productions have been scenes from the Greeks to Samuel Beckett, coproduced with the McCarter Theatre at Princeton; the *Dance Theatre of India*, coproduced with Carolyn Kaye; *Opera Plus*, coproduced with Karen Klauss; *Mime's Eye View* by Tony Montanaro; *Drum Song*, a musical directed by David Moss; and the Little Theatre of the Deaf (q.v.).

Paid internships, in-service training for teachers and recreation leaders, residencies in schools, theatre in education, and programs designed for children with special needs are among its current educational services. Lynne Kramer, the executive director, was active in The Children's Theatre Association of America (q.v.).

PROJECT INTERACT/ZACHARY SCOTT THEATRE
Address: P.O. Box 244, Austin, TX 78767
Founding date: 1976

Project InterAct at the Zachary Scott Theatre Center is committed to bringing high quality theatre to the children of Texas. Its choice of material is an attempt to present a cross section of theatrical content and style and to reach an age range from four to eighteen. Traditional titles like *Jack and the Beanstalk* and *A Christmas Carol* appear on a season's schedule along with some of the newest and most interesting modern scripts. Among this latter group have been *Step on a Crack, I Didn't Know That!*, *The Boy Who Talked to Whales*, *Dandelion* (a Paper Bag Players (q.v.) script), *Tales That Ought to Be True*, and *The Odyssey*.

The company is available for touring engagements during certain months of the year. It offers in-house workshops in creative drama, improvisation, and acting for both children and young adults. The Zachary Scott Theatre has the following facilities: a proscenium stage, a thrust stage, and an arena stage, on which Project InterAct offers five attractions a season.

THE PUERTO RICAN TRAVELING THEATRE
Address: 141 W. 94 St., New York, NY 10025
Founding date: 1967

Although The Puerto Rican Traveling Theatre is not a children's theatre per se, it is included here because it offers fare for the family and some plays are specifically directed to children. Most performances are given in Spanish, though some of the children's plays are also given in English. The annual summer tours visit parks in the New York metropolitan area. Actors perform fantasies and folktales on a mobile platform stage with taped musical accompaniment.

Founded in the late sixties, The Puerto Rican Traveling Theatre describes itself as the oldest bilingual professional theatre in the country. It has aimed to present the best in Hispanic dramatic literature from Puerto Rico, Latin America, and the United States. The company has produced world premieres of plays by Pedro Pietri and Eduardo Gallado. Additionally, it has presented English translations of contemporary classics including Puerto Rican playwright Rene Marques' *The Oxcart*. In 1981 the company toured over fifteen cities throughout Spain: Seville, Madrid, Huelva, Palma de Mallorca, and the Canary Islands. It has also received invitations to perform at the Festival de Manizales in Colombia and the Festival Cervantino in Mexico City.

Two hundred-fifty students age fourteen and up receive free training at The Puerto Rican Traveling Theatre. They come from all parts of the New York metropolitan area for classes in acting (Spanish and English), dance, body movement, music, and improvisation as well as workshops on job interviews and auditions. The teachers are both performers and educators. There is also a playrights' unit that gives beginning and advanced writers an opportunity to receive criticism, evaluation, and staged readings of their work. It is the only Hispanic workshop devoted to the development of new playwrights at the present time. The overall commitment of the company is to the economically disadvantaged Hispanic population, both youth and adult.

PUMPERNICKEL PLAYERS
Address: New York, NY
Founding date: early 1960s. Closed by 1980.

The Pumpernickel Players, founded in the sixties, were familiar to New York children's audiences for nearly twenty years. With a preference for traditional material, they presented such well-known favorites as *Peter and the Wolf*, *Hansel and Gretel*, *The Sorcerer's Apprentice*, and *The Pied Piper of Hamlin*. Productions were not traditional, however, for the company utilized masks and multimedia design, stereophonic sound, black light, and projected images in order to provide spectacular stage effects and a variety of listening experiences.

Pumpernickel Players performed throughout the New York area, at schools, Manhattan's Town Hall, the Tappan Zee Playhouse, the Henry Street Playhouse, and the 92nd Street "Y." They also performed at Harvard and in various locations in Europe in the summer of 1973. Sponsors often saw them in the annual PACT Spring Previews.

PUSHCART PLAYERS
Address: 197 Bloomfield Ave., Verona, NJ 07044
Founding date: 1974

Pushcart Players is a company of professional actors, musicians, writers, and technicians dedicated to bringing the best of theatre to young audiences. It is a traveling troupe that visits schools, hospitals, libraries, and museums throughout New Jersey, New York, Pennsylvania, Delaware, Maryland, Connecticut, and as far south as West Virginia and South Carolina. Its credits include performances at New York's Lincoln Center for the Performing Arts, Citicorp Center, South Street Seaport Museum, and the New York World Trade Center. It has presented two prime time television specials for which it drew an Emmy nomination.

A typical Pushcart production is an original musical comedy filled with song, dance, and fun. An ingenious use of costumes, props, and settings makes performing possible in any space. Scripts are based on the works of great writers such as Leo Tolstoy, Mark Twain, Shalom Aleichem, Katherine Mansfield, and O. Henry. In order to meet its stated objective, the introduction of theatre as an art form to young audiences, Pushcart is willing to spend an hour with the audience prior to a scheduled performance, during which questions may be asked of the cast. Discussions following the performance are also available, if desired. "Color, vitality, catchy tunes" are words used to describe the group. In addition to the sessions mentioned, Pushcart is also available for workshops and residencies.

Q

QUIET RIOT

Address: VNI, 360 Central Park West, #16G, New York, NY 10025
Founding date: 1979

Quiet Riot is a touring mime team that has gained a reputation for comedy theatre. It belongs to the roster of Young Audiences of Eastern Pennsylvania, under whose auspices it has given hundreds of programs throughout the country. Programs range from large auditorium performances to small group work with handicapped children. Creativity and humor are stressed in sketches that include mime, dance, improvisation, live music, and storytelling. The team of two artists offers entertainment for both elementary school and high school students. Adolescent problems and experiences are incorporated under the title *Made in America*; children's programs are geared to all grades from kindergarten through junior high.

The team has appeared on television and acted in and choreographed the award-winning film *Balloon People*. Quiet Riot is available for workshops for children and offers adult classes in mime theatre for teachers, parents, and professional actors.

R

THE RAINBOW COMPANY CHILDREN'S THEATRE
Address: 821 Las Vegas Boulevard North, Las Vegas, NV 89101
Founding date: 1976

The Rainbow Company of Las Vegas is different in thrust, organization, and services from the majority of children's theatres. It has received national acclaim for the quality of its work with handicapped youngsters; in 1982 it was selected for the fourth consecutive year by the National Committee "Arts for the Handicapped" to be a model site. The Rainbow Company brochure states that this designation has been given to only ten sites in the country and is awarded for "exemplary programming in the arts by, with and for the handicapped." Classes in creative drama, mime, technical theatre, makeup, costume, and playwriting are held for children from preschool through high school.

The primary goal of The Rainbow Company has always been the concentrated and conscientious development of young audiences, accomplished through the production of theatrical presentations of high professional quality and through classes in the theatre arts. Plays are toured to schools embracing the widest variety of socioeconomic backgrounds. For K–3, shows tend to be participatory. For the upper grades, more formal presentations are given. Workshops for teachers are available.

RALEIGH CHILDREN'S THEATRE
Address: Raleigh, NC
Founding date: 1948

Established in 1948, the Raleigh Children's Theatre was a community-supported project. On the board were representatives from the Junior League, the Junior Women's Club, the Raleigh Little Theatre (an adult dramatic society), The Girl Scouts, the Parent-Teacher Association, the school system, the city library, and the recreation department, each furnishing a service. Elementary school children and high school students performed in three productions a year, as well as in the summer theatre during the vacation months.

See also Theatre in The Park.

REPERTORY THEATRE COMPANY OF ST. LOUIS. *See* THE IMAGINARY THEATRE COMPANY.

RHODE ISLAND COLLEGE THEATRE FOR CHILDREN
Address: Providence, RI 02908
Founding date: 1969

Rhode Island College Theatre for Children was founded by Raymond Picozzi with the primary objective of presenting high quality, exciting theatre to the children and youth of southeastern New England. Each academic year one major production is mounted in the Little Theatre (capacity 80–150) for a run of two performances a day for up to two weeks. Children are bussed in to see the production. The thrust of the theatre is to offer a variety of presentations fully mounted so that children and youth can begin to appreciate and develop an aesthetic philosophy. Study guides and program notes are sent two weeks before the show to groups that have booked the production.

There is an effort to find new scripts, innovative ideas, and/or adaptations of (sometimes controversial) books, poems, and stories. Each summer there is a children's season in conjunction with the regular Summerfest. Guest directors and playwrights are often invited during this period.

The mode of presentation varies with the script. The Little Theatre can be used in a variety of ways (thrust stage, arena stage, complete environmental stage, as well as ordinary proscenium). Sometimes in the summer two plays are presented in repertory. In 1984–1985 a touring segment was added. In addition, Rhode Island College has also established a segment called Family Theatre. This allows for more ambitious plays such as Rodgers and Hammerstein's *Cinderella.* Plays written by college students and directed by student actors are also a part of the program. Sometimes these are for children.

RITES AND REASON
Address: Box 1148, Brown University, Providence, RI 02912
Founding date: 1970

George Bass, a native of Tennessee, is a poet, lyricist, director, and playwright. He brought a missionary zeal to his task of getting Rites and Reason off the ground.

Rites and Reason is a company that uses as many creative arts as possible—dance, poetry, music, lights, and prose. It is a company of multitalented youth. Their works include adaptations of Afro-American folktales told through drama, dance, and music. Rites and Reason has won acclaim from the American College Theatre Festival for the best original play from the New England region; Lola Hatcher, a member of the company, also won an award as best performer. It is not currently producing children's plays, although it is still in existence.

ROADSIDE THEATRE
Address: Box 743, Whitesburg, KY 41858
Founding date: 1975

Roadside Theatre was developed in Appalshop, a 1969 federally funded workshop in photography, film, books, and magazines describing life in Appalachia. The purpose of Appalshop was to train local people for work in the media. As there were few job opportunities in the area, however, the project was not feasible and was discontinued. In 1972 the administrators of Appalshop appealed to the National Endowment for the Arts and private foundations for grants to launch a community radio station. It was at this time that Don Baker, a former Washington arts counselor, returned to his home in Virginia across the border from Whitesburg. Seeing the rich resources of the region, Baker decided to add theatre to the project. He made use of the folktales told by the mountain people and the pictures and filmstrips that had already been made in Appalshop, converting them into a theatrical format that would appeal to local audiences.

The result of Baker's work was a unique style of presentation. Roadside's first show, *Mountain Tales*, presented in the summer of 1974, was a combination of storytelling with music, given out of doors for 500 men, women, and children in the area. The second show a year later marked the formal founding of the theatre. That production, *Red Fox/Second Hangin'*, departed from fantasy and dealt with local history. Succeeding shows for family and children's audiences have made use of the material that abounds in the region. The common thread that runs through all of Roadside's productions is the search for, and pride in, cultural identity. Roadside is one of the companies that has benefitted from the National Endowment's new category, Ongoing Ensembles.

While not strictly speaking a children's theatre, Roadside for the past ten years has offered plays for school children with residencies in playwriting, storytelling, and performance. The company tours nationally, although the majority of performances are given in the southern and mid-Atlantic states.

ROD RODGERS DANCE COMPANY
Address: 62 E. 4th St., New York, NY 10003
Founding date: 1972

The Rod Rodgers Dance Company has been in existence since 1968, although it was not legally incorporated until 1972. The company is known for its interracial ensemble and its percussion dance plays, in which the dancers play instruments, "creating their own musical environment," as they describe their entrance on stage. Rodgers, the founder and artistic director, has received wide acclaim for his *Poets and Peacemakers*, a social piece that combines several different art forms. Other titles of works by this company are *Langston Lives!*, featuring the poetry of Langston Hughes; *Against Great Odds*, inspired by the struggle of black artists and scientists in America; and *The Legacy*, reflecting the courage of Martin Luther King, Jr., and Mahatma Gandhi.

While Rod Rodgers Dance Company is not a children's theatre in the narrow sense, it qualifies in the broad sense for its equally balanced components of entertainment and education for youth. Indeed, it has been featured on several showcases of children's entertainment. The company tours extensively throughout the United States in community centers, in schools, and on university campuses. In 1979 it was selected by the United States International Communications Agency for a six-week goodwill tour to Senegal, Nigeria, Kenya, Zambia, Syria, and Portugal.

ROUND HOUSE THEATRE
Address: Montgomery County Government, Department of Recreation, 12210 Bushey Drive, Silver Spring, MD 20902
Founding date: 1970

The Round House Theatre serves both children and adults. In a 1984–1985 brochure, it stated its purpose for the children's component as follows: "to provide students and faculty with an opportunity to experience the excitement and power of live theatre. Through the medium of performance, workshops and residencies, the program's goal is to reinforce the use of imagination, ensemble, interaction and creative problem solving in the regular classroom." Improvisation, characterization, discussion of performance, and an opportunity to create an original performance piece are among the experiences offered.

The Theatre Training Program runs from October to April and includes a wide variety of classes for children and teens. This ends with a Children's Theatre Festival and Teen Performances for family and friends. The Summer Training Program includes both classes and a community production. The tours go to elementary and junior high schools. In 1984–1985 the children's series of plays was expanded to eight. Some titles are traditional, but others are original. Some are musicals, and puppets and magicians may be included as well in a season's offerings.

RUTH FOREMAN'S PIED PIPER PLAYHOUSE

Address: Bay Vista Campus of Florida International University, N.E. 151st Street and Biscayne Blvd., North Miami, FL 33181
Founding date: 1949

Ruth Foreman, known locally as "The First Lady of Florida Theatre," founded the Dramatic Academy, Lemonade Theatre, and the Pied Piper Playhouse in Miami in 1949; the Studio M. Playhouse in Coral Gables ten years later; and the North Miami Playhouse in 1967. Despite the fact that she produces plays for both adults and children, Foreman's strong interest in the latter has resulted in extensive work in children's theatre, television, and radio programs for children, and a six-week summer actors' workshop. Children's performances are given throughout the year and number altogether more than 200.

While titles of plays for young audiences tend to be traditional, Ruth Foreman has written plays on themes and characters of particular interest. *Meet Young Chopin*, for example, was written upon the discovery of a ten-year-old boy who, she said, "played Chopin like Chopin would have liked to have heard it played," whereas *Einstein* was written to celebrate the Einstein Centennial. Her training of young people has been recognized by doctors and social workers, who often call on her to conduct special classes for the handicapped. The Pied Piper Players include persons of all ages, and productions list musicals as well as straight plays.

S

ST. NICHOLAS THEATRE COMPANY
Address: Chicago, IL
Founding date: 1974. Closed in 1980.

The St. Nicholas Theatre Company was listed in the 1978 CTAA directory as offering one hundred performances a year. It was identified as a professional company that offered classes as well as public performances. Three productions were mounted every season, with thirty performances of each given in the home theatre and ten on tour. St. Nicholas closed its doors in 1980 and did not reopen.

ST. OLAF COLLEGE CHILDREN'S THEATRE INSTITUTE
Address: Northfield, MN 55057
Founding date: 1978

St. Olaf College has operated a summer theatre for children since 1978. From a group of 36 children and a staff of six in the first year, it grew to 160 children and a staff of twenty-eight in the summer of 1983. The Children's Theatre Institute is designed to capture the natural drive of children's play and develop it around the fundamental elements of theatre arts. The institute offers a full program of classes and performances for the child interested in theatre.

Classes include creative drama, music, creative dance, and technical theatre for boys and girls from six to sixteen, arranged for different age and experience levels. The full-day participants present four full-scale productions. A musical production is developed in the Studio Theatre and presented in that location on certain dates during the month of July. A second production rehearses and performs in the theatre. The third and fourth productions are traveling shows that perform later in the summer in Northfield, Faribault, and surrounding area towns. Some of the plays given in the past few years have been *Trudy and the Minstrel*,

Three Tales from Japan, The Beeple, The Great Cross Country Race, The Phantom Toll Booth, H.M.S. Pinafore, and *Snow White and the Seven Dwarfs.*

In 1983 the Children's Theatre Institute was sponsored in cooperation with the Southeastern Minnesota Arts Council, Inc., through funding from the Minnesota State Arts Board and the Minnesota legislature. Both a continuing education course and a regular St. Olaf College course are offered in connection with the institute.

THE ST. PAUL CHILDREN'S THEATRE
Address: St. Paul, MN
Founding date: the 1920s

Sponsored by the St. Paul Players, an adult community theatre, this group was organized as an experiment to compensate for the poor entertainment offered by local cinemas. A community enterprise, the theatre was conducted for and by children insofar as possible. Good children's plays as well as original plays written by the children themselves were presented. The opportunity to produce their own work was a stimulus to active participation, for the experiment prospered for several years.

SAN DIEGO JUNIOR THEATRE
Address: Casa del Prado, Balboa Park, San Diego, CA 92101
Founding date: 1949

The Civic Conservatory of Theatre Arts for Youth, a nonprofit corporation, is an activity of San Diego's Park and Recreation Department and is totally self-funded except for the facilities of the Casa del Prado, which are provided by the city of San Diego. Young people from ages eight to eighteen are eligible to join. The theatre offers workshops in mime, acting, playwriting, puppetry, television production, and technical theatre, and occasional classes in phonics and the classics. Conservatory students are encouraged to participate in one of the six plays produced by San Diego Junior Theatre yearly. The actors are cast through open auditions, and crews for stage, costume, and house management are selected from applicant interviews.

Some recent productions have been *Little Mary Sunshine, The Wizard of Oz, Good News, Mary Poppins, Li'l Abner,* and *The Sound of Music.* Although production is an important component, the San Diego Junior Theatre considers itself educational.

THE SAN FRANCISCO MIME TROUPE, INC.
Address: 450 Alabama St., San Francisco, CA 94110
Founding date: 1959

The San Francisco Mime Troupe started out doing silent mime in a style based on that of Charlie Chaplin, with the idea of bringing life back to the theatre. Mime was chosen because it demanded that the vitality be in the performance: no scenery and no dialogue, only the actors' skill and energy to hold the attention of the audience. The company now does original plays and circus acts, but mime remains the basis of its style. The troupe believes that the meaning and the humor should be clear without words.

In 1962 the troupe took its shows out of doors into the parks of the city during lunch hours and over weekends. The actors quickly learned that in order to hold the interest of an audience that is neither captive nor has paid to see the show, they must first of all be twice as good at what they do as the actors in a theatre. Next, they must present material that is important to people. Following these precepts, The San Francisco Mime Troupe has become the oldest theatre in the city that is still in existence.

Years of playing in the parks, on the streets, on college campuses, and in libraries, churches, and community centers taught them that the average person enjoys and agrees with their presentation of topics and does not reject them as radical or outrageous. The Mime Troupe creates comic plays about serious issues and current events. It deliberately chose comedy because people enjoy it and because laughter is a potent weapon and satire is often an effective way of dealing with a controversial issue.

The troupe gives free performances in the Bay area parks during the spring and summer, passing the hat; they tour around a larger area during the fall and winter, booking engagements and offering circus acts and children's clown and puppet shows. The company is collectively run, nonprofit, and unsubsidized. It believes that the support and inspiration for popular theatre must come from the audience. Although not children's theatre in the traditional sense, it does perform for children and family audiences.

THE SAN FRANCISCO PLAYERS GUILD
Address: San Francisco, CA
Founding date: 1949

Although it was actually established in 1949, The San Francisco Players Guild belongs to a later period because of the growth and scope of the program in the sixties. After twenty seasons the guild was sponsoring a touring company of professional actors skilled in performing for a wide range of age levels and a variety of ethnic backgrounds. It sent out educational materials to schools in advance of its appearance in the belief that live theatre stimulates learning and creativity. It would appear that the guild was right, for it went from 37 performances of *Circus Day* in 1949 to 300 performances of *Katya, the Wonder Girl* in 1969.

SAN FRANCISCO STATE COLLEGE THEATRE
Address: San Francisco, CA
Founding date: before 1915

It was the belief of Mrs. John J. Cuddy that drama could be used as an outlet for children's energy and as an effective educational tool. This resulted in a practical workshop being founded at San Francisco State College. Mrs. Cuddy wrote her own plays, while her students and children from the community performed them. Her interest in Greek myths led to the dramatization of six of them. The activities of the workshop are of historical interest in that they were begun before 1915 and were therefore among the earliest recorded in the United States. Children's theatre continues to be important at San Francisco State University (*see also* Children's Repertory Theatre of San Francisco State University).

SAN JOSE REPERTORY PHANTASY COMPANY
Address: P.O. Box 28247, San Jose, CA 95159
Founding date: 1974

The San Jose Repertory Phantasy Company is a professional group of actors dedicated to producing the best quality of drama possible for young audiences. It hopes to become a permanent resource for the communities of San Jose and Santa Clara County, representing the interests, tastes, and values of the region in its selection, presentation, and interpretation of classical and modern works.

According to Lee Kopp, the producer, it originated with a classroom experiment in storytelling at San Jose University in 1966. The students focused on folktales from around the world. After graduation, in 1970, three of the alumni formed their own group and began touring schools, parks, and shopping malls informally throughout the state of California. Shows combined storytelling, pantomime, live music, improvisation, and audience participation. The little company was highly successful, leading to the formation of the Phantasy Company in 1974. Pamela Wood, one of the original trio, began a group of her own, J. P. Nightingale (q.v.) in the Los Angeles basin; Dennis Johnson, a second member of the trio, formed Sky Forest Phantasy in San Bernardino (later moved to West Virginia); while Lee Kopp remained to head the Phantasy Company in the San Francisco Bay area.

Since 1974 the Phantasy Company has performed in over 1,400 schools; an average year is reported to include 130 schools, with 200 performances of at least two different programs. Phantasy shows stress positive human values and the universal nature of mankind. Stories by the great storytellers of literature are adapted to play for different age levels; performances can be offered indoors or out, on a stage or in an all-purpose room. In addition to these performances, the company has produced several television specials. Bookings are arranged by Young

Audiences of San Jose and San Francisco, with city, corporate, and private grants to help defray costs.

Recent productions have included *Shakespeare for Children, Songs and Stories from Around the World,* and *My Sister Makes Me Sick* (an original new script). The company also offers educational services, paid internships, and theatre in education programs for children from age six through high school. It has permanent facilities, and tours from September to June.

SANTA MONICA PLAYHOUSE
Address: 1211 Fourth St., Santa Monica, CA 90401
Founding date: 1960

The Santa Monica Playhouse was listed in the 1978 CTAA directory as offering 275 performances a year. By 1985 it had expanded its activities to include four to six shows during the year, with 225 performances on weekends at the playhouse and 52 performances a year on tour. The touring unit, a mobile theatre, visits schools and hospitals throughout Southern California. The company also offers programs for students in the upper grades, for holidays, and for "family theatre." Plays are original, and there are generally ten in the repertoire.

Individualized educational programs, seminars, and workshops are available for all age levels and may be arranged either in conjunction with a production or by themselves. The Santa Monica Children's Theatre has been awarded three Mayor's Commendations for cultural contributions to the community.

SATURDAY THEATRE FOR CHILDREN
Address: 131 Livingston St., Brooklyn, NY 11201
Founding date: 1960

This community theatre program was launched in New York City in 1960 by the All-Day Neighborhood Schools and the Bureau of Audio-Visual Education of the Board of Education. It was established to bring some of the city's cultural resources to thousands of children who would otherwise not be able to experience them. The program had reached 450,000 children by the end of the first decade. In 1970 it was reported that 60,000 children were seeing plays, operas, modern and ethnic dance companies, and puppet shows, and hearing concerts during the academic year. Prices were kept as low as thirty-five cents in order to assure seats for all interested children. The success of and continuing interest in this enterprise has enabled the administration to keep it going. It is a sponsoring organization with an aesthetic goal, although substance is as important to the board as the entertainment value.

In 1982 The Children's Theatre Association of America (q.v.) gave a special citation to Paula Silberstein for her efforts in behalf of the Saturday Theatre for Children. Silberstein, a retired member of the Department of Cultural Resources of the New York City Board of Education, now devotes all of her time to the project.

SCHOOLTIME THEATRE
Address: R.D. 2, Box 289, Irwin, PA 15642
Founding date: 1980

A new Equity children's theatre company appeared in the Irwin-Pittsburgh area in the fall of 1980. Its opening show was a musical review entitled "Schooltime Showtrain," an original program of songs, dances, and vaudeville skits. The director, Mary Beth Kayson, had a background in theatre arts and music and had as her aim to bring the excitement of live entertainment into the schools, giving students the opportunity to see and enjoy the performing arts. In addition to schools, however, the company performs in hospitals, churches, and community centers. Unlike many of the touring companies operating today, Schooltime Theatre makes use of colorful costumes, elaborate props, and sound equipment. Performances are designed for audiences from first through sixth grades.

While the three performers are willing to meet with the audience (which they insist be limited to 450 children) afterward for questions and answers, they do not consider themselves an educational company. The show may deal with history, different geographic areas of the country, health, safety, citizenship, or patriotism, but it is entertainment first, with the learning embedded in the material. Didactic theatre is not the company's interest or primary objective.

SCOTTSDALE THEATRE FOR CHILDREN
Address: Scottsdale, AZ
Founding date: 1968. Closed in 1978.

The Scottsdale Theatre for Children was designated as an educational and professional company. Founded at the time of the greatest activity of the children's theatre movement in the United States, it reported more than 120 performances a year of its three productions. It offered classes and conducted an extensive touring program. By the late seventies it had ceased operation.

SEATTLE CHILDREN'S THEATRE
Address: 4649 Sunnyside Ave., N., Seattle, WA 98103
Founding date: 1975

Seattle Children's Theatre was formerly the Poncho Theatre, a facility of the Seattle Department of Parks and Recreation. Its programs are funded, in part, by grants from the National Endowment for the Arts, a federal agency; patrons of civic, cultural, and charitable organizations in the Northwest; and the Washington State and King County Arts Commissions. Its objective has always been to provide the best possible theatre experiences for children and young people who live in the Northwest, by employing the finest artists and teachers and establishing a working and learning environment that supports the creative imagination of the audience. The theatre operates year-round and offers six productions a season. Performances take place at the Poncho Theatre.

Programs and educational services include paid internships in acting and directing, professional training, residencies, and theatre in education. The company works with all ages from five to eighteen. Recent productions include both well-known and new scripts, traditional and experimental. Among the former have been *Great Expectations, Pinocchio, The Tempest, Tall Tales from Mark Twain, The Comedy of Errors*, and *Dracula. Mother Hicks* by Suzan Zeder, one of the most popular contemporary children's playwrights, was performed in the 1982 season; her earlier play, *Step on a Crack*, was also given by Poncho. An extensive promotional program has acquainted the country with this theatre and the quality of literature that it chooses to present to the children of Seattle.

In 1984 Seattle Children's Theatre added a unique summer arts program for young hearing impaired and deaf students called Theatre-in-Sign. A three-year pilot project, Theatre-in-Sign is partially underwritten by a grant from the King County Arts Commission as part of its Special Populations Program. The establishment of a permanent theatre of the deaf with productions of excellence and a program of theatre education is the long-range goal of the project. Theatre-in-Sign will include a sign language workshop/performance for adult deaf artists, a sign language theatre production for children and adults, and interpreted performances of the Seattle Children's Theatre main-stage season for school and public performances. Interpreted performances will include pre-performance discussion as well as the standard post-performance discussion between audience members and artists.

SEATTLE JUNIOR PROGRAMS. *See* SEATTLE JUNIOR THEATRE.

SEATTLE JUNIOR THEATRE
Address: Seattle, WA 98109
Founding date: 1939

The Seattle Junior Theatre was founded in 1939 as Seattle Junior Programs, Inc. It was established for the purpose of providing superior entertainment for children and was a sponsoring agency rather than a producing company. It resulted from the interest of a group of civic leaders who had the support of the public schools. The stated purpose from the beginning was to provide children of the community with entertainment that was both educational and artistically of good quality.

In addition to plays, programs included music, dance, science, and other areas of interest. The founders hoped to raise standards of entertainment and to develop young audiences. Junior Programs, Inc., was reported to have reached 4,200 children in its first season, and many more later, after Junior Programs, Inc. (q.v.), of New York had suspended operations. The initial success was followed by changes and an expanded program which incorporated production as well as sponsorship.

Today, faced with the competition of professional and semi-professional theatre companies in Seattle, it has had to curtail the number of performances it sponsors during a season and to cut expenses. As an all-volunteer organization, Seattle Junior Theatre does not have the strong financial and professional support of some more recently organized groups. Its importance can hardly be overestimated, however, in view of the fact that it introduced good children's theatre to the city, paving the way for future groups. It patterned itself after the New York organization, which was considered the best in the nation at the time.

SEATTLE REPERTORY THEATRE
Address: Bagley Wright Theatre at Seattle Center, 155 Mercer St., Seattle, WA 98109
Founding date: 1963

The Seattle Repertory Theatre's operation for young audiences is known as the Mobile Outreach Bunch, or MOB. Although MOB has been in operation since 1963, all of its performances in recent years have been given in schools throughout the state under the sponsorship of the Washington State Cultural Enrichment Program. The MOB shows are designed for junior and senior high school students rather than for elementary school children. They deal with tough questions important to young people: prejudice against minorities, rebellion against authority, and so on. *The Newcomer* by Janet Thomas, a play commissioned by the Repertory Theatre for MOB, dealt with the subject of prejudice and was one of the company's most popular offerings. Because of its success in Seattle, it was later staged at the Honolulu Theatre for Youth (q.v.) and attracted interest in other communities. The staged objectives of the company are entertainment and education, which they combine in programs such as those cited, rather than using traditional material or familiar scripted plays.

SEEM-TO-BE PLAYERS, INC.
Address: 630 Elm, Lawrence, KS 66044
Founding date: 1973

The Seem-to-Be Players' stated objective is "to provide children at varying stages of development with insights into the nature of the human condition." This they believe can most effectively be done through dramatic play designed to encourage the audience to involve itself empathetically with real actors. Eight months of the year they give a Saturday matinee at the Lawrence Art Center. Each month the program is varied to interest several grade levels. Within the hour-long performance the audience enjoys a sing-along and becomes acquainted with the company. This is followed by two short plays. One of these plays is usually a folk or fairy tale, an original script, or an improvised piece. Between the two plays the company performs skits for the children, which may be a potpourri of songs and audience participation activities.

Players do creative drama workshops in the area, varying materials to suit the age level and group size. Sometimes a process-oriented approach is used; other times, a combination of process and demonstration. Plans for teacher workshops were also made when the theatre was established. In line with the philosophy of encouraging audiences to use their imaginations, the players use only skeletal props and costumes. These are easily toured, making it possible to perform in almost any location and space. The company is available in the area for several months of the year and performs only for children.

SESAME STREET LIVE
Address: VEE Corporation, 810 Lumber Exchange Building, Minneapolis, MN 55402
Founding date: 1980

The touring shows presented by VEE Corporation, in cooperation with the Children's Television Workshop, consist of one and a half hours of music, songs, dancing, drama, and audience participation. Jim Henson's Sesame Street Muppets are among the featured players. Big Bird, Cookie Monster, Bert, Ernie, the Count, Oscar the Grouch, and other familiar television personalities materialize when a group of nineteen young performers puts the "live" into "Sesame Street Live."

SHAKESPEARE AND COMPANY
Address: The Mount, Lenox, MA 01240
Founding date: 1978

Shakespeare and Company states its thrust to be multiracial, classical training and performance within a school's program. It claims to be the nation's only classical theatre committed to the training of a multiracial ensemble of actors and teachers. Two major workshops for professional actors and a series of workshops in professional training institutes are designed to continue and strengthen this commitment. It is presently giving performances in the Berkshires but plans to extend tours throughout the United States and the English-speaking world, where it will introduce students to the understanding and vitality of Shakespeare, his language, and his times.

The company in the short period of its operation has received commendation for its performances at the American Shakespeare Festival in Stratford, Connecticut, in Lenox, and in Prospect Park, Brooklyn, under Joseph Papp's auspices.

In the summer of 1984, 20,000 persons attended the company's productions of *Romeo and Juliet* and *A Midsummer Night's Dream*, plus an original script dramatizing Edith Wharton, her circle, and the Berkshires at the turn of the century. During the 1984 school year, 70,000 students in the New England region took part in the Shakespeare-in-the-Schools program, and 10,000 Berkshire County students participated in this unique performance and hands-on workshop experience. The company operates on a twelve-month basis.

SHEFFIELD ENSEMBLE THEATRE
Address: 1350 Bourbon St., New Orleans, LA 70116
Founding date: 1972. Closed in 1983, reopened in 1986.

Sheffield Ensemble Theatre (formerly the Southern Educational Theatre) represented a new style in children's entertainment. The company developed a distinctive approach, which bore no resemblance to any other well-known group in existence. It was fast-paced and lively, high-spirited and modern. Through the creation of a new musical each season, the Sheffield Ensemble tried to keep abreast of the times and the changing mores and interests of children. Some of the titles of shows were *Bananas*, *Illusions of Beauty*, *Videosyncrasies*, and *Beans*, all written and composed by the directors of the company, Buddy and David Sheffield; conventional scripts were never used.

Costumes were bright-colored and sets minimal, if used at all. A concept and brisk movement rather than a narrative characterized the performance. Although some points were made, the directors believed that it was important to gain the attention of an audience before any social or moral lessons could be taught. Audiences, accustomed to television shows, responded to the Sheffield technique, which, though designed for children, appealed to all ages.

During its eleven years of operation, the company was available for residencies the year around. It was fully professional and offered more than 350 performances a year. *Bananas* was shown at a Children's Theatre Association of America (q.v.) conference, and *Beans* at a PACT spring showcase. Despite enthusiastic audiences, the company ceased operation in 1983, when the directors went into television programming for children. It reopened three years later.

THE SHOESTRING PLAYERS

Address: The Levin Theatre, Rutgers University, New Brunswick, NJ 08901

Founding date: 1980

The Shoestring Players is a professional ensemble troupe working in association with the Mason Gross School of the Arts of Rutgers University. Joseph P. Hart, the artistic director, joined the company in 1980, at which time he expanded the group into a traveling ensemble, appearing the year around in New Jersey, New York, and Pennsylvania. The company has performed as guest artists at the McCarter Theatre in Princeton, at B. Altman's in New York, and for the International Festival at the Annenberg Center in Philadelphia.

The players use folktales exclusively as material, but the focus is on little-known stories rather than on the traditional and frequently produced adaptations. They use no settings or props and wear only basic costumes, adding accessories to suggest a change from one country or period to another. The format generally includes three comic pieces and one serious tale, broken at midpoint for a creative drama session with the audience. This period may be used as an intermission, but it is available to the young audience as an opportunity to join the actors in a unique participatory experience. The nature of the Shoestring's material makes it possible for performances to appeal to very young as well as older audiences. The Shoestring Players' brochure explains that in having actors become caves and castles, tunnels and mountains, faucets and rivers, fish and birds, animals and people, theatre is brought back to its oldest and purest form.

SMALL WORLD PLAYERS

Address: University Theatre, Colorado State University, Ft. Collins, CO 80522

Founding date: 1972

In operation since 1972, Small World Players has become a regular part of the school year in the area. It performs in all of the Ft. Collins public elementary schools, keeping the troupe fully booked every spring. The company uses a story theatre style of performance, dramatizing popular children's literature for its young audiences. The 1984 program included excerpts from such children's favorites as *Charlie and the Great Glass Elevator* by Roald Dahl, *Harold and the Purple Crayon* by Crockett Johnson, and *The Snowy Day* by Ezra Jack Keats. The main thrust of the program is the dramatization of nondramatic literature to assist children to see the dramatic potential inherent in all types of literature and to encourage them to read the rest of the books and other works of the author.

In 1978 sixty-five performances a season were reported; by 1985 there appeared to be fewer, though the program and its format were considered successful.

SOUTH COAST REPERTORY (SCR)
Address: 655 Town Center Dr., P.O. Box 2197, Costa Mesa, CA 92628
Founding date: 1964

Founded in 1964 by David Emmes and Martin Benson, the South Coast Repertory is a professional, nonprofit resident company presenting plays for audiences in Orange and Los Angeles counties. It is committed to serving the theatre arts as a source of cultural enrichment. In addition to a series of six main-stage productions a season for adult audiences and its series of five experimental works in the theatre's Second Stage, South Coast Repertory also espouses many community outreach programs. Among these are the Educational Touring Program for children; the Theatre Discovery Project for secondary school and college students; and the three branches of the SCR Acting Conservatory—the Young, Evening, and Summer Conservatories. Since 1969 SCR has presented new, original plays for child audiences in Southern California.

SOUTHERN EDUCATIONAL THEATRE. *See* SHEFFIELD ENSEMBLE THEATRE.

STAGE ONE: THE LOUISVILLE CHILDREN'S THEATRE
Address: 721 West Main St., Louisville, KY 40202
Founding date: 1946

Stage One has been in existence for nearly forty years; in 1980 it became a fully professional Equity theatre for children. It strives to provide an aesthetic and enjoyable experience for young people of the city. It also hopes to develop a habit of theatre-going in the future; an important aspect of this latter goal is to help American audiences recognize that the theatre is an institution in which there is more to be found than entertainment. Theatre also provides an opportunity to examine social and personal values. Moses Goldberg, the director, is an advocate of age level programming and to that end chooses plays carefully for narrow age groups. He attempts to develop the sensitivity of his audience and move them from one level to the next until they become committed theatre-goers.

Stage One offers six productions a season. The company tours as well as playing in the home theatre. It offers internships in acting, costuming, and promotion; it is also available for in-house workshops and gives classes in drama for children and adults. Plays produced in the past few years include traditional titles, such as *Beauty and the Beast*, dramatized by Goldberg, *Rumpelstiltskin*, and *Christmas Firebird*; Broadway plays such as *The Diary of Anne Frank*; dramatic adaptations of foreign plays such as *Vasilisa*; and plays of Shakespeare. Goldberg is a playwright whose plays are published and widely produced throughout the United States. He is the author of a landmark college textbook, *Children's Theatre: A Philosophy and a Method*, and was an active member of The Children's Theatre Association of America (q.v.) and is on the board of ASSITEJ (q.v.).

STAGE SOUTH

Address: South Carolina Arts Commission, 1800 Gervais St., Columbia, SC 29201
Founding date: 1973

Stage South, a producing company, was originally the State Theatre of South Carolina. It was listed in the 1978 CTAA directory as offering 140 performances a year for children. In 1980 it became a sponsoring organization and no longer produces plays of any kind. This shift represents a common change as more and better touring productions became available and organizations preferred to focus on sponsorship of superior entertainment rather than compete with it.

STAGECOACH PLAYERS

Address: Parks and Recreation Department, 1045 E. Dayton St., Rm. 120, Madison, WI 53703
Founding date: 1949

This theatre company began operation in 1949 and is described in its brochure as "the oldest traveling troupe of its kind in the country." It is identified as both educational and community theatre, with teenagers as performers. The 1978 CTAA survey listed 110 performances on tour each season. Today the players offer two productions year, totaling 125 performances. These are given through the Parks and Recreation Department in playgrounds and at the Farmers' Market on Saturdays. In addition, there are performances in the Children's Hospital, on beaches, and at other locations in and around Madison.

The summer of 1984 saw the inauguration of a deluxe new coach. Built in Florida by a corporation that specializes in circus wagons, it possesses features that make it possible to set up and move from one site to another with ease and dispatch. Because of the heavy summer schedule, plays are double cast. Performers and technical staff often stay on for as long as five or six years. Among the popular plays toured by the Stagecoach Players are *The Reluctant Dragon*, *The Emperor's New Clothes*, *Robin Hood*, *The Ransom of Red Chief*, *Prisoner on Pirate Island*, and *Mystery of the Haunted House*. Well-known children's classics and fairy tales rather than experimental or new plays characterize the repertory and may account for the continued interest and support of the community.

STORY THEATRE PRODUCTIONS, INC.
Address: P.O. Box 4603, Parker Playhouse, Fort Lauderdale, FL 33338
Founding date: 1971

Story Theatre Productions is made up of eight professional performers and a stage manager. As the name suggests, the material used consists of fairy tales and fables. These are adapted for performance, but along with the entertaining narrative there is always an underlying theme. These may be stories of greed, gullibility, fear, conflicts, poetic justice; they are selected to convey to children what society considers right and wrong, illustrating through beauty and ugliness, both physical and spiritual, a simple basic morality.

Story Theatre provides improvisational programs, popular theatre, and theatre games. It also provides the necessary educational services such as pre-performance materials, study guides for teachers, workshop outlines, and post-performance suggestions. Performances are said to be geared to all grade levels. When Paul Sills brought his Story Theatre to Broadway, he proved the appeal of the material to audiences of all ages when it is handled with imagination and artistry.

STUDIO ARENA THEATRE
Address: 710 Main St., Buffalo, NY 14202
Founding date: 1926

Studio Arena Theatre is a professional theatre that places primary importance on developing the avocational and preprofessional interests of both young people and adults. A chronology of Studio Arena Theatre reveals that it is one of the oldest in the nation. At the turn of the century in Buffalo there were several social groups that met from time to time to read plays and poetry for their own entertainment. In this category was the Studio Club, formed about 1918. By 1922 several of the leading members of the club felt that Buffalo was ready for a full-scale amateur theatre. A professional director was hired, a small theatre was rented, and the Buffalo Players became an active organization. By 1926 the trustees realized that some kind of reorganization was needed. Jane Keeler, head of the drama department at Buffalo State Teachers College, had been active with the players and was prevailed upon to resign her position to head the new organization, The Studio Theatre School. This would be not only an amateur company but a drama school as well.

The endeavor was highly successful, winning the Belasco Cup in 1930. This was a national competition for community theatres held in New York for a number of years. By 1932 the theatre had outgrown its space and moved to a large downtown theatre, The Gaiety, which was empty at the time. Six years and several moves later, the theatre relocated to an empty church. In the mid-sixties there was a desire on the part of the trustees to convert the Studio Theatre into a professional theatre. Through a Federal Economic Development Administration grant, a new theatre was built in a complex across the street from the original site. By the mid-eighties student matinee performances of each production were included as part of the main-stage season. Original scripts were developed through improvisation for elementary school children and preteenage audiences. A long-term goal for the school is to develop a young company that will tour the western New York region.

Subscriptions, group prices, plays for both adults and children, and a long record of meeting the community's interests and needs have succeeded in making the Studio Arena Theatre of Buffalo a major force in the cultural life of the city and one of the most comprehensive theatre programs in the country. Expansion has been made possible by government and Rockefeller Foundation grants.

SUNNYVALE COMMUNITY PLAYERS JUNIOR THEATRE
Address: P.O. Box 60399, Sunnyvale, CA 94088
Founding date: 1967

The Sunnyvale Community Players are dedicated to providing the widest opportunity for amateurs of all ages to participate in and enjoy theatre. The company produces six shows a year, consisting of a summer musical for young adult performers and artistic staff aged thirteen to twenty-four, three shows for adult performers, and two musicals for young performers aged eight to eighteen. The children's theatre program shares equally in group resources.

Each of the children's productions is presented ten or twelve times in the modern, fully equipped, 200-seat theatre. Most rehearsals also take place here, sharing the space with the California Young People's Theatre (q.v.), a renowned group of professional adults who perform for children. Some of the shows performed in the past include *The Wizard of Oz, Bye, Bye, Birdie, Superman* (the musical), and *Charlie and the Chocolate Factory*, as well as an original workshop musical, *House of Tomorrow*. Sunnyvale Community Players has been in existence since 1967, first exclusively as a children's group and two years later incorporating adult and young adult shows as well.

The group aims to provide the best entertainment value for the community as well as the most valuable educational experience possible for the participants. Sunnyvale Community Junior Theatre is constantly adding and modifying its program to meet the needs of the children and young adults of the area.

SUNSHINE TOO
Address: One Lomb Memorial Dr., P.O. Box 9887, Rochester, NY 14623
Founding date: 1980

Sunshine TOO is an outreach program sponsored by the National Technical Institute for the Deaf at the Rochester Institute of Technology. It was founded to promote awareness of the hearing impaired and to offer positive role models for deaf children and youth. Three deaf and three hearing actors make up the company; all shows are performed in sign language and voice simultaneously. Sunshine TOO is a professional touring group that presents more than 650 performances a year for approximately 70,000 people. It appears on television, conducts residencies sponsored by state departments of education, and performs in public schools, colleges, before deaf groups, and at national and regional conferences.

The National Technical Institute for the Deaf states that it is the only college in the world that offers a full program of theatre, dance, and music for deaf students. This background has made it possible to develop the unique programs and workshops that within a period of only five years from the date of its founding achieved popularity and renown. Programs are designed for grades K–6 and 7–12. Teaching materials and information about deafness are sent out to schools in advance of the shows. Workshops include The Deaf Experience, in which cast members lead participants through a series of experiences to help them understand the feeling of the deaf in a hearing world; Sign Language, in which participants are taught selected signs; Sign Mime, in which mime and sign language create a new means of expression; and Sign Songs, in which sign language and songs are combined to create a new art form. Members of the workshop learn special selections.

SYRACUSE STAGE
Address: 160 Forrest Way, Camillus, NY 13031
Founding date: 1979

Syracuse Stage produces six main-stage productions a year (from October through May). It also puts on a children's production each spring (not one of the main-stage shows), which tours elementary schools in the area. The children's production is cast from the Syracuse University Drama Department, and the actors receive their Equity cards as a result of that experience.

As a nonprofit organization, Syracuse Stage has the flexibility to present the broadest spectrum of plays because it does not seek to make money. Also, unlike the commercial theatre, it is able to keep ticket prices within the budget of the average audience member. Finally, it is a regional theatre, meaning that it is a part of a fast-growing organization of theatres, the League of Resident Theatres, or LORT.

The 1980–1981 season marked the opening of the new 499-seat John D. Archbold Theatre. This $1.3 million renovation resulted in the creation of Syracuse's finest theatrical facility. Meet-the-cast discussions, cabaret, and variety shows are added features for family audiences.

Titles of both adult and children's plays attest to the stated objective: quality plays, professionally produced. Overall, Syracuse Stage is committed to the concept of nurturing new voices and new ideas, and it promises to continue to seek the work of developing playwrights. The children's wing is dedicated to the same philosophy. In advance of touring performances, the theatre sends out educational materials prepared for the use of school administrators and teachers; special features are described, with historical background and other information that will enable them to prepare students for the experience. Grants from foundations have made it possible for Syracuse Stage's children's shows to continue at a time when inflation has made budget cuts necessary for so many producing companies and school systems.

T

TEATRO DOBLE
Address: Back Alley Theatre, Inc., 1365 Kennedy St., N.W., Washington, DC 20011
Founding date: 1968

Teatro Doble, a program of Back Alley Theatre, Inc., of Washington, D.C., introduced plays in Spanish and English for children from four to twelve years of age in the sixties. Back Alley toured children's shows in the summer of 1968 and has toured them extensively since then for the District of Columbia Board of Education as well as for area churches and community centers. Various funding agencies have supported its comprehensive program of bilingual entertainment consisting of folklore, song, dance, puppetry, and mime. Like the first children's theatres in the United States, Teatro Doble's goals were learning and entertainment, combined with social consciousness.

Programs are for both English-speaking and Spanish-speaking children, but it is not necessary for children to be bilingual to enjoy them. A related goal is to foster exchanges of information about Latino and American ways and to develop language skills in Spanish and English. It is an example of one way in which community theatre is serving the children and young people of America today.

TEMPLE CHILDREN'S THEATRE
Address: Temple University, Dept. of Theatre, Philadelphia, PA 19122
Founding date: 1976

Temple Children's Theatre began in 1976 as part of the undergraduate performance program. The focus is on new or unusual scripts that emphasize actor-audience relationship and present creative challenges in both staging and acting. Two shows a year are produced: one each semester with a diversified performance program. Each show is given six public performances, seven private in-house performances for school groups, and several weeks of touring to area schools.

Temple represents no particular point of view other than the production of the best available scripts; in the recent past it has presented plays as different as *The Arkansaw Bear, Step on a Crack, The Ice Wolf, The Marvelous Adventures of Tyl, The Doctor in Spite of Himself*, and *The Hairy Man*. The 1984 season included an original rock musical version of *The Musicians of Bremen*. The children's work is an important part of the Temple University theatre program.

THEATRE ARTS OF WEST VIRGINIA, INC.
Address: P.O. Box 1205, Beckley, WV 25801
Founding date: 1955

Theatre Arts of West Virginia was incorporated in 1955 and offered its first production in 1961. A professional company, it played during the summer months to family audiences with a special children's event in addition to the other productions. The thrust of the company was announced as entertainment, which included education, and drama which was designed to raise the social consciousness of the audience.

Today the theatre has two components, the Acting Company and the Puppet Company. Companies tour in their own van, offering plays for older and younger audiences from September to June. Shakespeare and modern plays are in the repertory of the Acting Company; traditional plays like *Jack and the Beanstalk* and *Peter Pan* are popular offerings by the Puppet Company. Extensive teaching materials are readied at the beginning of the season and are sent to schools and community centers to prepare young audiences in advance of the performance. Follow-up activities are also suggested to extend the experience. Writers' workshops and other special workshops are tailored to sponsors' requirements on request. Summer tours are also offered for children's audiences; these take place in parks and playgrounds.

THEATRE FOR YOUNG AMERICA
Address: 7204 West 80th St., Overland Park, KS 66204
Founding date: 1974; incorporated in 1977

This is a year-round Equity company performing mostly dramatized classics of children's literature. It has recently added plays dealing with specific social issues (for example, *Bubbylonian Encounter*, a play about touching and sexual abuse). It also offers acting classes. Over 200 performances annually are reported. The company places emphasis on music, mime, and choreography.

Some of the all-time children's favorites have been given by the theatre: *The Ugly Duckling, The Pied Piper of Hamlin, Cinderella, Alice in Wonderland,*

and *The Prince and the Pauper*. Newer favorites have been *Snoopy*, *The 500 Hats of Bartholomew Cubbins*, and *The Lion, the Witch and the Wardrobe*. A special staging of *A Midsummer Night's Dream* is planned for the summer of 1986, with a cast made up of students in the acting classes. Theatre for Young America is part of the Kansas Touring Program; this program is reviewed by a panel of experts and recommended on the basis of performance skills and readiness to tour. Study guides for teachers are sent in advance, with workshops available on request.

THEATRE FOR YOUNG AUDIENCES AT SAN DIEGO STATE UNIVERSITY

Address: College of Professional Studies and Fine Arts, San Diego State University, San Diego, CA 92182

Founding date: 1971

The Theatre for Young Audiences offers three or four plays a season at the university and in the schools. Both traditional and new plays are included; for example, in the 1983–1984 season *The Miracle Worker*, *The Three Musketeers*, *The Two Maples*, and *Maggie Magalita* were listed. In 1984–1985 *Just So!* (a program of songs and stories by Paul Tracey, an Englishman born in Africa), *Peter Pan*, and *The Ice Wolf* were the attractions. Subscriptions are sold in different series presented at the university theatre. The school plays tour as well, and special theatre enrichment workshops are provided. These include creative drama activities and backstage tours at the university. The goal of the program is to produce the best in children's theatre literature so that both the university and the community are provided with quality entertainment for elementary and secondary school students. The program was founded and is still directed by Margaret McKerrow of the drama department.

The plays to be performed in the Theatre for Young Audience's season are selected for several reasons. They need to be challenging and interesting enough for university students to act in, they need to conform to the technical requirements of the design faculty and staff, as well as the facilities, and finally they need to be quality theatre pieces worthy of the standards of the department and the audiences who see them. The theatre tries hard to stage only the best, and frequently produces the newest fine plays for children. At the same time they make every attempt to vary the shows from classics to new plays, from farces to tragedies, and to include foreign plays in order to expose the audience to the wide variety of wonderful material now available to the Theatre for Young Audience's producer.

THE THEATRE FOR YOUNG PEOPLE
Address: UNC-G, Greensboro, NC 27412
Founding date: 1962

The Theatre for Young People, housed in the Pixie Playhouse, is one of the best known children's theatres in the country, offering over 160 performances annually. The company tours as well as playing in the home theatre. It is one of the child drama programs approved for Winifred Ward Scholars because of its comprehensive offerings and the quality of its work. Described as educational and professional, it emphasizes both drama and theatre in its program. Through the Department of Communication and Theatre the university student may be awarded the M.F.A. degree in acting/directing, with emphasis available in child drama. Three qualified M.F.A. candidates are accepted each year, and their work includes courses in creative drama, children's theatre, puppetry, and advanced creative drama. They participate actively on stage and off in Theatre for Young People's productions. During their second year, qualified candidates are invited to direct one of the three productions. An internship is required and can be fulfilled in the North Carolina Theatre for Young People (a professional company which tours throughout the Southeast), the University of North Carolina's summer theatres, or an accepted internship elsewhere. Graduates of the forty-eight-hour program are currently employed as directors, actors, and creative drama specialists throughout the country.

In 1974, with the help of a grant from the North Carolina Arts Council, a newly named Theatre for Young People Touring Repertory Theatre presented Aesop's *Falables* and *Tarheel Tales* to 37,000 children. The latter play was an audience participation/arena style show, which was sponsored for a five weeks tour by the state's Department of Public Instruction through funds from the Edwin Gill Professional Touring Theatre Program. Some of the other titles that have been offered are *Peter Pan, Reynard the Fox, The Land of the Dragon, The Dancing Donkey, Alice in Wonderland,* and *Mr. Popper's Penguins*. While the years since its founding have brought many changes, the goal of providing quality theatre experience for children has been maintained. By 1984, 183 performances were reported. Photographs show elaborately mounted productions in the theatre, with the touring plays staged more simply.

Professor Tom Behm, director of the program, is a past president of The Children's Theatre Association of America (q.v.) and a former editor of *Children's Theatre Review*.

THE THEATRE FOR YOUNG PEOPLE OF HERKIMER COUNTY
Address: Box 324, Herkimer, NY 13350
Founding date: 1976

The Theatre for Young People of Herkimer County is a semi-professional theatre supported each year by the New York State Council on the Arts, the New York State Division of Youth, and the United Arts Fund of the Mohawk Valley. It does a minimum of six productions each season. It also makes school tours and does drama in the classroom, as well as offering workshops for teachers. Since its founding it has given sixty-two productions involving some 800 adults, young people, and children as performers. These impressive results began with a bake sale to raise forty dollars; by 1985 it had spent close to half a million dollars to bring drama and theatre to the county. One of its notable productions was Lorraine Hansberry's *What Use Are Flowers?*, which was presented at the East Central Theatre Conference in 1977. The number of yearly performances varies from forty to eighty.

THEATRE FOR YOUTH, UNIVERSITY OF TEXAS AT AUSTIN
Address: College of Fine Arts, Department of Drama, Austin, TX 78712
Founding date: 1945

The University of Texas at Austin offered its first children's play in 1945, but it was not until 1963 that youth theatre became a major focus. Under the direction of Coleman A. Jennings, now chairman of the department, youth-related projects have expanded: the Department of Drama produces up to four plays for young people yearly and offers classes and workshops in creative drama and dance. Each spring the Department of Drama takes a children's show to five elementary schools in the city; all grades are in the audience. The major objective of the Theatre for Youth program, however, is to bring children to the university so that they can be exposed to a complete theatre experience. An average of thirty-five schools attend each production, depending on which one of the auditoriums is used. According to Jennings only sixth graders attend; this is so that no children are missed. The hope is that every child in Austin will visit the university at least twice for theatrical productions.

Preceding the shows, Junior League volunteers go to the classes scheduled to attend. Slides and other visual materials are used to give a short presentation about the experience. Afterward, if teachers desire it, a follow-up to the show is offered. Here graduate students conduct a question and answer period and perhaps a creative drama workshop. In addition to the shows for school children, four to six public performances also take place. Plays offered in recent years have included *Reynard the Fox*, *The Honorable Urashima Taro*, *Yankee Doodle*, *A Toby Show*, and *The Arkansaw Bear*.

The department also offers classes and workshops so that young people may participate actively in theatre and dance. Faculty members teach university-level courses in creative drama and drama education. As a laboratory for these classes, professors and students go to the various elementary schools to work with young people, either after school or during school hours, if the teachers wish to tie them into the curriculum. The department offers programs leading to the M.A., M.F.A., and Ph.D. degrees. Areas of study include theatre for youth and teacher training as well as theatre history, criticism, playwriting, directing, stage and costume design, and stage lighting. The University of Texas is included in the list of programs certified for Winifred Ward Scholars.

THEATRE IV
Address: 6 N. Robinson St., Richmond, VA 23220
Founding date: 1975

Theatre IV operates both a theatre for adults and a theatre for children. Unlike the majority of companies with these two components, the children's productions account for 85 percent of the total audience. Seven original musicals for young people ranging from kindergarten through high school are given each year in the Richmond area and on tour in several southeastern states. The growth pattern has continued steadily from its inception, resulting in the company's becoming Virginia's largest professional touring theatre.

Children's programs include the Great American Heroes series, which brings to life people and events studied in school. Teachers' guides are prepared for use in connection with this series and are sent to schools in advance of the performance. The "Wiggle Club Season" includes such children's classics as *Pinocchio, The Pied Piper, Sleeping Beauty,* and a Christmas holiday show. A further offering is a recently developed program of plays dealing with serious social issues affecting children. "Hugs and Kisses," a child sexual abuse prevention piece, was designed for elementary school age children and has a question and answer period following the presentation. "Runners" was written for grades 6–12 and deals with runaway prevention. This is also followed by a discussion period. Both shows have been cited for their excellence. "Hugs and Kisses" was the featured production at the third National Conference on Sexual Victimization of Children held in Washington, D.C., in 1984; "Runners" was co-produced by the National Network of Runaways and Youth Services. In 1979 Theatre IV received the Sara Spencer Award by The Children's Theatre Association of America (q.v.); it was cited as "The Most Outstanding Children's Theatre in the Southeastern United States." The company was featured in the January 1985 issue of *Good Housekeeping* magazine.

THEATRE IN A TRUNK, INC.
Address: New York, NY
Founding date: 1969. Suspended activities in 1983.

Theatre in a Trunk was formed in New York City for the purpose of presenting original theatre pieces for children. It grew into a full-time resident company of professional actors, musicians, dancers, and educators, who explored themes close to the interests of younger children and used material to supplement the school curriculum. Totally mobile and compact, Theatre in a Trunk productions centered around an old-fashioned trunk that held all the costumes and properties necessary to the play. Children were often seated on three sides of the playing space and were invited to become involved physically as well as intellectually and emotionally in the action.

Theatre in a Trunk's Bicentennial play dealt with the American Revolution and was designed for children of all ages or "family theatre." This was performed in various historic sites in the New York area for an entire season. In 1983, as a result of inflation and the lack of a home base, activities were officially suspended.

THEATRE IN THE PARK
Address: P.O. Box 12151, Raleigh, NC 27605
Founding date: 1948

Theatre in The Park was founded in 1948 as the Raleigh Children's Theatre (q.v.). The scope of the theatre and its name were changed in 1974. It is housed in the old National Guard Armory, which has a main stage with flexible seating for 200, a studio theatre, a dance studio, set and costume shops, and administrative offices. Theatre in The Park maintains a staff of four and is governed by an eighteen-member board of directors.

It is a community theatre which further strengthened its commitment to the young people of Raleigh by opening a school in 1984 to provide quality theatre arts experiences on an ongoing basis. The Theatre School offers classes and workshops for both children and adults. Courses are designed to allow students to grow through various levels at their own rate of development. Classes include creative drama, improvisation, acting for both beginners and more experienced students, speech, pantomime, voice, aerobics, costume design and construction, set design, vocal techniques, and makeup. Future plans include expanded offerings for grades K–5, outreach productions, and a Teen Company.

A theatre arts summer day camp is held at Theatre in The Park for young people who want to perform or to explore the performing arts. The winter season offers four main-stage productions (classics, musicals, original works), two children's shows, and a mini-series consisting of three plays in repertory in February. The staff consists of highly trained professionals who care about sharing their skills with others in the community.

THEATRE MASK ENSEMBLE
Address: Arthur Shafman International, Ltd., 723 Seventh Ave., New York, NY 10019
Founding date: 1978

Under the direction of Carol Uselman and Jerry Mouawad, its founders and artistic directors, Theatre Mask Ensemble combines mime, dance, movement theatre, and masks. The performers were awarded the highest ranking by the Drama Film Association of New York in a national mime film competition. They also received a "Willie" Award for excellence in Portland, Oregon, and National Young Audiences acclaims their children's theatre programs. Their residencies include lecture/demonstrations, workshops, and master classes in mime theatre. Theatre Mask Ensemble is part of the Western States Arts Foundation, the Texas Arts Exchange, and "Oregon on Tour" programs.

THEATRE OF THE YOUNG. *See* EASTERN MICHIGAN UNIVERSITY THEATRE OF THE YOUNG.

THEATRE OF YOUTH COMPANY (TOY)
Address: 681 Main St., Buffalo, NY 14203
Founding date: 1972

The Theatre of Youth Company was formed to provide experiences in theatre for young viewers and to help them develop taste, discernment, and interest in dramatic production. TOY performs and tours a minimum of three shows a year to schools, community centers, and at public sites. The company provides participatory plays for elementary grades. Follow-up workshops are available for grades K–8 in creative drama and mime; all workshops are process oriented. It also offers teacher workshops in creative drama techniques. TOY sends teacher information packets in advance for each production mounted. Legends and myths are often used to introduce children to theatre, after which improvisational techniques extend the stories. The company works with children during this part of the program.

By the mid-eighties TOY was offering the following diversified bill: *Rumpelstiltksin*, *Wiley and the Hairy Man*, *The Cherry Orchard*, *Peter Pan*, *Free Niagara* (on TOY's Museum-Go-Round series), and *Private High*, a social drama on the perils of alcohol and drug abuse, for high school student audiences. In 1983–1984, 130 performances were given with 37,373 children and young people in attendance.

THEATRE ON WHEELS
Address: 10001 Westheimer, Suite 2920, Houston, TX 77042
Founding date: 1979

Theatre on Wheels falls in the category of educational and professional presentation. It is a touring company of professional actors and teachers who specialize in performance and instruction for children. Because the primary sponsors of its activities are schools, all programming emphasizes educational values first, followed by the social, aesthetic, and entertainment values of a particular production or class.

The company has presented a combination of award-winning plays such as Suzan Zeder's *Step on a Crack* and Aurand Harris' *Punch and Judy,* with other original musicals and nonmusicals written by its current playwright-in-residence. The latter are sometimes adaptations; on one occasion a play was presented that resulted from a fourth grade level creative writing project in a Houston school district. All scripts are complemented with professional quality sets, costumes, and a portable lighting system. Theatre on Wheels provides at least 150 performances annually.

THEATRE RESOURCES FOR YOUTH (TRY)
Address: Department of Theatre and Communication, Paul Creative Arts Center, University of New Hampshire, Durham, NH 03824
Founding date: 1965

According to Susan E. Goldin, the director, and Carol Lucha-Burns, the artistic director, Theatre Resources for Youth originated in 1965–1966 under an Elementary and Secondary Education Act (ESEA) Title III grant and operated as such for three years. Its early commitment was to touring children's theatre, directing existing companies, performing children's plays and teaching creative dramatics. Although it was a highly successful program, TRY's original funding ran out during 1969–1970.

In December 1970 TRY was reorganized and restructured to become a self-supporting outreach program of the Department of Theatre and Communication at the University of New Hampshire. In the summer of 1971 the "Little Red Wagon" made its debut as a touring children's theatre vehicle for the state of New Hampshire. The present wagon has a similar format (but different content) and a newer truck. The "Wagon" show consists of puppetry, story theatre, music, and involvement theatre. This hour-long structure has always allowed for versatility and variety— both during summer outdoor performances and academic year indoor performances. All the "Wagon" performances are geared toward an elementary school age audience and are specifically designed for involvement/participation.

In 1976 the "Wagon" program was enhanced by the creation of the touring CARAVAN program, a six-vehicle multiarts touring program geared toward family style audiences. The original summer CARAVAN consisted of a separate vehicle in each of the following areas: theatre, dance, music, poetry-mime, visual arts, and crafts. Although originally a summer program in association with the New Hampshire Commission on the Arts, CARAVAN expanded to a year-round program maintaining a variety of art forms and establishing a self-supporting status under TRY. Since its conception CARAVAN has extended its content to include Shakespeare, magic, comedy, puppetry (both performances and lecture demonstrations), musical comedy, comics, and clowns, as well as two "catch-alls"—"Potpourri" and "Things and Things." (CARAVAN has twice toured a Brazilian musical quartet from New Hampshire's sister state, Ceara, Brazil, under the auspices of the Partners of the Americas Program.)

All of the programs ("Wagon" and CARAVAN) are approximately an hour long and are designed to adapt to whatever environment the program is requested to perform in. Generally the performances are held at playgrounds, recreation areas, town commons, libraries, schools, churches, hospitals, shopping malls, and state parks.

TRY is a self-supporting agency which raises all of its money through its performances and workshops. The "Wagon" and CARAVAN programs (depending on the number of vehicles in performance in a given year) can do between 350 and 900 shows a year for audiences ranging from 75,000 to 200,000 people. The program is New Hampshire—based and thus does at least 80 percent of its performances in-state, with the other 20 percent in the bordering states of Maine, Vermont, and Massachusetts. TRY has specifically chosen its performance style and touring format for the purpose of integrating "live" theatre and the creative arts within the communities' own environment. Philosophically, it is TRY's belief that the interaction and shared experience with the audiences, both interpersonally and artistically, are what give meaning to the creative arts.

THE THEATRE SCHOOL AND THE THEATRE SCHOOL PLAYWORKS, DE PAUL UNIVERSITY. *See* GOODMAN SCHOOL CHILDREN'S THEATRE.

THEATRE 65. *See* THE CHILDREN'S THEATRE OF EVANSTON.

THEATREWORKS/USA (formerly Performing Arts Repertory Theatre)
Address: 131 W. 86 St., New York, NY 10024
Founding date: 1962

Theatreworks/USA is a nonprofit, professional organization, formerly known as PART (Performing Arts Repertory Theatre of New York). By 1984 Theatreworks/USA had produced over forty original musicals, including *The Amazing Einstein*; *Freedom Train*; *The Pen and the Sword*; *The Sorcerer's Apprentice and Other Magical Tales*; *Jim Thorpe, All American*; *Marlin*; *First Lady*; and *Aesop and Other Fables*. Its first show, *Young Abe*

Lincoln, demonstrated the company's innovative style and format. It proved to be so successful that a series was developed entitled Preludes to Glory. These plays dealt with the lives of famous persons when they were young or before they had achieved renown. Young people responded to them, as did sponsors. This combination of substance and entertainment, presented professionally, proved the contention that children's audiences could be held by more than trivial or light amusement.

Theatreworks/USA tours are supported in part by grants from the National Endowment for the Arts and the New York State Council for the Arts. In addition to its own shows, Theatreworks/USA offers an extensive guest artist series. These include puppet performances, clowning and circus skills, African folktales in song, dance, and story, scenes from Shakespeare, and storytelling. This is one of the most comprehensive producing and sponsoring organizations in the country. One of the reasons why it has been so successful, in addition to its content and performance skills, is the care given to productions during the tryout period. Jay Harnick, the artistic director, travels to schools to see how plays are received, and if and where changes need to be made. He admits to a belief that good theatre will touch, perhaps even change children's lives. To this end, he seeks out the finest authors, composers, choreographers, lyricists, and actors to bring the qualities that can enhance the lives of young viewers. Over 850 performances are given on tour during a season, with 10 to 20 in New York.

A highlight of its long history was an invitation to present selections from *First Lady*, a musical about Eleanor Roosevelt, at a luncheon hosted by Nancy Reagan in the White House on October 9, 1984. The luncheon, held in honor of the centennial of Mrs. Roosevelt's birth, entertained many distinguished guests, including former first ladies, and as many as sixty members of the Roosevelt family.

TOUCH, THE MIME TRIO OF THE ART SCHOOL
Address: Art School, Carr Mill, Carrboro, NC 27510
Founding date: 1976

TOUCH is a professional touring affiliate of the Art School in Carr Mill, a nonprofit center for performing and visual arts. Since 1976 it has accepted engagements from New England to Mississippi, with performances and a variety of residency options.

TOUCH performances generally consist of three parts: (1) playing in the audience before the show begins; (2) performing a series of short pieces chosen from the repertoire; and (3) improvising on words or suggestions from the audience. These pieces range from amusing episodes to serious situations.

TOUCH has over two hours of material in a variety of short pieces. The three performers, along with a musician and a lighting designer, provide a different show for each of the following grade levels: K–2, 3–6, 7–9, and high school. The content of classroom workshops in lower and upper schools often stems from questions asked by the students. The following areas are usually explored: mime technique, body awareness, body language, relaxation and energy, self-expression, use of the imagination, and improvisation. TOUCH has worked successfully with physically and mentally handicapped persons, particularly the hearing impaired. Teacher workshops and master classes are available as well as programs for family audiences. TOUCH hosted the Southeast Regional Mime Festival, served on a panel on mime for the Southeastern Theatre Conference, performed at the Piccolo Spoleto Festival in Charleston, South Carolina, and was one of the fifteen mime companies selected to appear at the International Mime and Clown Festival in Elkins, West Virginia.

TOUCHSTONE
Address: 908 East Fifth St., Bethlehem, PA 18015
Founding date: 1976

Touchstone is a professional company formerly known as the B&B Mime of the People's Theatre Company. It started as the Lehigh Improvisational Street Theatre Troupe under the direction of the late John Pearson. The past few years have seen Touchstone's *Peace Train*, *Whoopsi Kerplonk*, and *Yellow Moon Jamboree*, all of which drew large crowds to the outdoor sites where the company performs. In the summer of 1983 over forty performances were given in the cities of Allentown, Bethlehem, and Easton, and several other Lehigh County locations; the program has been supported in part by the Pennsylvania Council on the Arts. The company has appeared in the Schenley Concert Hall at the University of Pittsburgh. In 1981 it was awarded one of the coveted Fringe First Awards at the Edinburgh International Festival of the Arts in Scotland for its original program of mime and dance, *Of Arrows and Roses*.

Although not children's theatre in the traditional sense, Touchstone always attracts large children's audiences in its parks and playground performances, and what might be described as family theatre, of course, includes young people.

THE TRAVELING PLAYHOUSE
Address: 104 Northampton Drive, White Plains, NY 10603
Founding date: 1949

The Traveling Playhouse is a company that began activities in the late forties and has survived into the eighties. It was founded and directed by Kay Rockefeller, who still directs its operation. The 92nd Street "Y" (q.v.) of New York offered it a home base at the time, although, as the name indicates, it has always been a touring company. An original grant from the Rockefeller Foundation enabled The Traveling Playhouse to initiate its program of plays for children from ages six to sixteen. Within a few years it became completely self-supporting.

From its inception The Traveling Playhouse has been committed to the production of children's classics, traditionally and elaborately staged. Both fairy tales and favorite stories like *Tom Sawyer*, *Treasure Island*, and *Ali Baba* have been staples in its repertoire. Its production of *Robin Hood* has been seen on numerous occasions on NBC-TV. Whereas many children's theatre companies have changed both their content and performance style, The Traveling Playhouse has remained faithful to its original intent. It is a professional troupe that offers at least 250 performances a year. An Equity children's theatre, it is seen regularly on the PACT showcase in New York each spring.

TRIBAL PLAYERS
Address: Boston, MA
Founding date: 1968. No longer in operation.

When the Tribal Players of the Theatre Workshop, Boston, Inc., was founded, it was unique in its aim and revolutionary in its approach to children's theatre. The group's goal was to involve everyone equally in an experiential performance, defined by director Barbara Linden as environmental theatre. The company believed that taking the audience through the play from beginning to end would create a deeper understanding of the situation and a stronger identification with the characters. By involving children in the totality in this way, environmental theatre differs from participatory theatre, which has a structure with specific places for audience input and movement.

The first play, *Tribe*, explored the history of the American Indian in terms the group believed children could understand. The following year a piece entitled *Creation* was the opening attraction. This play dealt with the problem of pollution and was communicated through words, mime, movement, sound, and improvisation with the audience as a necessary part of the production. Actor/leaders guided the audience to enact the roles and deliver the lines and perform the actions. A grant from the National Endowment for the Arts and sponsorship by the Arlington Street Church supported the effort. Both plays were subsequently published by New Plays, Inc. Material was organized by Barbara Linden and put into dramatic form for other groups who had had no experience with the Tribal technique. Although environmental theatre never became a popular form, the experiment attracted attention at the time.

TROY STATE UNIVERSITY PIED PIPERS CHILDREN'S THEA-TRE ENSEMBLE
Address: Troy, AL 36081
Founding date: 1970

Troy State's Pied Pipers Children's Theatre Ensemble has been under the direction of David Dye since its founding. Forty to sixty performances a year are presented; these are directed toward pupils in grades K–6, during school hours. Funding is provided by the Alabama State Council on the Arts and Humanities and sponsors' fees. The ensemble is composed of eight to twelve actors, all of whom are university students.

The performances are fifty minutes in length and consist of original and well-known children's stories, performed without scenery or properties. Three stories are often connected in a variety of ways to provide unity. The tour area includes the southern half of Alabama and infrequently parts of Georgia and Florida.

TUFTS UNIVERSITY MAGIC CIRCLE
Address: Medford, MA 02155
Founding date: 1952

Tufts University in Medford, Massachusetts, introduced a unique summer drama program for children in 1955. Twenty-five children from age nine to fourteen were accepted by audition to produce three plays in five weeks. Two performances were given every week. It was said to be the only program of its kind in New England, emphasizing drama and theatre arts. Like other camps, the Magic Circle program included recreation and a daily rest period, with the noon meal served in one of the university dining halls. The performances of the youthful actors were open to the general public on Thursday mornings.

By the mid-sixties the number of performances had decreased, but the project was described by some members of The Children's Theatre Association of America (q.v.) as the quintessential children's theatre because children were involved in all aspects of production. The association met at Tufts for its annual conference in August 1956, at which the Magic Circle was one of the featured performing groups. Tufts continues to have a strong theatre department with emphases on all areas of theatre.

THE TWELFTH NIGHT REPERTORY CO. (TNRC)
Address: 12732 Moorpark Street, Studio City, CA 91604
Founding date: 1973

TNRC is a multiracial professional ensemble of performers, writers, directors, and administrators. It has produced over one hundred original stage and television productions in the past five years.

Twelfth Night Repertory shows are designed to entertain as well as to enlighten, dealing with both educational and social issues. The company has tackled subjects such as human relations, environmental awareness, multicultural understanding, substance abuse, responsible sexual decision making, peer pressure, and American history. Its shows for adults have included industrials for major corporations and original plays with social themes. In 1981 the company turned its attention to television.

In addition to stage and television work, TNRC's commitment to young people includes a performing arts camp every summer at Jane Fonda's ranch at Santa Barbara. It gives over 1,000 performances annually.

A TWO RING CIRCUS
Address: No. 9–75 Rumson Rd., Atlanta, GA 30305
Founding date: 1981

A Two Ring Circus is actually story theatre, presented by two actor/musicians who play multiple roles. Their material consists of folktales of the world and a program called *Stories of the South*. Quick costume changes and live music enhance the performance. The company develops its own scripts in an effort to make the stories relevant to contemporary child audiences. Workshops and residencies of a week, as well as touring engagements, are available throughout the year. Technical requirements are minimal.

U

UNITED MIME WORKERS

Address: P.O. Box 2088, Station A, Champaign, IL 61820
Founding date: 1971. Closed 1986.

The company had a repertory that included plays for children, plays for high school students, and plays for adults. For children, a modernized version of *The Emperor's New Clothes* was presented as *The President's New Clothes* and is costumed in current garments. For college students and general audiences, popular offerings were *Mime Is No Object, The Reproduction of the Working Day,* and *A Visual Performance of Compositions.* The company was available year-round for both performances and workshops or residencies. Stage requirements consisted of a performing area of at least twenty feet by sixteen feet, microphones, tape recorders, and flexible stage lighting.

UNIVERSITY OF HAWAII THEATRE FOR CHILDREN

Address: John Fitzgerald Kennedy Theatre, 1770 East-West Rd., Honolulu, HI 96822
Founding date: 1972

The department of drama and theatre of the University of Hawaii at Manoa offers an extensive program in theatre for children. The degrees of master of fine arts and master of arts are available with a concentration in theatre for children. The doctorate in Western theatre is also offered, allowing for a concentration in theatre for children. Courses available on both undergraduate and graduate levels include creative drama, creative movement, puppetry, and theatre for children. The goals of the program are to stimulate interest in an appreciation of drama in education, to promote research, and to provide practical training in theatre, dance, and puppetry.

Faculty, graduate students, and guest artists direct productions for child audiences on both the main stage and the laboratory theatre. Since

1972 the University Theatre for Children has produced both original and established works: musicals (*Patchwork: Friends, Feelings, 'n Me*; *Patchwork: It's a Great Day*; *Theatre Magic*; and *Androcles and the Lion*); two operas (*Little Red Riding Hood* and *Adventures in a Garden*); five dance/ dramas (*Peter and the Wolf*, *Ceilbert's Christmas*, *The Ugly Duckling*, *Why the Evergreens Keep Their Leaves in Winter*, and *Friends*). Other productions have included *Reynard the Fox*, *Dracula's Treasure*, and a Thai play. University students have created puppets for the Honolulu Symphony, the Honolulu Zoo, and the local public broadcasting station.

The University Theatre tours regularly on Oahu and the neighboring islands. The puppet troupe has toured annually since 1973, performing ethnic legends and giving workshops. In the spring of 1977 a grant was awarded to tour *Adventures in a Garden* to the neighboring islands. A company of twelve performed to over 8,000 children. A second tour was sponsored in the fall of 1977.

Professional guest artists perform and lecture regularly in Hawaii. Recent visitors have included Kermit Love (creator of Sesame Street's Snuffalufagus and Big Bird), Caroll Spinny (Sesame Street's puppeteer for Big Bird and Oscar), Jim Henson, (The Puppet Man), Jim Gamble's Marionettes, Nancy Renfro, Nikki Tilroe, Dorothy Heathcote, and the mime troupe Mummenschanz. Professional troupes from Asia have included the Awaji Puppet Theatre and the Kathakali Masked Dancers.

According to Professor Tamara Hunt, offerings have expanded in the past few years. The department has a strong production program (several plays produced annually for children; opportunities for students to pursue individualized projects in hospitals, schools, and television stations and to work with puppet troupes, the Honolulu Theatre for Youth, and other outstanding community organizations). The University of Hawaii is listed among the Winifred Ward Scholarship institutions.

THE UNIVERSITY OF KANSAS THEATRE FOR YOUNG PEOPLE
Address: The University of Kansas, Murphy Hall, Lawrence, KS 66045
Founding date: 1954

The University of Kansas Theatre for Young People celebrated its thirtieth year of operation in 1984. The theatre department is one of those approved for Winifred Ward Scholars and had the distinction of training the first Ward Scholar, Roger Bedard, in 1979. Jed Davis, chairman of the department, went to Kansas in 1960 as lighting designer and director of children's theatre. Eventually he gave up the former to concentrate full-time on the latter. He wanted the theatre to make more of an impact on the community and to that end initiated a working relationship with the Lawrence District School System. In the beginning schools bussed children to university performances; more recently, however, under the auspices of the Kansas Arts commission, university plays went on the road. Both means of reaching children of the community are employed today. This association of "town and gown" has not only been worthwhile for both partners, but some of the current performers in the Theatre for Young People were former spectators in school audiences.

During the thirty years of its existence the Theatre for Young People has produced sixty-one plays. The first play given on campus was *Rumpelstiltskin*. Early productions at Kansas, as elsewhere, included many dramatizations of children's classics and folk and fairy tales. The production of *Peter Pan* in 1964 was the first children's play to be included in the major series on the University of Kansas main stage. In recent years the number of productions has increased and with it the scope of the program. Today one finds some of the newest scripts by such American children's playwrights as Aurand Harris and Suzan Zeder on the season's schedule. The Kansas program has received numerous awards and honors. Jed Davis has been president of The Children's Theatre Association of America (q.v.) and The American Theatre Association (q.v.). He is coauthor of one of the landmark texts on children's theatre production, *Theatre, Children and Youth*, written with Mary Jane Evans and published by Anchorage Press in 1982.

UNIVERSITY OF MINNESOTA YOUNG PEOPLE'S THEATRE
Address: 110 Rarig Center, 320 S. 21 St., Minneapolis, MN 55455
Founding date: 1931

Plays for children have been given at the University of Minnesota for many years, first under the direction of Kenneth Graham, a well-known authority in the field. The program has undergone many changes since its beginning, responding to the interests and needs of the city and the university students. One of the attractive features in the sixties and seventies was the Peppermint Tent, a facility that offered plays to audiences of children during the summer months. Student actors performed and were, in fact, regular members of the summer company. In 1976 it was moved for convenience to the Stoll Thrust Theatre in the Rarig Center Theatre Complex. In 1981 the Peppermint Tent was discontinued for lack of funds.

So far as the winter program is concerned, the University Theatre mounts an annual production for children in the early spring under the title of the Young People's University Theatre. This program caters to group reservations from area schools, grades 2–7, although there are usually additional performances for the general public. The theatre furnishes teaching aids and suggested activities to the teacher in charge, making the performance an educational experience as well as an entertaining one. Past performances have included *You're a Good Man Charlie Brown*, *Androcles and the Lion*, *Tales of the Old West*, and *Reynard the Fox*.

The productions are directed by M.F.A. candidates in directing or by guest directors.

Fifty to sixty performances a year are reported although some of the other university productions could fall into the category of family theatre. Many teachers, professors, directors, and children's theatre playwrights have studied at Minnesota in past years.

UNIVERSITY OF NORTHERN IOWA, THEATRE UNI
Address: Cedar Falls, IA 50614
Founding date: 1947

Theatre UNI is a combination of programs, including an innovative curriculum, major theatrical productions, and many experimental student projects in the theatre arts. The theatre arts curriculum is aimed at instructing the prospective teacher as well as the student interested in pursuing a career in the professional theatre or a graduate degree. Although there is no undergraduate major in creative drama/children's theatre, a variety of coursework is offered to students interested in emphasizing this area of theatre. Courses include creative drama, children's theatre, and practical experience in touring a play for child audiences. Additional independent study advanced work can be pursued in each emphasis. One production slot per year is devoted to a theatre for youth script. Past seasons have included *The Arkansaw Bear, The Sleeping Beauty, Working*, and *The Great Cross-Country Race*.

UNI also offers a master's degree in child drama and is on the list of certified programs for Winifred Ward Scholars.

UNIVERSITY OF UTAH YOUNG PEOPLE'S THEATRE
Address: Pioneer Memorial Theatre, Salt Lake City, UT 84112
Founding date: 1943

The Young People's Theatre at the University of Utah has been presenting children's theatre consistently for nearly forty years. C. Lowell Lees and Vern Adix, both well-known names in educational theatre, joined forces in 1945 in the first children's production, *Anne of Green Gables*. Adix, a professor in the university theatre department for four decades, only recently stepped down as executive director of the Young People's Theatre after supervising more than 150 children's productions.

Xan S. Johnson, the current director of both the Young People's Theatre and the child drama program, ushered the theatre into a new era with the addition of a University Theatre-in-Education Touring Company, designed to bring live performances directly into schools throughout the state. Thus both traditional titles and educational programs comprised the new approach.

During the Young People's season, four productions are offered annually in two theatres. Two shows play on the Pioneer Memorial Theatre's professional stage, and two shows designed for older youth play in an intimate 200-seat theatre. The University Theatre-in-Education Touring Company goes to over forty schools, performing to over 30,000 young people. There is, in addition, a Theatre School for Youth, an intense year-round program run by graduate students and faculty for highly motivated and talented youth between the ages of six and eighteen. During the school year, classes are offered after school for youngsters six to twelve years old. In June of each year, a school is conducted eight hours daily, five days a week, for twelve- to seventeen-year-olds. Touch, a touring company that performs primarily in elementary schools, presents material designed to educate young people about sexual abuse and incest.

The university grants the M.F.A. and Ph.D. degrees in child drama. It is on the list of approved programs for Winifred Ward Scholars.

UNIVERSITY OF WASHINGTON
Address: Seattle, WA 98195
Founding date: 1932

Although the program in theatre was established in the early thirties, there were two new developments at the university in the fifties. One was the establishment of creative dramatics as a required course for all recreation and education majors; the other was the inauguration of a touring program of children's plays. The purpose of the latter was to introduce live drama into the communities of the Northwest and to bring this art form to children who otherwise would probably have no opportunity to see a play.

Although the University of Washington was a pioneer in the field and a leader in children's drama and theatre for thirty years, the program was dropped in 1981. Reasons were not given, but the amount of theatrical activity for children in the Seattle area could have led to its termination. Geraldine Brain Siks and Agnes Haaga, nationally known theatre educators, were responsible for the development of the program; after their retirement, they were followed by Suzan Zeder, a popular children's playwright, and Susan Pearson. Many teachers and directors in the field today received their theatre education at the University of Washington between 1932 and 1982. While the department is still strong, the emphasis has shifted from child drama to theatre for adults.

UNIVERSITY OF WISCONSIN AT MADISON
Address: Vilas Communication Hall, Madison, WI 53706
Founding date: 1973

The University of Wisconsin at Madison has both a creative drama program for the training of elementary teachers and a strong emphasis on children's theatre. One major production for young audiences is given each semester. Performances are scheduled so that elementary school children can be bussed to the university. After the performance, tours of the theatre and art museum across the street are made available. The second semester production is performed for the general public only. In addition, productions have been taken to the Kennedy Center in Washington, D.C., and to the International Festival of the Child in Sibenik, Yugoslavia. Titles have included both classics and new plays, including *Tom Sawyer, Beauty and the Beast, Winnie the Pooh, Step on a Crack, The Arkansaw Bear*, and *Snoopy*. The University of Wisconsin–Madison has one of the programs certified for Winifred Ward Scholars. John Tolch, who directs children's plays, has been editor of *Children's Theatre Review* and is an active member of the organization regionally and nationally.

V

VIRGINIA POLYTECHNIC INSTITUTE AND STATE UNIVERSITY

Address: Blacksburg, VA 24061

Founding date: 1979

Virginia Tech's Program in Child Drama leads to an M.F.A. degree in theatre arts. The program is three years in length and offers emphases in theatre for children and creative drama, with work in production, management, and drama-in-education. In addition to the formal, individualized course work, each M.F.A. candidate is required to fulfill an internship with a professional theatre or arts organization. In addition to courses within the Theatre Arts Department and the internship, students are enrolled in courses (according to need) in such other university units as the School of Education and the child development and recreation programs. Finally, the Theatre Arts Department maintains close liaisons with local schools, with state, regional, and national arts agencies, and with professional children's theatre companies.

The Program in Child Drama at Virginia Tech is highly individualized according to the needs and goals of each student. A course of study for a child drama graduate student may include various combinations of the following:

Core courses in the theatre curriculum such as styles of theatrical production, directing, and arts management;

Theatre courses in child drama such as children's theatre, creative drama, and puppetry;

Courses from related disciplines such as education, recreation, and child development;

Individualized studio assignments and projects

Short-term residencies and task-oriented projects with professional theatre companies;

Full term internship with a professional children's theatre or an arts agency;
   and
A final project.

The Theatre Arts-University Theatre produces an average of twenty plays per year, including a wide range of plays for young audiences. These plays are produced as part of both the main stage and the studio seasons. The department also regularly hosts performances by professional children's theatre companies.

The Program in Child Drama is on the approved list for Winifred Ward Scholars, and Roger Bedard of its faculty was the first recipient of a Ward Scholarship.

W

WASHINGTON THEATRE OF YOUTH
Address: Seattle, WA
Founding date: 1936. Closed by the end of the 1930s.

The Washington Theatre of Youth came into existence as the result of the interest stimulated by the Repertory Playhouse Civic Theatre of Seattle. It presented Shakespearean plays for Seattle children and toured productions to neighboring towns during the early thirties. Portrayed as the first state theatre in the United States, this experiment in theatre and education later organized seventeen areas, with performance centers in each. Local sponsors handled the business arrangements as the company toured the seventeen areas. Although the project was hailed with enthusiasm, there were no later references to its work.

WICHITA CHILDREN'S THEATRE
Address: 9112 East Central, Wichita, KS 67206
Founding date: 1945

The idea of a theatre for children in Wichita came from Maude Gowen Schallenberger, a community leader and arts organizer. It was Irene Vickers Baker, however, who turned the dream into reality. Together the two women handled the business details and the production of plays. In the early years performances took place in the local high school auditorium; later a touring program was added and plays were taken to elementary schools.

Still later, the need for a school of performing arts in Wichita was expressed and, in an effort to meet the need, classes in creative drama, acting, and dance were organized. In 1966 the Wichita Children's Theatre Guild of ninety-six members assembled. Its objectives were to provide a permanent organization to support the children's theatre program and to broaden the public's understanding of its value. From this meeting a group of citizens and educators began an active fund-raising campaign, which led to the building of a theatre in 1971. The Wichita Children's Theatre is one of the few fully equipped buildings in the United States designed exclusively for the production of plays for young audiences. Moreover, the organization has been in existence for over forty years, offering classics and traditional stories with special emphasis on the visual effects. The Wichita Children's Theatre offers over one hundred performances annually. In 1977 a book describing the history of this successful community theatre was published. Beautifully illustrated, *The Wichita Children's Theatre* by Irene Vickers Baker shows the progress of an enterprise that has met the artistic, social, and educational needs of a town.

THE WILL GEER THEATRICUM BOTANICUM REPERTORY THEATRE COMPANY
Address: 1419 North Topanga Canyon Blvd., Topanga, CA 90290
Founding date: 1973

An educational and professional group, the Will Geer Theatricum Botanicum Repertory Theatre Company was founded and developed from a theatre workshop where aspiring actors could learn their craft and experienced professional actors could pass on their knowledge and keep their skills and techniques tuned. The group, which named itself for the popular character actor of the time, presented Shakespeare and other classical plays free of charge to the public. The grounds of the theatre contained many of the plants mentioned in the plays of Shakespeare, hence Theatricum Botanicum, or "theatre of plants."

In 1978 the company started paying the experienced actors who were devoting much of their time to the project. Apart from the academic curriculum for young, aspiring actors, other educational programs were developed by the company. These included the Youth Drama Camp (a summer program for children from age eight through sixteen), an intensive Shakespeare seminar, and School Days Field Trips in the spring. The Will Geer Theatre cannot be construed as a children's theatre, but the fact that entertainment and classes in the theatre arts were offered to children and young people places it among theatres in which they were included during the seventies.

WOLF TRAP FARM PARK FOR THE PERFORMING ARTS
Address: Vienna, VA 22180
Founding date: 1971

An extensive summer program of performances for persons of all ages has been offered at Wolf Trap since 1971 under the auspices of the National Park Service. Events are planned to take place in the Theatre in the Woods and in the Meadow Tent. Although most of the evening entertainment is geared to adults and family audiences, the daytime events are planned for children. These include musical programs, mime shows, acrobatics, puppetry, and theatre appropriate to several age levels. A beautiful outdoor setting with picnic facilities and acres of well-kept wooded land distinguishes this theatre and makes it an attractive site for area residents during the summer months. Performing companies for the children's shows are drawn from both the professional stage and local universities.

After a damaging fire in 1981, the theatre at Wolf Trap was closed. It was completely rebuilt and officially opened again in the summer of 1984. All previous services were restored at that time, again making Wolf Trap Farm Park one of the most beautiful resources in the country, offering, in addition to its splendid physical facilities, a superior quality of summer entertainment for adults, children, and family audiences. Children from local camps are bussed in by arrangement with the administration, so that attendance is both high and steady during the summer months. Wolf Trap is the only park for the performing arts in the United States.

WORLD MOTHER GOOSE
Address: 1625 Broadway, Seattle, WA 98122
Founding date: 1979

World Mother Goose is a nonprofit, tax exempt, professional theatre company designed to promote participation in and appreciation of the performing arts in preschool aged children. The company develops its own material from rehearsals, which include improvisation, mime, and the use of contemporary and traditional children's literature. The focus of the material is not only entertainment but the solving of problems familiar to young children. The final result is educational storytelling that is fun and fulfills its goal to develop enthusiasm for live theatre in very young children. It is this audience of children from two to ten that makes World Mother Goose a unique company in the Seattle area. Most of the productions are adapted by the artistic director, Mollie M. Hughes. Twelve full-time and eight part-time actors comprise the company, which offers other educational services in addition to its performances. These include apprenticeships in directing and workshops in acting with parents of young children. The company gives over fifty-five performances annually in both indoor and outdoor settings.

Y

YELLOW BRICK ROAD SHOWS

Address: P.O. Box 5728, Huntington Beach, CA 92646
Founding date: 1976. Closed in 1980.

Yellow Brick Road was a popular professional touring company during the seventies. Two productions a season were reported, with over 250 performances. Every show was developed by the company and designed to meet the interests and needs of a particular age level. Follow-up packages of suggested ways in which the production might be extended and enhanced were sent to teachers; in addition, complimentary creative drama sessions were provided by the company following the performance, if requested. Budget cuts for education in California resulted in the disbanding of the company in the spring of 1980, with the suggestion of a resumption of performances in the future. Classes were offered while the theatre was in full operation, but these were also dropped later because there was no resident facility in which to hold them.

YORK LITTLE THEATRE

Address: 27 S. Belmont Street, York, PA 17403
Founding date: 1932

Like many of the early community theatres in America, the York Little Theatre was established in the early thirties but did not introduce plays for children on a regular basis until much later. There is some controversy as to when the children's activities were actually started, for plays were presented in what is described today by a resident of York as a "hit and miss pattern." The first actors were high school students who enjoyed dramatics; longtime volunteers in the theatre recall the pleasure these young people received from performing for children and how many of them got their start in future careers through this community organization. It was not until 1962, however, that a regular program of plays for children was scheduled, though from all reports, good work and strong community interest preceded it and led to its development.

The first full-time artistic director to be hired was Elbert Smith. Now deceased, he was director of the theatre for over twenty-five years. As part of his work, he organized the first touring show for children, *Aladdin and His Wonderful Lamp*, in 1962. The first full-time children's theatre director was Robert Miller, who led activities between 1974 and 1982. He directed plays and supervised classes. When he left to go to the New York Performing Arts High School, activities were reduced but were restored in the 1984–1985 season.

Productions for both children and adults were originally given in an old academy, with rehearsals often held in schools. A later move to larger quarters offered both main-stage and studio space. Periodic renovation has resulted in greatly expanded backstage and lobby areas.

Today the children's plays are an important part of the York Little Theatre program. A full season performed by adult actors includes classic folktales, with an occasional modern musical or current title appropriate for older children. For example, the 1984–1985 brochure listed the following: *Hansel and Gretel, Beauty and the Beast, Jack and the Beanstalk*, plus *Annie*, and, on three special Saturdays, *The Puppet Factory*. In addition to public performances, the York Little Theatre today offers classes in dramatic play, theatre games, and creative movement for grades K–2; creative dramatics, introduction to acting and dance for grades 3–5; acting, improvisation, jazz and musical theatre dance for grades 6–8; and advanced acting for junior and senior high school students.

THE YOUNG ACT COMPANY
Address: 100 West Roy, Seattle, WA 98119
Founding date: 1966

The Young ACT Company of A Contemporary Theatre is the oldest professional theatre company performing for young audiences on the West Coast. Since 1966, its original productions have been performed by a company of Equity actors selected annually from national auditions. Its scripts have introduced live theatre to tens of thousands of school children, teachers, and parents throughout the western United States, Alaska, and Canada. The Young ACT Company also has performed at international festivals and at the Kennedy Center in Washington, D.C., and it was awarded the 1980 Jennie Heiden Award for excellence in professional children's theatre from The Children's Theatre Association of America (q.v.). Each year, besides touring, the Young ACT Company also performs in residence at ACT Theatre in Seattle. It gives 150 performances a year.

YOUNG AUDIENCES, INC.
Address: 115 E. 92 St., New York, NY 10028
Founding date: 1952

Young Audiences, Inc., is a national organization that has not concerned itself with children's theatre until recently. Its headquarters are located in New York, but it has established chapters in different cities across the country. By the early eighties there were thirty-eight chapters of Young Audiences with 2,800 professional artists participating in its programs. Originally dedicated to music, it later broadened its services to include the other performing arts. Over 6,000 workshops and 12,000 performances of music and drama were reported in 1982, and the totals were rising.

Young Audiences has been described as conservative in its approach, but this may be interpreted as preferring established artists and classic works to the unknown and experimental. Under any circumstances, Young Audiences promotes only the best, and it enjoys an excellent reputation among sponsors. One important aspect of its work is to provide research techniques for the development of arts education programs, which it then shares with professionals in the field. Young Audiences merits inclusion here both for the services it has rendered in the field of performing arts and because it now concerns itself with children's theatre.

YOUNG PEOPLE'S THEATRE (YPT)
Address: P.O. Box 608, Brunswick, ME 04011
Founding date: 1972

The Young People's Theatre was founded by Al Miller, who still directs activities including theatre production, workshops, and related activities, primarily for children. YPT describes itself as the only touring theatre in the state of Maine with children performing for children. It is a nonprofit organization that employs a full-time artistic director and a part-time business manager. YPT does not have a facility of its own but rents space over a store in Brunswick, where costumes are stored and rehearsals are held during the warm months. Most of the work during the school year is done out of Mt. Ararat School (grades 6 to 12) in Topsham, Maine. The company holds winter classes that run for six weeks; clowning classes that run for four weeks in the spring; and summer classes that run for six weeks.

In 1983–1984 two shows were toured: *Alice in Wonderland* in the fall went to dozens of schools in the state, with four performances in Connecticut. *Too Much!*, a play about "overdoing," toured in the spring and offered several public performances. Another original script, *The Pollution Solution*, written by the cast and Al Miller, was booked for engagements in New York and Michigan during the 1984–1985 season.

The YPT brochure carries the following statement regarding its philosophy: "The Young People's Theatre helps a child to trust his own perceptions, his own instincts—to find an answer that comes from his own feelings before he checks it against anything else, be it a book, a movie, or an adult. . . . All good, honest, true art, and human values come from the inside out. And that is a little magic."

YOUNG PEOPLE'S THEATRE OF CENTER STAGE (YPT)
Address: 700 N. Calvert St., Baltimore, MD 21202
Founding date: 1963

Since 1963 Young People's Theatre of Center Stage has entertained thousands of school children throughout the state of Maryland with performances of live theatre. Each year a new play is selected by the theatre's artistic director, Stan Wojewodski. In the past these selections have ranged from an adaptation of Homer's *Odyssey* to an original musical. Despite rising inflation, YPT has maintained quality and has not cut the number of performances. This has been accomplished by the support of the board and by grants from national, state, and local sources.

YPT offers a play complete with costumes and setting specifically developed to entertain and challenge young viewers; workshops where actors encourage students to explore their own imaginations through movement, sound, and language; and study guides suggesting pre- and post-performance activities to enrich the student's experience long after YPT has gone. Workshops and performances each take place within one class period of approximately forty-five minutes.

By the end of the seventies 280 performances during the school year were reported.

YOUNG PEOPLE'S THEATRE OF NEW YORK CITY. *See* CITY CENTER YOUNG PEOPLE'S THEATRE.

YOUNG PEOPLE'S THEATRE ON TOUR
Address: Department of Speech and Drama, California State University, Chico, CA 95929
Founding date: 1972

The Young People's Theatre on Tour and the Pegasus Players, originally two separate programs, are now combined as a result of budget cuts. While the program has been moved off campus, the nature and quality have been maintained. The Young People's Theatre has traveled over 15,000 miles and given over 400 performances for more than 350 schools and 100,000 young people since its founding in 1972. The performances are fifty minutes in length and carry such titles as *Princesses, Princes and Peasants in Song and Story*. The Pegasus Players, on the other hand, aim at providing a unique and high quality theatrical experience for high schools, colleges, and communities (family audiences). Recent titles such as *Clarence Darrow: A One-Man Play* and *Benjamin Franklin* indicate the thrust of the Pegasus Players. Still under the direction of the Department of Speech and Drama at California State University, Chico, the intent, organization, and extent of the new, combined programs are unchanged.

In addition to performances, one-day residencies are available. Workshops in storytelling and dramatic activities are also offered for teachers, students, and parents. Like many other theatre departments today, California State has combined programs in an effort to maintain quality while cutting operational costs.

YOUTHEATRE. *See* THE DETROIT YOUTHEATRE.

Z

ZACHARY SCOTT THEATRE. *See* PROJECT INTERACT/ZACHARY SCOTT THEATRE.

Appendixes

APPENDIX 1

Other Extant Children's Theatre Companies

The following companies provided little or no information on request. There was sufficient evidence of continuing operation, however, to warrant listing them among extant groups at the time this work was undertaken. It is probable that there are other groups that meet the criteria of fifty performances a year and five years in existence but are unknown to state arts councils and Actors' Equity Association. If they are not members of theatre associations or have closed, information about them is difficult to obtain.

The American Company
Address: P.O. Box 310, Fairhope, AL 36532
Founding date: 1974
   The American Company was listed in the 1978 CTAA directory as offering 200 performances a year.

Children's Theatre of Maine
Address: P.O. Box 1925, Portland, ME 04104
Founding date: 1930
   The Children's Theatre of Maine was listed in the 1978 CTAA directory as offering 175–200 performances a year.

Mr. & Mrs. Fish
Address: SMVTI, Fort Rd., S. Portland, ME 04106

Jack Hill
Address: 605 Waukegan Rd., Glenview, IL 60025
Performing Arts Group
Address: P.O. Box 21482, Concord, CA 94521
Founding date: 1975
   The Performing Arts Group was listed in the 1978 CTAA directory as offering 250 performances a year.

Portland Stage Co.
Address: P.O. Box 1458, Portland, ME 04104

The Robin Hood Players, Inc.
Address: Scottsdale, AZ 85253

Founding date: 1964

This professional children's touring theatre serves all ages and reported 4,500 performances a year in the 1978 survey conducted by The Children's Theatre Association of America. It is still in existence according to the state arts council, though it performs mostly outside the state.

The Theatre of the Enchanted Forest
Address: P.O. Box 336, Orono, ME 04473

Theatrical Productions for Children, Inc.
Address: 7731 Eastland Terr., Chicago, IL 60053
Founding date: 1971

The thrust of the company's program is entertainment. It is professional and reports over 125 performances annually.

Yates Musical Theatre for Children
Address: 19 Morse Ave., E. Orange, NJ 07017

APPENDIX 2

A Chronology of Events

The following chronology lists the founding dates of selected historical theatre companies, organizations, and events affecting theatre for children in America. For example, the first gathering of children's theatre leaders at Northwestern University in 1944 and the founding of ASSITEJ in 1964 represent highlights when viewed from the perspective of the eighties. Although other researchers might make some different inclusions, it is probable that there would be a consensus regarding the majority of them, for they are generally accepted to have been milestones in the history of the children's theatre movement.

1903   Founding date of the first children's theatre in the United States, The Children's Educational Theatre in New York
1905   Maude Adams' production of *Peter Pan* on Broadway
1910   The founding of The Drama League of America
1915   The Neighborhood Playhouse erected in New York
1920   The Association of Junior Leagues of America initiated planned dramatic activities for children
         Emerson College in Boston offered plays for children
1921   The founding date of the Clare Tree Major Children's Theatre
1921   Montrose J. Moses' publication of *A Treasury of Plays for Children*
1922   Theatre Tulsa incorporated
1923   Founding of The King-Coit School of Acting and Design in New York
1924   Goodman Memorial Theatre in Chicago began program of theatre for children
1925   Founding date of The Children's Theatre of Evanston by Winifred Ward
1927   Publication of Constance D'Arcy Mackay's *Children's Theatres and Plays*
1931   Founding date of the Nashville Children's Theatre
1932   Founding date of the Wichita Children's Theatre in Wichita, Kansas
         Eva Le Gallienne's production of *Alice in Wonderland* in New York
1935   Fort Wayne Civic Theatre was established; programs for children given the following year. In 1971 renamed Fort Wayne Youtheatre
         Founding of the Children's Theatre Press by Sara Spencer in Charleston, West Virginia (later renamed the Anchorage Press, Inc., after the move to Anchorage, Kentucky)

The Federal Theatre for Children established by Congress

1936   The opening of the new home of The Palo Alto Children's Theatre
       The founding date of Junior Programs, Inc.

1937   The Children's Centre for Creative Arts established at Adelphi University

1939   Establishment of Seattle Junior Theatre Programs, Inc.
       The closing of The Federal Theatre for Children

1943   Founding of The Children's Experimental Theatre of Baltimore by Isabel
       Burger

1944   Meeting of children's theatre leaders on the campus of Northwestern
       University

1945   Birmingham, Alabama, Children's Theatre founded
       Theatre for Youth established at the University of Texas at Austin

1946   Founding of Stage One: The Louisville Children's Theatre

1947   Founding date of Children's World Theatre

1950   Establishment of the Children's Theatre Committee of the American
       Educational Theatre Association (AETA)
       The Jean Arthur and Boris Karloff production of *Peter Pan* on Broadway

1952   The Children's Theatre Conference (CTC) established as a division of
       the American Educational Theatre Association (AETA); later to be
       named The Children's Theatre Association of America (CTAA)

1955   The first showcase of children's theatre plays in New York under the
       aegis of CTAA, Region 14
       Mary Martin production of *Peter Pan*
       Honolulu Theatre for Youth established

1956   Charlotte Chorpenning Cup awarded to an outstanding children's theatre
       playwright

1958   Zeta Phi Eta–Winifred Ward Award for Outstanding Achievement of a
       new children's theatre company in existence for at least four years
       Founding date of the Paper Bag Players

1960   Dedication of the Nashville Theatre building for the exclusive use of
       children

1961–69   Formation of state arts councils in all fifty states

1962   Performing Arts Repertory Theatre (PART) established in New York
       City

1963   Founding date of New Plays for Children, Inc.

1964   Formation of ASSITEJ (Association Internationale du Theatre pour
       l'Enfance et la Jeunesse)
       Inclusion of children's plays in the program of The Living Stage in
       Washington, D.C.

1966   Jennie Heiden Award given for the first time for "Excellence in Profes-
       sional Children's Theatre"

1968   *A Directory of Children's Theatres in the United States*, a publication of AETA

1969   Alliance Theatre of Atlanta, Georgia, included theatre for children

1970   The Little Theatre of the Deaf performance at Lincoln Center

1972   ASSITEJ Congress held in Albany, New York

1973   Founding date of Metro Theatre Circus in St. Louis
       The Southern Educational Theatre of Biloxi, Mississippi, established

1974   Founding date of the Empire State Youth Theatre in Albany, the first state mandated theatre for children in America; later renamed the Empire State Institute for the Performing Arts (ESIPA)

1975 The Nebraska Theatre Caravan established in Omaha with a Junior Theatre Center

Formal opening of the new theatre complex of The Children's Theatre Company of Minneapolis

1976 Incorporation of New Plays, Inc. (formerly New Plays for Children)

1977 Establishment of the Kennedy Center programs for children

1978 Sara Spencer Award given for exceptional achievement of an established children's theatre company

Awarding of the first Winifred Ward Scholarship to Roger Bedard

1979 The first annual CTAA sponsored showcase

1981 The Sandy Duncan production of *Peter Pan* on Broadway

1983 The establishment of ASSITEJ/USA as an independent organization

1984 World Festival of Children's Theatre organized by ASSITEJ/USA and the New Orleans World's Fair

1986 Closing of CTAA as a result of the termination of ATA

Reforming of a new children's theatre association entitled the American Association of Theatre for Youth (AATY)

APPENDIX 3

Personalities Roster

The following Personalities Roster lists the men and women who have been most instrumental in furthering children's theatre in the United States. Although hundreds of others have contributed to the movement, the persons cited here, either through their activities or their writing, made contributions which are generally known and recognized as important.

Jane Addams—Director of Hull House in Chicago and one of the first strong supporters of children's theatre in the United States.

Robert Alexander—Director of the Living Stage, a project of Washington's Arena Theatre during the sixties, seventies, and eighties; known for his experimental work in children's theatre.

Flora Atkin—Well-known children's playwright in the sixties, seventies, and eighties; associated with Adventure Theatre of Maryland.

Roger Bedard—First Winifred Ward Scholar; editor of the anthology *Dramatic Literature for Children: A Century in Review.*

Tom Behm—Professor and director of The Young People's Theatre at the University of North Carolina, Greensboro; a past president of The Children's Theatre Association of America and former editor of *Children's Theatre Review.*

Campton Bell—Pioneer in children's theatre; University of Denver professor and director of the Children's Theatre Conference in 1949.

Betty Bobp—Founder of the Harwich Junior Theatre on Cape Cod, the first "straw hat theatre for children." Professor emeritus of child drama at Emerson College.

Isabel Burger—Director of the Children's Experimental Theatre of Baltimore in the early years of the movement; later an author and activist.

Gerald Chapman—First director of the Young Playwrights' Project (from 1981 to 1984), sponsored by the Dramatists Guild of New York.

Charlotte Chorpenning—One of the first children's playwrights in America; author of "rules for writing plays for child audiences"; associated with the pioneering period at Northwestern University and the Goodman Children's Theatre in Chicago.

Orlin Corey—Director of The Everyman Players; publisher of the Anchorage

Press after Sara Spencer's death; a past president of The Children's Theatre Association of America.

Gayle Cornelison—Chairman of *Children's Theatre Directory*, 1978; director of California Young People's Theatre in San Jose.

Rita Criste—Retired professor of creative drama and children's theatre at Northwestern University; featured teacher in the film *Creative Drama: The First Steps*.

Jed Davis—Professor, author, leader in children's theatre; a past president of The Children's Theatre Association of America and the American Theatre Association; retired from University of Kansas.

John Clark Donahue—Founder and, until 1984, artistic director of the Minneapolis Children's Theatre Company and School, one of the best and best-known young people's theatres in the United States.

Nat Eek—A past president of The Children's Theatre Association of America and of ASSITEJ/USA, which organization he helped to begin activities, including program and services; professor at the University of Oklahoma.

Mary Jane Evans—Professor and director of children's theatre at California State University, Northridge; coauthor (with Jed Davis) of *Theatre, Children and Youth*.

Hallie Flanagan—Director of the Federal Theatre of the thirties. This project included a children's theatre component with sites in several cities throughout the United States, some of which outlived the parent organization.

Moses Goldberg—Professor, director, and author of books, plays, and articles on theatre for children and youth.

Kenneth Graham—Professor at the University of Minnesota; he wrote one of the first dissertationa on theatre for children and was chairman of one of the first departments offering work in this area.

Agnes Haaga—Professor emeritus of child drama at the University of Washington in Seattle; a past president of The Children's Theatre Association of America; one of the founders and fund-raisers for the Winifred Ward Scholarship Committee.

Jay Harnick—Producer, Theatreworks/USA, one of the oldest and largest producing companies offering theatre for children and young people in the United States.

Aurand Harris—Well-known children's playwright; recipient of many awards; described as our "most produced playwright for children."

Ruth Beall Heinig—Professor of child drama; a past president of The Children's Theatre Association of America and former editor of *Children's Theatre Review*.

Alice Minnie Herts—Founder of the first children's theatre in the United States, The Children's Educational Theatre in New York City (1903).

Ann Hill—A past president of The Children's Theatre Association of America and of The American Theatre Association; a founder of the Nashville Children's Theatre.

Rowena and Russell Jelliffe—Founders of the Karamu Theatre in Cleveland, Ohio, including its children's theatre; probably started the first black theatre in America.

Coleman A. Jennings—Professor of child drama at the University of Texas in Austin; former editor of *Children's Theatre Review* and editor of anthologies of plays for children's theatre; a past president of The Children's Theatre Association of America.

Judith Kase-Polisini—Instigator of research and seminars on child drama in the seventies and eighties; a past president of The Children's Theatre Association of America.

Edith King and Dorothy Coit—Founders and directors of The King-Coit School of Acting and Design in New York; from the twenties to the late fifties.

William Kolodney—For many years Education Director at the 92nd Street "Y" in New York; strong supporter of children's theatre in the United States.

Virginia Glasgow Koste—Professor of children's theatre, playwright, and author of *Dramatic Play, Preparation for Life.*

Paul Kozelka—A past president of The Children's Theatre Association of America; professor emeritus, Teachers College of Columbia University.

Joanna H. Kraus—Award-winning children's playwright of the sixties, seventies, and eighties; professor of child drama and theatre.

Nellie McCaslin—Professor; author of books, plays, and articles on children's theatre; a past president of the Children's Theatre Association of America.

Dorothy McFadden—Founder of Junior Programs, Inc., a professional children's theatre company in the late thirties and early forties.

Barbara McIntyre—Educator; a past president of The Children's Theatre Association of America; author of a text and numerous articles on creative drama for the special child; associated with the University of Pittsburgh, Northwestern University, and the University of Victoria.

Constance D'Arcy Mackay—Early supporter of children's theatre in America; children's playwright.

Percy Mackaye—Playwright and exponent of the pageant, including pageants for children in the early years of the children's theatre movement.

Clare Tree Major—Director of the Clare Tree Major Theatre for Children, one of the first touring companies of its kind, operating continuously from the early twenties to the mid-fifties.

Judith Martin—Founder and director of the Paper Bag Players Children's Theatre, New York City, from 1958 to the present.

Miriam Morton—Author of books and articles on theatre for children in the Soviet Union; translator of Russian plays for children.

Harold Oaks—Director of children's theatre at Brigham Young University, one of the largest and best-known departments in the West; officer of The Children's Theatre Association of America, on both regional and national levels.

Christine Prendergast—Coauthor with Helane Rosenberg of *Theatre for Young People: A Sense of Occasion.*

Helane Rosenberg—Educator; coauthor with Christine Prendergast of *Theatre for Young People: A Sense of Occasion.*

Dorothy Thames Schwartz—A past president of The Children's Theatre Association of America; coeditor with Dorothy Aldrich of *Give Them Roots and Wings.*

Ann Shaw—A past president of ASSITEJ/USA; editor of two books on theatre and the handicapped; vice president of ASSITEJ/International.

Geraldine Brain Siks—Professor emeritus of child drama at the University of

Washington in Seattle; playwright and author of books on children's theatre and creative drama.

Patricia Snyder—Founder of the Empire State Institute for the Performing Arts in Albany, New York (the first state mandated children's theatre in the United States).

Sara Spencer—Playwright and founder of the Children's Theatre Press, later renamed the Anchorage Press.

Viola Spolin—author of *Improvisation for the Theatre* and originator of theatre games.

Grace Stanistreet—Founder and director of Adelphi University's Children's Centre for the Creative Arts from 1937 to 1980. Author of books and articles, and proponent of arts education rather than theatre education as a single subject.

Lowell Swortzell—Professor of drama and theatre at New York University; playwright and author.

Lillian Wald—Director of the Henry Street Settlement in New York and a strong supporter of children's theatre activities in the early years.

Stuart Walker—Playwright, who also wrote plays for children in the early years of the movement; director of the Portmanteau (touring) Theatre in New York.

Winifred Ward—Professor of children's theatre and creative dramatics at Northwestern University; founder of The Children's Theatre of Evanston; author and founder of The Children's Theatre Association of America.

Brian Way—British author, playwright, and director of plays for the child audience; best known for his audience participation approach and his book on the subject.

John Weil—Founder of Metro Theatre Circus of St. Louis, a well-known touring children's theatre company.

Patricia Hale Whitton—Founder and publisher of New Plays, Inc., a publishing house dedicated to the publication of new and nontraditional plays, and books on children's theatre and child drama.

Barbara Salisbury Wills—First president of AATY and professor at the University of Texas at Austin.

Lin Wright—A past president of The Children's Theatre Association of America, editor of *The Professional Theatre for Young People Directory*, 1984; professor at Arizona State University.

Suzan Zeder—Children's playwright in the seventies and eighties; best known for her use of current themes and problems.

APPENDIX 4

Associations Involved in Children's Theatre

A number of associations have been or are currently involved in children's theatre activities, although only The Children's Theatre Association of America (CTAA) and ASSITEJ are exclusively devoted to this branch of the theatre. The others may include it, often scheduling productions for young audiences, or panels and group discussions on the subject at regional conferences. They also occasionally provide space for articles on children's theatre in their journals and newsletters.

The Drama League of America (1910–1931) was founded to help the many community theatres that were springing up all over the United States during this period, some of which included plays for children. The Association of Junior Leagues of America has always been actively involved in puppetry and children's theatre, though the participation has varied from city to city according to the interests and needs of the community. As a volunteer service organization, the Junior League contributes to a variety of social and cultural enterprises as well as children's theatre. Young Audiences, Inc., began as an agency founded to promote good music for young people, but it has gradually been adding other performing arts and artists to its list of attractions. It now has offices in thirty-eight cities, but not all include theatre. CTAA was composed of both individual and organizational members, and included representation from educational, community, and professional theatres. There are also a number of state and regional organizations that affiliated with the American Theatre Association (ATA), whose membership, like that of the divisions, may be organizational or individual. Some professional children's theatre companies belonged to CTAA; some did not. Others joined, dropped out, then renewed their memberships at a later date. The International Amateur Theatre Association (IATA) includes theatre on all levels but supports young people's work through biannual drama-in-education conferences rather than the production of plays. Membership in ASSITEJ is small but comes from professional, educational, and community theatre.

Actors' Equity Association is a union and, as such, is concerned solely with the welfare of its members: salaries, working conditions, and benefits. Not many professional children's theatre companies belong to Equity, and the number varies from year to year. At the present time there are about fifty companies with Equity contracts. Whatever the relationship of these various associations to children's theatre, they have all provided supportive services of one kind or another and, in the case of the Junior League and CTAA, have been responsible for the growth and development of many young companies.

In 1986 American Association of Theatre for Youth (AATY) was founded following the demise of CTAA.

APPENDIX 5

Geographical Directory

The listing that follows shows where historic children's theatres were located and where current theatres operate today. The largest concentrations have been and continue to be on the East and West coasts, with a substantial number of companies in several cities in the Middle West. Thus we can see that children's theatre has followed adult theatre in its location as well as in content and form. Although some states in this survey show surprisingly few theatres for young audiences, there were often dramatic activities of different sorts in these areas. These might be recreational programs with a drama component, occasional productions of a children's play, or classes in mime, creative drama, and puppetry. Some of these programs and activities have been described as being very good indeed, but those theatres not producing plays on a regular basis were not included in this appendix. Theatres listed here but not profiled in Part Two of this volume are asterisked.

ALABAMA

The American Company, Fairhope*
Birmingham Children's Theatre, Birmingham
Children's Musical Theatre, Inc., Mobile
Troy State University Pied Pipers, Troy

ALASKA

Alaska Junior Theatre, Anchorage
Arts Alaska, Inc., Anchorage

ARIZONA

Arizona State University Children's Theatre, Tempe
Childsplay, Inc., Tempe
Mesa Youtheatre, Mesa
The Phoenix Little Theatre, Phoenix
The Robin Hood Players, Inc., Scottsdale*
Scottsdale Theatre for Children, Scottsdale

ARKANSAS

Arkansas Arts Center Children's Theatre, Little Rock

CALIFORNIA

American Conservatory Theatre, San Francisco
American Living History Theatre, Hollywood
Burbage Theatre for Children, Los Angeles
California Creative Arts, Los Angeles*
California State University at Chico, Chico*
California State University at Northridge, Northridge
California Young People's Theatre, San Jose
Child Drama Center, Fresno*
Children's Repertory Theatre of San Francisco State University, San Francisco
The Children's Theatre of the West, Sacramento
Crackerbox Company Children's Theatre, Chico*
East Bay Children's Theatre, Inc., Oakland
East West Players, Los Angeles
Firebird Theatre Company, Hollywood
Improvisational Theatre Project, Mark Taper Forum, Los Angeles
The Inner City Cultural Center, Los Angeles*
J. P. Nightingale, Canoga Park
Junior Programs of California, Inc., Los Angeles
Kaleidoscope Players, Fullerton
The Magic Carpet Play Company, San Francisco
Mime Musica, Santa Monica*
Old Globe Theatre, San Diego
The Palo Alto Children's Theatre, Palo Alto
Peppermint Palace Community Theatre, Chico
Performing Arts Group, Concord*
Phantasy Company, San Jose
Pickle Family Circus, San Francisco
Players USA, Studio City*
San Diego Junior Theatre, San Diego
San Diego State University Children's Theatre, San Diego*
San Francisco Attic Theatre, San Francisco*
San Francisco Mime Troupe, Inc., San Francisco
San Francisco Players Guild, San Francisco
San Francisco State College Theatre, San Francisco
San Jose Repertory Phantasy Company, San Jose
Santa Monica Playhouse, Santa Monica
South Coast Repertory, Costa Mesa
Sunnyvale Community Players Junior Theatre, Sunnyvale
Theatre for Young Audiences at San Diego State University, San Diego
The Twelfth Night Repertory Company, Studio City
The Will Geer Theatricum Botanicum Repertory Theatre Company, Topanga
Yellow Brick Road Shows, Huntington Beach
Young People's Theatre on Tour, Chico

COLORADO

The Colorado Caravan, Boulder
Denver Center Theatre Company
Junior Entertainment, Inc., of Denver
Small World Players, Ft. Collins

CONNECTICUT

The Bridge, West Hartford
East-West Fusion Theatre, Sharon
Grumbling Gryphons, Brookfield
Little Theatre of the Deaf, Waterford
The Long Wharf Access Theatre Company, New Haven

DISTRICT OF COLUMBIA

The American Theatre Association
The Children's Theatre Association of America
The Federal Theatre for Children
The House of Play
Howard University Children's Theatre
Interplay Productions
The John F. Kennedy Center Programs for Children and Youth
Library Theatre, Inc.
The Living Stage Theatre Company
Palisades Theatre Company*
The National Junior Theatre of Washington, D.C.
Paul Robeson International Center for Performing Arts*
Programs for Children and Youth (Kennedy Center)
Teatro Doble

FLORIDA

Asolo Touring Theatre, Sarasota
Coconut Grove Playhouse/Burger King Touring Company, Miami
Florida State University Children's Theatre, Tallahassee
Fort Lauderdale Children's Theatre, Fort Lauderdale
Hippodrome Theatre-in-Education, Gainesville
The Little Palm Theatre, Boca Raton
Ruth Foreman's Pied Piper Playhouse, North Miami
Story Theatre Productions, Fort Lauderdale

GEORGIA

Academy Theatre for Youth, Atlanta
The Alliance Theatre Company/Atlanta Children's Theatre, Atlanta
Open City Children's Theatre, Atlanta
A Two Ring Circus, Atlanta

HAWAII

Honolulu Theatre for Youth
University of Hawaii Theatre for Children, Honolulu

ILLINOIS

Alice Liddell Theatre Company, Chicago
The Children's Civic Theatre of Chicago
The Children's Theatre of Evanston
Child's Play Touring Theatre, Chicago
The Drama League of America, Evanston
Goodman Theatre for Children, Chicago
Hull House, Chicago
The Illustrated Theatre, Evanston
Imagination Theatre, Inc., Chicago
The Jack and Jill Players, Chicago
Jack Hill, Glenview
La Monte Zeno Theatre, Chicago*
National College of Education Children's Theatre, Evanston
On Stage!, Chicago
Paramount Traveling Theatre Company, Aurora*
Peripatetic Task Force, Chicago*
St. Nicholas Theatre Company, Chicago
Theatrical Productions for Children, Inc., Chicago*
The Truck, Incorporated, Wilmette*
United Mime Workers, Champaign

INDIANA

The Children's Museum–Lilly Theatre, Indianapolis
The Children's Theatre of Gary
Children's Theatre of Terre Haute
Fort Wayne Youtheatre
Happiness Bag Players, Terre Haute*
Indiana Repertory Theatre, Indianapolis*
Indianapolis Junior Civic Theatre
Martin W. Kappel and Victoria Calvert Mimes, Indianapolis*
Midsummer Mime Theatre, Indianapolis
The Participation Players, North Manchester
The Peppermint Stick Players, St. Mary-of-the-Woods

IOWA

Black Hawk Children's Theatre (Waterloo Community Playhouse), Waterloo
Davenport Community Theatre*
Davenport Junior Theatre
University of Northern Iowa, Cedar Falls

KANSAS

Continental Theatre Company, Manhattan
Music Theatre for Young People, Wichita*
Seem-to-Be-Players, Inc., Lawrence
Theatre for Young America, Overland Park

The University of Kansas Theatre for Young People, Lawrence
Wichita Children's Theatre

KENTUCKY

Blue Apple Players, Louisville
Roadside Theatre, Whitesburg
Stage One: The Louisville Children's Theatre

LOUISIANA

The Children's Theatre Guild of New Orleans
The Everyman Players, Inc., New Orleans
Playmakers of Baton Rouge
Sheffield Ensemble Theatre, New Orleans

MAINE

Celebration Mime Theatre, Portland
Children's Theatre of Maine, Portland
Maine Acting Company, Lewiston
Mr. and Mrs. Fish, Portland
The Portland Children's Trailer Theatre
Portland Stage Co.
The Theatre of the Enchanted Forest, Orono
Young People's Theatre, Brunswick

MARYLAND

Adventure Theatre, Glen Echo
Archaesus Productions, Inc., Rockville
Children's Experimental Theatre of Baltimore
CTA Theatre for Young People, Baltimore*
Gary Young Mime Theatre (formerly Archaesus Productions), Rockville
In School Players of Adventure Theatre, Glen Echo*
Plexus Mime Theatre, Takoma Park
Round House Theatre, Silver Spring
Young People's Theatre of Center Stage, Baltimore

MASSACHUSETTS

The Boston Children's Theatre, Chestnut Hill
Boston Youth Theatre
Chamber Theatre Productions, Inc., Boston
Crosswalk Theatre of Young Audiences, Cambridge
Emerson College Children's Theatre, Boston
Emerson Stage, Boston*
First Night, Inc., Boston
Harwich Junior Theatre, Harwich
Just Around the Corner Company, Brookline
Little Flags Theatre, Roxbury
Living Poem Theatre, Greenfield*

Loon and Heron Theatre, Brookline
Mudhead Masks, Cambridge
Nettie Greenleaf's Children's Theatre, Boston
The New England Theatre Guild for Children, Boston
Shakespeare and Company, Lenox
Tribal Players, Boston
Tufts University Magic Circle, Medford

MICHIGAN

The Actor's Trunk Company, Bloomfield Hills
Albion Productions, Inc., Southfield
Detroit Recreation Department Theatre
The Detroit Youtheatre
Eastern Michigan University Theatre of the Young, Ypsilanti
Flint Youtheatre
Other Things and Company, Rochester
Prince Street Players, Ltd., Detroit
Siena Heights College, Adrien*
Southfield Repertory Theatre, Southfield*

MINNESOTA

Central High School Performing Arts Center, St. Paul
The Children's Theatre Company, Minneapolis
CLIMB, Inc., St. Paul
Community Theatre of Duluth
Fuller Young People's Theatre, Minneapolis
The Junior Repertory Theatre of Minneapolis
Old Log Theatre, Excelsior
St. Olaf College Children's Theatre Institute, Northfield
The St. Paul Children's Theatre
Sesame Street Live, Minneapolis
University of Minnesota Young People's Theatre, Minneapolis

MISSOURI

The Imaginary Theatre Company (Repertory Theatre of St. Louis)
Metro Theatre Circus, St. Louis

MONTANA

New Western Energy Show, Helena

NEBRASKA

American Community Theatre Association, Omaha
Emmy Gifford Children's Theatre, Omaha
The Nebraska Theatre Caravan, Omaha
The Omaha Children's Theatre
Omaha Junior Theatre Center*

NEVADA

The Rainbow Company Children's Theatre, Las Vegas

NEW HAMPSHIRE

Kitchen Sink Mime Theatre, Portsmouth
Little Red Wagon Caravan, Durham
The Players' Theatre of New Hampshire (relocated in Belgium)
Theatre Resources for Youth, Durham

NEW JERSEY

Crates n' Company, Bayonne
Creative Theatre for Children, Inc., Englewood
Creative Theatre Unlimited, Princeton
George Street Playhouse Children's Theatre, New Brunswick
Glassboro Children's Theatre*
The Growing Stage, Chester
Inner City Ensemble, Paterson
The Learning Theatre, Paterson
National Artists Management Company, West Orange*
Project IMPACT, Midland Park
Pushcart Players, Verona
The Shoestring Players, New Brunswick
Yates Musical Theatre for Children, East Orange

NEW YORK

Adrienne Morrison's Children's Players, New York
The Association of Junior Leagues of America, New York
Auburn Civic Theatre, Inc., Auburn
Billie Holiday Theatre for Little Folks, Brooklyn
Binghamton Children's Theatre Council
Briggs Management, New York
The Broque Opera Company, New York
The Brownsville Laboratory Theatre, Brooklyn*
The Buffalo Studio Theatre, Buffalo*
CERT (Community Experimental Repertory Theatre, Inc.), Poughkeepsie
Characters Unlimited, New York
The Children's Centre for Creative Arts, Adelphi University, Garden City
The Children's Educational Theatre, New York
Children's Theatre International, New York
Children's World Theatre, New York
City Center Young People's Theatre, New York
Clare Tree Major Productions, New York
Creative Arts Team, New York
Don Quijote Experimental Children's Theatre, New York
Edwin Strawbridge Theatre for Children, New York
Empire State Institute for the Performing Arts, Albany
Equity Library Children's Theatre, New York

Fanfare Productions, New York
The First All Children's Theatre, New York
The Floating Hospital Children's Theatre, New York
Fourth Wall Repertory, Inc., New York
GeVa on Tour, Rochester
Gingerbread Players and Jack, New York
Harlem Children's Theatre, New York
The Heckscher Children's Theatre, New York
The Henry Street Settlement, New York
The Henry Street Settlement, Louis Abrams Arts for Living Center, New York
The Ishangi Family Dancers, New York
Jewish Repertory Theatre for Young Audiences, New York
Junior Programs, Inc., New York
Kaleidoscope Dancers, New York
Kids for Kids Productions, Inc., Lake Grove
The King-Coit School of Acting and Design, New York
Lincoln Center Institute, New York
Little People Productions, New York
The Mad Hatters, New York
Maximillion Productions, Inc., New York
Merry-Go-Rounders, New York
The Merry Mimes, New York
The Merry Wanderers, New York
New York University—Program in Educational Theatre, New York
The 92nd Street "Y," New York
The No-Elephant Circus, Rye
Off Center Theatre, Inc., New York
Pan Asian Repertory Theatre, New York
Paper Bag Players, New York
Peel and Smith, New York
The Penny Bridge Players, Brooklyn
The Peppermint Players, New York
Percival Borde and Company, New York
Performing Arts Foundation, Huntington
Periwinkle Productions, Inc., Monticello
The Pixie Judy Troupe, New York
Playmakers Repertory Theatre, Westchester County
The Portmanteau Theatre, New York
Practical Cats Theatre Company, New York
The Puerto Rican Traveling Theatre, New York
Pumpernickel Players, New York
Quiet Riot, New York
Rod Rodgers Dance Company, New York
Rodger Hess Productions, New York*
Saturday Theatre for Children, Brooklyn
Stone Soup Players, Albany*
Studio Arena Theatre, Buffalo
Sunshine TOO, Rochester

Syracuse Stage, Camillus
The Theatre for Young People of Herkimer County, Herkimer
Theatre in a Trunk, Inc., New York
Theatre Mask Ensemble, New York
Theatre of Youth Company, Buffalo
Theatreworks/USA, New York (formerly Performing Arts Repertory Theatre)
Tic/Toc Players, Rochester*
The Traveling Playhouse, White Plains
Young Audiences, Inc., New York

NORTH CAROLINA

Children's Theatre Board, Inc., Winston-Salem
Land of Oz, Banner Elk
Raleigh Children's Theatre
The Theatre for Young People, Greensboro
Theatre in the Park, Raleigh
TOUCH, Carrboro

NORTH DAKOTA

Fargo Moorhead Community Theatre, Fargo

OHIO

Akron Children's Theatre, Barberton
American Repertory Theatre of Cincinnati*
ArtReach Touring Theatre, Cincinnati
Cain Park Children's Theatre, Cleveland Heights
Civic Children's Theatre of Youngstown
Columbus Junior Theatre of the Arts
The Curtain Pullers of the Cleveland Playhouse
Fairmount Theatre of the Deaf, Cleveland
Heights Youth Theatre, Cleveland Heights
Karamu House Children's Theatre, Cleveland
Little Miami Theatre Works, West Liberty

OKLAHOMA

The Children's Theatre of Tulsa
Oklahoma City University

PENNSYLVANIA

The Almost Free Theatre of the Germantown Theatre Guild, Philadelphia
The American Theatre Arts for Youth, Philadelphia
The Children's Repertory Theatre Company, Drexel Hill
The City Theatre Company, Pittsburgh
Dan Kamin, Pittsburgh
Fulton Opera House—Theatre for Young Audiences, Lancaster
Grace Price Productions, Pittsburgh
Hedgerow Theatre, Wallingford

Knickerty Knockerty Players, Pittsburgh
Mae Desmond's Company, Philadelphia
Pennsylvania State University Theatre, University Park
The People's Light and Theatre Company, Malvern
Philadelphia Theatre Caravan
Philadelphia Youth Theatre
The Pittsburgh Playhouse Junior Children's Theatre
Schooltime Theatre, Irwin
Temple Children's Theatre, Philadelphia
Touchstone, Bethlehem
York Little Theatre, York

RHODE ISLAND

The Great Interplanetary Soapbox Revival, Wakefield
Looking Glass Theatre, Providence
Project Discovery, Trinity Square Repertory Company
Rhode Island College Theatre for Children, Providence
Rites and Reason, Providence

SOUTH CAROLINA

Greenville Fine Arts Center
The Patchwork Players
Stage South, Columbia*

TENNESSEE

ASSITEJ/USA, Nashville
Bijou Theatrical Academy, Knoxville
Memphis Children's Theatre
Nashville Academy Theatre
The Play Group, Knoxville

TEXAS

Casa Mañana Playhouse, Fort Worth
Children's Theatre Festival, Houston
Creative Arts Theatre and School, Arlington
Dallas Theatre Center Teen-Children's Theatre
Midland Community Theatre of Texas
The National Children's Theatre Association, Dallas
Project InterACT/Zachary Scott Theatre, Austin
Theatre for Youth, University of Texas, Austin
Theatre on Wheels, Houston

UTAH

Brigham Young University's Whittlin' Whistin' Brigade, Provo
University of Utah Young People's Theatre, Salt Lake City

VERMONT

The Green Mountain Guild, Inc., White River Junction

VIRGINIA

The American Association of Theatre for Youth, Blacksburg
The Barter Theatre, Abingdon
Children's Theatre of Richmond
Jack Tales Touring Theatre Troupe, Ferrum
Theatre IV, Richmond
Virginia Polytechnic Institute and State University, Blacksburg
Wolf Trap Farm Park for the Performing Arts, Vienna

WASHINGTON

Black Arts West Theatre Unlimited, Seattle
Central Washington University, Ellensburg
Piccoli Junior Theatre Guild, Seattle
Poncho Theatre, Seattle
Seattle Children's Theatre (formerly Poncho Theatre)
Seattle Junior Theatre
Seattle Repertory Theatre
University of Washington, Seattle
Washington Theatre of Youth, Seattle
World Mother Goose, Seattle
The Young ACT Company, Seattle

WEST VIRGINIA

New World Theatre Company, Berkeley Springs
Theatre Arts of West Virginia, Inc., Beckley

WISCONSIN

The Great American Children's Theatre Company, Milwaukee
Imagination Theatre, Milwaukee*
K.I.D.S. Repertory Theatre, Madison
Milwaukee Imagination Theatre, Whitefish Bay
Pick-a-Pack Players, Milwaukee
Stagecoach Players, Madison
University of Wisconsin at Madison
Wisconsin Children's Theatre, Madison*

Bibliographies

The first list comprises articles, brochures, pamphlets, unpublished records, and books containing historical background material used in the preparation of Part One. This is followed by selected bibliographies of books on children's theatre, creative drama, and theatre in education; and of directories, journals, newsletters, and unpublished doctoral studies relevant to children's theatre in America, all of which are available to scholars. A list of the major publishers of plays for young audiences is also included.

SOURCES UTILIZED FOR HISTORICAL OVERVIEW OF CHILDREN'S THEATRE

1. Documents, Catalogues, Pamphlets, and Newsletters

American National Theatre and Academy. *The ANTA Story*. New York: American National Theatre and Academy, 1956. [Unpaged pamphlet.]

Arberg, Harold. *Support for the Arts and the Humanities*. Washington, D.C.: Government Printing Office, 1968.

ASSITEJ (Association Internationale du Theatre pour l'Enfance et la Jeunesse). *Newsletters*. [1970–1985, from ASSITEJ/USA and International Centers.]

Children's Theatre Conference Regional Newsletters. [Newsletters for individual regions from time publication was begun to 1985.]

Children's Theatre in the U.S.A. [Pamphlet prepared by the United States Center for ASSITEJ, 1965.]

Coming to Our Senses: The Significance of the Arts in American Education. New York: McGraw-Hill, 1977. [A panel report, David Rockefeller, Jr., panel chairman.]

Davis, Jed H., comp. *A Directory of Children's Theatres in the United States*. Washington, D.C.: American Educational Theatre Association, 1968.

Gault, Judith, comp. *Federal Funds and Services for the Arts*. Washington, D.C.: U.S. Department of Health, Education and Welfare, 1967.

Hill, Ann S. *European Children's Theatre and the Second Congress of the International*

Children's Theatre Association. Washington, D.C.: American Educational Theatre Association, 1968.

Landers, Jacob. *Higher Horizons Progress Report.* New York: Board of Education of the City of New York, January 1963.

Pacesetters in Innovation. Washington, D.C.: Government Printing Office, 1966, 1967, 1968.

2. Miscellaneous Unpublished Material

Adventure Theatre. Scrapbook collection of mimeographed materials and pictures in Glen Echo Park, Maryland, theatre archives.

Association of Junior Leagues of America. "Children's Theatre and Puppetry Statistics." Compiled in typewritten form for the author.

Brochures from theatre companies. Available on request.

Children's World Theatre. History prepared for the author.

Comer, Virginia Lee. "Highlights of the American Educational Theatre Association Children's Theatre Conference in Seattle, Washington, August 1–5, 1946." New York, Children's Theatre Conference, 1946. Mimeographed report.

Drake, Mrs. Reah Stanley et al. "Promoting Good Theatre for Children in Binghamton." Binghamton, New York, Children's Theatre Council, 1939. Mimeographed record of activities.

Equity Library Theatre. "Equity Library Theatre for Children." Mimeographed information distributed by Equity Library Theatre, 1956.

Junior Programs, Inc. "Records and Press Releases." Mimeographed material from the files of Dorothy McFadden.

Junior Programs, Inc. "Scrapbook of Programs and Press Notices." New York, Theatre Collection of The New York Public Library.

Living Arts Project, Dayton, Ohio, 1970. Scrapbook.

Major, Clare Tree. "Scrapbooks of Programs, Press Notices, Photographs and Mimeographed Materials." New York, Theatre Collection of The New York Public Library.

Plowitz, Kathryn A. "Artists-in-Schools: Background Information." Washington, D.C., National Endowment for the Arts, April 7, 1980. Mimeographed report.

Saturday Theatre for Children. New York, New York City Board of Education. Mimeographed reports.

Seattle Junior Programs. Report. Seattle, Junior Programs typewritten report, 1970.

Shohet, Max. "Scrapbook of WPA Children's Theatre." New York, Theatre Collection of The New York Public Library. Miscellaneous collection of clippings, letters, press releases, mimeographed questionnaires, and research files.

Stanistreet, Grace. "What Is Adelphi's Children's Theatre?" Garden City, New York, Adelphi College, n.d. Mimeographed material.

State Arts Councils. Reports prepared for the author in response to requests for information.

Tribal Players. "Scrapbook Collection." Boston, Tribal Players, 1970.

3. Books on Early Theatres for Children

Addams, Jane. *The Second Twenty Years at Hull House*. New York: Macmillan Co.,
    1930.
———. *The Spirit of Youth and the City Streets*. New York: Macmillan Co., 1909.
———. *Twenty Years at Hull House*. New York: Macmillan Co., 1910.
Chorpenning, Charlotte. *Twenty-One Years with Children's Theatre*. Anchorage, Ky.:
    Anchorage Press, 1955.
Fisher, Caroline, and Hazel Robertson. *Children and the Theatre*. Rev. ed. Stanford,
    Calif.: Stanford University Press, 1950.
Flanagan, Hallie. *Arena*. New York: Duell, Sloan and Pearce Co., 1940.
Heniger, Alice Herts. *The Kingdom of the Child*. New York: E. P. Dutton and Co.,
    1918.
Herts, Alice Minnie. *The Children's Educational Theatre*. New York: Harper and
    Brothers, 1911.
Kase, Robert. *Children's Theatre Comes of Age*. New York: Samuel French Co.,
    1956.
Mackay, Constance D'Arcy. *Children's Theatre and Plays*. New York: D. Appleton
    Century Co., 1927.
———. *How to Produce Children's Plays*. New York: Henry Holt and Co., 1915.
McCaslin, Nellie. *Children's Theatre in the United States: A History*. Norman: Uni-
    versity of Oklahoma Press, 1971.
Mauer, Muriel, for Seattle Junior Programs, Inc. *Children's Theatre Manual*. An-
    chorage, Ky.: Children's Theatre Press, 1951.
Moses, Montrose J. *Concerning Children's Plays*. New York: Samuel French, Inc.,
    1931.
Siks, Geraldine Brain, and Hazel Brain Dunnington. *Children's Theatre and Cre-
    ative Dramatics: Principles and Practices*. Seattle: University of Washington
    Press, 1961.
Wald, Lillian. *The House on Henry Street*. New York: Henry Holt and Co., 1915.
———. *Windows on Henry Street*. Boston: Little, Brown & Co., 1934.
Ward, Winifred. *Theatre for Children*. New York: D. Appleton Century Co., 1939.
    3d rev. ed. Anchorage, Ky.: Children's Theatre Press, 1958.
Whitman, Willson. *Bread and Circuses*. New York: Oxford University Press, 1937.

4. Articles

Adamoska, Helenka. "Junior League Children's Theatre." *Drama*, Vol. 21 (April
    1931), 37.
Alexander, Selma. "Need for a Children's Theatre." *Drama*, Vol. 21 (May 1931),
    16.
"American Children's Theatre." *Literary Digest*, Vol. 117 (June 1934), 32.
Arnold, Frank R. "Play Service in Utah." *Education*, Vol. 39 (December 1918),
    244–48.
Bailey, E. V. "How to Organize and Operate a Children's Theatre." *Emerson
    Quarterly*, Vol. 6 (January 1927), 10–14.
Baker, George P. "What the Theatre Can Do for the School." *Ladies Home Journal*,
    Vol. 30 (January 1913), 26.

Barclay, Dorothy. "Children's Theatre Progress." *New York Times Magazine* (September 10, 1950), 47.

Barty, Margaret. "Children and the Post-war Theatre." *Theatre World*, Vol. 39 (August 1943), 7–8.

Behner, Elsie. "For and By." *Players Magazine*, Vol. 32 (November 1955), 41.

Bell, Campton. "Conference and Progress." *Theatre Arts Monthly*, Vol. 33 (September 1949), 53.

Benet, Rosemary. "Children's World Theatre." *Saturday Review*, Vol. 33 (January 21, 1950), 47.

Best, Mrs. A. Starr. "The Drama League at 21." *Drama*, Vol. 21 (May 1931), 35–39.

Black, Donald, and Rose Kennedy. "Footlights for Small Fry." *Colliers*, Vol. 121 (February 7, 1948), 54.

Bloyom, Marian. "Yakima Children's Theatre Gets Its Start." *Players Magazine*, Vol. 27 (April 1951), 156–57.

"Boys and the Theatre." *Atlantic Monthly*, Vol. 107 (March 1911), 350–54.

Braden, George. "Municipal and School Outdoor Theatres in California." *American City*, Vol. 38 (March 1920), 98–100.

Brinkerhoff, Mary. "Talent Unlimited." *Recreation*, Vol. 43 (February 1950), 534.

Broadman, Muriel. "Children's Theatre—Who Needs It?" *Backstage*, Vol. 27, No. 8, section 2 (February 21, 1986), 1, 22, 31.

Brush, Martha. "The Eighth Annual Children's Theatre Meeting." *Educational Theatre Journal*, Vol. 4 (December 1952), 342–49.

———. "The Seventh Annual Children's Theatre Meeting." *Educational Theatre Journal*, Vol. 3 (December 1951), 192–97.

Buchanan, Roberta. "Point of View." *Players Magazine*, Vol. 32 (December 1955), 63–64.

Butterworth, Bette. "Theatre in the Round We Go." *Recreation*, Vol. 47 (June 1954), 342–43.

Cabell, Elvira D. "The Children's Educational Theatre." *English Journal*, Vol. 1 (April 1912), 251–55.

Carmer, Carl. "Children's Theatre." *Theatre Arts Monthly*, Vol. 15 (May 1931), 410–20.

Carville, Virginia. "The Key to Karamu House." *Extension*, Vol. 50 (March 1956), 20–21, 42, 45–46.

Caswell, Margaret. "Boston Revives the Medieval Pageant Wagon." *Recreation*, Vol. 27 (July 1934), 204–5.

Caulkins, E. Dana. "Recreation in Westchester County." *Recreation*, Vol. 27 (August 1933), 221.

"Century of the Child in the Playhouse." *Current Opinion*, Vol. 54 (February 1913), 121–23.

Chancerel, Leon. "Youth and the Theatre." *World Theatre*, Vol. 2 (December 1952), 3.

"The Child and the Imaginative Life." *Atlantic Monthly*, Vol. 100 (October 1907), 480–88.

"Child Labor on the Stage." *Survey*, Vol. 24 (July 23, 1910), 635–36.

"Children's Civic Theatre of Chicago." *Drama*, Vol. 17 (October 1926), 30.

"Children's Educational Theatre." *Atlantic Monthly*, Vol. 100 (December 1907), 798–806.

"A Children's Folk Theatre." *Recreation*, Vol. 26 (April 1932), 4–5.

"Children's Players of New York City." *Drama*, Vol. 21 (April 1931), 28.

"Children's Theatre." *Charities and the Commons*, Vol. 18 (April 6, 1907), 23–24.

"Children's Theatre." *Drama*, Vol. 16 (October 1925), 32–33.

"Children's Theatre." *Drama*, Vol. 21 (December 1930), 30.

"Children's Theatre." *Drama*, Vol. 21 (February 1931), 29.

"Children's Theatre at the University of Tulsa." *The Playground*, Vol. 22 (March 1928), 697–98.

"Children's Theatre Cooperates with Book Stores." *Publishers Weekly*, Vol. 134 (August 27, 1938), 579.

"A Children's Theatre for Children." *Drama*, Vol. 20 (November 1929), 53.

"Children's Theatre in Nine States." *American Magazine of Art*, Vol. 26 (January 1933), 42.

"Children's Theatre—1945." *Recreation*, Vol. 40 (October 1946), 388.

"Children's Theatre of Chicago." *Drama*, Vol. 17 (October 1926), 12.

"Children's Theatre Planned." *Literary Digest*, Vol. 117 (June 1934), 32.

"Children Unhappy When Unions Hold Up Pocahontas." *Newsweek*, Vol. 5 (January 5, 1935), 25–26.

Chipman, Sands. "Story Books Come to Life in a Children's Theatre." *Drama*, Vol. 21 (April 1931), 27–31.

Chorpenning, Charlotte. "Adults in Plays for Children." *Educational Theatre Journal*, Vol. 3 (May 1951), 115–19.

———. "The Special Audience." *Theatre Arts Monthly*, Vol. 33 (September 1949), 51–52.

Ciaccio, Mary Eleanor. "Ninth Annual Children's Theatre Meeting." *Educational Theatre Journal*, Vol. 5 (December 1953), 355–63.

Clarke, T. "I've Got the Best Job on Earth." *National Parent-Teacher Magazine*, Vol. 49 (November 1954), 16–19.

"Cleveland Theatre for Youth." *Design*, Vol. 40 (March 1939), 1–2.

Coburn, Randy Sue. "It's Not Just Kid Stuff at This Children's Theatre." *Smithsonian*, Vol. 13, No. 5 (August 1982), 52–59.

Cohen, Helen Louise. "Education in the Theatre Arts." *Theatre Arts Monthly*, Vol. 8 (October 1924), 392.

Collins, Lillian Foster. "The Little Theatre in School." *Drama*, Vol. 20 (November 1929), 52.

Comer, Virginia Lee. "A Children's Theatre Takes to the Road." *Recreation*, Vol. 34 (September 1940), 363–65, 402.

———. "Organizational Problems in Children's Theatre." *Dramatics*, Vol. 48 (November 1948), 13.

———. "The White House Conference and Educational Theatre." *Educational Theatre Journal*, Vol. 3 (October 1951), 218–23.

"Community Children's Theatre." *Recreation*, Vol. 28 (September 1934), 269.

Daggy, Maynard Lee. "The Story of the Theatre of Youth." *Players Magazine*, Vol. 13 (March-April 1937), 5.

"Decade of Children's Theatre." *Theatre Arts Monthly*, Vol. 38 (November 1954), 84.

De Publio, John. "The Sponsor's Role." *Players Magazine*, Vol. 31 (May 1955), 186.

"Disciplined: King Coit Children's Theatre."*New Yorker*, Vol. 30 (May 22, 1954), 24.

"Drama and Language: Learning in Action." *English Language Arts Bulletin*, Vol. 26, No. 2 (Fall 1985). [Special issue entirely devoted to children's theatre and creative drama.]

"The Drama Tourney." *The Playground*, Vol. 22 (March 1929), 699–703.

Drennan, Bertha. "Plays for Children." *Commonweal*, Vol. 14 (June 24, 1931), 205–6.

Dunham, Myra. "A Children's Theatre in a Great Store." *Emerson Quarterly*, Vol. 10 (November 1929), 9–10.

Elicker, Virginia Wilk. "City-wide Dramatic Program at Lakewood, Ohio." *Players Magazine*, Vol. 21 (May 1945), 24.

Eustis, Morton. "Wonderland—Broadway in Review." *Theatre Arts Monthly*, Vol. 17 (February 1933), 101–3.

"A Fairy Tale Interpreted in the Light of the Present." *School and Society*, Vol. 53 (January 18, 1941), 77.

Finley, John H. "A Modern Perspective on the Public Recreation Movement." *The Playground*, Vol. 24 (December 1930), 509–10.

Fisher, Caroline, and M. S. Theltgen. "How Two Children's Theatres Are Functioning in Wartime." *The American City*, Vol. 58 (June 1943), 97–98.

Fitzgerald, Burdette. "Children's Theatre Conference." *Players Magazine*, Vol. 24 (December 1947), 64.

———. "Oaks from Acorns." *Players Magazine*, Vol. 24 (March 1948), 135.

Freitag, Beverly. "How One Children's Theatre Became Successful." *School and Society*, Vol. 39 (April 7, 1934), 427–30.

Gerstenberg, Alice. "The Chicago Junior League." *Drama*, Vol. 18 (January 1928), 118.

Gilbertson, Alice. "Curtain Going Up." *Recreation* Vol. 37 (November 1943), 432–34.

Golden, Ben. "A Children's Theatre on Tour." *New Theatre*, Vol. 10 (October 1935), 8–9.

Gordon, Dorothy. "Creating Audiences for the Future." *Drama*, Vol. 21 (June 1931), 12.

Gordon, F. E. "Best for a Dime." *Parents' Magazine*, Vol. 14 (March 1939), 20, 32, 34.

Gots, Judith. "More than Make Believe." *Recreation*, Vol. 47 (September 1954), 433–34.

Griffin, Alice. "Theatre U.S.A." *Theatre Arts Monthly*, Vol. 33 (September 1949), 50–60.

———. "Theatre U.S.A." *Theatre Arts Monthly*, Vol. 37 (October 1953), 81–85.

———. "Theatre U.S.A." *Theatre Arts Monthly*, Vol. 38 (May 1954), 82–86.

———. "Theatre U.S.A." *Theatre Arts Monthly*, Vol. 39 (August 1955), 74.

———. "Theatre U.S.A." *Theatre Arts Monthly*, Vol. 40 (November 1956), 95.

———. "Theatre U.S.A." *Theatre Arts Monthly*, Vol. 41 (February 1957), 67.

Haaga, Agnes. "A Directory of American Colleges and Universities Offering

Training in Children's Theatre and Creative Dramatics." *Educational Theatre Journal*, Vol. 10 (May 1958), 150–63.

———. "Twelfth Annual Children's Theatre Meeting." *Educational Theatre Journal*, Vol. 8 (December 1956), 321.

Harrington, Mildred. "Mrs. Major's Stock Company Plays to Children Only." *American Magazine*, Vol. 105 (February 1928), 60.

Harrison, Gloria. "Recreation Goes Dramatic." *Recreation*, Vol. 37 (May 1943), 66.

Hayes, R. "King-Coit Children's Theatre." *Commonweal*, Vol. 60 (May 21, 1954), 175.

Heiderstadt, D. "Curtain Going Up." *Wilson Library Bulletin*, Vol. 18 (May 1944), 642–43.

Heniger, Alice Herts. "The Drama's Value for Children." *Good Housekeeping*, Vol. 57 (November 1913), 636–43.

Herendeen, Anne. "Adults Not Admitted." *Theatre Guild Magazine*, Vol. 8 (December 1930), 31–32.

Herts, Alice Minnie. "The Children's Educational Theatre." *The Atlantic Monthly*, Vol. 100 (December 1907), 798–806.

———. "Making Believe." *Good Housekeeping*, Vol. 66 (March 1917), 22–23.

"How Much Children Attend the Theatre, the Quality of the Entertainment They Choose, and Its Effect on Them." *The Pedagogical Seminary*, Vol. 16 (September 1909), 367–71.

Humphrey, Edith. "Children's Theatre Comes Home." *High School Thespian*, Vol. 15 (March 1944), 4–5.

Israels, Belle L. "Another Aspect of the Children's Theatre." *Charities and the Commons*, Vol. 19 (January 1908), 1,310.

Johnson, J. L. "Summer Theatre for Children." *The American Home*, Vol. 23 (May 1940), 62.

Johnson, Raymond. "Report from the South." *Theatre Arts Monthly*, Vol. 33 (September 1949), 56.

Jones, Beatrice A. "A Community Children's Theatre." *Recreation*, Vol. 28 (September 1934), 269.

Jones, Clair. "What Do Children Want in Children's Theatre?" *Children's Theatre Review*, Vol. 22, No. 4 (Fall 1973), 11.

Jones, Wyatt. "The Junior League Story." *Town and Country*, Vol. 110 (August 1956), 52–53, 88.

"Junior Drama League." *Drama*, Vol. 20 (October 1929), 28.

"Junior League Theatre Conference." *Drama*, Vol. 20 (February 1930), 139.

"Junior Repertory Theatre of Minneapolis." *Drama*, Vol. 21 (April 1931), 29.

"Karamu House." *Life*, Vol. 30 (June 18, 1951), 67.

Kennedy, H. S. "Children Need Recreation in Wartime." *The American City*, Vol. 57 (July 1942), 64.

Kogen, Dean. "Playing in the Streets." *Players Magazine*, Vol. 45 (June-July 1970), 219–22.

Kraus, Joanna. "Taking Children's Theatre to the Moon." *Players Magazine*, Vol. 45 (April-May 1970), 186–87.

Kupper, Herbert. "Fantasy and the Theatre Arts." *Educational Theatre Journal*, Vol. 4 (March 1952), 33–38.

Laflin, Lewis. "The Goodman Children's Theatre." *Drama*, Vol. 19 (October 1928), 12–13, 32.

Landy, Robert. "Measuring Audience Response to Characters and Scenes in Theatre for Children." *Children's Theatre Review*, Vol. 32, No. 3 (Summer 1977), 10–13.

Layman, Pauline. "A Unique Children's Theatre." *Emerson Quarterly*, Vol. 6 (May 1928), 3–6.

Levy, Jonathan. "A Theatre of the Imagination." *Children's Theatre Review*, Vol. 27, No. 1 (Winter 1978), 2–5.

Lewis, George. "Children's Theatre and Teacher Training." *Players Magazine*, Vol. 27 (October 1950), 11.

Lippman, L. B. "Children's Theatre." *Saint Nicholas*, Vol. 51 (February 1924), 427.

Lobdell, Robert. "Planning a Show Wagon." *Recreation*, Vol. 48 (January 1955), 32–33.

Loney, Glenn. "The Long Wharf Theatre." *Players Magazine*, Vol. 45 (June-July 1970), 223–28.

"Los Angeles Children's Theatre Guild." *Drama*, Vol. 21 (April 1931), 30.

McCabe, Lida R. "Making All the Fairy Tales Come True." *Arts and Decorations*, Vol. 18 (October 1922), 14–15.

McCaslin, Nellie. "Aurand Harris: Children's Theatre Playwright." *The Children's Literature Association Quarterly*, Vol. 9, No. 3 (Fall 1984), 114–16.

———. "Children's Theatre in Indianapolis." *Players Magazine*, Vol. 22 (January 1945), 24.

McFadden, Dorothy. "Europe Challenges American Parents." *National Parent-Teacher Magazine*, Vol. 21 (June 1937), 10–11.

———. "The Future of Professional Children's Theatre." *Players Magazine*, Vol. 20 (February 1944), 9.

Mackay, Constance D'Arcy. "Children's Theatre in America." *Woman's Home Companion*, Vol. 54 (June 1927), 22.

———. "Drama in Which Young People Can Participate." *Drama*, Vol. 16 (October 1925), 32–33.

———. "The Most Beautiful Children's Theatre in the World." *Drama*, Vol. 14 (February 1924), 167.

"Make Believe Land." *Recreation*, Vol. 39 (December 1945), 459.

Mackenzie, Catherine. "Children's Own Theatre." *New York Times Magazine* (January 19, 1947) 30.

McSweeney, Maxine. "Matinees for Children." *Recreation*, Vol. 35 (May 1941), 91–93.

Major, Clare Tree. "Children's Theatre." *New York State Education*, Vol. 22 (October 1934), 45–47.

———. "A Children's Theatre at Columbia." *Columbia University Institute of Arts and Sciences Institute Magazine*, Vol. 2 (October 1929), 10.

———. "Children's Theatre in Nine States." *The American Magazine of Art*, Vol. 6 (January 1933), 42.

———. "Child's Play." *Theatre Arts Monthly*, Vol. 35 (October 1952), 32.

———. "Playing Theatre." *Columbia University Institute of Arts and Sciences Institute Magazine*, Vol. 3 (February, 1931), 9.

———. "A Saturday Morning Children's Theatre." *Columbia University Institute of Arts and Sciences Institute Magazine*, Vol. 1 (May 1929), 9.

Marks, Paul. "Taking Children's Theatre Plays on the Road." *Players Magazine*, Vol. 17 (October 1940), 6, 10, 28.

Meader, Dorothy. "Duluth Children's Theatre." *School Arts*, Vol. 38 (November 1938), 85–87.

Meadowcraft, Clara. "At the Children's Matinee." *Saint Nicholas*, Vol. 41 (February 1914), 351–57.

Mohn, Margaret E. "Children's Theatre—Minnesota Plan." *Players Magazine*, Vol. 26 (May 1950), 194–95.

"Moral from a Toy Theatre." *Scribners*, Vol. 58 (October 1915), 405–12.

Morrison, Adrienne. "Drama for the Youngest Set." *Theatre*, Vol. 52 (September 1930), 40, 62.

Morse, William W. "Educational Theatre." *Outlook*, Vol. 89 (June 11, 1908), 572–77.

Moses, J. Garfield. "The Children's Theatre." *Charities and the Commons*, Vol. 18 (April 6, 1907), 23–34.

Moses, Montrose J. "Children's Plays." *Theatre Arts Monthly*, Vol. 8 (December 1924), 831–35.

Moyne, Sheila. "The Never-Never Land to Iran." *Arts and Decoration*, Vol. 24 (December 1925), 36.

Murray, Myrtle. "She'll Be Riding Six White Horses When She Comes." *Recreation*, Vol. 27 (September 1933), 290.

Nancrede, Edith D. "Dramatic Work at Hull House." *The Playground*, Vol. 22 (August 1928), 276–78.

"National Drama Week." *The Playground*, Vol. 19 (February 1926), 625.

Newmayer, Sara. "For Children It Is Not Make-Believe." *New York Times Magazine* (December 5, 1948), 24–26.

Newton, Peter. "The Toy Theatre, A Children's Playhouse Where Children's Fairy Tales Come True." *The Craftsman*, Vol. 28 (April 1915), 36–41.

Oberreich, Robert. "Unique Children's Theatre." *Recreation*, Vol. 45 (November 1951), 319.

Ogden, Jean. "A Theatre for Children." *Recreation*, Vol. 38 (February 1944), 623.

"Our Thespians in Dead Earnest." *Literary Digest*, Vol. 85 (May 16, 1925), 26–27.

Palmer, Winthrop. "Make Believe for Children." *Drama*, Vol. 18 (March 1928), 173–74.

Partridge, Pauline. "The House of Fairies." *Sunset*, Vol. 56 (April 1926), 38–39.

Patten, Cora Mel. "The Children's Theatre Movement." *Drama*, Vol. 18 (November 1927), 51.

Patten, Hazel R. "A Program Carries On." *Recreation*, Vol. 39 (January 1946), 513–15.

"The Play of Imagination in the Tiniest Theatre in the World." *Survey*, Vol. 34 (September 18, 1915), 551.

Plotkin, Charlie. "Putting the Fine Arts into Education through Junior Programs." *Progressive Education*, Vol. 17 (April 1940), 251–54.

Pollette, John. "Tryout Plays for Children's Theatre." *Players Magazine*, Vol. 27 (October 1951), 8.

Powell, Anne. "Federal Children's Theatre in New York City." *Recreation*, Vol. 30 (October 1936), 344–45.

Powell, Jessie. "The Children's Players." *Emerson Quarterly*, Vol. 11 (November 1930), 17–18.

Price, Grace. "Helping the Beginning Playwright." *Players Magazine*, Vol. 28 (November 1951), 38.

Pyle, M. T. "Theatre School for Children." *Recreation*, Vol. 39 (August 1945), 230–31.

"Racketty-Packetty House." *Outlook*, Vol. 103 (January 11, 1913), 58.

"Report of the Seventeenth Annual Convention of the Drama League of America." *The Playground*, Vol. 20 (July 1926), 237–41.

Resnick, Jack. "Children's Theatre—New York." *Federal Theatre Magazine*, Vol. 2 (December 1936), 3.

Richards, Stanley. "450,000 Miles of Children's Theatre." *Players Magazine*, Vol. 31 (December 1954), 66–67.

"Richmond's Children's Theatre—Second Edition." *Recreation*, Vol. 37 (November 1943), 434–74.

Robertson, Hazel. "It Belongs to Them." *Recreation*, Vol. 35 (December 1941), 545–46.

Rockefeller, Kay. "Live Drama for Children." *Child Study*, Vol. 30 (Spring 1953), 18–20.

Rogers, James Edward. "The Psychology of the Drama." *The Playground*, Vol. 19 (February 1926), 625.

Rounds, Charles. "A Theatre for Children." *Education*, Vol. 54 (September 1933), 57–59.

Royal, Patricia. "Children's Theatre Goes Traveling." *Recreation*, Vol. 39 (January 1946), 535–36, 550–51.

Sands, Mary K. "Dramatics for the Few or the Many?" *Players Magazine*, Vol. 8 (November-December 1931), 2.

Savage, Mrs. George. "Audiences for Tomorrow." *Players Magazine*, Vol. 22 (September-October 1945), 14, 20–21.

———. "The Business Side of It." *Theatre Arts Monthly*, Vol. 33 (September 1949), 54.

Schoell, Edwin. "College and University Productions, 1953–54." *Educational Theatre Journal*, Vol. 7 (May 1955), 149.

"Schools and the Drama." *Review of Reviews*, Vol. 45 (March 1912), 367–68.

Schott, V. W. "Peter Pan Players of Wichita, Kansas." *The American Library Association Bulletin*, Vol. 26 (October 1932), 768–72.

Shade, Edwin. "Children's Theatre, A Community Project." *Players Magazine*, Vol. 28 (December 1951), 66.

Shell, Alyce. "A Community Children's Theatre Grows." *Recreation*, Vol. 33 (February 1937), 555–56.

Sherwood, Robert. "A Message from Robert Sherwood." *Recreation*, Vol. 44 (January 1951), 40.

Siks, Geraldine Brain. "Out of Your Cage." *Players Magazine*, Vol. 31 (January 1955), 89–90.

———. "A View of Current European Theatre for Children and a Look Ahead in the United States." *Educational Theatre Journal*, Vol. 19 (May 1967), 191–97.

Smith, C. C. "Child Actors in the King Coit Productions." *Theatre Arts Monthly*, Vol. 2 (September 1927), 720–23.

Smith, Milton. "The Place of Drama in Leisure Time." *Recreation*, Vol. 27 (January 1934), 462.

"Snow White." *New York Dramatic Mirror*, Vol. 67 (November 13, 1912), 6.

Spencer, Sara. "A Decade of Children's Theatre." *Theatre Arts Monthly*, Vol. 38 (November 1954), 84.

Spottiswoode, Raymond. "Children in Wonderland." *Saturday Review of Literature*, Vol. 31 (November 13, 1948), 60.

Strawbridge, Edwin. "Do Your Play for, Not to, the Children." *Recreation*, Vol. 47 (October 1954), 484–86.

"Tall Stories for Small Audiences." *Dance Magazine*, Vol. 28 (February 1954), 57.

"Ten Cent Drama for San Francisco Children." *Survey*, Vol. 34 (April 24, 1915), 80.

"Theatre and Education." *Outlook*, Vol. 115 (March 7, 1917), 411–13.

"The Theatre as an Educative Agent." *Current Literature*, Vol. 45 (October 1908), 441–44.

"A Theatre for All Children." *Literary Digest*, Vol. 47 (January 11, 1913), 74–75.

"The Theatre of Youth Players." *The Playground*, Vol. 22 (February 1929), 629–30.

Thomas, Cate. "Report from the New England States." *Theatre Arts Monthly*, Vol. 33 (September 1949), 55.

"Three Years of the Drama League." *The Nation*, Vol. 98 (March 26, 1914), 322–23.

"To Reorganize Children's Theatre." *Charities and the Commons*, Vol. 20 (June 6, 1908), 307–8.

"Toward a Community Theatre." *Recreation*, Vol. 39 (August 1945), 235–36.

"Unique Children's Theatre." *Recreation*, Vol. 45 (November 1951), 319.

"Unlocking the World of the Wonderful through the Children's Theatre." *The American City*, Vol. 40 (January 1929), 106–7.

Van Hercke, Ethel. "A Different Kind of Little Theatre." *Recreation*, Vol. 33 (January 1940), 549–50.

Waldron, Webb. "Children's Delight." *Readers Digest*, Vol. 34 (January 1939), 33–36.

Wallace, Richard. "One Hundred Thousand Children Can't Be Wrong." *Cue*, Vol. 4 (August 8, 1936), 8–9, 14–15.

Ward, Winifred. "A Passport to the Never-Never Land." *Drama*, Vol. 21 (April 1931), 25–26.

———. "The Sixth Annual Children's Theatre Conference." *Educational Theatre Journal*, Vol. 2 (October 1950), 199–207.

Watkins, Mary Jane. "The Tenth Annual Children's Theatre Conference." *Educational Theatre Journal*, Vol. 6 (December 1954), 348–54.

Weed, Helen. "Theatre by Children in Tacoma." *Players Magazine*, Vol. 26 (January 1950), 89.

Weller, Charles. "A Children's Playhouse." *Survey*, Vol. 35 (February 19, 1916), 615.

Welty, Susan. "Children's Theatre Notes." *Players Magazine*, Vol. 18 (October 1940), 19.

———. "In the Children's Theatres." *Players Magazine*, Vol. 17 (November 1940), 19.

Wernaer, Robert. "Work of the Drama League in Boston." *The Nation*, Vol. 99 (September 10, 1914), 310–11.

"Where Children Play at Giving Plays." *Literary Digest*, Vol. 86 (August 1, 1925), 25–26.

Wilson, Margery. "Children's Theatre in the Round." *Educational Theatre Journal*, Vol. 2 (May 1950), 104–7.

Winthrop, Palmer. "Make-Believe for Children." *Drama*, Vol. 18 (March 1928), 173.

Woody, Pam. "An Interview with the Improvisational Theatre Project at the Mark Taper Forum." *Children's Theatre Review*, Vol. 26, No. 1 (Winter 1977), 5–6.

Wright, L. "The Forgotten Audience." *Dramatics*, Vol. 24 (October 1952), 26–27.

Wyatt, E. V. "Adventures of Marco Polo." *Catholic World*, Vol. 154 (November 1941), 216.

———. "Children's Audiences." *Catholic World*, Vol. 145 (February 1937), 669–70.

———. "The Rose and the Ring at the Cosmopolitan Club." *Catholic World*, Vol. 155 (April 1942), 87–88.

Young, Betty, and Virginia Ray. "Henry Street Playhouse Presents Fine Saturday Children's Programs." *Parents' Magazine*, Vol. 31 (March 1956), 22-b, 22-d.

Young, Margaret. "The Child in the Theatre." *Players Magazine*, Vol. 8 (June 1932), 3–4, 21.

Young, Stark. "Nala and Damayanti." *The New Republic*, Vol. 84 (May 8, 1935), 370.

5. Periodicals

Beginning in the sixties the following periodicals have published articles on various aspects of children's theatre on a regular basis. The most current and authoritative information is to be found in them.

Children's Theatre Review (the official journal of The Children's Theatre Association of America), until summer 1986.

Theatre for Young Audiences Today (the official journal of ASSITEJ/USA), Office of Creative Arts Team, 715 Broadway, New York, NY 10003.

Improvise!, P.O. Box 2335, Providence, RI 02906.

Youth Theatre Journal (the official journal of AATY), Virginia Tech, Blacksburg, VA 24061.

The following periodicals publish occasional articles on various aspects of children's theatre:

Theatre Journal (the official journal of the American Theatre Association), until summer 1986. Now located at the University of Oklahoma, School of Drama, Norman OK 73019.

Theatre Crafts (the theatre journal of Rodale Publications), Holmes, PA 19043.

SELECTED SOURCES FOR THE STUDY OF CHILDREN'S THEATRE

1. Books on Children's Theatre and Creative Drama

Baker, Irene Vickers. *Wichita Children's Theatre: The First Thirty Years*. Wichita, Kans.: Wichita Children's Theatre Guild, 1977.

Broadman, Muriel. *Understanding Your Children's Entertainment*. New York: Harper & Row, 1977.

Chorpenning, Charlotte B. *Twenty-One Years with Children's Theatre*. Anchorage, Ky.: Children's Theatre Press, 1952.

Corey, Orlin. *Theatre for Children—Kids' Stuff or Theatre?* Anchorage, Ky.: Anchorage Press, 1974.

Cornelison, Gayle, comp. and ed. *A Directory of Children's Theatre in the United States*. Washington, D.C.: American Theatre Association, 1978.

Davis, Jed, and Mary Jane Evans. *Theatre, Children and Youth*. New Orleans: Anchorage Press, 1982.

Epstein, Lawrence S., comp. and ed. *A Guide to Theatre in America*. New York: Macmillan, 1986.

Evans, Dina Rees. *Cain Park Theatre: The Halcyon Years*. Cleveland: The Halcyon Press, 1980.

Fisher, Caroline, and Hazel Robertson. *Children and the Theatre*. Palo Alto, Calif.: Stanford University Press, 1950.

Forkert, Maurice. *Children's Theatre That Captures Its Audience*. Chicago: Coach House Press, 1962.

Foundation of the Dramatists' Guild. *Young Playwrights' Festival*. Preface by Gerald Chapman. New York: Avon Books, 1983.

Goldberg, Moses. *Children's Theatre: A Philosophy and a Method*. Englewood Cliffs, N.J.: Prentice-Hall, 1974.

Hale, Patricia, ed. *Participation Theatre for Young Audiences*. Rowayton, Conn.: New Plays, Inc., 1972.

Healy, Daty. *Dress the Show*. Rowayton, Conn.: New Plays, Inc., 1976.

Heinig, Ruth Beall, ed. *Go Adventuring! A Celebration of Winifred Ward: America's First Lady of Drama for Children*. New Orleans: Anchorage Press, 1977.

Heniger, Alice Minnie Herts. *The Children's Educational Theatre*. New York: Harper & Bros., 1911.

Johnson, Richard. *Producing Plays for Children*. New York: Rosen Press, 1971.

Landy, Robert. *A Handbook of Educational Drama and Theatre*. Westport, Conn.: Greenwood Press, 1982.

Lifton, Betty Jean, ed. *Contemporary Children's Theatre*. New York: Avon Books, 1974.

McCaslin, Nellie. *Children's Theatre in the United States: A History*. Norman: University of Oklahoma Press, 1971.

———. *Theatre for Young Audiences*. New York: Longman, Inc., 1978.

O'Toole, John. *Theatre in Education*. London: Hodder & Stoughton, 1976.

Rosenberg, Helane, and Christine Prendergast. *Theatre for Young People: A Sense of Occasion*. New York: Holt, Rinehart & Winston, 1983.

Siks, Geraldine Brain, and Hazel Brain Dunnington, eds. *Children's Theatre and Creative Dramatics*. Seattle: University of Washington Press, 1961.

Special Edition of ASSITEJ/USA, edited by Kenneth McLeod and C. J. Stevens, for ASSITEJ World Congress held in Lyons, France, June 1981. Nashville, Tenn. Entire issue devoted to children's theatre in the United States.

Swortzell, Lowell, ed. *All the World's a Stage*. New York: Delacorte Press, 1972.

————, ed. *Six Plays for Young People from the Federal Theatre Project (1936–1939): An Introductory Analysis and Six Representative Plays*. Westport, Conn.: Greenwood Press, 1986.

Ward, Winifred. *Theatre for Children*. New Orleans: Anchorage Press, 1958.

Wright, Lin, ed. *Professional Theatre for Young Audiences*. Tempe: Arizona State University, 1984.

2. Books on Theatre in Education

Allen, John. *Drama in Schools: Its Theory and Practice*. London: Heinemann, 1979.

Bolton, Gavin. *Drama as Education*. London: Longman, 1984.

————. *Towards a Theory of Drama in Education*. London: Longman, 1980.

Courtney, Richard. *Play Drama and Thought*. New York: Drama Book Specialists, 1974.

Hodgson, John. *The Uses of Drama*. London: Methuen, 1975.

Hunt, Albert. *Hopes for Great Happenings: Alternatives in Education and Theatre*. New York: Taplinger, 1977.

Jackson, Tony, ed. *Learning through Drama*. Manchester, England: Manchester University Press, 1980.

James, Ronald. *Developing Drama*. London: Nelson, 1975.

Kelly, Elizabeth Flory. *Dramatics in the Classroom*. Bloomington, Ind.: Phi Delta Kappa Educational Foundation, 1976.

Linnell, Rosemary. *Approaching Classroom Drama*. London: Edward Arnold, 1982.

McCaslin, Nellie, ed. *Children and Drama*. 2d ed. Lanham, Md.: University Press of America, 1985.

McGregor, Lynn; Maggie Tate; and Ken Robinson, eds. *Learning through Drama*. London: Heinemann, 1977.

Male, David C. *Approaches to Drama*. London: Allen & Unwin, 1977.

O'Toole, John. *Theatre in Education*. London: Hodder & Stoughton, 1976.

Robinson, Ken. *Exploring Theatre and Education*. London: Heinemann, 1980.

Shuman, R. Baird. *Educational Drama for Today's Schools*. Metuchen, N.J.: Scarecrow Press, 1978.

Wagner, B. J., and Dorothy Heathcote. *Drama as a Learning Medium*. Washington, D.C.: NEA, 1976.

Webster, Clive. *Working with Theatre in Schools*. London: Pitman, 1975.

3. Unpublished Doctoral Studies

Abookire, Noerena. "A History of Children's Theatre Activities at Karamu House in Cleveland, Ohio—1915–1975." New York University, 1980.

Bedard, Roger L. "The Life and Work of Charlotte B. Chorpenning." Lawrence: University of Kansas, 1978.

Gamble, Michael W. "Clare Tree Major's Children's Theatre." New York: New York University, 1976.

Graham, Kenneth. "An Introductory Study of the Evaluation of Plays for Children's Theatre in the United States." Salt Lake City: University of Utah, 1947.

Guffin, Jan A. "Winifred Ward: A Critical Biography." Raleigh: Duke University, 1976.

Jennings, Coleman A. "A Critical Study: The Dramatic Contribution of Aurand Harris to Children's Theatre in the United States." New York: New York University, 1976.

Kraus, Joanna H. "A History of the Children's Theatre Association of Baltimore from 1943–1966." New York: Teachers College, 1972.

Rodman, Ellen. "Edith King and Dorothy Coit and the King-Coit School." New York: New York University, 1979.

Rubin, Janet E. "The Literary and Theatrical Contributions of Charlotte B. Chorpenning to Children's Theatre." Columbus: Ohio State University, 1978.

Swortzell, Lowell. "Five Plays: A Repertory of Children's Theatre to be Performed by and for Children." New York: New York University, 1963.

Van Tassel, Wesley. "Theory and Practice in Theatre for Children: An Annotated Bibliography of Comment in English Circulated in the United States from 1900 through 1968." Denver: University of Denver, 1969.

4. Lists and Directories

Actors' Equity Association Lists of Companies under Equity Contract. New York: 1984 (revised annually).

Black Theatre Alliance Touring Brochure. New York: Black Theatre Alliance, 1984.

Directory of Children's Theatres in the United States, compiled and edited by Gayle Cornelison. Washington, D.C.: Children's Theatre Association of America, 1978.

Professional Theatre for Young Audiences, edited by Lin Wright. Tempe: Arizona State University, 1984.

Theatre Profiles 6. New York: Theatre Communications Group, 1984.

Theatre Resources Handbook Directory, edited by Charles M. Watson and Sister.

Kathryn A. Martin. Washington, D.C.: National Endowment for the Arts, Artist-in-Schools Programs, 1979.

Lists of current members available on request from Regional Governors of Children's Theatre Association of America.

Lists of children's theatre companies known to state arts councils available on request from council offices.

5. Journals and Newspapers

AATY Journal. Theatre Arts Dept., Virginia Tech, Blacksburg, VA 24061.

ASSITEJ/USA Bulletin. This bulletin is published three times a year, serving as an instrument of communication among ASSITEJ/USA members and theatre artists and colleagues concerned with theatre for young people throughout the world. Sent to members only. Office of Creative Arts Team, 715 Broadway, New York, NY 10003.

Children's Theatre Review. This was the journal of The Children's Theatre Association of America. It was published quarterly and sent to all members of CTAA. Articles and news items were relevant to teachers, leaders, and producers of child drama and children's theatre (1951–1986).

Dramatics. First published in 1929 and issued monthly thereafter, *Dramatics* is intended for students and teachers on the secondary school level. It does, however, include articles on children's theatre, television, film, and puppetry from time to time. International Thespian Society, 3368 Central Parkway, Cincinnati, OH 45225.

Improvise! A newsletter published quarterly, featuring articles and news of creative drama, it occasionally carries articles on children's theatre. Obtained by subscription. Box 2335, Providence, RI 02906.

On Stage. This is the journal of the American Community Theatre Association. Articles describe activities of this division of theatre and include the work of practitioners on all levels. Omaha Community Playhouse, 6915 Cass St., Omaha, NE 68132.

Players Magazine. This is the magazine of the National Collegiate Players. Players International Publications, 8060 Melrose Ave., Los Angeles, CA 90046.

SSTA Journal. The Secondary School Theatre Association had its own journal, which was published three times a year. It included articles for and by teachers at the high school level and was sent to all members. For future publications, Judith Rethwisch, 1719 Stemwood Way, Fenton, MO 63026.

Theatre Crafts. This is a periodical that deals primarily with crafts and the technical aspects of the theatre. Occasional articles about theatre on all levels and areas make it interesting to directors of theatre for children. Rodale Publications: Holmes, PA 19043.

Theatre Journal. This was the journal of the University and College Theatre Association. Although directed to the professor and producer on that level, it contained occasional articles on theatre for children and carried reviews of textbooks on child drama. For future publications, School of Drama, University of Oklahoma, Norman, OK 73019.

Theatre News. This was the newspaper of The American Theatre Association. Published nine or ten times a year and sent to all members of all divisions, it contained news items and short articles, leaving feature stories and scholarly articles for divisional periodicals.

Youth Theatre Newsletter. Theatre Arts Dept., Virginia Tech, Blacksburg, VA 24061.

6. Publishers and Distributors of Children's Plays

Anchorage Press, P.O. Box 8067, New Orleans, LA 70182
Baker's Plays, 100 Chauncy Street, Boston, MA 02110
The Coach House Press, Inc., P.O. Box 458, Morton Grove, IL 60053
David McKay Company, Inc., 750 Third Ave., New York, NY 10017
The Drama Book Shop, 723 Seventh Avenue, New York, NY 10019
The Dramatic Publishing Company, 86 E. Randolph Street, Chicago, IL 60601

Dramatists Play Service, 440 Park Avenue, New York, NY 10016
Involvement Dramatics, Oklahoma City University, N.W. 23rd & Blackwelder,
    Oklahoma City, OK 73106
Music Theatre International, 199 W. 57th Street, New York, NY 10019
New Plays Incorporated, P.O. Box 273, Rowayton, CT 06853
Pickwick Press, Box 4847, Midland, TX 79701
Pioneer Drama Service, 2171 S. Colorado Blvd., Denver, CO 80222
Plays, Inc., Publishers, 8 Arlington Street, Boston, MA 02116
Rodgers & Hammerstein Library, 598 Madison Ave., New York, NY 10022
Samuel French, Inc., 45 W. 25th Street, New York, NY 10011
Stage Magic Plays, P.O. Box 246, Schulenburg, TX 78956
Tams-Witmark Music Library, Inc., 757 Third Avenue, New York, NY 10017
Theatre Arts Books, 153 Waverly Place, New York, NY 10011
Young Audience Scripts, 9140–146 A Street, Edmonton, Alberta, Canada

Index

Page numbers set in *italic* indicate the location of main entry.

About the Author

NELLIE McCASLIN, Professor of Educational Theatre at New York University, is Past President of the Children's Theatre Association. She is the author of numerous children's books and college textbooks, as well as general works of children's theatre and dramatics, including *Creative Drama in the Classroom, Theatre for Children in the United States, Theatre for Young Audiences,* and *Shows on a Shoestring.*